THE STRATIFICATION OF BEHAVIOUR

International Library of Philosophy
and Scientific Method

EDITOR: A. J. AYER
ASSISTANT EDITOR: BERNARD WILLIAMS

THE
STRATIFICATION
OF BEHAVIOUR

A SYSTEM OF DEFINITIONS

PROPOUNDED AND DEFENDED

by

D. S. Shwayder

LONDON
ROUTLEDGE & KEGAN PAUL
NEW YORK: THE HUMANITIES PRESS

First published 1965
by Routledge & Kegan Paul Ltd
Broadway House, 68–74 Carter Lane
London, E.C.4

Printed in Great Britain
by Richard Clay and Company, Ltd
Bungay, Suffolk

DEDICATED TO
WILLIAM R. DENNES, GILBERT RYLE AND J. O. URMSON

CONTENTS

CONTENTS

CONTENTS

PART FIVE: THE USE OF LANGUAGE

PREFACE

The material set out in this volume was originally meant to be the introduction to a book on the theory of Language. The main line of development still points in that direction, Part V being an attempt to define the use of Language as a form of behaviour. As this 'introduction' grew progressively more general and oppressively more bulky, it became evident that I would have to publish it on its own, if I were to publish it at all. I hope that this volume will be of interest to some readers who are not particularly concerned with the theoretical analysis of Language and thought—psychologists as well as philosophers. In the concluding pages I outline how my definition of Language as a form of behaviour may be applied to achieve a General Theory of Language, and the detailed implementation of those thoughts will be published in a separate volume, now in preparation.

Taken on its own, this work is a study of part of what has currently come to be called Philosophy of Mind or Philosophical Psychology—an ancient subject recently revived. Beginning with Professor Ryle's *Concept of Mind* and following through the publication of Wittgenstein's *Investigations*, Miss Anscombe's *Intention*, and Professor Hampshire's *Thought and Action*, and a series of volumes edited by Mr. R. F. Holland under the general title of *Essays in Philosophical Psychology* (to mention only the most widely read and influential items), Philosophy of Mind has become the dominating wave of contemporary Anglo-Saxon philosophy. But, as I said, this is an ancient subject; most of us first encounter it with a reading of that part of *The Republic* where Plato sets forth his analysis of the soul. It persisted through the ancient and mediaeval discussion of practical reason and reached something of a high point in the writings of philosophically sophisticated psychologists such as William James. From then until the end of the Second World War it fell into decline. That was so partly because psychologists had multiplied in sufficient numbers to enforce their demands for their own space in the University and their own place in the fashionable world of Science; but the decline is also partly to be traced to local developments in philosophy stressing methodological issues and the self-conscious application of formal logic. Philosophers' inevitable concern with the Mind was diverted into generally fruitless discussions of methodology in psychology and the problematic relation between mind and body, all this resulting in little more than sceptical barricades or programmatical reductions, unless a diluted and abstracted sense of reality is to be reckoned an achievement. It has now once more become possible to investigate 'topics' in the Philosophy of Mind, after the manner of Aristotle or James, promising a harvest of detailed proposals which may be assessed on their own merits.

Philosophy of Mind also appears to be replacing Theory of Knowledge and Formal Logic as a central, unifying area of philosophy. In one respect, the history of philosophy resembles the history of mathematics. Mathematics is familiarly if amorphously divided into fields, notably those of Geometry, Number Theory, Analysis, Algebra, Set Theory, and Logic. Each of these fields, possibly excepting Number Theory, has at some historical period actually tended to dominate the whole of mathematics or has been thought to do so by certain thinkers. Thus it was common through the time of Newton to formulate mathematical questions of every kind in geometrical terms. The succeeding epoch of Analysis was opened by the work of Descartes and Leibniz (among others) who achieved this change partly by an analytical reformulation of Geometry itself. Analysis in its turn, together with the greater part of classical mathematics, has been successively submitted to algebraic and set-theoretic reformulations. Following leads of Peano, Frege, Hilbert, and Russell, the investigations of Tarski and his school have resulted in another proposed recasting of mathematical theories of every kind in terms of questions over what can be formulated within certain systems of logic. Something similar has happened in philosophy. Here, too, we have a familiar if amorphous division into fields—Metaphysics, Ethics, Theory of Knowledge, Logic-cum-Theory of Language, Philosophy of Mind. Each of these, possibly excepting Ethics, has in different historical periods tended to occupy a central, unifying position in the whole subject. Philosophy of Mind, though it has a long and respectable history, has finally and only recently come foward as a claimant. Intimations of this can be found in many contemporary philosophical writings. The right of Philosophy of Mind to occupy this central place would be substantially vindicated by the success of this book and its sequels, for I hope to show how the theory of action here set forth supplies a groundwork for the systematic investigation of questions traditionally belonging to Logic and the Theory of Language, Metaphysics, and the Theory of Knowledge. But do not mistake my sense. This theory of action is not a monolithic study of Everything philosophical—not at all, no more than Set Theory narrowly regarded is the whole of mathematics; rather, it affords methods hopefully fruitful for the study of many things.

My development of the basic doctrine and its contemplated application in subsequent volumes may seem almost indecently ambitious. I would have preferred it otherwise. But these applications have come forward on their own, almost as challenges to be met. Here, as everywhere, the proof is in the proving.

I am aware that this book, even without its sequels, is intimidatingly long and distressingly difficult. But the difficulty is not due to the length—rather to the contrary. I have compressed the presentation whenever it seemed possible, curtailing the examination of examples and by-passing interesting questions (I say practically nothing about the emotions and avoid applications to Ethics). But, allowing that there be value in the attempt to set out a systematic theory of behaviour adequate for the analysis of the use of Language, it is inevitable that we should pass through certain points. My attempt to do the job is apt to be inadequate or false more for what it leaves out than for what it includes. Though I go into greater detail in the examination of certain topics—notably reasons—than is required for the analysis of Language, only my discussion of motives is off the main line of development; I have elected to leave that in because I am convinced that motives can be profitably discussed only against the background of some such theory of action as is constructed in Part II of this book.

I am writing, not for the 'plain man', but for professionals—chiefly teachers and students of philosophy, though I am hopeful that my efforts may be of interest to comparably professional psychologists, linguists, and social scientists generally. I make no apologies for arid technicalities. There is an opinion, held by surprisingly many people who ought to know better, that almost anyone could pick up a book of philosophy and read it with interest and profit—say Kant's *Critique of Pure Reason*; and if a book of philosophy is so dry as to be difficult to comprehend, that is to be marked down against it. I am inclined to the contrary opinion, and would contend that the apparent limpidities of Hume and Russell do more to cloak confusion than they do to illuminate truth. I know that my willingness to multiply distinctions, proliferate examples, and spell out definitions with some exactness will not win me many readers. But I honestly feel that my distinctions are probably too gross, my examples too few to be entirely typical, and my definitions too compressed; I cannot but fear that the general account would need revision, were it to stand at all, if it were tested by application to problems outside of those for which it was immediately designed. All this said, I am sure that anyone having, as a mathematician might say, a 'certain sophistication', who was interested in the problems I shall bring under review and who had a taste for technicalities could read this book. Little in the way of professional knowledge is presupposed.

I claim no originality either in point of doctrine or method. Theses similar to those which I enunciate and try to prove have been advertised from the time of Plato. In method, my efforts are in the tradition of Aristotle and Kant, though I have actually been very little influenced in matters of doctrine by either. Like Aristotle and Kant, I seek a general account of how we think about certain parts of the world, an account which necessarily reaches beyond any body of data we may actually possess, no matter how large. But data, in the form of examples, must be invoked at every point both to illustrate the doctrine and to render it plausible; and the theory is put forward to be tested against further examples. My account will seem different only in being rather more systematic than the work of other philosophers I know, possibly excepting Spinoza and Kant. I make no apologies for the system, though I have feared to become blinded by my lucubrations. I know of no other way to proceed but systematically, though I respect those recurrent condemnations of systematic philosophizing by thinkers from Plato to Wittgenstein. Lacking the literary equipment which Wittgenstein could employ to strip a particular case down to its essentials, I am not disposed to ape his methods, and must repair to the use of systematic distinction and generalization.

A brief word, now, regarding format. The work naturally divides into sections and not into chapters. I have grouped the sections into five parts. I follow the policy of preceding each section with a brief summary. Should the reader want to go back to review, he may do so by reading the summaries. I also believe that it is possible to digest the content of the book by simply reading through these summaries in order. I suggest that every reader should try out that method, returning to read only those sections, if any, in which he has a particular interest or for which he wishes to pursue the argument in detail.

I make every effort to explain technical usage as it is introduced, though I may sometimes fail by oversight. Lacking skill in coining terminology when it is needed, I often make technical adaptations of vernacular vocabulary items; I hope that these adaptations when explained will not prove difficult obstacles. Some may already have wondered about my way of capitalizing 'Language'. The reason is simply this: In talking about the use of Language, it becomes necessary to observe and to mark the distinction between languages in the sense that English, German, and Esperanto are languages and Language as a form of behaviour which is equally well served by employment of different languages.

As this work progressed, I more and more despaired of ever becoming sufficiently prepared to finish it. I deal with matters that have been topics in the history of philosophy from the beginning and which are currently being worked over by psychologists, linguists, and logicians, subjects with which I have only an exiguous familiarity. I have had to content myself with reading certain standard works which, for all I know, may already be out of date. I fairly tremble at the thought that I have not begun to realize even the extent of my ignorance. But to defer the task for the sake of further study would have been to abdicate it; I could never become prepared enough.

As it is, this work flows from more sources than I can trace. I have drawn heavily on a growing corpus of journal literature, as well as on the already mentioned books of Ryle, Wittgenstein, Anscombe, Hampshire, and others. The more important pieces for my purposes, *e.g.*, Mr. Grice's 'Meaning', are cited in the text, but certainly I have been influenced in one way or another by articles which receive no mention. I have been more influenced by Austin than by anyone else, both from his writings and from conversations. His book of lectures *How to do Things with Words* was published just at the time I was writing the final version of my theory of conventional behaviour and the use of Language. But I had already had the opportunity of reading a set of notes taken down by Professor Charles Caton from an earlier version of those lectures that Austin gave at Oxford. I once thought to include an appendix digesting the main themes of those lectures and pointing out in detail how my views differed from Austin's. But the book which has now appeared speaks for itself, and an occasional footnote will suffice to signal my infrequent disagreements.

I have benefited from discussions with students, friends and colleagues in more ways than I could possibly track down. Parts of this material were presented to two seminars and three classes, and the comments and criticism of participating students have led me to make many changes and additions, all for the better. I am especially grateful to Professors William P. Alston, Robert L. Vaught, and W. I. Matson. When I was just beginning to write this book, I several times had the chance to discuss with Alston at great length on crucial issues; where we originally differed, he has usually turned out to be right; I suspect that he would continue to find much to disapprove of in what follows. Vaught was able in short order to point out a serious obscurity in the initial stages of my systematic presentation; I hope that the remainder is not as obscure as the beginning was. Matson's reading of the typescript resulted in so many improvements that I cannot record them.

I wish, finally, to thank Mrs. Ruth Crippen for her excellent typing

PREFACE

of successive versions, Miss Genevieve Rogers for her valuable
editorial assistance, Mr. John Chambless for verifying references,
and the Institute of Social Sciences on the Berkeley campus
of the University of California for a continuing grant used to
defray costs of preparing successive typescripts.

Berkeley, California

Part One

CONCEPTUAL EPIPHENOMENALISM

---

1. THEORY AND COMMONSENSE

[My aim is to supply a set of definitions of concepts for the theoretical typification of behaviour. My efforts will be systematic and deliberately theoretical. A theory has the character it does partly in contrast with commonsense, though the theory lives in dependence upon commonsense, which provides the ultimate field of application and the controlling examples against which the theory is tested. The contrast is to be brought out by considering how and to what the theory is applied, by noticing the manner in which the theory enables us to see phenomena in novel ways thereby enhancing our conceptual and material control over those phenomena and by observing the unusual distinctions it affords. Finally, a theory, unlike commonsense, must be technical and dispose of technical usage. Notice is taken of dangers created by the occurrence of technical usage in theorizing, and a variety of strategies are described for guarding against those dangers.]

In this volume, I shall be making a deliberate attempt to establish a foundation for a kind of theoretical investigation of animal behaviour and especially human behaviour. The programme aims to work out a string of hopefully viable definitions of types of behaviour ultimately sufficient for giving a definition *per genus et differentiam* of Language as a type of behaviour, here to be called the use of Language. While the theory is aimed in a definite direction at a definite target, I believe that the methods to be employed are adaptable for hitting other targets on the same range.

1

This description of my programme shows that I shall not be engaged in a descriptive study of actual happenings, after the manner of a chronicler, say; I shall, rather, be engaged in a theoretical, abstracted study of types. We are, in short, embarked upon a journey of abstract theorizing, however wrong-headed or even disreputable that may appear according to certain current fashions of thought regarding the nature of philosophical inquiry. The intent of this work is unashamedly theoretical and systematic, as well as philosophical. In the next section something will be said by way of explaining 'philosophical'. Now I wish to draw out part of what is involved in calling this work a *theory*.

Theories are of countless kinds and of enormously different character, depending both upon the subject-matters studied and upon the methods employed for fixing and formulating data and principles, problems and results. But, as it seems to me, any theory has the character it does partly in contrast with what we vaguely call commonsense. Theory, whatever else it does, provides a kind of supplement to commonsense. We all know how the physicist's ideas of force and mass supplement the ordinary man's ideas of effort and weight. The use of the theory has indeed brought about changes in our everyday ways of thinking about the world, as, for example, is witnessed by the modern man's familiarity with the idea of acceleration. The theory opens up new possibilities which commonsense would not have envisaged, *e.g.*, weightless bodies, and it enhances our control, both material and conceptual, of the field of phenomena in question, all of which is amply illustrated by the history of modern technology. At the same time, no theory however abstract can live except off its relations to commonsense, for commonsense fixes the field of application which defines the theory and supplies examples only against which the theory may be tested and proved. Commonsense, as we say, 'assumes' that ordinary bodies fall if dropped or left unsupported. Inability to account for the correctness of that 'assumption' and for deviations from it, *e.g.*, the rising of balloons, would be grounds enough for rejecting a physical theory. Commonsense 'assumes' that winter follows fall: incapacity to cope with that fact would be fatal to the claims of any theory designed to cover the field of climatological phenomena. The lesson, for our purposes, is that we must always take very seriously indeed these 'assumptions', the distinctions and generalizations implicit in our everyday ways of thinking about ourselves and our fellows.

But the difference between commonsense and theory should not be obscured. The contrast is visible in many places. I should now like to mention a small number of features which, I believe, any theory, in contrast with commonsense, will have, features which, therefore, I

2

unashamedly announce, will mark the putative results that ensue in the development of this work.

Commonsense is an amorphous body of mostly inherited but always altering presumptions which we are constantly but almost unthinkingly making in our everyday particular encounters with the world. The principles of any group's commonsense at any time, while they may be false and certainly admit of exceptions, are not taken as standing in need of justification. Any accepted theory, by way of contrast, exists as a general body of established doctrine and technique, designed to be deliberately applied to particular cases and always presuming a delimited field of application. But it is another fact about theories in general that they would be wrongly taken to be simple compilations of the cases to which they are applied. A theory is seldom if ever a verbal file-box of natural kinds, nor is it a bare chronicle of cause and effect. Rather, it affords us ways of grouping and explaining phenomena, and no application is ever entirely beyond question. This, upon reflection, will be seen to be part of what is involved in saying that it must be that a theory can be applied: It must enable us to see in the phenomena what we might otherwise have missed. One must, of course, in setting forth a theoretical account, always have examples in mind, and the more abstract the account the more necessary examples become; that is the control. Examples so presented are not bare matter in motion, but also, in being cited as examples, intimate ways of applying the theory. Thus, to illustrate, 'action' will be introduced to include such types as reaching out for food, tying a shoe, moving a piece in a game of chess, and making a promise, which I assume any reader could readily recognize examples of; I shall contrast such items with, e.g., being knocked down, sneezing and stumbling, and shall thereby try to get you to see all these different examples in certain ways. In our more detailed work, we must always keep examples before us, to see whether they can easily and naturally be viewed in the suggested ways. The method is never foolproof, for the chosen example may not be entirely typical, and there may be any number of cases which cannot naturally and easily be cast and viewed as the theory would demand. That is only as it should be. It affords the possibility, by way of counter-example, of disproof, and no theory is worth the work if it cannot by its very nature be disproved. Commonsense, by way of contrast, seldom if ever requires a readjustment of our conceptual vision—of the 'understanding'—and is never susceptible to global repudiation.

'Coming to see things in a certain way' is, derivatively, a hallmark of theoretical investigation. It is that readjustment of our understanding which commonsense need not make, for commonsense embodies the everyday adjustments which we learn to make automatically in the course of growing up. As a general but not inevitable rule this 'coming to see' is not the 'result' of theoretical endeavour, but a preliminary to gaining such results; it is, we might say, what makes results possible. Consider, for example, the traditional physicists' way of regarding bodies as being in a relation of mutual gravitational attraction. Many of the classical so-called 'thought experiments' are compelling devices for impressing these new ways of seeing things upon our understanding. In what follows, I shall, among other things, be trying to get the reader to see our identifications of behaviour in certain systematic, slightly novel ways, *e.g.*, as involving certain kinds of belief on the part of the animals observed, or as involving the possibility of success and failure.

Theoretical work usually carries with it the use of distinctions unfamiliar to commonsense and the obliteration or neglect of other distinctions taken for granted in everyday life. The introduction of measurement usually has that result. But even in taxonomic science, the investigator is on the look-out for possibly subtle, hitherto unnoticed *differentiae* while casually turning a blind eye to the grosser features of things which almost everyone can spot. Now we neglect everyday distinctions at our peril, and no more so than in philosophy; at the same time, novel distinctions must establish themselves as fruitful or decisive. But that only confirms that theory requires justification in ways that commonsense cannot. Theory must be proved in application.

Finally, theory is inescapably *technical* in ways that commonsense cannot be. Commonsense belongs to Everyman; while it may be sharp or dull, improved or impaired, it comes without express instruction and results from experience; but one must be instructed in and trained up to the intricacies and technicalities of a theory. An important mark of this difference is that theory must inevitably dispose of a body of technical terminology or, at any rate, technical usage. But the fact of technical usage may go unrecognized and unremarked, alas, even by the author of a theory, because the terms employed may be borrowed from the vernacular. That is especially apt to happen in subjects like philosophy and political theory. Here lies danger. An elementary methodological rule is that technical usage must be explained and illustrated if not defined. Vernacular borrowing exposes one to the danger of overlooking this demand. As protection, it would perhaps be wise to employ terminology whose technical character could not be mistaken. But there are perils lurking there too. Technical sounding talk is all too frequently a mask for empty thought. We all are familiar nowadays with the heavy use of jargon in the so-called social sciences, and how often it fraudulently

4

poses as exactness when it is nothing more than confusion. The mere cacaphonous sound of a word does not excuse us from giving explanations either. In this work the reader may be sometimes offended by what he feels are barbarisms. I do not apologize, at least so long as I provide the required explanations. I do nonetheless strongly feel that one should when possible employ language, whether or not overtly technical, which will almost automatically, as it were, etymologically point to the field of application, language which may counteract the tides of speculation and tend to keep us anchored to reality. Failing the terminological inventiveness of a Pierce or an Austin, we may, especially in philosophy, largely have to fall back upon vocabulary items of the common language we all understand. So here we are pulled in two directions. The somewhat uneasily compromised position I have fallen into is this: First, always to illustrate my meaning with examples, and especially to introduce jargon in the light of examples. Second, always to explain how my use of a familiar term, e.g., 'purpose', differs from the vernacular. Third, whenever possible to employ what we might call 'naturally' technical terms, or terms which have in philosophical usage taken on a technical ring. The *noun* 'act' is an important example. It is seldom used in the market place and then only for quite special kinds of deed, but is known to everyone by associations with its cognate verb. Other examples are 'statement', 'rule', 'conventional'. Adjusting the usage of such terms is fair game when it really does facilitate investigation, provided one explains or illustrates his meaning and does not fly in the face of usage. I hope always to follow this procedure. I shall also try to give express warning of what might otherwise be unsuspected technical usage.

But, you will say, there is another danger that ought not to be overlooked. While the adjustment of vernacular items to the requirements of theory may have explanatory power and give us a more transpicuous view of the field of investigation and free us from entrammelling irrelevancies, still, What is to assure us that the essential question hasn't been hidden and the author's account foolishly buttressed behind a wall of arbitrary usage? The thought is a frightening one, and I admit to being troubled by it. Perhaps indeed I shall sometimes think that I have isolated something important when in fact I shall isolate nothing at all but a figment of my theorizing imagination. A useful rule for minimizing this threat is to have good, indisputable examples at hand, and that I shall always try to do.

The technical adaptation of vernacular usage must be contrasted with two other kinds of case. Though theory involves technical usage, it does not follow that it involves technical usage only. (While programmes for formalization could have just that perhaps salutary result, they are only rarely carried out and then not always to the perfect satisfaction of the reader.) I shall for the most part be writing in English, and I shall never hesitate to avail myself of whatever parts of the vernacular I fancy myself to be master of. That is perfectly acceptable procedure, though it does cast a shadow, that one may in all innocence fail to realize that he has hazardously wandered from the well marked paths of vernacular usage. But still the principle is clear, that we may non-technically employ non-technical language *ad lib*. That is the first kind of case I want to contrast with the technical adaptation of familiar language. The second is that common-sense notions, possibly philosophically problematical in the extreme, may be vernacularly settled in usage which we simply assume, *e.g.*, 'can', 'responsible', 'know', 'believe', 'cause'. Certain of these ideas will be brought under theoretical review. But they need not be in order to get on with the task at hand. The only guide I follow here is to give explanations of these ideas—not words and not usages—when and to the extent that I find it useful or interesting to do so.

2. CONCEPTUAL EPIPHENOMENALISM

[Our theory will be philosophical and behavioural. It will be philosophical in that the direct subject matter is to be our ways, usually our commonsense ways of thinking and talking about behaviour, and only indirectly behaviour itself. It will be behavioural in contrast with phenomenological, in that we shall always take as immediate subject of investigation the third person observer's ways of thinking about animal behaviour. Unlike in classical behaviourism, we do not eschew the use of 'mentalistic language'. Our efforts will be to establish the conditions under which a conceptualizing observer of behaviour would be entitled to characterize that behaviour in certain ways. We attempt to explain what it is to see certain kinds of behaviour in the animal movements which constitute it. The method will generally be to consider what would be implied by an observer's true report on some behavioural episode. This theoretical position could be called *conceptual epiphenomenalism*.]

The ensuing theory will be philosophical and behavioural. I must now explain the intended force of 'philosophical' and 'behavioural', regrettably not without risk of controversy. I unhesitatingly accept the Aristotelian explanation of philosophy as the study of 'how we think about the world', and I mean our actual ways of thinking about the world. In its broadest dimensions, the field of philosophical investigation is the total range of possibilities latent in any operative form of conceptualization. Any new form of theorizing is allowed for in

6

advance. But these may be made subject of philosophical inquiry only by those who are familiar with them. I, for example, do not qualify as a philosopher of science.

There is another kind of philosophizing which I do not wish to denigrate but which falls outside my formula. That consists in *a priori* speculation over how we *might have* thought about the world if, *e.g.*, we were radically different in our physical nature and in our faculties. For all I know, the perceptual world of the porpoise may be so different from our own as to preclude any conceptual concourse between us. One can suppose that the logical or conceptual relations which obtain for us between x-rays and the visible spectrum would be reversed for creatures who could directly perceive the former but not the latter. But we can only speculate about such things, and then only for possibilities which deviate but slightly from the norms implicit in our standard ways of thinking, deviations of a sort already familiar from actually realized historical developments in science and commonsense, or from what we can discover by experiments on other types of animals. We cannot provide real live, controlling examples of the possibilities that are speculatively conjectured.

There have been two dominating moments in the history of western philosophy which I should call the sceptical and the metaphysical. Metaphysics, in the traditional pattern is, as I understand it, at least in part, the attempt to work out general and coherent *theories* of our ways of conceptualizing the world. Aristotle, Kant, and the high Scholastics are notable examples; I would also include Euclid, Leibniz, Newton, and Frege. In contrast, there have always been philosophers whose main concern has been to raise difficulties, leading to sceptical doubt about knowledge, morality, or what have you. Hume and the Sophists leap to mind. Such thinkers do not seek a coherent account of how we conceptualize the world, but, by twisting at certain important joints of the structure, stir suspicions that the whole apparatus is unreliable and infirm. Historically there have been other operative forces too, *e.g.*, all those schools of philosophy which are correctly read as manifestations of or as reactions to the spiritual, moral, or intellectual climate of their times. One thinks of neo-Platonism, *Weltanschaunungphilosophie* and existentialism, and the various philosophies of progress which were so plentifully spawned by the last century. I think that these systems qualify as philosophy—I certainly don't want to deny them any title they may claim—because they always have metaphysical and/or sceptical components. But taken entire, such developments, while possibly very interesting in themselves and to the historian of thought, are of no permanent philosophical importance, because they lead nowhere for being excessively parochial. Much more important for the general history of philosophy are those thinkers who have engrossed themselves in problems and difficulties of the same kind traded in by the sceptics, but whose inspiration is neither positively sceptical nor systematic. I think mostly of Plato and Wittgenstein. Both of these writers, as I read them, were obsessed with the challenge of scepticism; both tried to show that the sceptical challenge was unreal and ultimately unsound; but both understood how compelling the sceptics' arguments could seem; both wanted to break the charm which the sceptic casts over the understanding. Before anyone can engage in metaphysical philosophy he must be delivered from sceptical doubts of the philosophical kind. Plato made Aristotle possible. And Wittgenstein, I think, has made possible a resurgence of metaphysical thought in philosophy.

Whatever the validity of these historical asides, the character of this work is intended to be systematic and theoretical, hence, since philosophical, metaphysical. Philosophical 'problems' will trouble me only as hurdles to be got over, or as cases for testing the general coherence of the account.

I embark on this project with trepidation. Wittgenstein has amply demonstrated the pitfalls which terrorize the construction of philosophical theories. These theories fascinate you. They lead you to squeeze and pull at the facts to make them fit. But that is simply a danger that must be faced—and in theorizing of every kind. I am not convinced that it cannot be got around. It is notorious that both Plato and Wittgenstein, despite literary resources that enabled them to escape the lure of the systematic, never completely detached themselves from certain points of vantage from which they viewed the world nor completely avoided the compromising use of favourite models. I am therefore not convinced that philosophical theory is impossible; I am even inclined to think that it cannot be escaped; but since one may easily fool himself on this, the more reason to enter into these theories with all due deliberateness.

Theoretical philosophy has strong affinities with certain parts of mathematics, 'natural mathematics', I'd call it. Parts of the classical mathematical corpus strike me as substantive philosophical developments of permanent value. I think of classical geometry, analysis, and the modern topological theory of dimension as well as of mathematical logic. All these seem to me to qualify as accounts of how we actually think about the world, as witnessed by our concern to ascribe shapes, measurements, and dimensions to things, and to reason in certain ways. Natural mathematics and metaphysical theory are alike in seeking to understand and to formulate first principles regarding how we think about the world. I don't claim any originality for this thought that philosophy and mathematics are close cousins; it calls

8

for comment only because of certain locally current fashions of thought according to which philosophy is somehow strange. There are, of course, clear differences between the usual practices of mathematicians and of philosophers. Plato seems to me to have come close to putting his finger on one of them when he remarked that mathematics seeks to arrive at truths from accepted principles, whereas dialectic (philosophy) seeks to show the reasonableness of the principles themselves. The mathematician is naturally apt to be more delighted than the philosopher at an obscure but elegant formulation of principles, while the philosopher is not nearly so anxious to arrive at distant consequences. In both kinds of study, we are dealing with matters extremely close at hand which are therefore easily entangled with other parts of our lives. Any hope of success requires methods of control, procedural rules of organization and presentation. Mathematicians typically secure that control by limiting themselves in advance to a small number of key ideas whose relations are either expressly stated or unmistakably known, and by use of the method of demonstration. Philosophers typically secure control by constant appeal to examples and counter-examples. But philosophy can be done, as it were, mathematically; witness the theories of Frege, Russell, Poincaré, Lesniewski, and Tarski, whose contributions to logic and topology are of enormous philosophical consequence. On the other side, the modern mathematician's use of counter-examples—the wilder the better—is in method as philosophical as anything could be.

With all that said, let me state unequivocally that I shall not be working up anything like a mathematical theory of behaviour, though the later stages of my work, not to be included in this volume, will foreshadow something like a mathematical theory of assertion. I shall use every and any method I can. I shall not hesitate to appeal to all the commonsense and theoretical notions and knowledge I possess. Demonstration will sometimes be attempted. More often, in lieu of proof, I shall have to content myself with offering considerations *pro* and *con*. The control will be always to keep examples in mind and 'to watch my language'.

Because this will be a theory of our ways of thinking about behaviour, it will be a theory of behaviour only at second remove; our analyses will be resolutely conceptual, second-order, theories of theories, if you wish. The immediate field of application will be cases of what I shall technically call the identification and characterization of behavioural episodes and only indirectly those episodes themselves. I am not anxious to insist upon any particular set of categories for placing our way of talking about items of behaviour, though I am indeed anxious to say what such a category would be, and I should

9

be happy if my work suggested such categories to the working psychologist and grammarian. I shall, of course, always assume that there are such categories, particular examples of which I shall be constantly citing for purposes of illustration.

The method will be as follows: I shall suppose an animate creature is being observed by another animal who is making reports upon what he sees. We consider these reports, which we understand and which we assume to be true. Our aim is to ascertain what these reports imply. In the light of examples, we provisionally stipulate that the observed behavioural episode is of a certain kind if and/or only if the report has certain implications, which we may generically denominate as conditions. Lists of such conditions will be taken to define types of behavioural episode. What is to be submitted to analysis is always supposed to be determined by some true report upon some animate phenomenon which appears digested within some presumed well-determined system of identification and description. The ideas to be set forth and the lines I shall draw between them are schematic, as it were, relative to the physical transaction itself, which might be variously identified and described by different observers. The account we give of such a phenomenon will therefore not in general be unique to the physical transaction. Nor, again, does the physical transaction by itself determine what the correct account will be. For example: Sports reporters use a vocabulary for describing golfing acts, e.g., 'driving', 'putting', and 'approaching'. One of them might be heard to say, e.g., 'Snead is making his approach to the second green', meaning that Snead is now getting set to try to hit the ball onto the green. Of course some club will be employed, and it might be that Snead is making his approach with a nine-iron. That kind of movement with that kind of implement is made. But the reporter does not tell us that it is Snead's purpose to make the approach with just that club, though Snead regards the employment of just that club as best calculated to get him to the green, and the sports reporter may know that very well. Given the scheme of 'driving', 'approaching', 'putting', etc., for identifying golfing acts, the reporter would be making a quite different identification of the act were he to say, 'Snead is getting set to make a nine-iron approach to the green'. For, by saying that, he would be conveying to his listeners that it is part of Snead's purpose to make the approach with just that club: One might do that kind of act, for example, when practising nine-iron approaches. I shall later find it convenient to introduce the general term 'hybrid action' to cover the latter kind of identification of acts. To identify an act as of a hybrid kind presumes that there exists some other predominating scheme for identifying non-hybrid acts. But that is not determined by the physical transaction itself, which may

10

have the same shape in every case. Since observers may identify physical occurrences as acts in a variety of ways, there is no advance answer to the abstract question whether the transaction—set forth perhaps solely in kinematical terms—is or is not hybrid. Similar observations may be made about almost all the abstract distinctions I shall draw, *e.g.*, between behaviour and mere animal movement, between behaviour which does and does not qualify as action, between what is done and how it is done, between kinds of acts, *e.g.*, between conventional and non-conventional acts. These distinctions are not self-applying, and are not to be applied in the abstract; they presume not only a field of application, as does every theory, but already familiar ways of identifying and describing the phenomena in question. Indeed these verbal formulations are the immediate field of application, and we deal only indirectly with the presumed transactions I have called the phenomena. That I should draw these abstract distinctions surely indicates my confidence that they can be usefully applied to increase our understanding of what might be said about the concrete particular. My only wish is that it be clearly understood that this application is, as I put it, schematic and indirect.

A distinctive mark of philosophy—sceptical or metaphysical—is its second-order character. It is to be set apart from natural science in this respect, among others, that it seeks to render comprehensible and coherent what all interested parties must already understand. That, more than anything else, I believe, lies under contemporary doubts about the possibility of systematic philosophy. How can we seek to render comprehensible what we must already understand? But the argument, if made explicit, would be equally embarrassing for the claims of much mathematics. How then is it possible to become intellectually exercised by what we already must understand? Well, one may be master of a certain concept, *e.g.*, of the concept of the past, *i.e.*, be able to employ the word 'was' or the equivalent without mishap, but still be unable to say in so many words what is involved in the use of the word. The mathematician, again, may have a complete mastery of the use of $\aleph_0$, $\aleph_1$, *etc.*, complete practical control over the concept of infinity, and still wonder what infinite (cardinal) numbers are. We may be impelled to ask, 'What is time?', 'What is infinity?', and the answers may not be entirely easy to find. The questions make sense and the project of answering them is possible for the very reason that some have found it puzzling: to ask the question presumes a practical mastery of the concept, and we can check proposed answers against a very large body of data which is latent in that mastery. Our familiar ways of thinking about the world may be elicited in examples upon which we may hopefully agree.

PART ONE: CONCEPTUAL EPIPHENOMENALISM

The ways of thinking brought under philosophical review may themselves be highly technical. Hence, the philosophies of science, mathematics, the law, not to speak of philosophy itself. What is required is that the investigator have a working familiarity, an adequate mastery of the forms of conceptualization in question. But commonsense has been the more usual target. It is on this part of our intellectual lives that traditional metaphysics, epistemology and moral philosophy have historically centred attention. And for the most part so shall I. It is therefore somewhat inaccurate to describe what will follow as a theory of theories, for my dominating interest will be in our common, everyday ways of thinking about behaviour. These are not theories. This is not to be a philosophy of under-developed science, *e.g.*, not a philosophy of psychology.

In philosophy we may study our ways of thinking about anything at all—matter in motion, works of art, historical fact, or what have you. In this work we bring under systematic review our ordinary ways of thinking about animal behaviour. Behaviour, therefore, is indirectly the subject matter of investigation.

The methods to be employed will be, in a broad sense, 'behaviouristic', where 'behaviouristic' marks a contrast with 'phenomenological' and 'introspective'. We shall always be considering the observer's view of behaviour. The conceptualization of the behaviour we investigate will always be strictly and even ruthlessly third-person. Even when we consider how we think about our own behaviour, we must do so as an outside observer would. Usually there is no problem about this; but there may be when the subject is human behaviour, and especially, the use of Language. The reason, briefly put, is that an observer is not in a position to identify an act, especially a Language act, unless he is capable of doing such acts; there is then a temptation to conduct the analysis in terms of what an agent might say in the course of and incidental to doing that kind of act on his own. But in this kind of investigation it is always a mistake and usually a sign of muddle when one sets himself to imagine how 'it feels'. As Wittgenstein has taught us, we must always look for the (public) criteria, not only as exits from philosophical labyrinths but also as a condition for theoretical progress. Alternatively, we shall take as our data reports upon behaviour and not verbal manifestations of behaviour, *e.g.*, expressions of intention.

Though introspection is eschewed, our method will not be Watsonian behaviourism. I shall not hestitate to use 'mentalistic language', like 'purpose', 'believe', 'aware'. Mine is not a programme for founding a new science, nor does conceptual economy intrigue me. I simply want to understand what we mean when we say, *e.g.*,

12

'Smith is eating cheese' or 'Smith thinks that this is cheese'. I take all our common ways of thought hence our common ways of talking about behaviour as fundamental data, and I claim the right to employ that same language on my own. It is no part of my purpose to devise novel, economical, scientific ways of formulating facts about behaviour itself; I am not seeking foundations for psychology. Nor is my work on Language in particular to be regarded as a continuation of that rather tedious behaviouristic tradition stretching from *The Meaning of Meaning* through Morris' *Signs, Language, and Behaviour* and Russell's *Inquiry* to Quine's *Word and Object*. The method, to repeat, is to draw out and classify the implications of supposed true reports upon behavioural episodes.

Now I assume that the imagined observer's characterizations of behaviour are given in consideration of what he sees in the movements and the circumstances of the animal observed. I shall constantly be asking questions of this form: What must an (outside) observer see in the movements constituting the behaviour and in the circumstances of the animal in order that he should meaningfully or truly be able to say . . . In one respect I am much more conscientiously behaviouristic than any self-styled behaviourist I know of. The observed conditions warranting the characterization in question will always be ones taken to be open to the view of an imagined observer. The observer is to consider not only the imagined animal observed, but must give at least equal weight to the observable circumstances in which his movements occur.

My theory represents an attempt to explain and understand what it is to *see* certain things *in* the movements of animate creatures. What we thus see and report upon might be styled as a kind of epiphenomenon with respect to animal movements and situational elements. They are phenomena which we see as residing in the movements only because we have these ways of thinking about the movements. You can, if you need a name, categorize my account as *conceptual epiphenomenalism*. There may be other methods of finding answers to the questions that I want answers for. But I do not know what those other methods would be. I hazard that the notion of a conceptual epiphenomenon may capture what is sound in the so-called Argument from Analogy, without risking its extravagances.

Here then is the kind of question we shall ask: What must the conceptualizing observer of animal movements see in and around those movements that will license him to characterize the movements in a certain way, *e.g.*, as tying shoes. Those conditions will come out as implications of the observer's report. If the characterization meets certain requirements, then we shall be able to say that what the observer observed was an act: 'tying shoes' identifies a kind of action.

13

The following is a picture of the situation I contemplate, and summarizes the kind of investigation I shall be making:

A   O   We

A is an animal imagined to be moving in certain ways. *O* is an imagined conceptualizing observer of *A*, whom we are to think of as reporting what he sees *A* doing. *We* is a theoretical commentator on the reported observations of *O*. *We* is supposed to have available the apparatus of the ensuing theory. He applies that by drawing out the implications of *O*'s report. On the assumption that what *O* reports is true, *We*'s observations contribute to a theoretical analysis of *A*'s movements.

O says that *A* is eating: *We* says that what *A* is doing is an act.
O says that *A* is wiring a circuit: *We* says that *A* must know how to wire electrical circuits.
O says that *A* is kicking a ball: *We* says that *A* thinks that there is a ball in his immediate vicinity.
O says that *A* thinks that there is a ball in his immediate vicinity: *We* says that *A* may be meaning to kick a ball.

In what follows I shall retain these distinctions between the subject animal, the observer, and the theoretical purveyor of analyses, whom I shall often refer to as 'we'. The technical notions that I shall introduce, fixed by such terms as 'behaviour', 'action', 'conditions of success', 'conditions of doing', 'proficient', 'conformative', 'conventional', *etc.*, pertain to the activities of the meta-theoretical commentator, *we*, on the reports of an imagined conceptualizing observer, *O*.

As our project develops it will progressively explain a growing conceptual sophistication on the part of the imagined observer by dint of which that observer is enabled to descry and bespeak ever more sophisticated types of behaviour in the imagined object of his observations. We start on the bottom rung with bare animal movement

14

and climb step by step to behaviour and action and various types of action including types of the use of Language.

3. PSYCHOLOGY AND PHILOSOPHY OF MIND

[Our aims differ from those of the psychologist insofar as, first, we are concerned more directly with common ways of thinking about behavioural phenomena than with those phenomena themselves and, second, while psychology purports to seek causal explanations of behaviour, our efforts are definitional in intent. But there are bound to be encounters between the two, critical but prospectively fruitful. Philosophers are often sceptical about programmes in modern psychology, whose theories, in certain phases, seem destined to be replaced by something more physiological in form and, in other phases, seem little better than crude philosophy of mind. But philosophers may still profit considerably from exposure to modern psychology. Psychologists may observe and isolate forms of behaviour hitherto unnoticed in vernacular usage, *e.g.*, so-called compulsive and replacement behaviour. Also, among the growing multitude of psychological theories are some which may enable the philosopher better to focus his own thinking. Hopefully among the results to be claimed here some may be similarly useful to the working psychologist. In particular, it would be gratifying if these efforts demonstrated the inadequacies of any simple imitative theory of the learning of Language.]

This work is not meant to be alternative to or to be in competition with modern psychology. But the two kinds of study are not utterly separate. Both are somehow concerned with animal behaviour. At certain crossings my putative results will conflict with and at others hopefully complement those of modern psychology, especially so-called Learning Theory. Typically, the philosopher's point of view is importantly different from that purportedly taken by the working psychologist. While the psychologist is presumably directly interested in animal behaviour itself, our immediate concern is a second-order one, being initially concentrated upon our ways of thinking and talking about behavioural phenomena. Derivatively: The psychologist allegedly means to secure a foundation for the 'causal explanation' of animal behaviour; our efforts, by way of contrast, are to be resolutely definitional, seeking a foundation for the explanation of our ways, usually commonsense ways of thinking about animal behaviour.

Despite that important difference, the two kinds of theoretical account will sometimes come into contact, prospectively fruitful as well as negatively critical. I have certainly profited from a slight exposure to psychology, especially to Learning Theory as it is presently developing, and hope to be able to return the favour. Psychologists, too, must sometimes pause over the definitions of familiar types of behaviour; they too must begin immersed in our everyday, commonsense ways of thinking about the animate world, and I assume that they would welcome progress towards the better understanding of those ways of thinking.

Now I confess to sharing the scepticism which many contemporary philosophers apparently feel towards the general claims which the psychologist is apt to make for his subject. In reading systematic psychological literature I often suffer spasms of distress. The multitudes of elaborate experiments which are described and the proliferation of 'explanatory models' leave a lay reader, like myself, with a dark suspicion that all this is little more than a painfully contorted exercise in the eliciting of the obvious. Psychology ardently aspires to the status of an explanatory science, but it never quite seems to qualify. What makes me sceptical and susceptible to distress is, I think, a deep apprehension that modern psychological theory in its abstracter phases fails to achieve a permanent identity of its own. On the one hand, psychology's proliferating 'explanatory models' seem to be destined to enjoy only a short useful life. The more promising of these, when accurately set out, seem redolent with unrealized physiological possibilities. The bonds, interactions, *etc.*, of Learning Theory are hypotheses which simply cry out for supplementation and confirmation from the study of the physiology of the nervous system. I don't mean to sneer. It would be no small achievement were the psychologist able to formulate in his own language the salient features of the mechanisms which the physiologist must finally invest with body and explain. But if I am right, psychology is only a temporary expedient, a perhaps useful stopgap, fated to be abandoned for something better.

In another phase, much of psychological literature seems little better than bad philosophy of mind. History reveals that what is now happening over on the other side of the campus is not always so very different from what was already in progress before the division of the departments. That is to be expected. Just as the physicist surely contributes to the understanding of our everyday ways of thinking about matter in motion, so too the psychologist contributes to our everyday ways of thinking about our fellow creatures. He is certainly on the lookout for ostensibly duplicated pieces whose common presence possibly accounts for our talking in similar ways about different things, *e.g.*, about ourselves and our pets. But the psychologist doesn't always do this very well. For one thing, he seems unable

16

to achieve the elevated detachment which the physicist and the botanist enjoy. He seems almost too bothered by the facts. He wants to get above commonsense but somehow he cannot really. Consequently his attempts at theorizing in a different dimension often seem premature. The psychologist is also, like the philosopher, exercised by the obvious. That would be no cause for complaint were he not so often so pretentious in his claims, so confused in his language, and so speculative in his willingness to generalize. The psychologist cannot quite bring himself to see that to be properly scientific he must actually stop thinking about people, in much the same way that the physiologist thinks about ganglia instead. Now, because of his scientific presumption, the psychologist is likely to regard himself as excused from exercising the kind of care and caution which becomes more and more a trademark of modern philosophy. To the trained philosopher, the professional psychologist often appears extraordinarily naïve. I recall once attending a lecture on the psychology of language in which the speaker admitted that his account could not readily effect a distinction between the sense of 'Mary loves Johnnie' and 'Johnnie loves Mary': he hadn't even thought to ask himself about that. Philosophers are often, and rightly, charged with ignorance. But if the plaintiff is psychology, then there is room for countercharge. Many psychologists, I feel, could quickly profit from some simple instruction in drawing distinctions and seeing differences.

That is the negative side of the story, as read by one philosopher, that psychology in its general theorizing often seems to pass from callow physiology to decrepit philosophy without the enjoyment of a fruitful maturity. Perhaps what I say is unjust. But there is another side to the story, more agreeable to relate.

Psychologists do sometimes turn up facts of an unobvious kind, often of first-water interest to common life and to philosophy alike. I think chiefly of results which have come out of the physiological-cum-psychological investigation of perception, e.g., on colour vision. Recent work in so-called animal psychology is another case in point. Here too have been revealed facts not at all obvious to commonsense which are highly suggestive to the philosopher engrossed in traditional problems over space and time and the origin of our ideas. It is significant that in these cases one would be hard pressed to draw a distinction between the psychologist, the biologist, and the physiologist.

Differently and more autonomously, the psychologist may, in the course of his investigations, find it necessary expressly to take note of and to give name to forms of behaviour which, though as common as the air we breathe, may go unheeded by vernacular usage. Examples are what, following the psychologists, we now call *compulsive* and *replacement* behaviour, but I think especially of so-called VTE.[1]

It is also encouraging for a philosopher to discover psychologists having to draw roughly parallel distinctions. Thus what I shall call proficient behaviour and conformative behaviour seem to correspond, if only roughly, to what psychologists call learned behaviour and social behaviour, respectively. To come across such comparable distinctions and accounts rising from a source so apparently different is confirmatory in itself.

In one instance I am particularly grateful to Mowrer. Remarks of his suggest a clue which I had been missing for the definition of what will be called *proficient behaviour*. Additionally, certain of the 'theoretical models' proposed by learning theorists may be highly suggestive to the philosopher and by their very existence serve to correct or to confirm the direction of his speculations. A topic for Learning Theory nowadays is the relation between information (likened to a kind of stimulus) and behaviour (likened to a kind of response). Such theories seem to me to be attempted answers to the ancient problem of *practical reason*, or, as it is sometimes called, *practical syllogism*. The psychologist may fail to appreciate what kind of question he is trying to answer, and what his answer comes to philosophically. But that needn't matter very much. One such 'model' seems to me to be very like the theory of action which I shall develop in Part II. That is the so-called 'Drive-Cue-Response-Reward' theory ascribed to Miller and Dollard.[2]

I suspect that there is nothing that I define that could not somehow be framed in S-R (Stimulus-Response) terms, though, if what I propose is correct, then these formulations would often prove much more complicated than the psychologist could ever have expected.

Psychologists, when they are not simply bored, probably find philosophers more irritating than philosophers find them. That is sad. In compensation for what I have learned from them, I could only hope that they might also learn something from a working philosopher. My account, if right, would demonstrate that the S-R mechanisms to which the psychologist appeals, would have to be immeasurably more complicated than he might at first have thought. My proposed definitions for types of behaviour, while certainly not framed in psychological terminology, could possibly be of value for fixing the

---

[1] Vicarious Trial and Error Behaviour (see O. Hobart Mowrer, *Learning Theory and the Symbolic Process*, Chap. 6, III), the head-waggings and such like which are the visible manifestation of thought. It is important for my account that we can see people thinking, believing, *etc.*

[2] See Mowrer, *loc cit.*, pp. 104–108. Mowrer tells us that this theory is an adaptation of the Hull Theory of Learning. The drive corresponds to my *principle of reason*; the cue is my *reason*; the response is the *animal movements* constituting the act, or possibly the act itself; and the reward is the *measure of success*.

phenomena for which the psychologist might want to work out the machinery. These definitions, if correct, reveal the minimal complexity that would have to be accommodated. They would serve as a kind of control for any future science of behaviour. That goes especially for psychological accounts of the use of Language. Nothing could be more unconvincing to a philosopher than the simple-minded imitative theories now current in standard textbooks on the psychology of Language. Doubtless, learning the use of Language must involve imitation; but one of the most surprising things about Language is that imitation doesn't matter more than it does. Only when psychologists come to a better working conception of what Language is will they appreciate how very complicated any learning-theoretical mechanism will have to be to do justice to the facts. A psychologist to whom I have already alluded, and from whom I have learned, still talks about meaning as if it were always a matter of referring to an object meant (*loc. cit.*, Chap. 4, esp. VII). Psychologists also seem almost unconsciously to assume that using Language is a matter of one animal's getting through to, communicating with another, oblivious to the fact that they themselves may be busily writing down thoughts for their own private consumption, not to mention their failure to see that the use of Language is only one special way by which animals may communicate. Psychologists also are apt to be more concerned with the mere utterances of words than with the allowedly much more subtle behaviour of actually *saying something*. They seem, in short, as yet unable to cope with what it is to formulate and convey sense, living proof of how impoverished are their schemes. Presently available analyses of the use of Language in terms of mediation seem so extraordinarily crude and unconvincing that I scarcely know what to say about them, except to point out how they might be improved. Perhaps my definition of Language will give an inkling of how reticulated will have to be the bonds of any feedback stimulus-response–stimulus-response mechanism adequate for the analysis of linguistic phenomena.

In fine, I suggest that we all should continue to pursue the studies we prefer but not without hope that we can profit from trade. I look for relations of a kind similar to those mentioned above to obtain between that part of my work which is specifically on Language and the investigations of modern structural linguistics.

But enough in the way of comparative generalities. Let us proceed to our first task, that of defining *behaviour*.

19

Part Two

BEHAVIOUR AND ACTION

---

1. BEHAVIOUR

[An item of behaviour is defined as a sequence of movements of and/or in a particular animal of a particular type occurring over a connected interval of space and time, such that there is in force a presumption, based on our common experience with the type of animal in question, that such creatures, when placed in circumstances of the kind in question, could have been so trained that, being so disposed in advance, they could, by exercise of sufficient attention and expenditure of energy, have arrested or inhibited movements of the kind in question on occasions like that in question. The latter part of this definition is advanced as an analysis of what we would mean by saying that the animal might be held responsible for his movements.]

The indirect subject of this study, most generally described, is animal movement. The aim is to supply a framework for describing our ways of thinking about animal movement. More specifically, I wish to develop apparatus for characterizing our ways of talking about and especially our ways of typifying kinds of animal movement. But I wish these explanations to accommodate a certain level of animal movement which I call *behaviour*.

We must first try to say what it is for an animal to behave. In posing so abstract a problem, we show that we are concerned not only with animals' behaving but also with what is done when animals behave. I shall call what the animal does an *item of behaviour*. By defining *item of behaviour* we shall be on our way towards giving a theoretical analysis of what it is for an animal *to behave*, somewhat as by defining what a colour is we should be on the way towards giving a theoretical analysis of what it is for a body to have a colour.

'Behaviour' is a common word familiar to everyone. But in the hands of psychologists and philosophers it is invariably used technically to cover a rather special range of phenomena. We commonly speak of the behaviour of the planets or of the intestinal tract; again, we tell children to behave themselves, and we criticize their behaviour. The intended technical usage of 'behaviour' is nothing like so broad as to cover the first kind of example, nor does it have many of the special features suggested by the second kind of example. I want to employ 'behaviour' to cover only natural occurrences which consist of movements of or in animals, and then not all such movements. But I am not much interested in questions of comportment. Therefore, it will not do simply to appropriate 'behaviour' without explanations.

So far as I know, there is no vernacular item in the English language which exactly covers the intended range of phenomena. That is because we have not yet developed ways of talking and thinking *theoretically* about behaviour, abstractly regarded. A reason for that—as witnessed by the enormous vocabulary that we all regularly employ for identifying kinds of items of behaviour—is that our everyday interest in behaviour is so minute and so encompassing that a general theory would at once be very difficult to come by and of little practical service to our common understanding of people. In learning our mother tongue, we are taught to draw behavioural distinctions so finely that the need for a theory is not felt. But part of what I am attempting is just to articulate the skeleton of such a theory, not to enable us better to understand what we and our fellow creatures do and fail to do, but to enable us better to understand what we mean when we say that they have done such and such.

It is, then, not part of my programme to give an analysis of the ordinary English usage of 'behaviour'. But 'behaviour' is, failing better, a natural word to employ for categorizing a certain kind of animal movement. It is easily carried into the psychologist's or philosopher's technical account. I shall feel free to employ it in my own technical, philosophical way—which may or may not coincide with that of other writers—after I have told you what behaviour is. But that would be fatuous were I not confident in advance that my usage of 'behaviour' had clear and unequivocal applications for actual cases, and that my explanation, to be given below, constitutes clarification of a concept which plays an important role in life. Items of behaviour, in my sense, are easily found and are a subject of great interest to us all. That is confirmed by the fact that we have an abundance of language available whose predicative application to particular cases implies that the cases in question are items of behaviour in my sense.

Our programme of analysis requires nothing more, for our

imagined data are precisely reports, real or imagined, upon animal movement, which are presumed to carry certain implications. We shall consider examples of such reports to determine what those implications may be. With a provisional criterion in hand, we may then say whether items of a certain range of animate phenomena truly reported on in such and such ways do or do not qualify as behaviour. Let us then have some examples of animal movement which both do and do not qualify as behaviour.

Examples of kinds of animal movement which qualify as types of behaviour are stumbling, ingesting, going over to a person, kicking a ball, tying shoes, presenting salutations, integrating a partial differential equation.

Examples of kinds of animal movement which are not types of behaviour are these: being knocked over by a car or a bullet, the swelling of a lump on the head, the contraction of the colon in the course of normal digestion, turning over in sleep, swooning.

Because there is no customary word for what I want to mean by 'behaviour' (which I feel is much the same as psychologists and other philosophers have wanted to mean by the word), I appeal to the reader's intuitions and hope that his tally with mine. But that is not satisfactory, for I have discovered to my chagrin that actually there is no universal meeting of minds on this matter. My examples may therefore seem arbitrary, and the definition which they suggest no more than stipulative. Let me acknowledge that threat in advance, while expressing hopeful confidence that the ensuing analysis will prove itself in application.

At this place another problem rises to confront us. All the words we selected to illustrate animal movements that are and are not items of behaviour are used to *typify* animal movements in certain ways. They are, if you wish, names of types of animal movement. But there are, unfortunately, types of movement instances of which sometimes do and sometimes do not qualify as items of behaviour, at least as I preconceive the matter. Blinking, coughing, sneezing, yawning, falling asleep, and starting at a snake are examples. So words are not enough. Now, such types of movement would be useful as test cases for our definition, which could be applied to determine when such a movement does and does not qualify as an item of behaviour. But that presumes substantial advance agreement on the status of particular cases and hence a substantially common feel for the intended sense of 'behaviour'.

In order to impart this 'common feel' it will be useful to recall an ancient distinction in philosophy, and to suggest a device for selecting examples, which I shall call a verbal index. Behaviour, as a kind of animal movement, is to be contrasted with what *happened to* the animal. Behaviour, broadly speaking, is what animals do, in contrast with what they suffer. That suggests the following as a fairly reliable verbal index in English to examples of kinds of items of behaviour: Could we, after the occurrence of animal movement, receive an affirmative, unqualified answer of the form 'He —ed', to the question 'What did he do?'? If so, the verb which goes in the '—' signalizes a kind of behaviour. The use of 'unqualified' in the above statement is to be taken to imply that it would make no clear sense to qualify the answer. The possibility of saying, in answer to the question, 'He didn't do anything, he only turned over in his sleep', indicates that 'turned over in his sleep' is not a name for a kind of behaviour; in contrast, 'He didn't do anything, he only stumbled', sounds at best odd to my ear. Needless to say, this index to examples, though fairly reliable, is not infallible. Obviously, the test lets in too many different kinds of answers, including all those which sometimes do and sometimes do not identify an item of behaviour, *e.g.*, 'coughed'.

The question we must now answer is: What is observed that calls for the employment of a behaviour-signalizing verb? Alternatively: What is characteristically implied by a report which identifies an item of behaviour?

My proposal is this: An item of behaviour is a happening describable as a movement of and/or in a specifiable, single animal, occurring over a specifiable, single, connected interval of space and time, which movement is subject to a certain condition. I call the movement in question the animal movement constituting the item of behaviour. If such a movement occurs, we may say that the animal in question *behaves*.

I am not prepared to give definitions of *animal* and *movement*, doubtless hard to come by. Here unanalysed common understanding will have to suffice. I employ 'animal' and 'movement' according to what I believe is standard English usage. I would, however, observe the following: Movements always are movements of material bodies and ideally would be identified in highly explicit kinematical terms. Animals are material bodies, which I assume the reader will have no difficulty in distinguishing from other material bodies, and are always classifiable as falling within a certain type, some of which types I assume the reader can identify. Examples of types of animal are human beings, dogs, cats, kangaroos, and goldfish. Examples of what are not types of animal are buildings, molecules of sugar, and imbeciles (though, of course, whatever is an imbecile is an animal of some type).[1]

---

[1] When I was reading proof, the thought occurred to me that a necessary (but not sufficient) condition for a body to be an animal is that a typal identification by a conceptualizing observer would imply the possibility of explaining

Movements, including animal movements, may be arbitrarily decomposed into any (finite) number of parts, each of which is also a movement. A report which implies that an animal movement is an item of behaviour normally also implies that the movement is to be regarded as partially decomposed into parts of certain identifiable kinds. Thus to say that the animal kicked implies that his movement consisted in part of the movement of a leg. I shall call a collection of implied movements which are parts of the movement of an animal a *sequence of animal movements*. (This is not the mathematician's sense of 'sequence'.) The members of such a sequence of animal movements may occur concurrently or successively or overlap each other in time. Allowing that a single movement counts as a sequence of movements, we may stipulate that an item of behaviour is a sequence of animal movements. More exactly, an item of behaviour is an animal movement for which there exists a true report which implies that the movement in question may be represented as a sequence of movements, where that sequence of movements is subject to a certain condition.

A single animal movement might be truly characterized in a number of different ways. The alternative characterizations might imply complementary or alternative decompositions of the movement into sequences of movements. Our examples suggest, however, that usually only a single item of behaviour is to be identified in the body of a single animal over a single connected interval of time. That is true even when the movements are connected, as it were, solely through the body of the animal, as when one salutes by simultaneously lifting his arm to the head and clicking his heels, or as when one shifts gears by concurrently moving a foot onto the clutch and a hand to the gearshift. But there are cases when it would be more natural to speak of two such items of behaviour occurring concurrently, as when, in the course of shifting gears, one also quite independently addresses a remark to one's wife. This possibility is allowed for by our schematic definition of an item of behaviour. For more than one item of behaviour to be occurring at the same time with respect to a single animal, it appears that at least two necessary conditions must obtain, which conditions, I conjecture, are together sufficient. First there must exist true characterizations of the movement which imply that it is to be decomposed into at least two sets of parts, the only connection between which is through the body of the animal, *e.g.*, the movements of the arm and leg together and the movements of the tongue and larynx together. Second, we must be

---

certain of the body's movements in terms of *function, i.e.*, an animal is a body to which "teleological" explanations are appropriate. This is only a conjecture.

able to give independent identifications of each of the sets of parts as items of behaviour. A double item of behaviour is then to be distinguished from (1) a single item of behaviour for which there are two independent identifications (*e.g.*, by uttering a string of words, I at once express a malicious remark about one person and a complimentary remark to another); (2) separable sequences of movements which are connected only through the body of the animal but which are covered by a single identification (our example of shifting gears); (3) one segment of a sequence of movements which follows upon another segment of a sequence of movements which together are correctly identified by a single characterization (*e.g.*, the backward and then forward movements of the leg which together constitute an act of kicking); (4) cases where one description of an item of behaviour given with reference to certain movements is subsidiary to another characterization of an item of behaviour possibly but not necessarily also involving other movements as well (*e.g.*, turning on the radio *by* reaching out a hand and turning the switch).

We may summarize by saying that an item of behaviour is 'individuated' as a sequence of movements relative to an identification. A given animal movement may include two items of behaviour only if it may be decomposed into at least two sequences of movements each of which may be independently identified.[2]

It remains to specify the 'certain condition' alluded to in our schematic definition. What is implied in behavioural characterizations of animal movements? What, for example, is implied in saying that someone stumbled that is not implied in saying that he was knocked down by a car? The difficulty of specifying this condition is notorious. But holding to the idea that we are asking what a conceptual observer would have to see in the movements in order to characterize them behaviourally, and minding our examples of types of animal movement which are and are not types of behaviour, but especially types, instances of which sometimes are and sometimes are not items of behaviour, I hazard the following: The animal in question *might* (but need not) be rightly held responsible for the movements or for what issues from those movements. Cutting corners, I shall say that what the animal is or might be held responsible for are his movements, a compression licensed perhaps by the fact that items of behaviour are always constituted of animal movements. Thus, one might be held responsible for his movements if, upon entering a bus, he stumbles against a woman, scattering her packages. But if he were knocked into a woman by an oncoming car, he could not be held responsible

---

[2] At this point I can only hope that the reader will understand what I mean by 'identify' which is the near equivalent of 'typify'. My somewhat technical use of 'identify' will be explained in no. 4 below.

26

for *those* movements, though he possibly could be held responsible for walking into a position where he could be hit by the car. Where one might hold an adult responsible for sneezing at an inopportune moment, one could never hold a dog or an infant responsible for sneezing at any moment.

Perhaps I could stop there. Responsibility, after all, is an everyday notion familiar to all of us. But, unfortunately, it is an extremely problematical idea, very apt to engender paradoxes, and I should like to attempt some further resolution. I adhere to the position of the observer, and I ask what the observer must see in the animal and his movements in order that the animal might rightly be held responsible by anyone who understood the observer's report. I propose a refinement of the avoidability criterion: The movements for which an animal might be held responsible are ones such that there is a presumption, based on our common experience with the type of animal in question, that such creatures, when placed in circumstances of the kind in question, could have been so trained that, being so disposed in advance, they could by exercise of sufficient attention and expenditure of energy have arrested or inhibited movements of the kind in question, on occasions like that in question. So long as the presumption is in force, the animal might rightly be held responsible for his movements. For example: There is certainly no presumption that a man placed before an oncoming automobile could avoid being thrown down; but perhaps an elephant could. There is a presumption that adult human beings can avoid the movements which constitute stumbling; it is presumed that some animals can stifle sneezes and that others cannot.

Assembling what has been proposed, we may define behaviour as follows: An item of behaviour is a sequence of animal movements occurring over a connected interval of space and time such that there is in force a presumption, *etc.*

We establish the existence of an item of behaviour by showing that movements of or in an animal occurred, *etc.* The item of behaviour is individuated with respect to the minimum connected interval of space and time over which the constituting sequence of movements occurred, where every element of the sequence is, relative to a true typification, determined as a part of the animal's total movement. The item is identified as a particular by an exact kinematical description of the movements, given within one or another frame of reference. I am not able in short space to state criteria for typifying the item, *e.g.*, as stumbling, kicking, *etc.* Because an item of behaviour is individuated with respect to a single specific stretch of time, it cannot occur twice in time, but it may be re-identified (*e.g.*) as observed from different places.

27

I now append a number of observations about behaviour in general and responsibility in particular:

First, an animal might rightly be held responsible for what he does *not* do as well as for what he does do. *Responsibility* is a broader idea than *behaviour*. A complete account of responsibility would have to consider movements which the animal could have made but did not, as well as movements which he did make but could have avoided.

Second, whereas being *blameworthy* implies responsibility for something, the converse relationship does not obtain. Though I may be responsible for the movements which constitute my turning on the radio, I would not be blamed if I could not have known there was someone sleeping in the house.

Third, though animal movements constitute behaviour only if the creature *might* have been rightly held responsible, he *need* not be held responsible for his movements by the imagined observer or the observer's interlocutors, and generally will not be unless that behaviour issues in what would be regarded by some other animal as unfortunate, though even that is not sufficient. Furthermore, the allocation of responsibility may be in varying degrees, depending in many different ways upon the strength and generality of the basic presumption and the situation and history of the creature. This topic of responsibility and its degrees is as difficult as any in the whole of philosophy, and I am not prepared to supply a complete analysis.

Fourth, the imagined inhibition of the movement constituting an item of behaviour must be supposed to occur *in place of* the behaviour. Thus one could avoid being knocked over by a car by taking care not to walk into the intersection; but that is not enough to qualify his falling movement, upon being struck, as an item of behaviour; he must have been able to avoid being knocked over by the car upon the very approach of the car. The supposed substituted movement must at a minimum be thought of as overlapping the interval of space and time at which the actual behaviour occurred.

Fifth, actually to arrest or to inhibit the movements constituting the behaviour might call for counter-movements. That, too, would be behaviour, and of a more sophisticated sort we shall call 'action'. This illustrates what is commonly true, that restraint, forbearance or inhibition of behaviour is at a higher, more sophisticated level of behaviour than would be straightforward commission.

Sixth, an important consequence of our definition of behaviour is that the correctness of calling an item 'behaviour' is always relevant to the *type* and the *development* of the particular animal and to our actual *common knowledge* about creatures of the type of the animal in question. So, whether it is right to call it behaviour depends partly upon how we identify the particular animal as of a type; and it

28

depends upon our increasing common knowledge about that type once determined. As seal trainers learn more about their charges, they can teach them to be 'responsive' over a wider front, and they then increase our opportunities to speak about clever, or clumsy, or stupid seal behaviour. The stage to which the particular animal has developed also matters. Thus we have infants, adolescents and sub-normal human types, some of which we regard as almost subhuman. Infantile burping is not behaviour, but something which happens to the infant. Again, imbeciles can neither succeed nor fail in producing proofs of the Fundamental Theorem of the Calculus; that kind of behaviour is not open to an imbecile. It is because ascription of responsibility is thus relative to the type of the animal, its development and achievements, that some types of report on animal movement sometimes do and sometimes do not imply that what happened was an item of behaviour. The observer's words do not by themselves suffice. We need information about the subject of his report.

Seventh, what an animal might be rightly held responsible for alters with our changing presumptions about animals. Since we administer training in the light of knowledge we actually have, the satisfaction of the conditions regarding training, preparation, *etc.*, is also affected by the governing presumption. Recent writers on Free Will have stressed changes in our presumptions regarding human behaviour that result in a narrowing of the range of cases over which men might be held responsible. That is one-sided; for, as our ex-amples show, the field of responsibility is also widening along other fronts. If expenditures on public education are any index, it would appear that human beings are becoming responsible for more not less of what they do. Some may want to protest that an animal either is or is not responsible, regardless of what anyone may fancy he knows. I can only asseverate to the contrary: *Responsibility*, like *explanation*, is a concept whose application is *obviously* relative to what we know. And to those who would try to undermine the whole structure of our ways of thinking about animalkind by use of time-worn Laplacian arguments against Freedom of the Will, I would reply in similar vein that *explanation* like *responsibility* is a concept whose application is *obviously* relative to what we know. Perhaps an omniscient, omni-comprehenscient god would not hold lesser animals responsible for anything they do; but, so far as I can speculate, he might just as well hold them responsible for *everything* they do.

Finally, I must say something to elucidate 'presumption'. We define behaviour by reference to types of animal, but of course it is always individual animals that behave. Though an item qualifies as behaviour only relative to our general knowledge regarding the animal type, it

29

may be wrong to denominate as 'behaviour' what we might suppose was avoidable for some or most animals in question; our general knowledge is not an infallible measure of what an animal is responsible for. Usually the man who stumbles against a fellow passenger upon entering a bus is behaving clumsily, and might rightly be held responsible for the scattering of the packages. But falling against another by cause of an epileptic seizure is not stumbling nor any kind of behaviour at all; it is something which 'happens to' the poor man, and he cannot rightly be held answerable for the scattering of the packages. It was precisely for this reason that we had to speak about a 'presumption being in force'. The general story is this: In the light of our common knowledge about animals of this type, it is *prima facie* reasonable to call certain movements behaviour if the animal could have been trained to arrest movements of that kind. But special circumstances might defeat this *prima facie* presumption; in the usual case it is just that—that the presumption is defeated— which must be shown, that there is something special about the animal or his circumstances, *e.g.*, being taken by epileptic seizure. What must be shown is that the case is such that our common knowledge *does not* apply. Of course the demonstration is secured by bringing the case under our growing common knowledge about exceptions; but what these exceptions might be cannot be limited in advance. Behaviour and responsibility, to summarize the story, are, in Hart's apt term, *defeasible concepts*.[3]

An aspect of this 'defeasibility', prefigured by the heavily if implicitly conditionalized form of our definition of 'might be held responsible', is that the formula which defines responsibility does not by itself settle imagined cases for which the indicated conditions regarding the animal's situation, training, *etc.*, are not met. If the animal in fact was not properly trained, then, so far as our formula goes, it remains an open question whether he behaved. In some cases we shall say that he did and in others that he did not. To suppose otherwise would be to hold either that the animal is always responsible for his want of training and preparation or that he is *never* responsible for what he does if his training has been deficient— unsatisfactory alternatives. How we decide depends upon the particular case, and often we are not ready to decide at all. Criminal law in its modern developments well illustrates the difficulties that lie in the way of reaching an automatic decision. But for all that, decisions at law are ones which lawyers and other interested parties must sometimes make; and they work up general rules to fit different cases.

[3] See H. L. A. Hart, 'The Ascription of Responsibility and Rights', Chap. VIII, *Logic and Language*, First Series, ed. Anthony Flew; also my 'Moral Maxims and Moral Rules', *Ethics*, 1957, pp. 269–85, esp. pp. 278–83.

It surely is not for an amateur, seated comfortably in his study, to settle once and for all such important issue in advance of the facts. But our formula does suggest how we might describe what does happen; our growing experience with like cases intimates rules and suggests procedures by appeal to which we may decide whether inadequate training, *etc.*, is sufficient to nullify or to engender responsibility. Perhaps the chief merit of the formula is that it refuses to make any advance commitment on the substantive issues, for which, by the nature of the case, no advance commitment can be made.

2. ACTION: PRELIMINARY EXPLANATIONS

[An act is provisionally defined as an item of behaviour with a purpose. We individuate and identify an act as an item of behaviour; we identify what kind of behaviour it is by specifying the purpose, commonly by answering the question, 'What was the animal meaning to do ?'. Working criteria for the presence of purpose in behaviour are (1) items of the behaviour type in question may be said to succeed or to fail, and (2) the movements constituting the behaviour might be explained by the animal's knowledge or beliefs.]

I wish now to define a very common kind of behaviour which I shall call *action*. Particular episodes or items of this kind of behaviour will be called *acts*. We hold to the level of theory assumed in the last section. The supposed subject of our imagined conceptualizing observer is the act done, an item of behaviour, and not the animal which is acting, though in explaining what it is for an act to be done we should thereby put ourselves into position to give theoretical analyses of what it is for an animal to act.

'Act' and 'action' are central items in my vocabulary. The dictionary makes clear that, while both 'act' and 'action' are used to particularize behaviour, there are a number of cruces at which they separate. First, while 'act' always signifies *a doing*, 'action' may be used as well to signify *something done*, *e.g.*, a magistrate's action. Second, in obvious connection with this, action need not be what I shall call 'purposive', and indeed the word 'action' is frequently used to speak about physical transactions which in no way involve animals, *e.g.*, the action of the wind on the paint. 'Action' directs our attention to what happens, to the movements made and the results thereof. Third, action is always overt; things are 'put into action'; action is to be contrasted with *inaction*, with *thought* and *restraint*. It is, on the other hand, easy enough to speak of mental acts and acts of restraint. All this, as will soon appear, makes 'act' the better word

31

for purposes of particularizing items of behaviour. Why then use 'action' at all? Because it is what we could call a 'topic word', a generic term, this being part of its force as an abstract noun. Ours will be a theory of action, and not a theory of acts. The contrast resembles that between 'architecture' and 'building'. As a rule, then, when our imagined subject of observation is the particular, the choice will be 'an act'; but when talking about that subject itself, or some area or type thereof, 'action' will be employed.

Either of these words, 'act' and 'action', if passed off as part of the equipment we invariably employ when speaking about people and their comings and goings, will jar the careful speaker's linguistic sensibilities. Instead, we have a variety of more specific terms such as 'perform', 'execute', 'commit', 'enact', 'manoeuvre', 'deed', 'try'. 'Doing' is the usual English 'empty word' for raising questions about what I call acts. In daily life it would be a pompous pleonasm to ask what act he was doing. But 'doing' really will not do for us—it sounds and is too shallow. It does fine in daily life for reasons we have already reviewed. In daily life, there is very little need for talking theoretically about behaviour. But here the aim is to set forth a theory of behaviour, and to define certain levels of behaviour. Both on account of its vernacular associations and because of a long tradition, 'act' like 'behaviour' fits one terminological bill almost perfectly. Clearly, then, what follows is not an analysis of the ordinary use of the noun 'act', for (as far as I can determine) there is no such *a* use which is of special interest to the philosopher. On the other hand, 'act' always has been a natural for philosophers; it is a word which is easily carried into a philosopher's technical account, and I shall use it in my own philosophical way. My usage is, then, not designed to commit me on any substantive philosophical issue; rather, to the contrary. I wish, in particular, to avoid taking sides on the disputed question whether, in some natural sense of 'act', there are 'mental acts', though my inclination is to say that there are, examples being such items as trying to remember, concentrating on hearing the different voices in a string quartet, memorizing, and so on. Many of these types of 'mental act' seem to be or in some intimate way to involve the inhibition of overt acts, and especially Language acts as I shall explain them. 'Acts' in the presently to be adopted technical sense are always items of behaviour, hence 'overt', and will always involve detectable movement, however slight and minute. Mine, then, will be a technical use of 'act'. I should, nevertheless, be disappointed if the explanation of my use to be given below did not also constitute clarification of a concept which plays an important role in life. I believe that 'acts', in my sense, are easily found, and are a subject of great interest to the conceptualizing observer of behaviour.

Examples of kinds of action are ingesting, going over to a person, kicking a ball, tying shoes, presenting salutations, integrating a partial differential equation. These are all types of behaviour. But not all types of behaviour are types of action, *e.g.*, not stumbling. One may pretend to stumble or act as if he were stumbling, as an actor depicts a stumbler; that would be action, but it wouldn't be stumbling. What one feels about the examples of action in contrast with behaviour generally is that acts necessarily have a certain direction and directiveness, purpose, aim, intent. But it is hard to put a finger precisely on what this is.

Again, it would be useful to find some generally operating if not invariably accurate verbal index to action in vernacular usage, both to assure ourselves a subject matter wide enough to be interesting and to supply clues for a characterization. Speaking roughly, an item of behaviour is what the animal did; fastening on the usual force of the present participle, one might suggest that 'doing' would catch this ephemeral directiveness to which I alluded above. The verbal index would then be the possibility of giving an affirmative answer to the question, 'What was he (she, it) doing?'—an answer of the form, 'He was . . .ing', *e.g.*, eating, tying a shoe, feinting, presenting salutations. This form of answer suggests that something came about by virtue of active measures having been taken, that the movements were directed to something in view. The force of the participle intimates action. But on two counts the index is unsatisfactory. First, it is too broad. 'Sleeping' is a possible answer, but sleeping does not qualify even as behaviour. We might get around this by demanding, first, that no negating qualification be possible on the verb and, second, by insisting that an act always be an item of behaviour. The second count is more serious. 'What was he doing?' is importantly ambivalent. Usually the answer would tell us what happened in the course of the animal making the movements he did. Seeing an object on the ground, which he thinks is a football but which is really a sandbag, he kicks at it. What was he doing? Well, he was meaning to kick a football, but what he actually was doing was kicking a bag of sand. And even supposing that he was meaning to kick a sandbag, our answer would ordinarily imply that he actually got the sandbag kicked. But there are other kinds of case: We say he was approaching to the green, where the answer carries no such implication, *viz.* that he got the ball onto the green. The answer tells us only what he was meaning to do. Now, whenever an act is done, I want to assume that the animal must have been meaning to do something. But the answer to the question, 'What was he doing?' may or may not leave that undetermined and, if it does tell us what he was meaning to do, may or may not tell us whether he succeeded. The answer, by sometimes

33

leaving open and by sometimes foreclosing these possibilities, invites the curious conclusion that whenever anyone does an act he really does two things, what he means to do and what he actually does do. That is curious because in fact only a single item of behaviour may be in evidence. But we get the illusion of a second act. 'What was he doing?' in short comprehends answers to two distinct kinds of question, which, to obviate confusion, we would do well to keep separate.

I hold that whenever one does an act, he is meaning to do something. Let us then try *that* as a part of our verbal index, *viz.*, the possibility of giving an affirmative answer to the question, 'What was he (she, it) meaning to do?'. We may thus concentrate on one essential consideration and not declare ourselves on the question what the animal was actually doing, and therewith also excise any implication as to whether the animal succeeded in doing what he was meaning to do. As an index to examples, this also indirectly preserves the special force of the present participle, but without letting in examples we mean to exclude. Later I shall take a true answer to the question 'What was he meaning to do?' as also constituting an answer to our theory-cast question, 'What kind of act was done?'.

Unfortunately, 'What was he meaning to do?' is also ambiguous. To put it roughly, it may be used to inquire either what act he was doing (*e.g.*, taking money) or with what intentions he did the act (*e.g.*, with the intention of putting it back). I think we may get around that by laying it down that the question should be directed at a presumed item of behaviour and the answer should in some sense also tell us what the animal was doing. (He was taking the money, not putting it back.) Of the two possible answers to the question 'What was he doing?' only one will *also* count as an answer to the question, 'What was he meaning to do?'.

The answer of course leaves open the additional question whether the animal actually did do what he meant to do, and that too must have an answer. That suggests a supplemental, though probably redundant, verbal index. A straightforward employment of the verb which answers the question would usually though not invariably imply that the animal succeeded. But we know that other items of the same type of behaviour might have failed. We therefore need some way of countering the usual implication that the deed was brought off successfully. For the last, it suffices in English that we be able meaningfully to qualify the infinitive of the verb with some such auxiliary as 'trying' or 'attempting' or 'meaning'. I therefore suggest, as a verbal index of action, that we be able, after the fact, to answer the question, 'What was he (she, it) meaning to do?', with a phrase containing an English verb, the infinitive of which admits of a 'trying'

34

qualification, where the given answer would also answer the question, 'What was he doing?'.

Assured of examples, it remains to try to explain action. As a first stab, I propose the following: An act is an *item of behaviour*, the constituent movements of which are *brought about* by the particular animal in question, hereafter called the 'agent', to attain some one or other what I call *purpose*. There exists a true report which implies that the animal movement was an item of behaviour and that the animal in question had a purpose at the time the movement occurred. We may characterize action as 'behaviour with a purpose' or as 'purposive behaviour'. That presupposes what I have yet to supply—an adequate explanation of 'bring about to attain a purpose'. 'Purpose' in this context is technically employed, and must be explained: I shall have to set out criteria for the presence of purpose in behaviour. But for the moment it suffices to convey the tendency of what will be my definition of *action*. Not all kinds of items of behaviour are acts, *e.g.*, not stumbling into a stool, or nervous, aimless pacing of the floor. We need a *differentia*. My use of 'purpose' strongly suggests the presence of a kind of 'mental element', determining a sort of 'intent' on the part of the animal.

Leaving aside the problem of explaining purpose, the proposed definition clearly requires that an act should always be an actual happening in the physical world decomposed into a sequence of movements of or in some particular animal (the *agent*) occurring over a connected interval of space and time. We are thus limited to 'overt action'. Allowedly, I might have contrived a wider definition comprehending certain so-called 'mental acts', *e.g.*, trying to remember the French word for 'bachelor'. I do not attempt the wider definition because it is unnecessary for my immediate purposes and because it would be too difficult to achieve. I believe but shall not try to establish that mental action, suitably restricted, can be defined only derivatively from and in contrast with a definition of (overt) action.

Action, then, is a type of behaviour, behaviour the constituent movements of which are brought about to attain a purpose. But so far the formula is advanced only in anticipation of success, for 'purpose' is employed technically and I am certainly not entitled to assume that it explains itself.

Preliminary to supplying the wanted explanation, let me lay it down that a conceptualizing observer *would specify the purpose* of an act by giving the right answer to the question asked about the animal, 'What was he meaning to do?'. The '. . .' in the answer, 'He was meaning to . . .', schematizes a specification of purpose. So taken, . . . would imply nothing as to whether the act succeeded. It is important to remark on this because, as we have already seen, ordinarily most such words, used in context of a direct report, would imply that the act succeeded. Thus if I say, 'He was eating', employing one form of the verb 'eat', I would usually be taken to imply that he got the food into his mouth and down his gullet. But if I say 'eat' in answer to the question, 'What was he meaning to do?', I leave it as an open possibility that the food kept falling off his fork.

Now to specify the purpose of an act requires that an act was done, that purpose was present. We still need criteria or tests for the existence of action, *i.e.*, for the presence of purpose in behaviour.

Anticipating further elaboration, let me here and now lay down that an item of behaviour is purposive and hence qualifies as an act only if (1) it is behaviour of a kind items of which may be said to succeed or fail, and (2) a possible explanation of the occurrence of the movements constituting the behaviour is that the animal in question knows or believes such and such to be the case.[1] More correctly put, an item of behaviour A is an act only if there exists a true typification of A which implies (1) that every item of such a type either succeeds or fails (*not*: that every item either succeeds or that it fails), and (2) that the occurrence of the movement constituting A might be explained by reference to what the animal knew or believed to be the case.

The second stated condition is the more important one. But the first is also necessary. Certain kinds of animal movement might be explained by mention of what the animal knew or believed, and yet clearly do not qualify as action. Examples may be found among what G. E. M. Anscombe has called 'mental causes':[2] Seeing a face at the window or a snake in the grass, the animal gives a start. His coming to know that there is a strange face staring at him gives him a start. His knowing that there is a face in the window explains his movement. Often such movements do not qualify as behaviour; but sometimes they do, just when the creature could have avoided giving the start. Suppose it is behaviour; still, when he jumps, the animal is not meaning to do something, as is seen in the inappropriateness of asking whether he succeeded or failed. Later, after a fuller discussion of *purpose*, we shall amalgamate the two conditions to read: A true report implies that the movements constituting the behaviour might

---

[1] This use of 'believe' is already philosophically charged. Philosophers have come to employ 'believe' to cover a number of different things, the commonest of which is best formulated in English with 'thinks', *e.g.*, 'The cat thinks there's milk in the dish'. That is the kind of case I have most in mind. 'Believe' also covers such things as being of or (differently) having an opinion, being inclined to think, feeling that, and so on. It also covers, 'He believes . . .' literally taken, which I think, implies something like, 'He puts himself on the side of (saying, standing for, standing by, *etc*.) . . .'. Belief literally construed involves engagement, commitment.

[2] *Intention*, nos. 8–11. Also *Proceedings of the Aristotelian Society*, 1957–58.

be explained by the fact that the animal knew or believed that no condition obtained under which the purpose could not possibly be attained.

Provisionally then: An act A is an item of a type of behaviour, items of which may succeed or fail, where an explanation of the movement constituting A might be that the animal in question knew or believed something or other. We establish the existence of an act by showing that behaviour occurred and was of the indicated kind, *i.e.*, that such and such animal movement occurred over such and such connected stretch of time and . . . . We thus show the movements to constitute behaviour with a purpose. We individuate and identify the act as a particular item of behaviour, *i.e.*, with reference to what sequence of movements occurred where and when. We say what kind of act was done, identify it as a type, by specifying the purpose. It is, furthermore, always possible truly to say either that the act *succeeded* or *failed*, depending upon whether the agent was successful or unsuccessful, *i.e.*, depending upon whether the purpose was (as I shall put it) *attained* or not attained.

This explanation is not sufficiently concrete. We are situated with one foot on the doorway to a theory but the other still resting on a vestibulary verbal index. Too much still hangs upon the force of 'purpose'. Action, as we have been discussing it, is a higher rung on a kind of ladder of increasing behavioural sophistication: Bare animal movement, behaviour, action. A report implying that an act was done creates the possibility of giving positive answers to the questions, 'What happened, when and where, who did it, and for what purpose?', where each question marks a step up on the ladder. The concepts we have begun to examine and their leading questions, taken together, constitute a good part of the equipment which an adult human being brings to bear in his everyday encounters with the animal world.

The following further observations are in order:

(1) I said that an act is individuated and identified in the particular as an item of behaviour. Two different acts may indeed occur at one time or at one place, or even with partial overlap of time and/or place, as when two people shake hands or when a single animal's movement may be separated into two sequences of movements for each of which there exists an independent typification (see p. 25). However, two different acts cannot consist of precisely the same sequence of movements; nor can an act occur twice over in time.

(2) An act is identified as a kind but not individuated by specification of a purpose, *i.e.*, by answering the question, 'What was he (she, it) meaning to do?'. A single act may be of several distinct and

heterogeneric kinds, *i.e.*, the agent may have more than one purpose while doing a single act. An agent may at the same time, by way of giving away property, act both to benefit another and to reduce his own tax liability. However, this kind of duplicity must clearly be distinguished from another to be examined later, that in which an agent, in doing an act for one purpose, always does any number of subordinate acts: He does an act of benefiting another by way of giving away his property by way of signing his name to a document by way of moving his hand . . . In this last imagined case, the agent and his act have only a single purpose, *viz.*, to benefit another.

(3) Since an act is always behaviour, it immediately follows that an agent might be held responsible for his deed whether or not it succeeds. It is obvious that the intrusion of what I call purpose into behaviour alters the canons by which we might allocate responsibility, but the nature of that alteration is far from clear.

(4) According to my anticipated definition of action, only single animals may be said to act. However, there is no advance reason forevermore to disqualify extensions of usage allowing for the acts of collections of animals consolidated into packs, tribes, nations, corporations, *etc.* If we do later permit such an extension, we should then take care to distinguish the acts of the corporation from the acts of its members, *e.g.*, we must distinguish the member's act of joining the collective from the collective's act of hiring a president.

(5) I wish, finally, to reiterate a warning regarding what is *not* implied by the specification of the purpose(s) of an act. The vocabulary best suited for the specification of purpose in most of its usual employments seems to imply the attainment of the purpose specified and so the success of the act. Thus we speak of giving gifts, signing contracts, making promises, where the forms of speech employed would seem to imply that the agent got the gift given, the contract signed, or the promise made. These words, so employed, are, to use an idea of Ryle, 'achievement words'. But we do not want the specification of purpose to carry that implication. Nor will it always do (if it ever will) to prefix a 'try' or 'attempt' to the verb, for these words are apt to imply failure, which must be as extraneous to the specification of purpose as would be the implication of success; they would also mistakenly suggest that whenever an agent succeeds in an act *A* of kind *K*, he really must have done two things, *A* and trying to do *A*. Our resolution of this nasty, nagging kind of difficulty has already been given. Specification of purpose in vernacular terms is to be thought of as given *only* in answer to the question, 'What was he (she, it) meaning to do?'. The answer, if correct, and if it also constitutes a possible answer to, 'What was he (she, it) doing?', specifies the purpose and identifies the act while implying nothing as to success

or failure. The fact that the very same words in the very same senses could in other connections be used to report that the purpose so specified was attained and the act successful, foreshadows an important relation between the definition of a purpose and the possible success of an act having that purpose.

3. ACTION AND ACTIVITY

[The activities of life are distinguished from acts one might do, possibly when engaged in those activities. The background field of activity engaged in often provides the setting against which we may fix units of action. Also, we may begin to analyse a field of activity by specifying kinds of action necessarily or characteristically done when engaged in that activity.]

Before going on with the discussion of action as a type of behaviour, it will be well to notice a distinction, the neglect of which could later vex our progress or smudge the main lines of this account. It is the distinction between *action*, as we have begun to explain it, and *activity*.

We speak about a man's activities, such as gardening, golfing, walking, theatrical acting, carpentry, teaching. This is an important idea in our lives, and has nothing technical about it; and 'activity' is just the word for it. It is therefore not to be confused with our technical notion of action.

An act is not an activity, nor an activity an act. Activities are engaged in, had, cultivated; they may be frivolous or serious, professional or leisure; a man's activities are part of his life at large, and to know what his activities are is to know something of a personal kind about him. Acts are not engaged in but done or performed; they occupy definite stretches of time, and always begin and terminate at specific times; acts, unlike activities, may fail or succeed. (But one might succeed or fail *in* an activity.) One may do an act without necessarily being engaged in an activity, *e.g.*, blowing the nose. Not so obviously, one may be engaged in an activity without doing any particular (overt) act, *e.g.*, watching a chess match.

The distinction between action and activity is therefore drawn on two fronts. First, action is a technical idea, while activity is a commonsense notion. Second, whatever corresponds to action in our commonsense conceptions (collected in the full array of act-identifactory verbs and phrases vernacularly available) is not activity but rather a range of single, discrete, connected episodes consisting of movements in or of single animals.

39

Philosophers who have written about behaviour are frequently careless, suspiciously and significantly so, about this distinction, now and then falling back upon 'activity' when (in my usage) they ought to say 'act'. It gives them the illusion that they are walking along with the man in the street, for 'activity' is quite an ordinary word. But there are other forces at work here too. Present participles and gerund constructions generally are regularly employed for identifying both activities and acts, e.g., *golfing* and *putting*; and certain words are used for both, e.g., 'fishing'. But then it is always possible to clarify the situation by speaking of (e.g.) 'going fishing' and 'casting for fish'.

But the strongest force which works to confound the two ideas is the relation which obtains between them. First, one usually enters upon a field of activity by doing an act: One leaves the house and thereby starts on a walk. More interestingly, the field of activity often supplies the setting only against which we can in our theoretical endeavours measure units of action. Application of this theory always presumes a (verbal) identification of an act as of a kind, which is, however, not uniquely determined by the bare physical transaction. The question is, how do we know that one identification is right, and another not? Well, if we know that a man is playing golf, then we know that the units of action are shots of various kinds—drives and approaches, making estimates of distance, and saying upsetting things to his opponent. On the other hand, if he is engaged in the activity of practising golf, his acts are shots with particular clubs—nine-iron or spoon shots, directing the caddy where to pick up the ball, *etc*. Again, if a party is engaged in the activity of building a house, then among the kinds of units of action are fetching and laying bricks, throwing shovelfuls of cement into a concrete mixer, pouring parts of the foundation, *etc*. Because this is so, it would be wrong to say that the man who was mixing concrete was also laying foundations, even if the concrete he mixes is meant to be poured into the foundation.

I say, then, that the identification of an act sometimes presumes and is often facilitated by reference to a background field of activity. On the other side, if we wished to explain a familiar field of activity theoretically, as it were, we could proceed to do so by drawing attention to certain types of action which necessarily or characteristically are done when one is engaged in the activity. When playing golf, one must occasionally make a drive, and when lecturing on the history of philosophy one characteristically alludes to certain texts. However, we must not suppose that an activity can be simply defined as a sequence of kinds of action done when engaged in the activity.

The distinction between action and activity is one which, in a number of different kinds of case, shows us a way to terminate spurious sorts of regression of which philosophers are so fond. 'He opened the door to go for a walk, which he did for his own sweet pleasure; therefore his opening the door was really a part of the act of seeking pleasure'. Or, 'He started the mixer to make concrete to pour the foundation, to build the house, to receive payment, to buy food, to live; so all the time he was really engaged in The Act of Living'. Such linear deployments of 'ends' are typical philosophical figments that proceed by smudging more than one essential distinction. An especially important distinction which is smudged is that between *action* and *activity*. As useful general rules to keep us out of danger here: where action stops, activity fills in; again, always regard an act as something small in time and quite discrete, a unit for the analysis of activity.

4. IDENTIFYING AND DESCRIBING ACTION

[Attention is drawn to a fundamental distinction in our thinking between identifying things as being of certain kinds and describing them in certain respects. This distinction is applied to action, and it is held that we identify an act as being of a kind by specifying the purpose.]

So far as I can see, it is impossible to say anything about an object without allowing for the possibility of the question, 'What kind of thing is it?'. One may not know what kind of object it is, but only that it is blue; but in knowing that it is blue, one also generally knows that it is an object of some kind or other. The question over what kind may not always have an answer, but at least it may be asked.

Objects will usually be of many kinds, *e.g.*, the thing I see before me is a tree, a conifer and a spruce. Kinds are enormously various. But not everything we might say about an object counts as or even necessarily contributes towards saying what kind of object it is. To say that it is heavy or brown says nothing about whether it is or is not a lion.

This distinction between saying what kind of thing an object is and otherwise characterizing it, seems to be implictly fundamental in our thinking. Why that should be so is obscure. It is a challenging issue in theory of Language, and will be gone into more fully in a sequel to this volume. But some elucidation is in order here, and I should like to make a few rather disconnected observations for that purpose.

Generally, our conception of an object, regarded as a possible object of thought, is to be explained in connection with certain kinds of tests by application of which we are able to individuate

41

particular objects and to establish the existence and identity of
objects and to delimit collections of objects; we also have tests by
application of which we establish that objects have certain characteristics. Some of the latter kinds of tests are for establishing of what
kind an object is, and others are for establishing other features of an
object. I previously thought that kind-identifying tests are indispensable because necessarily an object is brought into our thinking
and individuated as of a kind, upon which foundation we may then
introduce tests for determining other features of the thing. I now
think that is wrong. It is conceivable that we should individuate
globs of stuff without yet being able to say that the thing is a lion, a
dog, a chair, or any other kind of thing, where of course a glob is
not a kind of thing. (Anyway, one may individuate a glob without
being able to think of it as a glob.) But when we proceed to questions
of particular identification, questions of the form whether $a = b$, then
I believe that usually, though not invariably, the question can be
raised and settled, the reidentification test applied, only against the
presumption of a prior typal identification. A bar of steel is not the
same object as the car fender which was melted down and formed into
the bar, because we think of these as two distinct *kinds* of object.

There is a distinction between characterizing an object as being of
a certain type and making a typal identification. The former presupposes that we can re-identify particulars; the latter does not, only
that we can individuate particulars. Thus a child may be able to identify the kinds of animals pictured in his book without yet being able
to grasp the question, 'Same or different?'. But obviously there is a
relation between typal characterization and typal identification. The
importance of the distinction is that it suggests that the tests by which
we would define kinds of things may be introduced at a low level of
conceptualization, before tests for reidentification have been introduced.

The topic of types is further complicated by the fact that, at a
rather high level of conceptualization, types may themselves be made
the subjects of propositions, as in 'The lion is a feline quadruped',
or 'The lion is indigenous to Africa'. But types so regarded, as
referents, are puzzling kinds of object. They are neither particular
instances of the type, classes of such instances, or characteristics by
virtue of the possession of which objects belong to the class. This is
revealed by the fact that types and their instances have some predicates but not all predicates in common. Thus both Leo and the type,
the lion, are feline quadrupeds. But Leo has certain features by virtue
of his occupying a certain place at a certain time, *e.g.*, being born of
Fatima, which are utterly extraneous to the lion; on the other hand,
the lion is indigenous to Africa, which it makes no sense to say of

Leo. Types occupy an intermediary position on several lines between particulars and characteristics, *e.g.*, *being a lion*. The explanation of the special nature of types regarded as objects is to be traced to the characteristically fundamental role of typal identification in our thinking. Particulars are usually introduced as of certain types. As a result of this, and putting it very vaguely indeed, upon introducing a particular as of a certain type, we therewith introduce also the possibility of saying a number of things about the particular and the type together, which features may be indifferently predicated of the particular or of the kind; but we also know that there may be other particulars of the same type variously individuated, generating the possibility of diverse predications.

The distinction between typal and non-typal characterization shows up at many places in our Language. In the vernacular usage of the languages with which I am familiar (in contrast with taxonomic science), typal characterization is regularly associated with what are called common nouns, and the predication of the characteristic calls for the use of an indefinite article, *e.g.*, 'That's *a lion*'; on the other hand, non-typal characterizations are regularly associated with adjectives and verbs, *e.g.*, 'That's *heavy*', 'That's *moving*'. Again, if we are uncertain of the use of a term which we know is associated with a non-typal characteristic, we ask, *e.g.*, 'What's the meaning of "lapidary"?'; but for typal characteristics, we ask, *e.g.*, 'What is a mongoose?'. Still, again, we characteristically ask, 'How do the French *say* lapidary?' and 'What do the French *call* a pineapple?'. It would be interesting to know if the distinction between typal and non-typal characteristics is found in all human tongues. But, whatever the answer, it surely does show through the language in which our theorizing will be done, and I shall simply assume that it can be readily discerned.[1]

The distinction between typal and non-typal characteristics is, I

---

[1] The distinction seems to exist in Chinese. If I have understood examples, the difference comes out in the following way. Chinese characterizing words fall into two general classes. Members of one class can occur only in company with at least one other characterizing term; members of the other class may occur without companions. Among the companion characterizing terms for members of the first class must be at least one member of the second class. Members of the first class are descriptive characterizing terms, corresponding to our adjectives and verbs; members of the second class are identificatory or typal characterizing terms, corresponding to our common nouns. The machinery of Chinese grammar seems well contrived for displaying the logical nature of the difference: to characterize, something must always be characterized; as a general rule, what is characterized is either directly identified as a kind or will be thought to be of some kind. Exceptions are handled, as in English, by the use of the equivalent of dummy common nouns, *e.g.*, 'thing'.

believe, the same one which Aristotle drew between what is predic-
able of an object (typal characteristic) and what is present in an
object (non-typal characteristic) (*Categoriae*, no. 2). It thus has an
important place in the Aristotelian doctrine of predication. But
latterly the distinction has been neglected by philosophers, perhaps
because it is made inconspicuous by its obviousness. That is unfortunate, because it is not at all easy to explain the distinction, and
almost any attempted explanations could have been useful. Let me
make a rather crude beginning, though, as I said, we shall go more
deeply into the matter in the sequel.[2]

First, typal characteristics, though not these alone, always attach
to a single, given object as a whole. Leo is a lion, but no part of him
is a lion in the way that parts of him may be grey or hairless; one
object is a table, another a table leg, and both may be wooden, but
the table leg is not a table nor the table a table leg. This also applies
to species of types. A species of a type is a subtype having special
characteristics which attach to objects as a whole. Thus a bobtailed
cat is a kind of cat by virtue of the fact that instances taken in their
entirety have characteristically short tails; on the other hand, 'mud-
splattered cat' fixes no feline species, because, while a particular may
be splattered with mud in whole or in part, he may be mud-splattered
without being splattered on any special part. This feature of typal
characteristics ties in with the fact that we may introduce typal
identification directly with the individuation of particulars. Here,
then, is one necessary, though not yet sufficient, feature of typal
characterization.

Second, if an object is of a certain type, then it must have other
subsidiary non-typal characteristics. A lion must have a size, colour,
shape, and it will presumably be born at a certain time and die at
another, and occupies certain locations at any given time in its
career.

Third, there are important relations between typal and subsidiary
non-typal characteristics of an object. We may, I think, say that the
type of a thing is recognized *from* certain of its subsidiary non-typal

[2] Use of the distinction has recently begun to appear in the literature, especially
in connection with questions over perception. See A. R. White, *G. E. Moore*
pp. 176f.; also S. Hampshire, 'Perception and Identification', *Proc. Arist. Soc.,
Supp. Vol.*, 1961, pp. 81–96. Hampshire *seems* to hold that particular identifications and statements of existence *always* imply a typal identification (see p. 93).
I would disagree. He suggests that typal identification of a body requires knowledge of the past history and causal relations of the object. I think that would be
true only for what Locke called 'complex ideas of substance' and not for his
'mixed modes'. I have already made some published attempts at explaining
the difference between typal and non-typal characteristics in *Modes of Referring*,
pp. 80f., 84f.; and also in 'Man and Mechanism', *Austr. J. Philos.*, 1963, pp. 2–11.

characteristics. However, as a general rule it is not true that, to be able to recognize and name the type of a thing, one need also be able to recognize and say from what features he recognizes the type. I am able to recognize a number of different kind of flowers, though I am unprepared even to notice characteristic features from which I suppose I identify what kind of flower.

Fourth, the point of greatest difficulty in coming to an understanding of typal characteristics is to explain the relation which obtains between typal and non-typal subsidiary characteristics. It is here that we run head on into all the ancient problems over essence and accidence. In general, there is no single, specifiable group of subsidiary features the possession of which by the object is either necessary or sufficient for it to be of a type. A lion may scrape off his mane in a thicket or lose his tail in a trap. However, there are certain features, which Locke called 'characteristical' or 'leading', which an object of the type must have pending explanation for their absence—thus the tail of a lion, the flat surface of a table. As a sufficient condition, we can say only that the object must have enough of an amorphous and always incompletely specifiable collection of features which objects of the type sometimes have, to present a certain gross appearance. These may comprise colour, shape, disposition, *etc.*

Finally, types themselves are of many different types. The most important rift here is between what Locke called (second) substances —lion, dog, man, tree—and mixed modes—machines, calendars, unicorns. The difference, roughly explained, is that mixed modes, unlike substances, are introduced into our thinking by way of the advance specification of subsidiary features, the absence of which from ostensible instances would either disqualify them entirely or be reckoned as infirmities or deficiencies. Substances, on the other hand, are introduced in connection with paradigm instances, any of whose subsidiary features may or may not come to be regarded as conspicuously important. Important corollary differences are (1) substances must have instances, whereas mixed modes need not; (2) substances cannot be exhausted by definition in terms of subsidiary features of particulars (following Locke, our ideas of substance are 'inadequate'), while mixed modes can.

While fully realizing how far my explanations fall short, I trust that the reader is almost infallibly able in practice to see the difference between typal and non-typal characteristics. In order to become explicit about the difference, I shall speak of *identifying an object as a kind or type* and of *describing an object*. [3]

[3] The sound of 'identifying' is enough to flag my usage as a technical one. It is more important to say that mine is no ordinary use of 'describing', departures

My use of 'identifying' in fact smudges a distinction we have already noticed, that between typal identification and typal characterization. Thus, asked of a passing object, 'What was it?', I answer, 'An elephant.' By way of contrast, I might later be asked *about* it, and say, 'It was an elephant, pink and somewhat decrepit.' The former might be called an identification *simpliciter*, and the latter an identificatory characterization or predication; the former kind of identification is, I have suggested, conceptually more primitive. But this distinction between identifications which are and are not 'about' particulars does not much matter for the present, and I shall neglect it except when it imposes itself upon us.

In full verbal, theoretical identification of an object as a type or a kind we say what kind of object it is, *e.g.*, a lion, a table, a planet. It is, I hope, clear that this is distinct from what I have sometimes called 'particular identification'. Particular identifications would be found were I to say what particular object it is, *e.g.*, Leo, or Jupiter. This latter kind of verbal performance can always be schematized as having the form '$a = b$'. For the moment, I am concerned entirely with typal identification. Any non-typal predication with respect to an object will count as describing that object. Thus, we might say that the object is fierce, brown, or is to be seen at midnight 80° above the eastern horizon. Identifying and describing are to be regarded as contrasting kinds of characterizing.

I now submit that the distinction between identifying and describ-

_____

from which seem to have become the privilege of philosophers. In describing something, in the ordinary sense, one produces a description. Now a description is always a description of some one thing or another—a face, a room, a building, a chemical substance—consisting in the specification of certain features of the object according to a fairly standardized customary schedule. We verbally draw in the main lines of the thing. Thus we describe a face by saying how it is with the eyes, the hair, the nose, the mouth, the complexion, *etc.*; we describe a chemical substance by giving its colour, smell, taste, texture, solubility in standard solvents, *etc.* For all the standardization that may be involved, one description may be better or worse than another, reflecting the sensitivity, acumen, and general skill of the observer. Much turns on what is said in the course of filling in the schedule. Thus, in describing the same face, one observer may say that the nose is cute and another that it is piquante. I would suspect that the latter would be the better description. Descriptions, for this reason, are credited to the describer. Now when philosophers use 'description' and its cognates, *e.g.*, in contrast with *evaluation*, *identification*, nothing like that is usually intended. Actually, both identificatory and evaluative characteristics might be mentioned in literally describing an object. Consequently, 'description' ('-ive', '-bing') takes on its whole meaning by contrast. That, unfortunately, is seldom apparent, so little so that philosophers commonly suggest that we can explicate, *e.g.*, 'evaluation' in contrast with 'description'. I am introducing *describing* in contrast with *identifying*, while claiming little for my efforts to explain *identifying*.

46

ing applies or can be made to apply to animal behaviour, and in particular to action.

Asked what he was doing, I might say 'Jumping', and perhaps add that he was doing it nimbly or clumsily, sporadically, convulsively, *etc.* 'Jumping' identifies his act, and 'clumsily' describes it. I might not have known what he was doing, but saw that he was doing it clumsily; I should then also know that there was some kind of thing that he was doing clumsily.

Earlier I observed that in English and the other tongues with which I am familiar we usually mark a typal identification by employing what grammarians call common nouns, *e.g.*, we say, 'It is *a table*'. Adjectives are typically employed for describing, but when animal behaviour is the subject the rule does not apply. Here verb forms do the identifying job, and, in English, the present participle or the infinitive. Thus, asked what he was doing, we may answer, 'Jumping', 'Hanging a picture', 'Fetching the mail', 'Scratching his head'. Again, we might say, in answer to the question, 'What was he meaning to do?', 'To jump', *etc.* For our purposes, the latter kind of answer is the more important. Adverbs and adverbial phrases, *e.g.*, 'clumsily', 'with malice aforethought', not surprisingly, are frequently used to describe acts.

Grammar must be adjusted to grammar, and we must not take this talk of noun, adjective, verb and adverb too seriously: it is useful for staking out, but establishes no final claims. Yet it is sometimes surprising how grammar does point to distinctions we might override, for example, to the transitions so easily made and so easily overlooked from speaking of people acting to speaking of their acts. When we wish to make the difference explicit, *e.g.*, by saying, 'His kicking the table was inexcusable', as against, 'He inexcusably kicked the table', grammar demands that we use an adjective to describe the deed, thus confirming the distinction.

All this said, we must allow that present participles and infinitives of verbs are not used exclusively for identifying acts; they also may be used for describing how or in what manner acts are done. For example, 'He paid for the meal by *charging it* to his expense account'. This distinction between identifying and describing acts with present participles will occupy us a good deal later.

I say, then, that we regularly identify acts as types by employment of infinitives or present participles. But for reasons already considered, we must exercise care. Often, even usually, the straight reportorial use of a present participle, as in, 'He was kicking a ball', tells us both what he was meaning to do and what he did do. But not always. Sometimes it tells us only what he was meaning to do ('He was kicking for a field goal'). Taking this into account, we earlier

47

decided to use the possibility of answering the question, 'What was he *meaning* to do?', where the answer would also tell us what he was doing, as our verbal index to examples of action. But now the words which answer the question might have been otherwise elicited, carrying different implications. Which of these implications if any contribute to the identification of the act? My proposal is that we identify the act by saying what he was meaning to do. He was, anyway, meaning to do something; and we must at all costs avoid the illusory duplication of action into what he meant to do and what he did. In order to get a bonafide identification of the act as a type, we must investigate the (generally) infinitive responses to the question, 'What was he (she, it) meaning to do?'.

In giving such an answer, thus identifying the act, we specify what I have called the *purpose* of the act; otherwise put, we specify what the animal meant to attain. I call such reports *specifications of purpose*. If asked what kind of act was done, we supply an answer by specifying the purpose, most commonly by use of the infinitive of a verb. All else is description. For example, if we go on to say how the act was done, in what manner, in what state of mind, we are *describing* the act.

Now the question arises, why should we call the specification of purpose 'identification' anyway? Actually, I think that to speak of identifying action is unnatural. Perhaps then it is open to me to assign any sense I choose to 'identifying action'? No. Apart from making the thing too hopelessly arbitrary for words, that would be to counterfeit a licence for regarding acts as more like other things than they may be. I would come in from the other direction: If acts as we think about them are like other things, then it should make sense to speak of identifying kinds of action. It certainly does make eminently good sense to ask, 'What was *he* doing?', and we often answer with a present participle. When we jack it up a notch and ask about action itself, we can expect to be able to give the same kind of answer. Unfortunately, there may be many answers to the question, 'What was he doing?', where we possibly want only one of these as an answer to, 'What kind of act did he do?'. For example, he was contracting his muscles *and* raising his leg *and* kicking the ball. Here once more we must appeal to our indexical question, 'What was he *meaning* to do?', which limits the answers. But why should answers to just that question be preferred for verbal identification of action? Because answers to that question occupy much the same position in our conceptualization of behaviour as do answers to the question, 'What kind of thing (table, chair, radio)?'.

First, there is always *an* answer to the question provided the behaviour qualifies as action, independently of whether the act succeeded or failed, or had any other particular descriptive characteristic.

Second, saying what he was meaning to do tells us something about the act as a whole in a way which telling us that he was moving his leg muscles need not, for he may also have been moving other parts of his body.

Finally, a highly abstract consideration: Typal identification regularly maintains quite close connections with questions of existence. Particulars, acts included, when shown to exist, regularly must be of one kind or another, even if we do not yet know of what kind. Now we have held that an act exists in the movement of an animal only if he is meaning to do something or other, *viz.*, he must have a purpose in our sense of 'purpose'. Therefore, satisfaction of the criterion of existence for action implies that there be a purpose which could be specified, thus giving assurance of the possibility of typal identification, if my proposal is accepted. Additionally, the test for existence should, if possible, suggest ways by which we could typally identify particulars. Now, behaviour qualifies as action only if there is a certain cognitive element present, *viz.*, knowledge or belief about the world, and if it might possibly succeed or fail. It will turn out that the knowledge and belief which the agent has must include items to the effect that certain conditions do not obtain, which, if they did obtain, would necessarily result in the failure of the act. But it will also turn out that we can theoretically identify the purpose itself— the purpose by specification of which we would typally identify the act—by listing these conditions. We thus maintain a very close connection between the existence and the typal identification of action.

Concerning my thesis that we typally identify an act by specifying the purpose, the following points should be noted.

First, as already stated, mine is no ordinary use of 'purpose'. The plain fact is that the vernacular supplies no single word for what I want to mean by 'purpose'. Mine is necessarily a technical usage, fuller explanations of which will follow below. Now, it is suspicious when there is no ordinary word for what would seem to be a very common idea. The danger is that one only thinks he means something and in fact does not. But in this instance, the problem is that we have too many locutions which overlap what I call purpose. Thus we may ask, 'What is he meaning to do?', 'trying to do', 'attempting to do', 'wanting to do', or 'purporting to do'; all these forms are often used to request a specification of the purpose of an act. This is evidence that 'purpose', as I employ it, has meaning.

Second, although by specifying the purpose we may identify the act as of a kind, we do not thereby identify the purpose itself either

C 49

particularly or as of a kind. That is another matter, which we must consider in due time. I shall later argue that we identify the purpose as of a kind by specifying conditions under which an act having that purpose could not succeed, *e.g.*, one could not succeed in eating if his mouth would not open, eating is a kind of purpose whose attainment by action requires the opening of the mouth.

Third, the participial form which might be employed to identify an act as of a kind might also be used to *describe* the *agent* as acting in that way. It seems likely that this latter use, in which we talk not about his act but about him, is the more primitive one, because we identify the act as of a kind by saying something about the agent, by answering the question, 'What was *he* (*she*, *it*) meaning to do?'.

Fourth, to get a particular identification of an act, it does not suffice to specify a purpose. We individuate an act and achieve the best possible particular identification of it by specifying its location as an episode, that is, as a happening in space and time. Everything which derives from the location of the episode together with the specification of the agent counts not as act-identification, but as act-description.

Fifth, we have noticed that some verbal accounts of behaviour imply an identification *plus*. Sometimes a single locution implies an evaluation or other kind of description of an act as well as an identification. Thus, we speak of *committing* (murder, adultery, *etc.*). Here we imply that a certain kind of act was done (homicide, say), having a certain 'quality'. Again, we may speak of 'making mistakes'; once more the governing verb shows that the observer views the act in a certain way, *e.g.*, as a crime, as a slip, *etc.* None of these verbs must be taken as purpose-specificatory, even though their employment implies a specification of purpose. Otherwise we stand to create illicit, illusory duplications. In addition to murderous acts of homicide, we would also have acts of murder.

Sixth, some confusion over the identification of action may arise in connection with a conflict between what one *hopes* as against what one *believes*. The place-kicker, standing on his own 40-yard line, hopes to kick a field goal, though he does not expect to succeed. What is he meaning to do? To kick a field goal, I would say. But some might protest that one cannot attempt what he has every reason to think he will fail at. Well, if he knows as a matter of necessary truth that he cannot succeed, *e.g.*, because there are no goal posts, then I agree, he is not meaning to kick a field goal. But if he has hopes, he thinks he *may* succeed. Succeed at what? Kicking a field goal. The answer to the question, what he was meaning to do, is: Kicking a field goal. Roughly put, what he hopes to do is what he is doing. That is because the hope reaches towards the outcome of the

50

deed. In this case he fails if his hopes are disappointed. But there is another kind of case involving *hope*. I pick up and drink what I hope is a cup of coffee. (Not: I hope to drink a cup of coffee.) If it turns out to be tea, my hopes are disappointed, but my act does not fail, provided I get the liquid into my mouth and down my gullet. On the other hand, were there no liquid in the cup at all, contrary to what I *believe*, my act would necessarily fail. What I believe in this case is that a condition is satisfied, which condition serves to define my purpose; but what I hope in no way determines the purpose, though it surely does figure in the state of mind in which I set about to attain that purpose.

Finally, we observed that present participles may be employed to describe how an act was done as well as to identify what kind of act was done. For example, he was making his approach to the green *by* swinging a nine-iron. But this kind of case must be distinguished from another, where, to put it very roughly indeed, what the agent means to do is to do something in a certain way. For example, engaged in the activity of practising nine-iron approaches, the agent does not simply make an approach by swinging a nine-iron, where he might instead have used a wedge; rather, he makes a nine-iron approach.

The most I can hope for at this point is that the reader will allow that I *may* have something in mind when I speak about the specification of purpose, and that he will agree that this *could* qualify as verbal typal identification of action. But purpose may still seem a questionable quantity. Our problem is to say more particularly what is involved in the specification of purpose, a task which will require me later to say also how we identify purposes, as against identifying acts (by specification of purpose).

5. EXPLAINING PURPOSE

[The presence of what we have called 'purpose' is essential for behaviour to qualify as action; and we identify an act by specifying the purpose. But this is no ordinary use of 'purpose', nor does there seem to be any other vernacular vocabulary item which does any better. That creates dangers, which are increased by the difficulty of separating the purpose from the other elements of the act, in particular the movements constituting the act. The only way to resolve the danger is to see that we must actually define purpose as a technical notion by laying down criteria for the presence of purpose and for the identification of purpose.]

What sets action off from other types of behaviour is the presence of what I have been calling 'purpose'. In the last section it was held that we typally identify an act by specifying the purpose, for which, we noticed, there are vernacular means available. We have therefore given a kind of contextual explanation of 'specifying purpose'. We may go on to multiply the relevant contexts, *e.g.*, we can speak about 'attaining' and 'not attaining' purposes. But those would be utterly redundant bits of terminology were we not able to show that something was thus specified, attained or not attained, *etc.* What would be specified, presumably, is a purpose present in the behaviour. The purpose would then be a piece of the world, a part of behaviour, something to which we could point, as it were, and describe if need be. It would seem, moreover, that purpose would pre-eminently qualify as that essential 'mental element' which we must see to be present in behaviour when we correctly identify it with act-identifying Language. This problem of saying precisely what that mental element is, is notoriously difficult; unfortunately, it is a problem for which we must provide a solution.

Perhaps we could let it pass if we could be quite certain that we understood 'purpose'. But it is already clear that mine is no obvious, ordinary usage of this quite ordinary term. Unhappily, there appears to be no other single term, in vernacular English at least, which could automatically be employed instead to indicate the presence of what I have been calling purpose.[1] Instead, we have a largish catalogue of words and idioms which are occasionally but not always alternative. Consider: 'On purpose', 'purposely', 'purposefully', 'with (or 'for') the purpose of', 'purportedly to', 'on account of', 'in order to', 'for', 'intend', 'with intent to', 'intentionally', 'wanting to', 'wishing to', 'desiring', 'meaning to', 'reason', 'end', 'aim', 'design', 'to have in mind', 'setting oneself to', 'with the resolution to', 'proposing to', 'trying to', 'deliberately', 'with the plan of', 'on the principle of', 'voluntarily', 'of one's own free will', 'knowingly', and so on. Each of these terms has its own special force. Some, like 'with the plan of', signal calculation and thought; some, like 'with the intention', try to get us to view the deed in a certain special way as only part of a larger picture also possibly including the ultimate situation of the agent as *he* views it (*e.g.*, 'I took it with the intention of replacing it later'). Still others show that the movements in question are being described as a way of doing something else. 'Purpose', in ordinary usage, seems to fall here, and it would be instructive to consider the force of the single phrase 'with the purpose of' as employed in reports on overt behaviour.

[1] I have seriously considered the word 'purport'. That would have the advantage of sounding rather more technical, for to speak about specifying and attaining purports would be obviously neologistic. But I am afraid it would only be an equally false but harsher sounding note.

The prosecuting officer before the court martial says, 'He fired the shot with the purpose of letting the enemy know the whereabouts of our troops'. The full statement tells us that what the agent was doing was letting the enemy know the whereabouts of our troops, and describes that act as being done by way of the accused's firing a shot. The firing of the shot was done, as I shall later put it, *collaterally to* informing the enemy. However, the statement is made because all that the court knows for sure is that the collateral performance was done, and there is a question why. The form, 'with the purpose of', disengages the act done from the active means taken, in order that the two might be expressly related as means to an end.

One reason I prefer 'purpose' over (say) 'intention' is that it really does signalize a request for identification of the act done; that is, to ask after purpose is to request a specification of purpose in my technical sense. But my usage surely does not jibe at all points with the vernacular. At two places in particular there are important differences.

First, if we ask with what purpose M was done, M is presented in act-identificatory language, and is momentarily regarded as what was done, rather than as the means. 'Purpose of the act' therefore suggests something beyond the act under examination, something to be discovered, something towards the attainment of which the success of the so-to-speak act would contribute; what we should ordinarily understand as the purpose of an act, M, would, in my usage, be the purpose of some other kind of act, A, which is indeed *the* kind of act being done by way of doing the so-to-speak act M. We may distinguish in any act between *what* was done and *how* it was done, between the 'end' and the 'means'. But it facilitates the identification of action to excise this implication of means to ends, and nothing need be lost. So long as what I call the purpose of the act is a purpose and so, in common usage, the purpose of the means presented in act-identificatory terms, so long as the relation is perfectly systematic in this way, then either way of talking could be squared with the other, and neither need constitute any essential distortion of the other. All that is lost is an easy way of presenting and focusing attention on a performance regarded at once as a type of behaviour and also as a means to something else, possibly still unknown. Putting it succinctly, the 'purpose' in my usage need not be something 'beyond' what is specifically alluded to in requesting 'for what purpose'; it is not something 'further' to be attained. Thus, to take a case: While the purpose of an act in my sense of 'purpose' will generally be to attain something beyond the mere completion of bodily movements, *e.g.*, one aims not only to do the work by which the nail is driven but also to drive the nail, it is still sometimes the case that one's only purpose is to make movements, *e.g.*, to wiggle one's ears. *That* is the purpose.

The second discrepancy between my usage of 'purpose' and the vernacular is more serious. I insist that purpose is to be found in even the simplest, most unnotable deeds, such as sugaring cereal ('To sugar the cereal' specifies a purpose); but in daily life we seldom if ever have occasion to specify purpose either directly or by implication unless the behaviour of the animal is for some reason uncertain, queer or conspicuous, say for purposes of allocating responsibility, or is in some other way worthy of comment. But usually one's purpose is obvious, ordinary and quite undeserving of notice or comment. We watch an animal eating, and there is scarcely room to question what his purpose is. And indeed, we would not often speak of purpose in such cases, because part of the very meaning of *all* the terms in my list on p. 52 is to suggest that the situation is in some way not clear or not perfectly ordinary, or would not be without the entrance of purpose-implying Language. We have just seen how 'purpose' itself implies that what the supposed agent was doing was not obvious.

The fact that we have no single word to cover what I want to mean by 'purpose', nor any other word for fixing what I fancy makes behaviour into action, but a slew of different terms having the one feature in common of implying or intimating something special or extraordinary, suggests that we are chasing a will o' the wisp. We may be creating a theoretical fiction which will make us its victims. The alleged mental element may be nothing at all.

But the feeling is strong and hard to suppress that there is this difference in behaviour and this admittedly rather ineluctable stuff I call purpose. Moreover, we have some protection against illusion. We have numerous examples of specifications of purpose. We have this verbal index, the possibility of giving answers to the question, 'What was he meaning to do?', whose answering verbs usually may be qualified with 'trying' or 'attempting' prefixes. Using that index, it would seem that (*e.g.*) 'eat' can specify a kind of purpose however ordinary and unremarkable. So perhaps it suffices to explain how my usage of 'purpose' differs from the ordinary one, as I have already done, and let it go at that.

That would be very well, except for a certain philosophical kind of difficulty. If we are to analyse action in terms of purposes, we ought to have an independent characterization of purpose. Now suppose that you are gazing at an item of behaviour. It may seem a hopeless task to pry the purpose off the act, to separate the two, as it were. To see that an act is done would seem in part to consist in being able to identify it, *i.e.*, to specify the purpose of the act. This is a force tending to compress the distinction between being an act and being a certain kind of act. In trying to preserve the distinction, we may end up by thinking of the act as what would be left if purpose were absent, *i.e.*, the bare physical transaction. This is supported by another force in our Language, the possibility of describing physical movement with verbs borrowed from the stock we use to identify action, *e.g.*, 'pounding' and 'kicking'. Now we can keep action and bare movement apart by judicious use of 'movement', *e.g.*, 'a kicking movement'. Can we also keep the act and its purpose apart? In one respect, obviously not; for *a* purpose must be present. But if we wish to allow that the same purpose could be present in other acts and that the act under examination could have been done with a different purpose, then we need an independent characterization of purpose itself, a characterization which will indicate ways of identifying different purposes independently of references to acts which may have those purposes.

To confirm this need, we may once more take note of another kind of difficulty (already encountered and to be met with again in the sequel) generated by the use of act-identificatory Language. To say, 'He was eating', while it would perhaps tell us what he was meaning to do, would also ordinarily imply that he actually got the comestibles down his gullet. To remedy this we may exploit the possibility of judiciously prefixing 'try' or 'attempt' or even 'mean to'. But this, while useful for neutralizing the obscuring implication of success, is not entirely innocent, for it frequently does imply failure, and that too is extraneous to the purpose. We must also take great care not to suppose that the act is to be identified as an *attempt* to do the act. It makes no sense to try to try to kick. Failure to see this encourages the opinion that what one *really* does whenever he acts is a mental act of trying. [2]

We have navigated between these two ways of saying too much by taking as our verbal index the possibility of answering the question, 'What was he (she, it) *meaning* to do?', and by insisting that the specification of purpose be given only in answer to that question, where the answer consists not in saying, 'He was meaning to ——', but only, '——'. But this ties the specification of purpose to particular items of behaviour and confirms the need for some independent characterization of *purpose* by which we may effect the separation of purposes from particular acts. We need, in short, an explanation of

<hr/>

[2] See H. A. Prichard, 'Acting, Willing, Desiring', reprinted in *Moral Obligation*, pp. 187–98; also 'Duty and Ignorance of Fact', *op. cit.*, *e.g.*, pp. 31 *et seq.* The question whether what one 'really' does when acting is a mental act of 'willing' will be resumed in no. 6.

the idea (concept, notion) of purpose, in my sense of 'purpose', and not merely an explanation of my use of 'purpose'.

A general procedure for giving such explanations is to specify the tests whereby we establish the existence and identity of objects of the problematic kind. To that end we must be quite specific as regards where the objects are to be found, *i.e.*, what we apply the tests to. There will be generally a preferred kind of location. Thus we establish the existence and the identity of bodies by probing into particular regions of space at given times; we establish the existence of colours by reflecting light off material surfaces in which the colours may be present; we test for the existence and identity of natural numbers by performing operations on numerical expressions. Though there be this preferred kind of location, the objects may be otherwise found, *e.g.*, we may see colour in a rainbow, refer to a number with a description, *etc.* From what has been said it will be obvious that we especially wish to be able to establish the presence of purpose in behaviour. Behaviour is the preferred location. At the same time, we assume that an animal may have a purpose although he does no act.

If an animal merely contemplates doing an act not yet done, he may yet have the purpose; or if he considers how he might act to attain the purpose, he may have that purpose even if he never acts. We may thus presumably isolate purpose from action, which is exactly what we wish to do. But the suggested way in which that might be done shows that it still is true that the primary manifestation of purpose is in action, *i.e.*, in connection with behaviour. I would want to hold that one could not discern the presence of purpose, without being able to discern purpose in behaviour. We first say of an animal that he has a purpose when we observe his reactions to objects. And for him *not* to act on a purpose he has requires that he inhibit overt action. He cannot do that while reserving the purpose without imagining himself succeeding in another act or by deliberate inaction, which *may* imply that he has Language, and thus has ascended to a quite high stage of act capability. It is somewhat the same as with colours: The primary manifestation of colour is in material bodies. But we can isolate colour from particularizations of matter, as we do when describing rainbows and sunsets. So, too, with the relation of purpose and action. The analogy may be extended. Just as colour can be manifested only in the presence of light, purpose can be manifested only in connection with an animal; a purpose is always 'instantiated' by being had by some creature.

What does this have to do with the existence of purpose? The analogy with colour gives a clue. A colour is possibly a colour of something. It is a property some object could have even if no object

56

does. We demonstrate the existence of a colour abstractly conceived in the only possible way, by showing that some object really has that colour. (That we could not actually do this does not of course disprove the existence of the colour, which would require that we show that *no* object *could* have the questionable colour.) We establish the presence of the colour in some body. We do that by performing certain tests, *i.e.*, reflecting standard light off a suitably prepared material surface. So, too, we demonstrate the existence of purpose abstractly conceived by testing for the presence of the purpose in behaviour, *i.e.*, by provoking some animal thought to have the purpose into acting with the purpose. To prove the purpose we must then make certain additional observations on the resulting behaviour. What is it we are then supposed to observe?

Earlier I stipulated that behaviour qualifies as action only if (1) the behaviour is of a type, items of which might be said to succeed or fail, and (2) the movements constituting the behaviour might be explained by the fact that the animal in question knew or believed something or other. I shall propose that these two conditions may be taken and fused into a single criterion for the presence of purpose, and hence for the existence of purpose abstractly conceived: That the movements might be explained by the fact that the animal believes that certain conditions are satisfied, the failure of which conditions would necessarily result in the failure of the act, *e.g.*, if an act is one of drinking, the agent believes that there is liquid in the vessel. I say, then, that what we must observe is that these beliefs might be the explanation of the movements, and our test is successful only if we actually do explain the movements in that way. We identify *what kind* of purpose by noting what conditions the animal believes to be satisfied, the failure of which conditions would necessarily result in the failure of the act, *i.e.*, we typally identify a purpose abstractly conceived by listing these 'conditions of success'. In the next section, we follow up this matter of explaining movement by reference to knowledge or belief. In no. 10, we shall lay down a criterion for identifying purpose. That done, we shall come into position (in no. 12) to amalgamate the two stipulated conditions for the existence of action. So far nothing has been said about how we might identify a purpose *particularly* as against typally, and for the excellent reason that purposes in general do not have particular identity, as will be explained in no. 10.[3]

---

[3] In this respect, purposes are rather like sensations and colours, in contrast with (say) eruptions on the skin and specified *bands* of colour.

PART TWO: BEHAVIOUR AND ACTION

6. IDENTIFYING THE 'MENTAL ELEMENT', WITH SPECIAL ATTENTION TO THE DOCTRINE OF ANSCOMBE

[The mental element, whose presence is required if behaviour is to qualify as action, is not adequately or usefully identified either as an originative 'mental act' or as self-consciousness. We consider the proposal of Anscombe that an act is done only if the question 'Why?' admits of a certain kind of answer. It is argued that Anscombe confuses answers which give the agent's *reason* for doing the act with answers that identify what kind of act was done. A modification of the criterion, implicit in the possibility of giving the first sort of answer, will be adopted in no. 7.]

My thesis is that action is a kind of behaviour which is marked, as we view it, by the presence of a certain sort of 'mental element', which I have chosen to call 'purpose'. The observer identifies an act as of a kind by specifying the purpose, which is done by giving a positive vernacular answer to the question, 'What was he (she, it) meaning to do?', asked about an item of behaviour, where the answer also answers the question, 'What was he (she, it) doing?'. Our present task is to give an analysis of our ways of thinking about behaviour sufficient to account for the employment of action-identifying verbs and verb phrases. Such an analysis is required because there is nothing corresponding to it in our commonsense ways of thinking, nor can it even be formulated in vernacular usage, which indeed discourages and obstructs the quest for central principles of analysis. We are not accustomed in daily life to theorize in this manner about the behaviour of ourselves and our fellows.

I wish now to consider some apparently possible answers to the question of what is commonly implied by an act-identifying report. Unfortunately, none of these answers has (to my knowledge) ever been formulated well enough to be decently evaluated. In considering these answers and in proposing my own, I assume that what we are inquiring after is what an observer must see in behaviour in order correctly to identify the item of behaviour in such a way as to imply that it is an act. We must conscientiously avoid putting ourselves into a position of wanting to know how it *feels* to the agent.

The first kind of answer does not require that there be anything in the behaviour-constituting movements themselves from which one may discern the presence of purpose. An act is done and purpose is present only if the animal does another, *mental*, act of setting himself, or trying to make the movements constituting the behaviour. We could describe this as an act of *trying* or *willing*. The mental act of trying causes the movements. (See previous reference to Prichard.)

58

I shall not review all the arguments against this proposal, for nothing in recent philosophy has been more thoroughly studied and constantly refuted than this kind of theory.[1] Nor do I wish to say that there are in no sense mental acts. (See p. 31.) But I do feel it unavailing to appeal to mental action in just this connection, as a *differentia* of (overt) action, and for the following reasons:

First, we need an operative, observer's criterion for an animal's doing a mental act, a criterion that must be independent of the other criteria by which the observer would establish that the animal does the (overt) act of which the mental act is an element. So far as I can see, the only possible candidate is the agent's testimony. But surely we wish to allow that animals incapable of giving testimony can do acts. Furthermore, testimony may be misleading or mendacious, and whether it is must be determinable otherwise than by further testimony.

Second, the answer smells suspiciously regressive. Mental action is certainly at least as much in need of explanation as action itself, and presumably the explanation would be very similar, thus inviting an appeal to second-order mental action, an appeal we may not wish to make only because the mental is already so usefully obscure.

Third, any operative explanation of mental action which could avoid the regress would probably have to trade upon a prior understanding of (overt) action. That is very strongly suggested by the fact that natural verbal identifications of mental acts, *e.g.*, in terms of 'trying', would also involve the use of language which is already employed for identifying (overt) action. In doing a mental act of trying, the animal could not be merely trying; he would always have to be trying to do something. Actually, the only plausible explanation of mental action I am familiar with would have it that mental action involves the possible suppression of those overt bodily movements that would constitute (overt) action. Mental action would therefore be secondary to (overt) action both in order of explanation and in the genetic order of the acquisition of capacity by observed animals.

Finally, *trying* (perhaps the most natural characterization of mental action) seems to be only an illusory kind of deed, created verbally out of the necessary possibility that any ordinary kind of action might fail. We may certainly draw a distinction between what one does and what he tries to do; but what he tries to do is what he means to do

[1] To mention only the most important books, Wittgenstein's *Investigations*, Ryle's *Concept of Mind*, and Anscombe's *Intention* are all sources of arguments against the view in question. Prichard's own writings make it clear that he was stating the view partly in reaction to objections of Cook-Wilson and others, who might also well be consulted on the question of the necessity for an originating mental act.

and that, in our understanding, is the kind of act done. I allow that there is a mental element we are trying to pin down. But to call it a mental act is only to give it another name, not to explain it. Possibly, what makes it seem that we have an explanation is that usually it makes no sense to say that the animal tried to try, thus apparently foreclosing further questions of the same kind, and thus achieving an answer. The more plausible interpretation would, however, be that, since we usually cannot meaningfully speak of trying to try, and since the possibility of prefixing 'try' to act-identifying verbs is a verbal index to action, *trying* is wrongly thought of as a second, shadowy kind of mental *action*. I maintain that the mental element, whatever it is, is nothing *like* action.

Against these arguments it might be countered that my objections turn to dust when we look back on the facts I have been stressing in earlier sections. The supposed originating mental act is most naturally described as an act of 'meaning', 'trying', or 'setting oneself to'. And it is held (*e.g.*, by Prichard) that this is what the agent really does, the behaviour constituting movements being then regarded as 'consequences' which, so to speak, merely happen to the animal. Now, I have indeed contended that an index to action is the possibility of answering the question, 'What was he (she, it) *meaning to do*?', where the answer may usually be qualified by one of the indicated auxiliaries (*e.g.*, 'try'), and that we say what kind of act was done by answering that question. It might then appear that my account lends strong support to the doctrine of mental action. At all events, the agent always means to do something, whether or not kinematic consequences ensue. The support is strengthened by my admission that there must indeed be a mental factor operating, which I shall later propose is in the nature of an *explanation* of the movements. Is this not the very theory I have been arguing against? No. But since the two doctrines are so easily confounded, I should like to dwell a bit longer on this topic of mental action.

The doctrine of mental action, following the argument above, becomes transfigured into the form: What one really does when he acts is an act of *meaning* (or *trying*), and it would, therefore, always be better to identify action with locutions like 'mean to . . .'. That seems very little different from what I have been advocating.

Now, I allow that what the animal does is, properly construed, what he means to do; but surely what he means to do is not an act of *meaning* to do. Looking at it grammatically, I wish to make three objections. First, while I hold that we identify action by answering the question 'What was he (she, it) meaning to do?', we do not answer the question by saying, 'He was meaning to . . .', but rather

60

by simply saying '...'. The 'meaning to' question is an index to answering verbs, e.g., 'eat', 'kick', etc. It would be wrong, I think, to suppose that the answer wants a prefix 'means to', 'tries to', etc. The effect of adding the prefix is, among other things, to nullify the suggestion that the act succeeded. But some verbs answering the 'meaning to' question do not carry the implication of success, e.g., 'pursue', and therefore do not readily admit of a 'meaning to' qualification.

Notice, secondly, that there are a variety of different available verbal qualifications. Additional to 'means to', we have 'try to', 'set oneself to', 'attempt to', 'seek to', and prepositions like 'at' and 'for' ('shooting at a target', 'kicking for a goal'). None of these comes to quite the same, and it is doubtful whether there is any single word consecrated to the job. 'Try', for example, when employed as auxiliary, usually carries a special suggestion of effort.

That recalls a third, most important objection to the proposal that what one really does is an act of meaning to do. Most of the mentioned auxiliaries, 'try to', 'mean to', etc., when attached to the answering verb void the usual implication of success at the cost of implying failure. The possibility of attaching the prefix assures the possibility that acts of this kind might fail; but by actually putting it there, we contrive to imply that it did fail. The explanation is that, for an act done, we can usually know whether it succeeded or failed, a fact which is taken into account by the natural economy of Language. In summary, then, while I appreciate that my explanation comes grammatically very close to the doctrine of the originating mental act, it is still not the same.

The doctrine of mental action encourages the idea that whenever one acts successfully he is actually doing two things, trying and succeeding. What the agent really does and is finally responsible for doing is the mental act of trying, although what he would do (or 'cause', as Prichard sometimes suggests) is what he tries to do. If one succeeds in his act, then, according to this theory, there are two acts done, and two quite distinct and problematically related ambits of action, only one of which really matters for allocation of responsibility.

That is an awkward conclusion, if only because it raises classical difficulties over the relation of mind and body. I have mentioned it already as a criticism of the theory that the mental element in action is an originating mental act. But, for all that, I think that the conclusion would be welcome in certain quarters. It usually makes little sense to say that the agent tries to try. The immediate consequence is that the alleged mental act of trying is one at which the agent cannot fail. That may block a regress but, in our account, also disqualifies

61

trying as a kind of action. But the partisan of mental action may turn the tables on us, and declare that, since when one acts he does what he does, no further questions can arise over whether he did what he did. The situation resembles what we find in epistemology: It cannot be that a statement known should be false; therefore, to assure ourselves the possibility of knowledge, we seek out statements which could not be false; it is only with reference to such statements that anyone can really know. So too here: We are looking, so to speak, for infallible acts; we are looking for what one *really* does, quite apart from ensuing 'consequences'. The objection here is obvious: There is no value in getting to know what could not be false, and, without statements that could be false, no claim to knowledge would be possible; so, too, without the possibility of failure, there could be no action.

The double ambit theory of action drives us to the conclusion that the operative language of 'does', 'doing', 'act', *etc.*, is systematically ambiguous. What one really does is a mental act, as a result of which the agent possibly (in another sense) 'does' another act (in another sense of 'act'). While some (*e.g.*, Prichard) would regard the second, 'external act' as no act proper but a mere *happening*—a natural conclusion if we simply disregard the kinematic 'consequences' and concentrate on the mental factor—that is quite at variance with the everyday distinction between what happens to an animal and what he does. So I think that the theory must still allow that, in *one sense*, what the animal *does* is to make the movements which result from the mental *act* of trying. Note that this systematic ambiguity of 'does', 'act', *etc.*, is necessitated by the theory. It is, therefore, properly speaking not ambiguity at all. There must be some tight connection between the act of *trying* and the other act that one tries to do. And of course the connection is implicit in grammar. One can try or mean to do only by trying or meaning to do *something*; on the other side, if the agent succeeds, what he does is what he tries to do. One must act, so to speak, for the 'consequences', and we cannot disregard them as a possibility or exile them somewhere beyond the dominions of action proper.

The double act is an illusion, a spurious duplication engendered by a fact of Language, that we can meaningfully raise questions over whether acts succeed or fail. But this fact of Language is, so to speak, misconstructed into a theory which would make that very Language utterly incomprehensible.

Let me finally concede that an animal may certainly have (what I call) a purpose without acting on it. Merely having a purpose might qualify as an example of a kind of merely mental action, though I think that it would be better to reserve 'mental act' for such phenomena as concentrating, memorizing, and running through intellectual tasks 'in the head'. But here I reiterate that we learn to ascribe purposes to animals in connection with acts *done*, and to ascribe purposes to inactive animals is to accord them a higher order of behavioural sophistication; also, to discern purpose without behaviour demands a higher order of conceptual sophistication on the part of the observer. Purpose and (overt) action are intertwined and knotted together.

So much, then, for an originating mental act as the wanted mental element always present in action. A second proposal holds that the mental element is *self-consciousness*: The animal in doing an act must know what he's about, and he must be conscious of himself as an agent. There is certainly something right in this suggestion, and it may, when suitably explained, be vindicated. But now we must ask what it is for an animal to be conscious of himself as an agent. The idea is far from clear. Allow that he must be aware of the world and move with something in view; but certainly, he need not explicitly consider himself moving. Many types of animal that do acts are never capable of this, and none of us is always so self-conscious. The most we could universally claim is that the animal 'moves with something in view', but he need not therefore be taking an internal peep at himself.

'Self-consciousness' threatens to obscure our subject, at least as viewed from our perspective. It invites a *report* from the putative agent regarding his own state of mind. But the original question was what a conceptualizing observer must see in the behaviour of the animal in order to discern the presence of the problematical mental element. We must hold resolutely to this latter, the third-person position. To break out of the egocentric circle, alter the question to read: Under what conditions do *we*, who have Language, begin so to describe the movements of an animal as to imply that they are purposive? That is, under what conditions do we describe an animal so as to imply that he is a creature who knows what he's about?

Here it might be suggested again that the words an animal may *utter* at once count as behaviour and embody a report on what the creature is conscious of. So amended, the proposal would be: If asked, the supposed agent will say that his purpose was . . . But that will not work for a reason already met with. It implies that the animal in question can or could make reports, and the test would, therefore, apply only to highly sophisticated creatures. But second, there is, as we already know, no single vernacular word for reporting purpose, and so, failing a complete list of act-identifying locutions, the criterion is inoperative.

In favour of the proposal, this much may be said. We shall later

63

discover that *if* an agent does have sufficient Language to make a report, he *could* directly be able to know what his purpose is and inform us what he was meaning to do. But in order even to understand that possibility, we must already be prepared to see action in behaviour and to explain the special force of act-identificatory verbs. Further discussion of self-consciousness as a criterion of action is deferred to no. 9, where we shall consider the idea of knowledge by reflection more directly.

The most intriguing and most widely currently discussed solution to the problem of identifying the mental element is that of Miss Anscombe, set out in her book *Intention*. This answer, suitably qualified and amplified, is the one I shall in fact adopt. Anscombe says, if I take her sense, that an animal behaves with purpose (does an 'intentional act' in her rather regrettable terminology) ('if'? and) only if it is possible to give a true and positive answer of a certain kind to the question, 'Why did he (she, it) do it?'. She makes the further somewhat suspicious suggestion, not entirely explicit, that the answer will specify the purpose (the 'intention'). But what kind of answer to the question 'Why?' is wanted?

'Why?' is often a request for an explanation. Explanations are of a variety of kinds: Explanations *which, how, where, when, etc.*, as well as explanations *why* or *how-come* narrowly conceived. An explanation *why*, broadly construed, brings a problematical item into a familiar connection. Such explanations are enormously various, and every day we come upon new ways of explaining things, which is to say that new patterns of circumstances become familiar to us. Animal behaviour is itself susceptible to a variety of kinds of explanation. Thus we may explain by mentioning common motives like avarice and vanity; or by citing physiological or psychological causes, dispositions and sets; or the bearing of social circumstances. Anscombe rightly eliminates some of these.[2] Following this line, it would appear that we ought to look for an explanation of a special kind. Now, explanation generally involves a complex of factors, the mention of any one of which may explain the phenomenon, but only on the presumption that others are operating. Thus, the passing of a car explains the ringing of a bell on the presumption that a photo-electric circuit had been rigged, the battery connected, *etc.* But in other circumstances, other things being taken for granted, the explanation might be that the circuit was rigged; and in yet other circumstances, that the battery was connected.

Let us now turn to action, and consider whether what I call pur-

---

[2] The most interesting is what she calls 'mental cause' (*op. cit.*, nos. 10, 11), a topic to which we shall intermittently return. Mental causation occurs, *e.g.*, when one leaps back upon seeing a snake in the grass.

pose is a possible explanatory factor. We take it for the moment that an answer to the question 'Why?' will identify the act done. Is it possible to turn up a constellation of factors, of which the element of purpose is one, where the mention of any one would explain on the presumption that the others were operating? Yes. That the dog was eating explains the disappearance of the food. Generally, the success or failure of acts of certain kinds done with a certain purpose is regularly associated with certain kinds of results, and the agent's having the purpose may therefore explain those results, always given certain other facts. Thus, the cross-bar's being off the standard is explained by an unsuccessful act of high-jumping; the presence of Koala bears in San Francisco is explained by someone's having brought them from Australia. But, and as Anscombe clearly sees, this is of no use here, for these explanations presume that we already have ascertained the presence of purpose in the agent's movements. The question 'Why?', if I understand Anscombe, is directed at something *in* the animal's behaviour, and not at something which results from that behaviour.

What then does she mean? There are, so far as I can see, two possibilities. These are quite different though easily confused; and I think that Anscombe confuses them.

In the first place, the question 'Why?' might request the *agent's reason for* doing the act, identified as of a particular kind. Examples of kinds of reason are: It tastes good; it's valuable; he promised to do it. A reason, in the intended sense, briefly put, *is a fact, the knowledge of which by an animal would explain his movements.* Perhaps, then, what Anscombe is telling us is that an act is always done for a reason, *i.e.*, there is always some fact, the knowledge of which by an animal would explain his making the movements constituting the behaviour in which the act is identified. When Anscombe holds that the order we impose upon events with the question 'Why?' and that which is drawn out by the formulation of an Aristotelian practical syllogism are the same (*op. cit.*, nos. 33 *et seq.*, also see no. 9 *supra*), she seems to be opting for the criterion as stated.

But now 'Why' may be used to request a reason in a quite different sense of 'reason'. Seeing someone running, and being quite unable to account for this, I ask another observer 'Why?', and am told, 'He is chasing Charlie' (*i.e.*, he is *pursuing* another person). This surely is quite different from the answer, 'It's a race'. With the latter we are given a reason in the earlier illustrated sense, a fact, knowledge of which on the part of the runner would explain his movements. But with the former, we are not told his reason for doing whatever it is he is doing, but rather are told that *what* he is doing is pursuing Charlie. Speaking philosophically, we might want to go on to say

65

that his running is explained as his means of pursuing Charlie. The connection of 'Why?' with explanation is preserved, but the sort of explanation given is of quite another order. It is an explanation *what*. The question 'Why?' here, in effect, requests an *identification* of the act. We earlier noticed that the identification of an act might indeed be an explanation *why*, not of the act itself, but of what results from the act.

Now, the character of this kind of explanation, which consists in the identification of what was done, is apt to be obscured by the fact that we also *describe* behaviour in *act-identificatory* terms, e.g., as *running*. No kind of act could be successfully done in all kinds of circumstances; and watching a man perform in a certain way, the observer would know that he could not simply be doing what he might seem to be doing, e.g., running; so the observer asks for an explanation, expecting to be told that the animal was performing in the manner seen as a way of doing such and such. There is no sense in the animal's simply running; the observer sees that the animal must be doing something by running and wishes to know what. His running, we are told, is, so to speak, part of his act of pursuing Charlie. The explanation resembles our accounting for the presence of a blank wall, the very description of which implies that it is an architectural structure, by saying that it is part of a house to be. Anscombe's examination of a case in which one's arm movements are explained as pumping is explained as getting water into a house, *etc.* (*op. cit.*, nos. 22–26), and remarks she makes elsewhere about 'means and ends' strongly suggest that precisely what she has in mind is that kind of answer to the question 'Why?'.

It is a serious defect in Anscombe's account that she does not distinguish these two kinds of answer to the question 'Why?'. Let us now examine the merits of each, taken separately, as an index to the existence of action. About the first kind of answer, that which gives a reason in the sense explained, this looks initially implausible. Cannot one simply rise from his chair for *no reason at all*? Though any kind of act might be done for some reason, e.g., I rise for the reason that a woman enters the room, not all particular acts, one might protest, are done for a reason. And, again, cannot the explanation of his acting be his mistaking the facts, or his ignorance of the facts? I do not believe that either of these criticisms will stand, and I shall explain why in no. 9 below. However, I should qualify my agreement with this analysis. First, while acts are always done for reasons or mistaken reasons in the sense indicated, it is not always the case that it is the presence of the reason which actually explains the act. One's reason for eating it may be that it is, as he sees, food; but the explanation for his eating here and now, at 4 *a.m.*, may be that he works a night shift.

Second, and more tellingly, reasons may similarly enter into the explanations of mental phenomena other than action. One kind of case is Anscombe's category of mental cause. My reason for jumping is that there is a snake there in the grass, as I see. Another kind of example is that of the so-called passions, *e.g.*, one is jealous, rancorous, *etc.*, for characteristic reasons which explain the jealousy, rancour, *etc.*, only if the animal is aware of them. So, while the possibility of assigning reasons or mistaken reasons in the intended sense of 'reason' may be necessary for the existence of action, it is by no means sufficient. Possibly, for achieving a sufficient condition, it will be enough to require that the reasons be of a certain type, ones which are closely tied perhaps to the possibility of success and failure in action.

It is the possibility of falling into the other interpretation of 'Why?' which calls for care. The doctrine that an act is behaviour of a kind which may be done as a means of doing something else is probably true, and tempting as an explanation. There is no act-identificatory, purpose-specifying phrase which could not on some occasion be used to describe the way in which an act was being done; to put it inaccurately, any kind of act might figure as a means towards something else. Even eating, for an agent might be eating as a means of putting his gluttonous guest at ease. A second force which pushes us towards the second interpretation of 'Why?' as a criterion of action is that it is very easy indeed to confuse ends as acts done with ends as reasons for doing whatever it was that was done. Thus I may be putting the man at his ease for the excellent reason that he is my guest; to say, 'He is putting his guest at ease' in fact suggests answers to both questions, and they are not then easily dissociated. It is rather like 'murder', which tells us that the act was one of *culpable homicide*. Or, to take a distant but interesting analogy, when one answers the question, 'How do you know?', by saying, 'I saw the broken glass', he not only supports his claim (the 'I saw'), but also indicates a sort of evidence (the broken glass). The naturalness of this kind of answer thus tends to make it more difficult to separate the questions, 'How do you know?' and 'Why do you think?'. So, too, in our case, we may have trouble separating the implied identification of the act from the implied indication of a reason for doing the act. We may regard the whole performance as just another richer *kind* of action.

But the second answer will not do as a criterion for the presence of purpose, at least without grave qualifications. Criticism comes to this: We answer the question 'Why?' by saying *what* he was doing; that is, we explain why he was doing it by saying what he was doing. But if there is an answer to that question, it is conceivable that we might have identified his act straight off; and then there would be no further answer of the requested kind to the question. After we have identified the act, giving an answer, having said what he was doing, then no further answers of *that kind* can be given to the question 'Why?'. *If* we allow that the question 'Why?' is being posed *apropos* of a report and if that is the kind of answer Anscombe intends, and *if* she furthermore wishes the answer to identify the act as of a kind, then she has it backwards: The act is finally identified when a certain kind of answer to the question 'Why?' is *refused*, not *given* application.

In fairness to her, it is not entirely clear that this is the answer she intends, nor is it obvious that she demands that the answer to 'Why?' should supply an act-identification. Moreover, it may be that the situation she envisages is not one of a report on action but one in which we are imagined to be spectators of an *episode*. We watch the animal moving, and ask why, implying that we see these movements as part of an act. When we are told that he is doing an act of a certain kind, then the movements are explained. I allow that the performance of any act might be so obscured from some observer that he might have reason to ask 'Why?' meaning 'What?', but I cannot think that Anscombe's analysis is the last word even for this case. Our observer could be given answers of many different kinds, *e.g.*, 'He's under pressure to make a good impression'. That the questioner should know which answers would satisfy him, he must already know what verbs bespeak action. This seems to leave us where we started, relying entirely upon our rough, verbal index (see p. 34), the application of which presumes that we are confronted with a report on behaviour. But we must not forget about the actual episodes to which the observer's characterizations are addressed, and there is this other question which could be put: What conditions must be met if we are to apply act-identifying language to behavioural episodes? The answer, to be given in the next section, implies that the animal is acting in the light of what he takes to be reasons. This comes close to the criterion of being able to give a first-kind Anscombian answer to the question 'Why?'.

7. AWARENESS IS A CONDITION OF ACTION

[Purpose is present in behaviour only if an observer could see that the constitutive movements could be explained by reference to the animal's awareness of something or other. Awareness or practical knowledge is explicated as an analogical extension upon full theoretical knowledge, *i.e.*, as an extension upon the imagined observer's capacity to acquire and retain information and to give expression to knowledge. So explained, awareness is a kind of propositional knowledge, from which it follows that awareness of objects always implies awareness of facts. Awareness may also imply beliefs. This yields the wanted conclusion that purpose is present and an act done only if the constitutive movements might be explained by reference to the animal's knowledge or beliefs. The stated condition is still not sufficient to distinguish action from other animal-seated transactions which also essentially involve the subject's awareness of the world.]

An act is done only if purpose is present in an item of behaviour. Purpose is present only if it would be correct to describe the animal with some one or other act-identifying word or phrase. When is it correct so to describe an animal? That is another way of posing the problem: What is it that a qualified, conceptualizing observer must find in the animal's movements and situation that will warrant this kind of description of the animal?

A first, rough kind of answer is that the observer must see that the animal is moving with something in view; his movements must have 'direction'. To present such a scene, it is necessary that the animal should, as we say, *know what he's about*. That kind of knowledge is what we must now try to explicate.

Take, then, an imagined observer. What he sees is that the animal is making such and such movements in such and such circumstances, and, possibly, that such and such happens as a result of those movements. For example, the animal moves in the direction of an apple and makes movements which result in the apple's being in his mouth and subsequently being reduced to pulp and caused to vanish down the creature's gullet.

But that is certainly not yet enough to say that the observer saw that the animal was eating an apple. We could give much the same kind of description of the operations of an applesauce-making machine. What more is needed, then? Nothing more in the way of movements, circumstances, or results. What the observer sees is that the animal's movements are in this instance *to be explained as being due to the animal's awareness of the presence of an apple*. The observer must be able to impose that kind of explanation on the kinematical and situational facts. To be able to discern a mental fact in the behaviour is to be able to give a certain kind of explanation. And, if we wish to give a theoretical account of what the mental element is, we must do so in consideration of the possibility of giving certain kinds of explanation. The mental element of purpose is brought into our thinking in connection with a certain kind of explanatory factor —awareness of the world. This does not mean or imply that awareness is not 'really' present in the observed phenomena. Gravitational attraction is something present in the world, which does not belie the fact that it is brought into our thinking, that it is something we learn to observe, in connection with learning to give certain kinds of explanation. So, awareness, hence purpose, is something we learn to observe in connection with learning to give certain kinds of explanation of animal movement. That, then, is a necessary condition for the existence of action. An animal knows what he's about and may be said to be doing an act, behaving with purpose, only when he physically reacts to an object present, a movement, etc., or, at a more advanced stage, physically reacts to the mention, thought of, etc., an object, etc., in such a way that a qualified, conceptualizing observer can truly say that the animal is aware of the presence of the object, etc., and that his being so aware might explain that he should react. An act-identifying report implies the possibility of explaining an animal's movements by reference to his awareness. In the simplest cases the purpose of the animal will be to come to have or to be in the neighbourhood of or to avoid the object of whose presence he is aware. To simplify matters, I shall frequently abbreviate the explanation by considering only cases where the creature reacts to an object present, his movements being such as would cause him to take that object into his possession. But we must not forget that there are other more sophisticated kinds of case of more abstracted awareness involving memory, thought, reference, etc.

The proposed criterion is very like that which William James set out in his celebrated chapter, 'The Will' (*Principles of Psychology*, Chap. XXVI). James tells us that consciousness is by its very nature impulsive (p. 526). He later expands this to the doctrine that, 'The terminus of the psychological process in volition, the point to which the will is directly applied, is always an idea' (p. 567). The 'evidence' is largely 'introspective'. But he cites numerous experimental cases where, when a subject animal's awareness of the world is shut off or impaired, his movements give the appearance of undirected flutter. The animal movements are seen not to constitute action. But that is coherent only if we keep well in mind that the appearance is given to a well-qualified, conceptualizing observer, the experimenting psychologist. Still, the thesis in its essentials is, I believe, correct: purpose ('volition') is discerned in connection with the animal's awareness of the world.

We have reached this conclusion and given it a coherent formulation only by holding pertinaciously to a supposed report of observation. Explanation, we earlier saw, always involves a conceptual structuring of a phenomenon. But we certainly do not want to say that only conceptualizing creatures are able to behave with purpose. The essential element, awareness, is introduced as an explanatory factor. But at the same time, this factor is something discerned to be present in the phenomenon; it is not itself a mere creature of Language, a mere 'idea', present only in the observer's explanation. Indeed, the factor may be present even though it does not actually explain. However, it cannot be discerned except by one capable of giving such explanations.

We now may explicate the concept of awareness and so of purpose by saying how it fits into explanations. Explanation, we saw, consists in bringing a problematical phenomenon into a familiar pattern of recognizable kinds of factor, barring mention of special considerations which may make us suspect that the pattern is not yet sufficiently familiar, or that the phenomenon under review is atypical, or that further explanations are required, or (possibly) that no explanation is required. In the case of behaviour what pre-eminently governs is the imagined observer's familiarity with the kind of the animal in question, qualified by any special knowledge he may have about that creature. If, as the observer knows, the creature is of a kind that is known to be insensitive to light or if his native visual capacities have been destroyed, then the observer would never say that the creature is looking at the moon or peering through a microscope.

'Aware of', though certainly a vernacular item and perhaps, therefore, not in need of explication, is nonetheless theoretically opaque. Some might protest that my use of the idea of awareness is a dodge; how, it might be asked, can a creature utterly without the use of Language strictly speaking be said to be aware of anything? I shall go into the topic of awareness more thoroughly in the next part (no. 2), but it will be well to attempt some preliminary explication here.

Awareness is a kind of so-called 'practical knowledge', a kind of knowledge which is manifested in the actual behaviour of animals. The acquisition of practical knowledge is surely genetically prior to the acquisition of 'theoretical knowledge', which involves a capacity to give verbal expression to what is known. But, I submit, we can explicate the concept of practical knowledge (the use of 'practical knowledge'), and so awareness, only as an analogical extension upon the concept of theoretical knowledge. We speak of an animal's being aware on analogy with human beings having and acquiring theoretical knowledge. More specifically, I would volunteer the following: If the observer O, of an animal A can presume that (1) a human being having Language, (2) put into the situation in which O finds A, and (3) reacting as does A, (4) could, on that account, be said to know or be acquiring information, p, where (5) there is no reason to think that A does not have non-conceptual capacities which a human would need in order to be able to know and to state p (e.g., eyes or the technical training required to make a chemical experiment);

71

then, we can say that *A* is *aware of p*. ('To know *p*' I take to mean 'to have acquired and retained the information that *p*'.) The analogy is founded on the presence in instances of practical knowledge of features which are identical with and not merely analogous to features of theoretical knowledge, *e.g.*, visual acuity.

At the most primitive stages of development, animals are aware only of the presence of objects or of their effluvia such as odours or sounds, or of other physical phenomena to which they are perceptually sensitive, such as light. They manifest this awareness in the movements they make towards or away from the object, *etc.*, in question. For animals capable of stating facts, this primitive kind of awareness may sometimes be superseded by knowledge or belief concerning various features of the situation in which the movements take place.

I stress that the agent need not have *theoretical* knowledge of the whereabouts of the object of whose presence he is aware and towards or from which his movements are directed. This is not altered by the fact that our *explanation* of practical knowledge or awareness is in terms of an analogy with theoretical knowledge, and therefore implies that a conceptualizing observer could have that theoretical knowledge. While the animal is said to have practical knowledge, it is *we* who call it that. We have Language as does the imagined observer; and for purposes of this account it is always observers' (verbal) identifications of the behaviour which are to be thought of as being under examination. Having transcended the observed animal's capacities, we suppose that the observer sees in the animal's movements behaviour which is analogous to what only those who have Language can do. The imagined report structures his behaviour according to a pattern of rationality.

One who observes that the animal is acting and what is being done must have theoretical knowledge of the presence of the actuating object and at least practical knowledge of the supposed agent and of his awareness of the object. Theoretical knowledge, though meta-theoretically primary, is still genetically secondary. If one can be meaningfully said to have theoretical knowledge of anything, it must be possible truly to say that he has practical knowledge of something; but not conversely.[1]

---

[1] I agree with Hampshire (*Thought and Action*), whose *leitmotiv* seems to be that knowledge is originally inseparable from action. But the variations he draws from this exaggerate truth and sometimes run counter to and invert the theme. He holds that in this primitive state of knowledge-cum-action, one must also be aware of himself as a spatial-temporal body, and of the spatial relations of things with respect to his body, and even of the relation of before and after itself; the agent must know that he is acting when he is acting and what his purposes are, and to do this he must also be able to see other animals as agents. Hampshire is a rationalist who sees everything as 'not contingently but necessarily' connected

We may speak of animals both being aware of objects and being aware that such and such is the case. These are the counterparts in practical knowledge to knowing particulars (*e.g.*, knowing Smith, Hume's *Treatise, etc.*) and knowing facts (*e.g.*, *that* Smith has blue eyes or that Hume's *Treatise* has three books). Let us call these *awareness of objects* and *awareness of facts*, respectively. There is a long tradition in philosophy according to which awareness of facts is founded upon and secondary to awareness of objects. A recent version of this is found in Russell's doctrine of Knowledge by Acquaintance and Knowledge by Description (see, for example, the article of that title reprinted in *Mysticism and Logic*). The basis of this view is, I believe, that animals could not be said to be aware of anything at all unless they were sensitive to and responsive to objects present. This responsiveness is then likened to awareness of the object. But it is quite clear that we are responsive to all sorts of things that we are not aware of, *e.g.*, a change in atmospheric pressure. The difference between such responsiveness and awareness is, I believe, that the animal to be aware must, as an observer could say, be apprised of the state of the world, *e.g.*, be apprised of the presence of the object to which he responds. But *that* an object is present is (possibly) a *fact*, not an object. I therefore deny that awareness of objects is in some way primary to awareness of facts. To be aware of an object is in minimal instances to be aware of the presence of an

---

with everything else. His error is almost exactly that of his philosophical forebear Leibniz: He projects the theoretical order into the realm of practice. One can, for example, know that his purposes are such and such only by taking a theoretical view of what he does. It is no good to plead that elements corresponding to our theoretical account must be latent in the practice, if this leads to the conclusion that the practice is its own theoretical analysis. The danger here is that we shall put ourselves into a position which will make it impossible to understand how the theory relates to the practice, and how higher-level theoretical capacities develop out of and presuppose a lower-order kind of practical knowledge. Hampshire's examination proceeds almost entirely from the agent or 'first person' position, and well illustrates the dangers that beset an 'introspective' analysis. It is presupposed that the animal in question, namely oneself, is capable of conceptualizing the phenomena; the introspective agent must therefore be assumed to have sufficient Language verbally to identify and to bespeak his own behaviour, and to give expression to his thoughts, intentions, *etc.* Of course such a one will necessarily have passed through all the stages of behavioural development which a command of so much Language necessarily involves. For him, the fabric of behaviour, which is his own behaviour, will indeed appear to be a network of necessary connections. But surely part of what we want to do is to separate these various factors just in order better to be able to discern how they are related and how all of them are presupposed whenever we engage in rather sophisticated behaviour involving the use of Language. Surely part of what we want to do is to explain how self-consciousness depends upon consciousness, *etc.*
I return to this topic of practical and theoretical knowledge in no. 2 of Part III.

object, which is to be aware of the fact that the object is present. At the same time, I want to hold that for one to be aware of any particular fact about an object implies that he is also aware of the object. More exactly, if the observer is able truly to say that the animal is aware of the fact *F*, then it follows that the animal is also aware of the object referred to in the observer's implied statement of the fact *F*.[2]

At the most primitive stages of development, animals are aware only of the presence of objects (*etc.*), otherwise not identified. At this level, there is no possibility that the animal should misidentify an object present, as to type and even less as a particular. Nor would it make sense to say that the animal is aware of the absence of objects, though he may 'respond to' absence. At higher levels of development the animal may, as the observer can discover, come to be aware of objects not only as present on the immediate stage of perception, but also as something thought of, or about, or as verbally referred to. Eventually, he will come to enjoy full theoretical knowledge, and then he too may become a qualified conceptualizing observer.

At the most primitive stage, where the animal is aware of the presence of an object, which awareness explains his movements towards or away from the object, he may be said to have a purpose and do an act. But he certainly need not be aware of the presence of purpose in himself or that he is acting with purpose. He need not be *self*-conscious. He can become aware of himself as having purpose only when he can be aware of his own movements as being made in response to objects, his awareness of which explains his movements.

We are not surprised to see puppy dogs move towards what we know is dog food or to move away from loud noises. Though such movements perhaps generally need no explaining, we know that they could be explained by reference to the puppy's awareness of the presence of the food or the noise. When there is such an established regularity, by knowledge of which we are entitled to say that animals of this kind regularly move towards or away from objects of this kind, the said objects qualify as *natural objects of desire* or *aversion*: they are 'natural goods' or 'natural evils' for that kind of animal.

But this goes only for regularities about 'kinds'. Particular animals can act to possess objects which are anything but 'natural goods' for their kind, and, knowing them individually, we can also know that they regularly do such untypical acts. (Needless to say, a

---

[2] Great care must be exercised here. The observer in saying what the animal is aware of must not imply that the animal is aware of as much as the observer is. Thus, an observer may misleadingly say that A is aware that Smith is at the door, even though A does not know who Smith is. The observer would better say: A is aware that an object, namely Smith, is at the door. 'Aware that . . .' is a 'non-extensional context'.

doctrine of 'natural good' is very far indeed from being an explanation of 'evaluation' or of good and evil generally, though it seems reasonable to suppose that evaluation presumes a domain of 'natural goods'.)

Awareness is a kind of knowledge, not by virtue of anything that the observed animal may have to say about the matter, but by virtue of a kind of analogical imposition on the part of the conceptualizing observer. Now if we can truly say that an animal knows p, it follows that we can also truly say that he believes (or thinks) p.[3] Thus, if an animal is aware of the presence of an object he also believes that there is an object present. But his awareness may carry a number of other beliefs along with it. The animal may believe that such and such *kind* of object is present, or that such and such particular object is present. The importance of this is that it immediately yields one of the earlier-stated criteria of action. Action is behaviour of a kind, the constituent movements of which might be explained by the animal's knowledge or beliefs. It also opens the way to providing additional tests (1) by which action may be distinguished from other phenomena, an explanation of which might be that an animal is aware, and (2) by which acts may be typally identified. Only if among the implied beliefs are beliefs to the effect that such and such conditions do not obtain, which, if they did, would inevitably result in the failure of the act, can the animal be said to be acting with a purpose, which purpose may be defined by listing just those conditions under which the purpose necessarily could not be attained.

To summarize what has been done in this section, the concept of awareness (consciousness) has been in a preliminary fashion defined

---

[3] I do not hold that knowledge and belief are the same: knowledge is a *state* of having acquired and retained information, whereas I would explain belief *dispositionally*. Subject to certain qualifications, knowledge, in the sense in which we ascribe knowledge to others, is a sufficient though not a necessary condition for belief. (The qualifications are called for because of the special force of 'believe' in contrast, say, with 'think', which allows for saying, *e.g.*, 'Though I know she did it, I cannot really believe it'.) The existence of an implication from knowledge to belief may, I think, be traced as follows: we may test for the presence of that disposition we call 'believing p' in various ways, by noticing what the animal does. One such test is that the animal acts as if he knew p. So, acting as if one knew p is sufficient for one to believe p. Since the test need not in fact be made, we may formulate the more general conclusion that if one would act as if he knew p, he believes p. This account of the relation between knowledge and belief, according to which belief is explained partially in terms of acting with knowledge, reverses the direction of traditional attempts to explain knowledge as belief *plus*. It might now also be argued that to say of someone that he knows p implies that he would act as if he knew p, where 'would' does not mean 'will'. The conclusion would be that if it is true to say that someone knows p, it follows that he believes p.

and brought into connection with the analysis of behaviour. Awareness is a factor, mention of which might explain the movements constituting an item of behaviour. Only if such a factor is present does the behaviour qualify as action. Awareness is a necessary condition for the existence of an act. It is not sufficient, for awareness occupies a similar position in the explanation of blushes, agitations, passions, and what Anscombe has called 'mental causation'. Perhaps certain of these kinds of animate phenomena do not qualify as behaviour, but it is doubtful that none of them does. (One might have kept from jumping back at a snake seen in the grass or from a peeping-Tom's face in the window.) We therefore need a further condition on behaviour to define action. We may generalize this to say that awareness is a necessary but not a sufficient condition for the presence of purpose, even though no act is done, *e.g.*, when the animal inhibits or forbears from making the movements which would constitute behaviour. Purpose is present only if the animal is aware of certain facts, and the awareness disposes the animal to make certain movements. We also noticed that awareness implies belief. Possibly we can eke out a sufficient condition for action by imposing certain conditions upon these beliefs, and also define types of purpose and action in terms of these beliefs. These possibilities will be pursued in nos. 10 and 12. But first I should like to explore the idea of *self-consciousness*, or knowledge of what one is doing, and to exploit what we have been developing to elucidate the topic of *reason*.

8. KNOWLEDGE BY REFLECTION AND PRIVILEGED TESTIMONY

[Arguments are brought against the doctrine that an agent must be self-conscious in the sense that he is, among other things, aware of himself as an agent and of the fact that he is acting to attain a certain purpose. It remains that an agent capable of conceptualizing behaviour can immediately and by mere reflection become aware of himself as an agent and of the fact that he is acting to attain a certain purpose. This possibility is traced to the consideration that an agent must be aware of certain things, and by observing the agent's awareness an observer could see that the agent was acting to attain a certain purpose; an agent capable of making such observations on his own can by mere reflection come to know that he is thus aware of certain things and thereby know also that he is acting to attain a certain purpose. Just because a common way of establishing that a putative agent is aware of certain facts is to ask him, his testimony as to what he is doing, determined in consideration of what he is aware of, has a privileged status in that it cannot be challenged without impugning the agent's candour or his use of Language.]

76

Some writers have held, explicitly or by implication, that animals acting to attain a purpose must be not only aware of some one object or other, but must also be in some sense self-conscious. According to this doctrine, to which we have already taken exception (see p. 63), an agent must, at a very minimum, be aware of himself; but it is often also held or implied that he must be aware of himself as an agent acting to attain a certain purpose. An agent must not only know what he's about, but he must also know what he means to do; he must know his purpose.[1]

The doctrine is wrong for reasons already mentioned. An observer discovers purpose to be present in behaviour only if he sees that the animal is aware of something. But it does not follow that the agent must therefore be aware that he is acting to attain that purpose or even that he be acting at all, that he be aware that he is aware of anything else or even of himself. Sometimes we are thus aware of ourselves, but surely not always; and some types of agent, I maintain, never are. To be able to be aware of oneself and even more of oneself as an agent requires a certain sophistication and capabilities not possessed by all types of agent. I am inclined to think that an agent capable of self-consciousness must already have the use of

---

[1] Hampshire seems to take this line. See n. 1 on p. 72. Indeed, the equation of consciousness with self-consciousness is a dominant theme in his account (see *op. cit.*, *e.g.*, pp. 75, 132f.). This mistaken equation is surprisingly prevalent, if usually by implication, in philosophical writings. Prichard's thesis (*op. cit.*, pp. 194ff.) that an agent always acts out of a desire to will what he does appears to be another example. Since Prichard holds that the presence of desire is necessary for action, his thesis implies that one cannot act unless he knows what he means to do; for, according to the thesis, that is what he desires to do. The Thomistic doctrine that the will is not only generated by an intellectual apprehension of a goal (which I accept) but also generates a consequential awareness of itself is possibly still another example. A similar mistake can be found in the writings of certain psychologists. Thus Slack, in a paper cited by Mowrer (*op. cit.*, p. 284), avers, '. . . that we do not know what the stimulus is unless we know what the response is and we do not know what the response is unless we know what the stimulus is.' There is here an ambivalence in 'know . . . is'. But sliding over that, we may, I think, take it that the response is the act and the stimulus is what the agent is aware of; his awareness explains the movements constituting the act. Then, to 'know what the stimulus is' would simply be to be aware in the indicated way, while to 'know what the response is' would be, *inter alia*, to be aware of one's purpose. But I am sure that to be aware of something and to have a purpose does not always require that the agent also be aware of the purpose itself.

This kind of mistake would abet the confusion we noted in Anscombe's account of 'intentional action' (see pp. 65f.), a confusion between knowing why an act was done (the animal's awareness of such and such) and knowing what kind of act was done. Unless I miss my guess, Anscombe actually makes this mistake, for she puts great stress on the agent's knowing his intention ('purpose') without observation —implying, I believe, that he at least could be aware that he was acting from a certain purpose.

Language, or at least be responsive to the use of Language. That an agent should be aware of himself (*e.g.*) acting to acquire object *O* requires that he be aware of *O* not only as an object present but also as an object sought. To get onto this trick, something more than the presence of the thing is needed; the object must be 'given' in a special way; and, so far as I can see, that can be accomplished only *via* a verbal reference. (The argument is far from demonstrative. I can see objections to the conclusion. Even if correct, it would not imply that an agent must have Language to become aware of *other* agents acting to acquire objects; here the whole transaction is on view.)

Why should a doctrine of self-consciousness have been so commonly and even persistently held? Partly because *we*, who have the use of Language and are capable of self-consciousness, take our own behaviour as the controlling case. Thinking about ourselves, as we say, 'introspectively', we there and then become self-conscious.

An argument in its support is that an agent must at least be aware of himself if he is to be aware of anything else; because that which he is aware of is perceived through the body or conceived through the mind. In response, I allow what is certainly true, that one is, in the most primitive case, aware of things by virtue of how they impinge on his body. But that by no means entails that the animal must also be aware of his body, and so of himself as one thing among others. Animals have to discover that they see the world through their eyes. One may be aware of things without reacting to his body, so long as the body reacts. But allow that he does react to his body: in our thinking we still draw a distinction between sensation and perception, perception being a species of awareness of something external while sensation is not; consistent with this, we do not count (*e.g.*) coughing and blinking as kinds of action. Here, I think, we mistake a condition (that the body respond to the world) which we know must hold if the agent is to be aware of the world, as part of what he is thus aware of. It is yet another example of imbedding the results of a theoretical account of a practice into that practice.

There are pressures at two other points whose resultant is to move us in the direction of some kind of doctrine of self-consciousness. First, a creature who does have sufficient use of Language can, *by mere reflection*, directly come to realize that he is acting and what he is doing. Second (anticipating a theme of no. 10 on the identification of purpose), one might argue: If an animal is really acting, he must in advance be prepared to recognize failure; and to know how he might fail is *ipso facto* to know *what* he is doing, which is a kind of self-consciousness.

I deny the cogency of this last argument. It is true, I allow, that one who can verbally identify an act surely will, in doing that, imply that it would fail for certain reasons. But consider this puppy dog scratching at the door: Here is the very picture of purpose, aim, intent. If the door opens the creature acts in just the way we might expect. But suppose the door stays shut, and all that happens is that the dog finally stops scratching, returns to his mat and falls asleep. He may then become aware of his mat and of the flea that greets him there; but he is not aware of the room he's not in. Nor, we may add, is trying to gain entrance at a door the most primitive kind of action we can conceive. (I hope it is clear that I am not saying that dogs cannot in any case become aware of failure, only that it would be unreasonable to say in the imagined case that the puppy was aware that he failed.)

What, now, of this matter of the agent's being able to come to realize by mere reflection that he is doing such and such? I have already considered this when I suggested that we, who are capable of conceptualizing behaviour, are apt to give too much importance to our own behaviour. Now, it is surely the case that one capable of reflection is capable of self-consciousness. But I do not think that reflection is a *necessary* condition for self-consciousness. That would be to ask too much. And to make the possibility of reflection a proof of self-consciousness in all action would be to weaken the claims which self-consciousness can make on its own behalf. Reflection, whatever it is, surely involves the consideration of propositions, and so implies that the agent has attained the level of being able to use Language. In particular, he must be able to say what he is doing, which (I suggest) implies that he is able to say what others are doing, *i.e.*, that he can apply tests for ascertaining the presence of purpose in behaviour. But, we have seen, practical knowledge comes before theoretical knowledge, where all that is generally required for the agent to be truly said to be acting is that he have practical knowledge. By demanding that the creature have a capacity for reflection, we have from the outset eliminated cases where consciousness of self seems most clearly absent, and in doing that we impose very narrow limits indeed upon the domain of action.

Reflection, I say, is sufficient, though probably not necessary, for self-consciousness. Now, it remains that we are conceptualizing observers of the behaviour of others and of ourselves, and are capable of reflection. For that reason, this idea of knowledge by reflection will be forever intruding itself upon our attempts to achieve an understanding of behaviour, quite independently of the doctrine that self-consciousness is a condition of action. It is a matter we must come to grips with.

To reflect is at least to entertain a proposition. It is a form of deliberate thought. It enters upon the behavioural scene in company with the acquisition of Language. One can reflect upon the behaviour of oneself or of others only if he is able verbally to identify different kinds of behaviour. But reflection is something special—not mere assertion or supposition; it is, if you wish, a manner of knowing things. Reflection is not looking or investigating; it is not a kind of testing or perceiving. It is, strictly speaking, not a way of *coming* to know at all, but rather it is coming to realize in a certain way what one must *already* know.

Since these thoughts were first set down a number of important works have appeared in which stress is placed on the alleged fact that purpose (among other things) can be known by an agent *without* observation. The agent neither must nor can seek out evidence that he is presently doing such and such, and there is no room for his applying a test.[2] I have no fondness for this curious idea of 'non-observational knowledge', for, in a paradoxical phrase, it fuses what is known with how it is known. There is nothing about the material world that can be known that someone could not come to know by observation. But let it pass, for it seems to be nothing but what I called 'reflection'. Reflection, surely, as we saw, is not gathering evidence nor making tests. I would therefore agree that one who has sufficient Language can have 'non-observational knowledge', knowledge 'by reflection', of what he is doing.

Confining ourselves to consideration of such creatures, *i.e.*, ones with sufficient Language to be able to identify acts of the kind they are doing, how can they know what they are doing without having to make tests or gather evidence? In essentials, the answer is very simple. The agent already has made the necessary observations, he already has acquired the knowledge, and needs only to realize that he has done so.

The central consideration is that one who can reflect, hence has Language enough, can immediately know what he believes himself to know or believe; for all he need do is to give expression to what he believes he knows or believes, and that will tell him. Let us now apply this to the case of action.

One cannot be said to act except in the awareness of certain facts implying that he knows and/or believes certain things. An observer who theoretically discerns the basis of knowledge or beliefs on which the animal is acting, thereby theoretically knows that the animal is acting and what kind of act he is doing. (The possibility of typally identifying an act from what we see the agent to be aware of has not

---

[2] I think especially of the earlier cited books of Anscombe and Hampshire. Since writing this, I have read an article by O. R. Jones, 'Things known without Observation' (*Proc. Arist. Soc.*, 1960, pp. 129–50), which appears to anticipate some phases of the following argument.

yet been explained. For the moment, I simply assume that such identifications can thus be made (see pp. 125f.).) So, an agent, by acting, shows awareness, hence knowledge and belief; if he is capable of theoretically knowing what he believes he knows and believes, then he can without further observation theoretically know that he is acting on these items of presumed knowledge and belief; hence, he can theoretically know what he is doing and has need for no observations additional to or beyond those by which he knows or comes to believe the facts; it is from his having that knowledge or belief that an observer would judge the behaviour to be of this kind. Again, confining ourselves to the simplest case involving only knowledge, if the agent *A* is doing an act of such and such kind, then *A* already knows, by observation, if you will, all the relevant facts by virtue of an observation of *A*'s awareness of which facts an observer would identify the act. The agent can come to realize what he knows by simply saying it to himself and hence proceed to identify his act. Let me now tell a fuller story, for what has been said goes too fast and misses an important point or two.

We saw that an observer identifies what is being done by observing that the agent is aware of certain facts. Therefore the agent is aware of those facts. Moreover, since it has been given that he has sufficient capacity to be able to identify kinds of action, he must also be able to specify the facts awareness of which defines action. Therefore, by reflecting upon what he presumes he knows and what he believes, he can immediately come to realize that he knows such and such, or at least that he has certain beliefs. Thus, he already knows all that an observer could know about the facts that call forth his movements. He can also come to realize that he is aware of those facts. For now, being aware of the facts in question, he realizes (as we can describe it) that his prereflective behaviour with respect to the facts was analogous to coming to have full theoretical knowledge of or beliefs in respect of those facts. Finally, he can, by reflection, come to realize that his awareness of the facts is what explains his making the movements he does; for, moving as he does, he usually need merely consider himself to realize that he is so moving. I say 'usually' and the necessary qualifications reveal that sometimes the agent may need some self-observation yielding consciousness of information additional to what comes by reflection, in order to see that he is acting and to identify his deed. There is always the case of the man who doesn't know where his members are. Psychology textbooks are full of examples of cases where animals do not know whether they are moving or what they are doing because of impairment of perception. (See again the early pages of James' chapter, 'The Will'.) But allow that our reflective agent can perceive his own movements and so can

81

directly come to realize that he is so moving. Then, since when he is aware (*e.g.*) of the presence of an object *and* that he is moving in a certain way, *and* since he can verbally identify action in such behaviour, he need only do so in order to realize and to say what he is doing.

I repeat, the reason the agent's knowledge is 'non-observational' is that he must already have made the necessary observations of the facts, *e.g.*, the presence of the object he seeks to have or to avoid. This is subject only to the one qualification that he may additionally have to observe his own movements, though generally, by knowing where he is and the nature of the object of his awareness, he already knows what kind of movements would be natural here, and so on reflection will realize as much.

There is a strong temptation, very hard to resist, to give special importance to the agent's testimony, when it comes to identifying what he means to do. It is not that we can never be misinformed by an agent, and testimony surely is not an ultimate test, for it does not even apply to creatures without the use of Language; still, it would often border on the absurd to challenge a man on his own ground. Such a challenge must be either to the agent's candour or to his way of expressing himself. The reason for this comes out of my analysis. The act is identified with respect to the agent's awareness of something, implying items of knowledge or of belief, true or false, about the world, possibly consisting simply in his being perceptually alive to an object. But awareness itself was defined on analogy with having theoretical knowledge, and a candid report is a normal manifestation of such knowledge. So, short of impugning the agent's honesty or simply failing to understand his words, there is no room for challenging his testimony. And here we also have one way of finding out what the agent is aware of when it might otherwise not be obvious, and so a way of discovering what he is meaning to do.

The most interesting issue here is over the relative worth of the possibly competing claims of an observer's report and a reflective agent's report when the agent does, and the observer does not, mistake the facts, *e.g.*, misidentify an object of awareness. The agent kicks what happens to be a bag of sand. He tells us that what he meant to do was to kick a football, while the observer says that he meant to kick a sandbag. Who is right? Here, too, I want to hold that the agent's testimony is preferred. But the issue is a bit intricate, and I defer discussion of it until no. 11, when we shall be better prepared to say how an agent's beliefs determine what kind of act he does.

Supposing that the agent's testimony does thus tend to prevail over that of an observer, our general conclusion regarding an agent's testimony is secure against challenge but not against disbelief. Without daring directly to challenge the agent, a third party might still put more faith in what the observer tells him. Testimony, because it reasonably may be disbelieved, is not proof. Nevertheless, it is a particularly telling kind of instrument for discovering what the agent meant to do. Again, if we wish to know what was being done, it is neither necessary nor sufficient to consult the agent, though his report, if available, will weigh heavily, and we would be ill-advised to neglect it. But finally we must retain the observer's position and take our stand on our general presumptions derived from our experiences with animals of the kind in question about the occasions upon which acts are done, about the expected normal consequences of such acts, the needs of the animal, and his prior and subsequent behaviour, *etc.* The normal presumptions may be questioned, but only on the ground of alleged and specific abnormalities, whose presence must in principle be ascertainable. Usually, there is no question what an agent means to do, for the purposes of most acts are perfectly patent, *e.g.*, the kind of action we call 'eating'.

So far we have been discussing questions only about the existence and identification of acts, *i.e.*, the possibilities of answering the question, 'What was he meaning to do?'. I have tried to explain why the conceptualizing agent may know the answers to these questions 'by reflection'. We have seen that his own testimony carries certain privileges. But clearly there is ever so much about an act which the agent cannot know merely 'by reflection'. In particular, he cannot always simply 'realize' whether or not his act succeeded, *e.g.*, whether or not he hit the bullseye on the target 100 yards down the range. Generally, the agent is in no better position than any other well-placed, experienced, and acute observer. I, too, may have to look to see that the object was moved by my kicking it. The conclusion is that the agent's testimony as to what he did in contrast with what he meant to do certainly has no privileges against dissent.

As a kind of counter-charm against exaggerated claims on behalf of the agent's identification of his act with the intimation that *only he could really* know, some have urged that animals come to do acts only by becoming aware that other animals do such acts. This is plainly overstated. At best it could apply literally only to kinds of action which one must *learn* to do. But it is not even true that in learning to do some kinds of acts (*e.g.*, a dog's learning to beg for food) an animal necessarily learns to recognize similar behaviour in other creatures. The thesis is really plausible only for those kinds of acts which an animal learns to do by following the lead of another.

But there surely is a germ of truth here. My analysis, if correct, shows that one cannot become aware of himself as having such and such purpose, *e.g.*, of doing an act of such and such kind, if he is not already prepared to recognize that purpose in the behaviour of other animals. He can structure his own behaviour in this way only if he can correctly so describe the behaviour of others. About the converse, whether his knowledge of the purposes of others depends upon the possibility of his having self-knowledge, I simply do not know; my conjecture is that it does not, the clue being that one must certainly have come to regard other creatures as animals before he can so regard himself, just as he must be able to see other objects in their places before he can regard himself as occupying a place, his own present place not being one of the places in his most primitive spatial world. But this is not enough for us to conclude that an agent could possibly identify purposive behaviour of a certain kind in another although not in himself; it may be that by the time one can identify *action* he must long since have come to regard himself as an acting animal, and, moreover, as an animal who could conceivably do any kind of action which he might identify. The answer, therefore, is not yet obvious, and awaits a more detailed investigation into the relations between levels of experience. (I would add that the evidence supports the view that the possibility exists that agents can identify behaviour in others even though not in themselves. There appear to be all sorts of things of a fairly sophisticated kind which a person might see in others though be apparently incapable of seeing in himself, *e.g.*, vanity. It remains to interpret the force of 'apparently incapable'.)

9. REASON IN ACTION[1]

[A reason is defined as a fact, knowledge of which on the part of an animal might serve as an explanation of his movements. We may also allow for the possibility of mistaken reasons. It then follows that an act is always done for true or mistaken reasons. This idea of reason, which resembles the second or minor premise in an Aristotelian so-called 'practical syllogism', is developed by drawing contrasts between (1) having a reason and acting on a reason, (2) having a reason and reasoning, (3) having reason for acting and having reason for believing, in connection with which remarks are made about statements, drawn as conclusions, about what one ought to do, (4) reasons and principles of reason, and (5) various kinds of principle of reason. A further distinction between reasons for doing an act and reasons for doing it in a certain way will be expounded in no. 17. As part of an attempt to give sense to the question how reasons can be justified, the question is raised, how do we recognize a principle of

---

[1] For an account rather like what follows, see Judith Jarvis, 'Practical Reasoning', *Phil. Quart.*, 1962, pp. 316–28.

reason for what it is? The answer is drawn out of the original definition of *reason*, with special attention to the knowledge which a competent observer would have to have about the species of animal in question in order to be able to say that the movements of such creatures could be explained by reference to their awareness of facts, which are reasons.]

We have explained action in connection with the idea of awareness. An act is done only when the movements of an animal might be explained as being due to his awareness and, in the most primitive case, as being due to his awareness of the presence of an object, of light or such like. Awareness itself was explained on analogy with situations in which a conceptualizing creature acquires knowledge or gives expression to what he knows or believes. To say of a creature that he is aware of something always implies that he knows or believes certain things, possibly only that an object is present, but possibly also a great deal more.

This account of action affords convenient introduction to the topic of *reason* as it has been discussed by philosophers, where *reason* is a concept associated with that employment of 'reason' in which one may be said to *have* a reason which may be *his* reason for doing something. [2]

Consider a case: A panting dog comes into the kitchen, sees a dish of water, moves towards it, and proceeds to drink. His reason for going where he does and doing what he then does is that this is water (as he sees). The fact that there is water in the dish is his reason. The dog is aware of the dish; and, though he might have been mistaken and only *thought* that there was water in the dish, in the imagined case there is no question but that he knows that there is water in the dish, and that item of knowledge contributes to the explanation of the movements we see him make. The fact that there is water in a certain place, which is the dog's reason, is a fact the knowledge of

---

[2] The word 'reason' like 'cause' is naturally employed whenever questions of explanation arise. 'Explanation for', 'cause of', and 'reason for' are near synonyms over a wide variety of cases. Thus we might say, 'The reason for [the explanation for *or* of, the cause of] there being so many meteorites is that we are passing through the tail of a comet'. Philosophers have regularly regarded both reasons and causes as something rather special, though their failure to realize that they are thus restricting these notions prejudices the coherence of their accounts. (Hume, for instance, often thinks of a cause as a happening which explains a subsequent happening. But he also often talks about 'cause' and 'causation' as if they were coextensive with explanation.) There are vernacular indexes already mentioned to the special, restricted sense of 'reason' that I wish to examine. The novelty of my efforts here will be to explicate 'reason' in the intended sense in terms of explanation: while reasons by themselves do not explain, knowledge of reasons does.

which would naturally be adduced to explain the fact that an animal such as this, in a state such as he is in, would make movements such as these.

Generalizing, I consider a *reason* to be a *fact* that is of a kind the *knowledge* of which kind of facts on the part of animals of certain kinds would in some instances be sufficient explanation of their doing acts of certain kinds. A reason, then, is a fact, a fact viewed in a certain kind of connection with animal behaviour. The connection is that knowledge of the fact by an animal would account for his making certain movements. Not all facts are reasons, for they do not all have that kind of connection with behaviour. What kinds of facts count as reasons is also obviously relative to the kind of animal—that this is money may be reason for my taking it, but not for a bear's taking it; but its being food might be a reason for either of us. Whether a fact is a reason is also relative to the conceptualizing observer's familiarity with the type of animal in question, for *reason* is defined in terms of explanation. To speak of reason brings to mind a certain kind of explanation.

Some philosophers have certainly talked about reasons (in the intended sense of 'reason') as if they were causes or other types of phenomenon whose presence at once explains and determines behaviour. Recently there has been a good deal of exception taken to this.[3] Now I agree that reasons (in the intended sense of 'reason') are not causes or any other kind of determining factor. I also agree that reason has a tight connection with cognition (awareness, knowledge). But I also hold that it is not possible to understand *reason* except in connection with what determines and explains behaviour and other animate phenomena. My proposal is that reason is something the cognition (knowledge) of which determines and thus explains animate phenomena. Reasons (in the intended sense of 'reason') enter into our ways of thinking in essential connection with the explanation of animal behaviour.

This does not imply that reasons exist only when some animal's knowledge of those reasons explains his movements. There are at least four kinds of case where having a reason does not explain. In the first place, an agent may indeed know the fact which is the reason, but his act may be of so familiar a kind as not to require explanation. The dog drinks; the reason is that this (as he sees) is water; but there is no call for explaining the act, at least in ordinary circumstances. The second case is that in which an agent knows a fact which is a reason, and his act does require explanation, but the kind of explana-

---

[3] To the extent of becoming a theme in contemporary philosophy. For representative examples, see R. S. Peters, *The Concept of Motivation*, and A. I. Melden, *Free Action*.

tion wanted would demand mention of other facts or circumstances which the agent is not necessarily aware of. Thus the explanation of my drinking water may be a heavy night before. Knowledge of reason is but *one* kind of explanation for animal behaviour; others are causes (of various kinds), dispositions (of various kinds), opportunities, emotional agitations, states of the body, motives. The third case is that in which an agent indeed knows a fact that is a reason, but he knows another fact that also is a reason, and it is by mentioning his knowledge of the latter fact that an observer would explain the agent's movements. He acts on another reason. That the woman has fallen is a reason for my helping her up; but it may be that the crowd is watching, which also is a reason. Or, I stop and help the woman, although my being late for an appointment is a reason for rushing on. The fourth kind of case, finally, is that in which there is a fact of the required kind, but the animal does not know it. Here mention of the reason explains nothing. But it is still quite all right to say that there is a reason, and, occasionally, even that the animal has a reason ('As I now see, I had every reason to sell last year; if only I had known!'). In both this case and in the previous case, the reason is not *his*. Here also we may speak of 'having reason' even when the agent does not act, either because he does not know the fact or is not moved by his knowledge to act for the reason.

If reasons may be present even though they do not even indirectly explain an act done, perhaps because the supposed agent is not aware of the facts which are the reasons, then it is wrong to hold that for a reason to be present it must have a tendency to move the animal into action, as Nowell-Smith seems to maintain in Chapter 8 of his book *Ethics*. What he calls a 'logically complete reason' would seem to be nothing more than being disposed to be moved into action by knowledge of a fact that the agent regards as a reason. This is a very natural mistake. It is natural, first, because our operating idea of a reason is indeed abstracted from cases in which an animal is moved to act for the reason in question; and to speak of reasons is to measure an animal's action or inaction against what would be explained by reference to his knowledge of those reasons, implying that the animal could know the reasons and perhaps occasionally even that he ought to know them. Second, Nowell-Smith considers only acts proper, that is, acts done; and here, we shall see, always there will either be reasons present and known (though not necessarily regarded as reasons by the agent), or the agent will have beliefs that would be of reasons were his beliefs true, though it may still be that mention of these reasons or putative reasons would not actually explain the act.

So, although reasons are not explanations, mention of an animal's knowledge of reasons might explain. What is possibly thus explained is an act, *i.e.*, behaviour with purpose. In assigning reasons, we conceptually structure the behaviour according to a pattern of rationality: the animal's behaviour is regarded as analogous to that of a creature who could deliberate and state on what facts he is acting, although we must always regard the animal's capabilities as commensurate with his kind. We treat him as acting on *knowledge*.

Hitherto I have illustrated the explanation of reason by examples in which an agent does *what* he does for certain reasons. His knowledge of the reasons explains his doing this; awareness of the reasons accounts for his acting with that purpose. But knowledge of reasons for doing such and such a kind of act is not the only kind of knowledge of reasons which is possibly manifested in action. One may kill a dog for the reason that it is rabid; but, knowing other things about dogs and drugs, he may do the act by injecting the creature with strychnine. What the agent knows shows itself not as a reason for doing the act, but, if you wish, as a reason for doing the act in a certain way. But his knowledge that dogs are creatures mortally allergic to strychnine may not figure at all, for he may act solely from the belief (for the reason) that the animal, whatever its kind, is rabid. Only in no. 13, after we have refined the distinction between what is done and how it is done, shall we be able to do justice to the distinction between reasons for doing an act and reasons for doing it in a certain way.

So far we have discussed reason in connection with *knowledge* of reasons. That is convenient, because reasons are facts possibly known. But the awareness that explains an agent's movements may imply that the agent has beliefs, true or false, in addition to what he knows. The agent may be said to act with or (more strongly) from those beliefs. Where the observed animal is a conceptualizing creature capable of stating his reasons, we could also say that he acts for what he *thinks* are such and such reasons. Now, if the agent's belief is true, what he believes is a fact; moreover, what the agent then believes, he could have known even if he does not know. Had he known rather than merely believed, that knowledge might have explained his movements. From this it follows that what he believes is a reason. When an animal knows or truly believes such and such, we shall say that what he knows or believes is a reason for which he acts. But now an animal may act from false beliefs, in misapprehension of the facts. Then surely it cannot be his knowledge of reasons which explains his movements. The explanation of the animal's behaviour might be that he believes such and such, which happens to be false. What he believes is not a reason, for it is not a fact. But still he looks as if he were acting for a reason. We might want to say that he believes that he has a reason. That might be true for creatures that can state their reasons, but it would inaccurately represent the situation of less sophisticated animals. The more exact statement is that what the agent believes would be a reason, were his belief true. When the explanation of his behaviour is that he has this belief, which happens to be false, let us, for the sake of brevity, say that he acts for a *mistaken reason*. Clearly a mistaken reason is not a reason.

Even where an agent acts for a mistaken reason, it is assumed that he is aware of something, and this awareness engenders the false beliefs from which he acts. That of which he is aware is a fact that he knows, and his knowledge explains his movements. So an animal acts always for (at least) *a* reason.

We may now reverse the direction of our analysis and recast it as a necessary condition for action. An item of behaviour is an act only if the animal in question acts for a reason, where he may also act for a number of reasons or a number of mistaken reasons. [4]

Some additional terminology will be useful. (1) When an agent acts for a reason, we shall say that this is *his* reason for acting. (Clearly, that it is his reason need not be *the* explanation.)

(2) A fact of kind F is *a reason for* doing acts of kind A if knowledge of some fact of kind F by some agent might explain his actually doing an act of kind A.

(3) An agent A *has a reason* for doing an act of kind K if there is a fact the knowledge of which by an agent A' of the same kind as A, and in no relevant respects differing from A, would explain A''s doing an act of kind K. A may equal A'.

(4) Finally, a rather difficult notion which is naturally called *acting with a reason*. A acts with a reason R if A is doing an act of kind K', where A believes R to be the case and R is a reason for doing acts of kind K and A would be inclined to do an act of kind K were he not doing an act of kind K' for some reason R'. K may equal K' and R equal R', allowing that one may act *with* a reason *for* which he acts. We need this idea of acting with a reason on account of the following: An agent may be aware of a fact R and appreciate that it is relevant to the deeds he contemplates; it is not that he merely believes R, where that belief is entirely incidental to his deed. He does not merely act *with* the belief R; he appreciates that R is relevant to his plan of action; at the very minimum he acts *in* the belief R, although he may choose to act in disregard of or in wilful opposition to the fact. I conjecture that an agent can do an act *with* a reason R *for* which he does *not* act only if he is aware of R *as* a reason, which of course is not a general condition for acting for a reason (see p. 97). The idea of acting with a reason becomes especially important when we

---

[4] This would be too obviously circular to serve as any part of a *definition* of action.

attempt to say what it is for an agent to act in deliberate violation of a rule.

These ideas of 'one's reason', 'being a reason for', 'having a reason', and 'acting with a reason' are patently highly schematic.

Here it could be objected that this account of the relation between reason and action makes no allowance for gratuitous acts, *i.e.*, acts done for no apparent reason. But here 'no apparent reason' means no *normal* or no *good* reason. It is prerogative of high behavioural sophistication that it allows us to act for the strangest reasons, perhaps even for second-order reasons, as when one's reason is that he would (as he sees or believes) be taken to act for another reason. It permits even the possibility of acting for the reason that others will believe that the agent acts for no normal reason. This possibility is allowed for by our general knowledge of our fellow-men, and is occasionally confirmed by our special knowledge of particular individuals. Finally, it should be noted that, in doing even the most gratuitous of acts, one acts in the light of and from what he knows and/or believes about the world.

I have chosen to discuss *reason* in connection with *action*. We have concluded that a necessary condition for doing an act is that the agent should act for a reason. I think that action is indeed the dominating case, but it is surely not the only kind of animate phenomenon that essentially involves reasons. Awareness of reason plays a closely parallel role for other kinds of phenomenon. The most obvious such case is *belief*. An animal believes one thing B_1 because he knows or believes other things, $B_2, \ldots, B_n$, which are his reasons for believing B_1. Another kind of case, already remarked upon several times, is that of 'mental causation', *e.g.*, one starts back for the reason (as he sees) that there is a snake in the grass or a face in the window. Another more familiar kind of case is that of the so-called 'passions', 'emotions', and 'agitations'—anger, mirth, jealousy, compassion, shame, fear. The occurrence of such phenomena always involves reasons in much the same way as does action. What might explain (*e.g.*) becoming angry is the animal's knowledge that he had just been insulted. One is angry only if he is angry for a reason or a mistaken reason. This consideration serves to mark off these passions and agitations from related moods, dispositions, and sets, *e.g.*, irascibility, envy, anxiety, *etc.*, for which the animal may possibly not have reasons or mistaken reasons. Passions (anger, say), like beliefs, may be manifested in action. We say that the animal behaves angri*ly* or acts from anger or in anger. The reason for the anger is then also a reason for the act. Rarely if ever, however, is the anger itself a reason for the act in which it is manifested, though (like belief) it may often be a factor serving to explain the occurrence of the act. But passions need not be so manifested in action. They may, if shown at all, be manifested in something that *happens* to the man, *e.g.*, one goes pale with fury or blushes with shame. Here again the reason for the occurrence of the passion is also a reason for the manifesting phenomenon, but the passion itself is not such a reason, though it may indeed serve to explain the occurrence of the manifesting phenomenon. Passions and the animate phenomena in which they are manifested differ from cases of mental causation. In cases of mental causation, the fact known—the reason—is not the *animal's* reason for doing what he does. On the other hand, the fact known—the reason—is indeed the angry animal's reason for being angry. If he be capable of giving a verbal response, he will not tell us that *his* reason for jumping was the face at the window, though what caused him to jump was his seeing the face at the window; on the other hand, he could tell us that his reason for being angry was the insult he received. In what follows, I shall concentrate primarily on action and secondarily on belief, and make only occasional contrasting references to other types of animate phenomena which necessarily involve reasons or mistaken reasons.[5]

According to our analysis, it is the belief or knowledge of a reason which might explain. Now, we know that one may have erroneous beliefs, beliefs which do not conform to reason. In that case, the movements constituting the behaviour might be explained by a *false* belief. Reason falsifies the belief. But we would not usually also want to say that the falsehood of the belief falsifies the act; that would be appropriate only were the act one of giving expression to the belief. While reasons may be evidence or proof for beliefs explaining action, they are not evidence or proof of action. Similar observations hold for mental causation, passion, *etc.*[6]

A reason is a fact, the knowledge of which might explain animal movements. We discern purpose in these movements and discover what purpose when we see that the movements might be explained in the indicated way. Knowledge of reason thus might explain the presence of purpose. Now, in answer to the question, 'Why?', asked of the act, we might specify either the purpose or the reason, as I have been explaining them (see pp. 65f.). But these are clearly different kinds of answer. Our explication shows that it would be wrong to equate the reason, or mistaken reason, for which one acts with the

[5] It was in a brief conversation with Professor Dan Taylor of Otago University that I first saw the possibility of extending the discussion of reason to cover relations of reason to types of phenomenon other than action. I remember his emphatically and correctly insisting that anger involves reasons. On this point, see M. Warnock and A. C. Ewing, on 'The Justification of Emotions', *Proc. Arist. Soc., Supp. Vol.*, 1957.
[6] In an unpublished work, *The Concept of Pleasure*, D. L. Perry makes much the same point in discussing the evidence for *enjoyment*.

purpose of the act, as some writers seem to have done (see Hampshire, *op. cit., e.g.*, pp. 129f.). Reason and purpose, though related, are different, and we would risk not seeing their relations by blinking their difference. Knowledge or belief of reason or mistaken reason explains the presence of the purpose, and not conversely. Moreover, an animal may have a reason for acting on a purpose but the purpose not be present; or the presence of the purpose may be explained by knowledge of another reason; or the explanation of the presence of a purpose might be of an entirely different kind, *e.g.*, he may be doing that because he is nervous. So, though the agent has a reason, mention of it would be quite out of the way. The general point of relation between reason and purpose is that for an animal to behave with purpose he must act for a reason or a mistaken reason.

We noticed that the question 'Why?' asked of an act might call for specification of either a purpose or a reason. Another force in our Language which may move us to equate reason and purpose is that many act-identifying locutions also imply that what was done was done for a certain kind of reason, or perhaps contrary to reason; also, present participles are often used, not to identify acts, but to place the reason. Thus, 'answering a letter' tells us that the act of writing the letter was being done for a certain kind of reason, also 'running for a score'; 'murder' tells us that it was an act of homicide, which there were reasons against doing; 'keeping a promise' does not identify the act, though it does describe it as being done for a certain kind of reason.

The notion of reason we have been examining is a familiar one, and an ancient topic in philosophy. It is, I believe, substantially the notion that Aristotle was elucidating when he set forth his doctrine of what others have called 'practical syllogism'. The key passage is chapter 7 of *De Motu Animalium*, where Aristotle discusses how one can be moved to action by what he sees to be the case. Action is taken upon the facts. Though no process of reasoning need intervene, it is useful to schematize the matter pseudo-syllogistically; but if we do so the conclusion is not a statement or a belief but the act itself; alternatively, if we formulate an observer's practical syllogism, the upshot is a statement of what the animal did, given in connection with a statement of his reason. Aristotle gives a number of examples, which do not all come to quite the same. But they are all cast (somewhat misleadingly) as arguments having two premises, one of which indicates that a certain kind of *want, desire*, or *principle* is operating (*e.g.*, 'I want to drink'); the other is a report on fact as perceived, conceived, or imagined by the agent ('This is drink'); and the conclusion is an act done (straightway I drink). This schematizes the agent's act, an act which is held to be done for a certain kind of reason. An observer might describe what had happened, in which case the conclusion would not be an act done but a statement that the act was done; but it is essential to see that in this case what we have formulated is not really an argument at all, but merely a statement of what the agent did and for what reason. It is not entirely clear how the doctrine of practical syllogism relates to Aristotle's theory of practical reason set forth in Book VII of the *Ethics*. I think they are in fact different pieces of one larger fabric. Among the theses insisted upon in the *Ethics* are, first, that a practical reason is a fact acted upon, and second, that it has its primary manifestation *in* behaviour. To be sure, it can be abstracted, but then it is not necessarily, in Ryle's phrase, 'operative' (see 'Conscience and Moral Conviction', Chapter 6, *Philosophy and Analysis*). This all squares very well with what I have been saying about *reason*, and prefigures most of the contrasts that I shall presently make explicit.

This doctrine of 'practical syllogism' has indirectly and perhaps unwittingly received the assent of some psychologists. In the introduction I alluded to the so-called 'Drive-Cue-Response-Reward' theory of action (see p. 18, and Mowrer, *op. cit.*, pp. 104–108). I believe we can draw a parallel. The Drive corresponds to what is mentioned in the 'major premise' of the 'practical syllogism', which formulates what I call the principle of reason (*e.g.*, 'I want to drink'); the Cue is the reason, knowledge of which might explain the movements, given by the 'minor premise' (*e.g.*, 'That's drink'); the Response is the sequence of movements which are explained by the knowledge of the reason and which, for our purposes, may be regarded as the act done, identified by the 'conclusion' of the 'practical syllogism'. The act, we know, either succeeds or fails; if it succeeds, the animal gets its Reward.

I have already intimated that a 'practical syllogism' is mistakenly called an argument. In one sense, an 'argument', strictly taken, is a sequence of statements (propositions, or other similar things) set out in a certain arrangement. One of these statements is designated as conclusion and the others are called premises. What 'follows' is that statement called the conclusion, and not (*e.g.*) the belief that that statement is true. But now we engage in setting out arguments in the faith that the statements designated as premises give reasons for *believing* that the statement designated as conclusion is true. We could, moreover, on occasion, explain that the animal believed the conclusion because he believed the premises. An argument is abstracted from this kind of explanation; valid forms of argumentation are sought in order to regularize and to justify our coming to have such beliefs. I stress that the argument itself is not a sequence of statements to the effect that such and such is believed. Rather, it is a sequence of statements set out with the implicit claim that some of the statements would give reason for believing one of them. It is obvious that one's believing the premises of a valid argument does not entail that one will also believe the conclusion. One need not believe what follows from what he believes. More strongly, even when we are entitled to hold that certain beliefs entail others, the relation between these beliefs apparently does not necessarily always conform to the 'laws of logic'. Thus, Smith's belief that Jones' promotion is a good thing might be held to entail that Smith believes that Jones was promoted; if Jones was not promoted, the latter mentioned belief is false; but it would not follow that the first belief, that Jones' promotion is a good thing, is also false. The 'law of contraposition' in one of its forms does not appear to obtain. [7]

If by 'syllogism' we mean a kind of argument, then a sequence of statements of what an animal believes, cited to explain his believing something else, is not a syllogism, nor is a sequence of statements believed, set forth as reasons for believing something else, a syllogism. To give them names, let us call creatures of the latter two kinds 'doxastic syllogisms'. Doxastic syllogisms are not syllogisms or arguments of any other kind. For all that, one certainly may set forth an argument properly taken counterpart to the schematization of a doxastic syllogism, as a guide in deliberation over what to believe or as a summary explanation of why an animal does believe such and such. In this last kind of case, what explains the animal's believing one fact is not the other facts he believes, which are his ostensible reasons, but rather his believing these other facts.

Much the same holds for so-called 'practical syllogism'. Only here the 'conclusion' is not the agent's believing something, but rather an act done. If a syllogism is an argument, then, strictly taken, what is schematized as a 'practical syllogism' is not a syllogism. Nevertheless, an argument might be set out either in the course of deliberating over what ought to be done or in explaining why an animal did what he did. We shall say something more about such arguments below (pp. 97f.). In an explanatory doxastic syllogism, the 'conclusion', the animal's believing such and such, is homogeneous in type with the items which explain the 'conclusion', *viz.*, he believes one thing because he believes other things. But in an explanatory practical syllogism, the 'conclusion' is inhomogeneous with the items which explain it; the agent *does* something because he *believes* something. Beliefs are most primitively manifested in behaviour. What is schematized as conclusions of practical syllogisms is behaviourally more primitive than what is schematized as conclusions of doxastic syllogisms. The homogeneity of a doxastic syllogism marks a gain in sophistication

[7] I borrow this somewhat dubious kind of example from Perry.

on the part of the supposed observed animal; but the inhomogeneity of a practical syllogism needs no forgiving.

A related point of difference between doxastic and practical syllogisms is that the beliefs indicated as both 'premises' and 'conclusion' of a doxastic syllogism, like statements and unlike acts, bear truth values. The relations between these beliefs do not always quite duplicate those other relations that obtain between the statements of an argument, in the light of which relations we are able to appraise the validity of the argument. But despite that, it is clear that doxastic syllogism is a step closer to argument proper than is practical syllogism. I trace that to the fact that doxastic syllogism describes something which is already a sophistication on the more primitive case of reasonable and unreasonable action. An act may fail for a number of different kinds of reason. We may want to concentrate on certain special factors, e.g., physical ineptness or erroneous conception. In doing this, it becomes natural to seek a single canon of appraisal. Our notions of truth and falsehood, as applied to beliefs, mark the partial achievement of that desideratum. It remains that beliefs, hence actions, may go wrong in other characteristic ways, e.g., they may be irrelevant.

Both doxastic and practical syllogism, as we have been talking about them, cover two distinct but related kinds of case—the deliberative and the explanatory. In deliberation, an *agent* reviews certain of what he believes to be facts, in the course of deciding what to believe or what to do. In explanation, an *observer* accounts for an animal's doing or believing such and such by mention of the animal's believing other things. Explanation is probably the more primitive case. An agent could not deliberate about his own behaviour or beliefs unless he were able at least to discern the determining effects on the beliefs or behaviour of other animals of their believing certain things, where those other animals might not be able to deliberate or to discern the effect of belief on behaviour and belief. In deliberation, the animal abstracts what he believes from his believing of it, whereas in explanation, the observer invokes the fact that the animal believes what he believes. Deliberation additionally involves the express weighing of reasons as good and bad, better or worse; not so in explanation. When it is necessary to make the distinction, I shall speak of (first-person) *deliberative* and (third-person) *explanatory* practical and doxastic syllogisms.

I shall now draw out a number of contrasts which are implicit in my account of reason and also (I believe) in the Aristotelian doctrine of practical syllogism.

In the first place, and as we have already noticed, one may have a reason and yet fail to act for that reason. For example, it may be a fact that I have promised to do something, and that is a reason for my doing it; but it may be that I have forgotten, or again, I remember and act, either doing the deed for some other reason, or failing to do the deed despite the reason. In all these cases, we say that the reason is not my reason. Some philosophers have held that a reason, in some full 'logically complete' sense of 'reason' must be acted for, must actually be the agent's reason.[8] These other possibilities do not destroy the relations between reason and action. A reason is a fact of a kind, knowledge of which might sometimes explain the behaviour of a 'reasonable' animal. Henceforth, failing notice to the contrary, I shall suppose that we are considering cases in which the reason that the animal has is indeed his reason for acting. That is, he is acting or has acted for the reason.

In the second place, for someone to have a reason and for it to be *his* reason does not require that he have engaged in deliberative *reasoning*, and still less that he have set forth his reasons in an *argument*. We do not always deliberate, and some animals cannot. Not all practical syllogisms are 'deliberative'; some are merely 'explanatory'. Ability to set forth an argument demands an advanced mastery of Language, and we must come to understand the idea of reason as it applies to all animals who can be said to act reasonably. Reasoning, whether deliberative or fully argumentative, is only one of the kinds of thing which we do: it is a way of finding out what is to be done or believed. To reason, whether or not argumentatively, requires suspension of the action or judgment which might be done or made with reason, but what we want is a notion of reason which will apply also to cases where animals, including ourselves, 'straightway act', but reasonably. It cannot be the case that acts done with a reason must always be ones in which the agent first finds reasons and then acts upon them. As we just saw, seeking a reason is itself a kind of action, which, depending upon circumstances, may or may not be reasonably done. To supplement this abstract argument, it is obvious that sometimes it would be quite unreasonable to deliberate about or to reason

<hr>

[8] *E.g.*, Nowell-Smith, *loc. cit.* In this connection, W. K. Frankena (in 'Obligation and Motivation in Recent Moral Philosophy', *Essays in Moral Philosophy*, ed. A. Melden) introduces the notion of an 'exciting reason', which seems to be a reason for which one acts. But, if this is a correct interpretation, Frankena is surely wrong to equate exciting reasons with reasons of interest and to contrast them with justifying reasons. Reasons of interest can justify; and (*e.g.*) 'moral' reasons can excite, *i.e.*, become one's reasons for acting. For further discussion of the issues at question, see Frankena's allusions in the cited article, including references to the writings of Aiken, Ayer, Blake, Clarke, Cross, Falk, Field, Frankena, Hare, Horsbourgh, James, Kant, A. Moore, G. E. Moore, Nowell-Smith, Reichenbach, Reiner, Rice, A. Ross, W. D. Ross, W. S. Sellars, Stace, Stevenson, and D. C. Williams, among others.

out the situation. The defending line-backer must immediately tackle the man whom he sees to be the opposing ball-carrier. This illustrates the most primitive kind of case, which probably remains the commonest in the lives of even the most intellectual of rational animals.

Most philosophers who have written about reason have made just this mistake of supposing that to have a reason one must have reasoned, and have been able to dress out his reasoning as an argument.[9] The mistake, I conjecture, abets the usual kind of wrong-headed theories which are legion in ethics, e.g., Emotivism. This theory and all others I know of which have given importance to the 'Language of Morals' seem plausible only as explanations of what it is to give reasons, and not at all as accounts of what it is to have reasons. The point usually urged is that Language that might seem to be used to formulate reasons is not really so used, but shows rather the agent's feelings, attitudes, prejudices, about the matter.

As part of this mistake, we easily smudge the distinction between 'being aware of a fact, which is a reason', and 'being aware of a fact as a reason'. That is to say, it is fatally easy to suppose that for one to have a reason as his reason he must be aware of it as a reason. Actually, to be aware of a reason as a reason is possible only for creatures who are able to take a somewhat detached observer's view of their own behaviour. The mistake to which I allude again witnesses an illicit projection of the observer's theoretical knowledge of the situation into the animal whose behaviour is being observed.

The mistake also testifies to a number of important facts about the concept of *reason*. First and most obvious, one might indeed sometimes reason (deliberate) from his reasons to the conclusion done or believed. In such instances, it is probably better to say that his reason for doing the deed is that he has reasoned in such and such a way; or, where an argument has been mustered, that the argument is sound (as he sees) is his reason for acting. But that there should be such reasons as these plainly depends upon the existence of the more primitive kind of case in which the facts, those set down as 'premises' in the 'syllogism', are one's reasons for doing or believing. So, we see, a reason can, but need not be, deliberated upon and reasoned from to a conclusion.

But by far the most important consideration, and one which underlies the possibility of *reasoning* to a reasonable conclusion, is that when a conceptualizing observer says that an animal has a reason, the observer theoretically casts the animal's behaviour according to a pattern of rationality which can be set forth as a kind of argument in which *statements* of the reasons figure as premises. It is *we* who use

---

[9] K. Baier is one of the latest; see, *e.g.*, pp. 93ff. of *The Moral Point of View*.

the word 'reason', and not necessarily the animal that is held to have the reason. It is a question of how we are to understand that behaviour; if we summon a reason of kind K, we are seeing the behaviour as of the kind which *we* might do upon deliberation or as the conclusion of an argument in which the reasons of kind K are explicitly considered. A reason, in the first place, is a *fact*. In saying that, we imply that a reason might be stated, by us if not necessarily by the animal for whom it is a reason. But any statement might figure as a premise of an argument. In the second place, to call a fact F a reason implies that F is something, mention of which would explain action only on condition that some creature was aware of F. Now an argument is one device by which an agent might be led from his knowledge of a fact to action upon that fact. But why, it will be asked, need the statement of the reason figure as premise of an argument, and why should we regard the operation of reason as mediated by an argument? Because our idea of an argument is the result exactly of our efforts to codify rationality. We learn to present arguments in the course of coming to be explicit about reasons. Having acquired this knowledge, we are then able to employ the word 'reason' in connection with the behaviour of animals who cannot reflect upon reasons, on analogy with cases of our own reasonable behaviour which has been submitted to that kind of analysis. We thus structure a natural explanation according to the pattern of a *logical account*, much as the physicist may structure a physical transaction according to the pattern of a derivation. The elements of the logical account are statements of facts, where mention of the knowledge of those facts would explain the phenomenon; or, if one be shy about 'facts', the elements of the logical account are statements whose truth implies the presence and operation of factors, where mention of an animal's knowledge of those factors would explain the phenomenon.

In coming to learn to think about reasonable behaviour and to analyse reason argumentatively, one may also come to learn to reason to conclusions. That is another, related kind of action. The theory enlarges the practice.

The final conclusion here is: While reasons are not the theoretical formulations of reasons, it is necessary that reasons could be theoretically formulated as premises of an argument, although not necessarily by an agent whose reasons they are.

The third contrast is pointed up by Aristotle's insistence that the conclusion of a practical syllogism is an *act*. An example of a deliberative practical syllogism might be: I am thirsty; water slakes thirst; that is water/ glug! The intended contrast is between reasons for *doing* and reason for *believing*, between 'practical' and 'doxastic syllogism'. Reasons for believing would be set out as premises for a 'doxastic syllogism', of which the conclusion is itself a belief. Among one's reasons for believing are facts which count as *evidence* for the belief. (It is no more necessary that reasons for believing be set out as the premises of an argument that has as its conclusion the statement believed than for reasons for acting to be so formulated. All that is required is that the reasons in question could be formulated as premises of such an argument. The last contrast holds equally of both kinds of reasons.)

Now philosophers frequently write as if they thought that reasons for doing are always ultimately nothing but reasons for believing. Two forces push them in this direction.

First, reasons for believing seem more closely connected to argumentation than do reasons for acting. An argument, we saw, is a connection of statements, where the premises give reasons for believing in the truth of the statement, which is the conclusion. All of us first learned to analyse arguments in consideration of examples in which the conclusions are statements. Allow it to be so: But why need an argument give reasons for believing any more than it does for acting? Let us not blind ourselves to the fact that one can formulate his reasons and then *either* believe, *or* act, or *neither*. All we have to do is follow Aristotle (who once again saw so much more clearly than many of his successors) and his commentators and adopt the term 'practical-syllogism', duly hyphenated, if you wish, to preserve appearances.

The second force is that we can indeed always formulate a doxastic syllogism counterpart to any practical syllogism, in which the conclusion (whether or not true or validly drawn) is that the agent has reason to (ought to, want to, is to, should, must, *etc.*) do an act of the kind which practical reason would call into existence. This shows that we can arrive at theoretical conclusions regarding what practical reason would demand. This does not destroy but supports practical reason's titles in its own dominions. I shall return to this matter presently.

We cannot reduce practical to theoretical reason without undermining the latter. It actually appears that we might be able to regard reasons for believing as a special kind of reason for doing. To say that someone has a reason for believing *p* is to say that he has one kind of reason for *saying p*. Reasons for believing are one kind of reason for saying. One may have other, better reasons for keeping silent, and may reasonably suppress the expression of belief. But belief is something one must learn to suppress the expression of, and he does so by learning *not* to act on reasons for saying what he believes, which are his reasons for believing. I do not mean to wipe out the distinction between practical and doxastic syllogism, only to say that whatever could have been the premise of a doxastic syllogism could equally have been the premise of a practical syllogism in which the conclusion would be an act of expressing belief. I would add that a 'live' argument (not a logician's example) seems to be precisely a case of expressing knowledge or belief on grounds of reasons set forth. To argue in this fullest sense is to *act*, *e.g.*, to assert, in a special way.

One may have reasons for believing all sorts of things: that the sun is over 90,000,000 miles distant, that $\sqrt{2}$ is irrational, that Jones is a fool, and that one ought to plug his ears when Jones is present. It is especially important for us to be clear about this last kind of example. One has reasons for believing that such and such is to (ought to, should, had better, must) be done. We may now formulate a counterpart argument, the conclusion which states what is to be done. Let us call such a conclusion a 'gerundive statement', and, glossing over differences, schematize all these statements, 'He ought to . . .'. What are the truth-conditions of such a statement? Assuming that we have a statement with truth-conditions, and putting the matter as broadly as I have done, it seems to me that there is only one answer: There is good reason for doing an act of kind . . . . To say, 'He ought to . . .', whether or not as the conclusion of an argument, is to say that he has good reasons for . . .[10]. Skipping questions about 'better and worse' reasons, the test clearly presumes that one who makes such a statement can recognize and formulate practical syllogisms. This does not mean that one who formulates such a conclusion in the course of reasoning about what he ought to do, will actually do it; he might merely believe that he ought to do it; if the deliberating agent in the imagined case did the act he supposed to be right, the deliberative practical syllogism would then be: (*e.g.*) 'One ought to act on what he sees to be good reasons; I see that there are good reasons for buying this coat'/whereupon the coat is straightway purchased. The point is that for one to be able to believe that he ought to . . ., he must know what it would be to act upon the reasons which are formulated as the premises of an argument. A syllogism proper with gerundive conclusion then turns out to be a type of device, available to most educated men, for providing theoretical analyses of reasonable action; such syllogisms are not schematizations of reasonable

---

[10] I do not wish to suggest that 'ought', 'should', 'must', 'is to', 'want to', *etc.*, do not differ in meaning. I am sure they do. Nor do I wish to say that everything which we might schematize as 'He ought to . . .' is properly speaking a statement, the truth or falsehood of which could be demonstrated. My only claim is that there is a fundamental kind of case in which a gerundive statement might be made. Contextual circumstances and other implications are indicated by the choice of word employed, and the test is to cast a balance of reasons.

action, for that is practical syllogism, but devices for showing that acts are reasonable.

Putting this all together, we can draw the conclusion that a reason is a fact which is germane to the truth of a statement that one ought to do something.[11] This conclusion shows how reasoning may have a bearing on action, for it tells us that a reason is a consideration which an agent might expressly consider in trying to come to a conclusion as to what he ought to do, which (following the pattern of practical syllogism) he then does. It is important that this conclusion about arguments with gerundive conclusions should be a position arrived at, not a point of departure. Arguments proper with gerundive conclusions are seen as presupposing for subject matter the sphere of reasonable behaviour.

The fourth contrast is between a reason and a principle of reason. Here I take exception to what *might* be the suggestion of Aristotle, although what I shall urge might be just what his account does suggest. I claim that what we would call the major and the minor premises of a practical syllogism are in certain respects essentially different, and that only minor premises state reasons.[12] The so-called major premise is a statement of what one 'wants', *e.g.*, 'I want water'; and the minor premise is a fact perceived, conceived, or imagined, *e.g.*, that this stuff before me is water; and the conclusion is my act of drinking. The conclusion follows directly upon the perception of the fact that this is water; however, that this being water should be a reason for my drinking certainly depends upon the fact that I am thirsty. Putting it so points up a difference between the contributions of the two premises, a difference which it is only too easy to overlook. But to miss the difference is to invite confusion of a kind comparable to that so well exposed by Lewis Carroll in his argument of 'What the Tortoise Said to Achilles'. (*Mind*, 1895; for commentary, see D. G. Brown, 'What the Tortoise Taught Us', *Mind*, 1954, pp. 170–79.) The confusion is precisely that of casting the principle of one's action as a further reason for doing the act,

---

[11] And that goes, too, for cases where there is no ready way of finally establishing the truth. When debating (real or imagined) cases of what one ought to do, we proceed by citing reasons of one kind or another; the problem is to ascertain the relative weight of these reasons, a problem complicated by the agent's own presumed view of himself, a factor not readily brought into the account we have been developing.

[12] I cannot decide what Aristotle would say if asked about this. Many philosophers have broken their heads trying to cast the major premise according to the same pattern as the minor premise. But it is interesting that in Aristotle's examples the major premise always has a different verbal form from the minor, being a statement of what one *wants*, or what *ought* to be done, *etc.*

which leaves one to find a new principle for acting upon a now augmented set of reasons.

The two premises are surely not in every way comparable. If the supposed practical syllogism represents a case, then the agent must see or at least believe that this is water; and, while he must be thirsty, surely he need not come to know or believe that he is thirsty. It might be replied that if he is thirsty, then he *must* know that he is thirsty. I doubt that. But we may allow that for him to act on the principle of reason, he must, so to speak, be keyed to that principle, he must be thirsty. But however we regard his state of being thirsty, as a kind of knowledge or not, the point remains. His being thirsty is not a fact which he must come to know as he must come to know that this is water, and upon which knowledge he then acts. His being thirsty is a state because of his being in which and by reference to which the fact that this is water is a reason for his drinking.

Here one might protest that the animal's thirst is no principle, but a mere fact, the fact that he is thirsty. Agreed: it is a fact in the light of which the conceptualizing observer can say that the animal's knowledge that this is water explains his drinking. It is, if you wish, in the observer's conception—for an explanatory practical syllogism —a principle of explanation. It is a fact in the light of which an observer can see that the agent's knowledge *explains* the deed.

My thesis is, then, that the 'major premise' of a practical syllogism formulates the principle by which the 'minor premise' is seen to be a reason for doing the act which is the 'conclusion'. I wish also to claim that in deliberation a fact is seen to be a reason for acting only in the light of some such principle of reason.

When an animal acts upon a reason falling under a principle of reason (*e.g.*, duty, honesty, advantage, hunger), we may call that the *principle of his act*. Such principles are invoked by observers as principles of act-explanation. (In explanatory doxastic syllogisms, the principle is perhaps better formulated as a question than as a statement of want.)

Now one may act on a certain principle without knowing what that principle is. But we, when formulating a third-person explanatory practical syllogism, surely must be able to state the principle. We might then hearken to that principle in our own deliberations. How then are we to interpret the principle when formulated as the 'major premise' of a first-person, deliberative practical syllogism? Precisely, I submit, as a principle of inference. That is, the principle of reason is stated as a principle by which one might reason from a stated reason to a conclusion which is the act or possibly a belief or a gerundive statement. This conception of principles of inference includes the logicians' preferred instances, *e.g.*, *Modus Ponens*. *Modus Ponens*, in particular, is a principle of reason according to which the truth of statements *p* and '*if p then q*' (as seen by the agent) are taken together as reasons for asserting *q*. If we now formulate the argument leading to the assertion of *q*, we might append *Modus Ponens* as a kind of extra premise. But, of course, if we do so, we must, to forestall a regress, set it off sharply from the other premises which are taken to to be statements that *p* and *if p then q* are true. [From this it should, incidentally, be clear that I do not believe that practical reason must always be schematized as proceeding from a single reason. A possible practical syllogism would be: major premise (principle of inference) —I am thirsty; minor premise*s* (reasons)—water slakes thirst, that is water; conclusion (act done or a description of that act)—glug! However, I suppose we may always conjoin the reason-stating premises into a single statement, while we cannot further conjoin that statement to the major premise, the Principle of Inference.]

Principles of reason may be more and less specifically stated. One thing which obscures the differences between the principle of reason that I am thirsty and the reason, that this is water, is that one's being thirsty is so much a matter of fact, so contingent and so highly specific as not to be easily contrasted with the fact which is the reason. Still I think it must be allowed that the meaning of 'thirsty' is such as to imply that one who is thirsty has reason for drinking what he sees to be potable liquid. Now, principles of reason can be more and more openly stated and, *pari passu*, progressively tautologized. Thus, 'I am thirsty', 'I have a craving for *x*', '*Ceteris paribus* one ought to act to possess *x*'. Another rather familiar example, which has been studied by philosophers, is the progressive tautologization of principles of reason for *saying* from apparently contingent statements about cause and effect to the Laws of Physics to the Principles of Deductive Logic. Perhaps the more specific and contingent principles of reason may always be interpreted by those who have attained a sufficiently high level of abstract conception as statements to the effect that the less specific, tautological principles apply. For example, that I am thirsty shows that this is a place where a craving for potable liquid is a relevant consideration. That is matter of fact. But that a craving for potable liquid gives one reason for drinking what he sees is potable, is no mere matter of fact. It is, within the limitations of a 'ceteris paribus' clause, 'analytic'.

My thesis is, then, that a reason is a fact, but a fact is a reason only in the light of a principle of reason, which is itself not a reason, though it may indeed be a fact.

Reasons may be classified according to the principles of reason in the light of which they are seen to be reasons. This introduces what is really a proliferation of contrasts between different kinds of reason.

There are as many kinds of reason as there are particular principles of reason.

It would be of no use to draw those out where they are specific, highly contingent matters of fact, *e.g.*, that John is thirsty or that sodium explodes when placed upon water. They are too varied, and are matters of knowledge which is too specific; they are, I grant, misleadingly called 'principles'. We want to begin sorting reasons according to principles the demonstration of which is, so to speak, verbal. We want principles which, when formulated as gerundive statements, will have the minimum generality of a 'ceteris paribus' tautology, *e.g.*, '*Cet. par.*, one ought to keep promises', '*Cet. par.*, one ought not to bring about dangerous chemical reactions', '*Cet. par.*, one ought to say that this ϕ is ψ when all observed cases of ϕ have been ψ'. But a partitioning of reasons even at this level of generality would be haphazard. I do not see any end to the list of, for example, moral principles, *i.e.*, tautologies like, 'One ought to keep promises', 'One ought to be honest', *etc.* What is worse, the truncated lists we could give, by themselves supply no clue to how we might go on. But the naturalness of labels like 'Moral Principle' suggests that these principles do fall into families for which we might hope to find a characterization. Among the most embracing of these families are those which philosophers often fix with terms like 'Morality', 'Law', 'Humanity and Sentiment', 'Interest', 'Desire', 'Logic', *etc.* There seems, moreover, to be no strain in speaking of, *e.g.*, Principles of Morality, Principles of Law, Principles of Prudence, Principles of Humanity, Principles of Economics, Principles of Analytical Mechanics, Principles of Deduction. These principles are facts of which one must have at least a practical knowledge in order to behave reasonably in certain spheres of action; and, at the level of theoretical knowledge, a failure to recognize these as true would be evidence that one did not have a theoretical grasp of what it is (*e.g.*) to set forth a deductive argument. If an animal never behaves in conformity with such a principle, that would be evidence that we could not truly say of him that he was engaged in the corresponding sphere of activity, or that he had attained a level of behaviour, where his movements could be explained by saying that he had reasons of this kind. Thus one whose behaviour is never in any way affected by the knowledge that what he does will affect his future welfare can hardly be said to be either prudent or imprudent. Recognition that prudence is a principle of reason is as much a matter of understanding the words 'will suffer' as the recognition of *Modus Ponens* is a matter of understanding 'if—then'.

I have chosen to formulate principles of reason in terms of what one 'ought' to do. For present purposes I could equally have elected *principles of reason*

to put it in the language of 'should' or 'right' or 'wrong'. I might also have used the form 'If you *want to* (do what's right, obey the law, serve your own best interest, say what is likely to be true, say what follows from what is accepted to be the case, *etc.*), then . . .'.[13] That formulation is in itself quite innocuous, but it might introduce a false suggestion into a philosophical mind, *viz.*, that all reasons and all acts are egocentric and selfish. For 'want to do' suggests that one is always acting to have that which he presently happens to want. It is quite true that if the mention of a reason explains what happened, then it was some particular animal's reason for doing some particular deed. And we might say, 'That is what he wants to do because he wants . . .' (he acts in consideration of such and such principle of reason). But we must not construe this to mean that he always must be acting to acquire an object of desire. While we do sometimes act for such reasons, and quite properly so, that is not invariably the case. It is only *one* kind of reason. Indeed, the purpose of one's act is not always to acquire something, even something as intangible as a good reputation. But, it might be held, one always does act to attain his purpose, *i.e.*, acts out of a desire to succeed. But this surely is a pseudo-object of desire. The object of desire, if there is one, is an object the acquisition of which would be the measure of successful action. Success in his act is not what the agent wants, though in getting what he wants he may succeed. To say that 'One acts to succeed', meaning that he wants success, is at bottom a misleading way of casting as a reason for acting what is part of what we mean by acting, that if one is acting he might succeed. To say, 'He acts to succeed' is to do no more than reiterate that he is acting, and success will seem an inevitable object of desire only because mention of it says nothing further about what he is acting for. As Butler long ago taught us, whether or not one's act is egoistic depends not upon the fact that he did something, but on whether he did it for a particular *kind* of reason, and we know that reasons may be of many kinds.[14] Acting for reasons of desire may be the most primitive kind of action.

[13] 'Want to' is better used to formulate principles of reason than gerundive conclusions, partly, I believe, because 'want to', unlike 'ought', may simply mark that *a* reason whether or not decisive, is present, and partly because 'want to' signalizes that the agent has at least a disposition to act for the indicated reason. The principle resides in the agent's state rather than in external circumstance.

[14] I go through all this partly because there is a suggestion, both in Aristotle and in Anscombe, that one always acts to acquire an object of desire, and that the desirability of the object is the reason. What gives this impression may be no more than that they are stressing, and for good reasons, the simplest case. But I get the feeling that they both do make the mistake of supposing that what one really desires is success in acquiring some desirable object; this defective equation is easily generalized to make success in action the 'object' of action whatever the measure of the success of action might be.

105

This is the kind of case in which the animal acts to acquire, avoid, or be in the neighbourhood of an object present, which is an object of desire or aversion. It seems true that one could not be meaningfully said to act for reasons of other kinds if it were not possible to regard him as an animal who would on some occasions act for reasons of desire. Thus to act for one's own long-term interests—to act prudently—requires that one should occasionally *refrain* from acting on desire. Similarly, to say of a creature that he acts for (what we call) moral reasons implies that he could act for (what we call) selfish reasons, but not conversely. Now we probably model our Language for attributing deeds to creatures on the most primitive case, the one in which one acts for reasons of desire, and this is a force pushing us towards egoism as a philosophical doctrine, and against which we must put up defences. The best general defence is, failing convincing arguments to the contrary, to refuse to allow that what one wants to do is always to acquire some object which one wants.

Another mistaken way of attempting to unify the concept of reason is found in appeals to the notion of *rule* to explain distinctions between *right* and *wrong*.[15] It is a kind of complementary exaggeration to the doctrine of self-interest we have just been criticizing. I held that whether an act is right or wrong may be decided only by an assessment of the agent's reasons. In Part III, no. 8, it will be maintained that the existence of a rule may indeed be a reason for acting. But not all reasons are of this kind, *e.g.*, if my reason is that this is water and I am thirsty, then, since neither the water nor my thirst is a rule, my reason is not that a rule exists. What misleads the advocate of rules into so absurd a position is this: A fact is a reason only in the light of a principle of reason. Now a principle of reason may indeed be regarded as an explanatory rule by a conceptualizing observer. It may also be regarded as a rule of inference by a deliberative agent. But we must take care not to inject into the thoughts of the acting animal what only conceptualizing observer or deliberative agent can discern. If we are mistakenly inclined to regard the principle of reason as the reason for acting, then indeed we shall be inclined (though not compelled) to say that all reasons are rules. An unfortunate result of this faulty equation of reasons with rules would be to undermine the explanation of rules as reasons in terms of certain special kinds of principle, *e.g.*, moral and legal principles as well as such principles as 'One ought to conform to rules'.

[15] See, *e.g.*, Peter Winch, *The Idea of a Social Science*, esp. pp. 49 *et seq.* Winch goes so far as to say that all acts are 'applications of rules' and are done 'relative to a social context', which pronouncements are only too consistent with his view that rules must be in operation whenever it makes sense to speak of right and wrong.

I conclude that principles of reason are various. Now a single act may be done for a number of different reasons, falling under different principles of reason. Put in charge of an incapacitated person, I may help him for reasons of duty and/or for reasons of kindness. Usually there is one reason and one principle which dominates an act; but not always.

Reasons may be better or worse, not in connection with explanation, but as reasons. One may have different reasons for doing the same act, some of which reasons are better and others worse. Or one may have reasons for doing an act and other better or worse reasons for forbearing. When we turn thus to question the quality of a reason, say for purposes of offering justification, it is no longer the believing of that reason but rather the reason, the fact itself, which comes under review. But that the fact should come under review as a reason implies that it is viewed in the light of some principle of reason. Ultimately what are weighed and contrasted are different, possibly competing principles of reason. The ultimate principle of reason, which does not even bear a 'ceteris paribus' qualification, is that one ought to act for the *best* reasons on balance. The measure of better and worse involves consideration both of the operating principle of reason and of the circumstances in which the agent finds himself. According to one account of morality (see Baier, *op. cit.*, Chap. 8, no. 1), action contrary to a principle of morality could be expected to create a conflict between (private) interests of different people. Morality reconciles interests. Therefore, *ceteris paribus*, it is better to act for a reason of morality than for a reason of (private) interest; reasons of morality so explained come into our thinking as superior to reasons of interest; we learn the relevant distinction between right and wrong in the course of learning to forgo the satisfaction of our own interests (desires, wants, appetites, ambitions, *etc.*).[16] Similarly, reasons of prudence are 'superior to' reasons of desire. But it would be irrational *always* to swallow one's hunger, say for the sake of reputation. The circumstances in which action occurs bear on the question whether one reason would be better or worse than another. It would be nice if we could hit upon a neat classification of reasons in which an unequivocal order of relative superiority could be discerned, as we can directly see that

---

[16] I doubt that this gets at the essence of morality. I am now inclined to think that morality is to be defined first in terms of refraining from harming others, to which we add specific principles of duty, obligation, *etc.* To this central idea of 'common decency' we would then adjoin principles of *honour, humanity, sacrifice, etc.* The advantage of Baier's explanation is that it invites a demonstration that reasons of morality are better than, and ought to prevail over, reasons of interest.

reasons of morality are superior to and ought to prevail over reasons of interest. However, 'natural classifications' of reasons are not so accommodating, for governing principles are often in varying degrees alternative. However distasteful it is, we know that the Principle of Law must sometimes prevail over the Principle of Human Sentiment, not only because of special circumstances but also because law must sometimes be impartial even in the face of hardship, and despite the judge's unofficial sympathy and pity.

'Justification' of action depends in part upon the appraisal of reasons. Typically, though not invariably, justification is a matter of the *agent's* citing reasons for his own deeds. (But not only reasons, for one may also cite precedents, common practice, ignorance, *etc.*) Some kinds of act done in certain circumstances patently require no justification. Still it is doubtful whether there is any kind of reason which could not be cited to justify or excuse an act of some kind done in some kind of circumstances. On the other hand, it is clear that an agent cannot cite or offer any kind of reason which may in fact be his reason to justify a deed. Thus, I explain and justify an act of taking food by pleading extreme hunger; that could be the justifying principle of my act. But, if I had snatched the food away from a child whom I knew to be hungrier than myself, then, although my reason and principle were as before, a similar reply would be at best a defiance of justification. Justification is not a topic upon which we can say very much in this work. Our perspective is that of the conceptualizing observer; but questions of justification are answered, even by an observer, partly from the perspective of the agent, giving his view of the deed and appealing to the facts which he could reasonably cite in his own defence.

Relatedly, one may fail to act on what he knows to be his best reason. The 'quality' of one's deed may be and usually is extraneous to our explanation and identification of it. It is these latter matters which here concern us most. So, with these observations of the obvious, I must leave this very important and difficult topic of 'good' reasons and the justification of action, which is only at the periphery of this work.

I wish, finally, to draw attention to the distinction between reasons for doing an act and reasons for doing it in a certain way. I try to enter the house for the reason that my wallet (which I need) is there; I do so by climbing in a certain window, for the reason (as I know) that that is the only way open. That my wallet is in the house is my reason for entering the house; that the window is the only way open is my reason for entering the house in the way I do. There certainly are both of these kinds of reason, despite the fact that some philosophers have held that reasons pertain only to the choice of means.

The possibility of both kinds of reason is to be traced to the fact that we may found our explanation of an animal's movements, both in relation to what he did and to how he did it, on his presumed knowledge or beliefs (see p. 149). But for all that, these are distinct kinds of reason. We easily see a difference between questions whether the creature did what was reasonable and whether he did it in a reasonable way. We appraise reasons on two fronts. I am not now prepared to explore this distinction between the two kinds of reason; that must wait until no. 17 when we shall have worked out an account of the distinction between what is done and how it is done.

We earlier noted that reasons may be better or worse and that reasons may sometimes be cited to justify action. It is clear, also, that we sometimes justify, first, by saying what we did, and second, by mentioning a principle of reason. Suppose someone accepts all this, but asks for a further reason; he would be demanding a justification of the principle of reason itself. Sometimes we can supply an answer. We might, for instance, show that one principle of reason is superior to another, or subsumable under another more general principle. But the global demand to justify principles of reason is not easily met. In citing a principle of reason, the justification seems to be already in hand, and any further justification could be given only by appealing to some further, broader principle.

When faced with this demand to justify reason itself, in contra-distinction to justifying action by citing a reason-cum-justifying principle, one is apt to go dumb. Does the question make any sense at all?

Yet this problem of 'justifying reason' is inescapable. I regard it as a merit of this account that it shows a way of giving sense to the question of what it would be to justify reason, and of supplying an answer. That answer will also impose a further constraint on the concept of reason.

To justify reason would be to show how the various principles of reason could be justified. What then is it to justify a principle of reason? Two different kinds of answer leap to mind. First, the justification might consist in showing that the principle is *true*. Second, it might consist in showing why we ought to conform to the principle. But neither of these answers will do. In the first place, principles are often already tautologies, and can always be tautologized. The demonstration of their truth then becomes a verbal matter. Why ought one not to steal? Because 'stealing' *means* *wrongful* taking. Nor is there scope for saying in general why we *ought* to follow reason, for, roughly put, what we 'ought to do' is what would conform to reason. Reason is, we might say, that by which we justify; it is, obscurely put, its own justification (whether

109

or not we ought *to reason*, *e.g.*, to deliberate, is, we have observed, a different question). One way round the impasse of a truism might be to follow those philosophers who try to reduce all reasons to reasons of personal interest, which somehow seem less problematical than, say, moral reasons. Another escape is to fall back on social considerations by way of an appeal to rules. We shall explain the plausibility of these suggestions below. Suffice it to notice here that they must be mistaken. Certain principles of reason are superior to interest, and even call for the sacrifice of interest; not everything in life is a matter of rule. We thus seem torn between tautology (What's right is right), stutter (It is reasonable to act on reason; we ought to do what we ought to do), or patent error (All reasons are reasons of personal or community interest). And that is a poor choice.

I believe there is an alternative way of giving sense to the question. We might recast it: How does one come to recognize that there is this kind of principle? But that is ambivalent, possibly returning us to the tautology we want to escape and possibly raising irrelevant questions about learning, causes, *etc.* The question I propose is this: How is it that conceptualizing observers come to consider behaviour as reasonable or unreasonable in just these ways; alternatively, what conditions must be met before we shall be willing to apply reason-laden epithets like 'steal' and 'thirsty' to animals? Not just any kind of taking is stealing, nor indeed, can just any kind of animal be (truly or falsely) said to steal.

Let us go back to the beginning. A reason is a *fact*. How do we come to regard certain facts as reasons? Well, a reason is a fact, knowledge of which on the part of animals of this kind on such occasions as these would explain movements of the kind we observe being made. The answer thus alludes to our general knowledge about animals of this kind or that. And it is clearly so; we do not speak of reasons except against such a background. Geese do not act in conformity with or contrary to the law of the land. Their migratory formations are not to be explained by reference to the rules of the road. Geese are not that kind of creature. But we should scarcely call a thing an animal if we did not conceive it as sometimes having desire for food and drink. It is part of our general conception of animalkind that animals should sometimes act on the principle of desire for nutriment. This is a kind of reason of (what I have been calling) interest. The above remarks begin to show why this kind of reason has so often been regarded as ultimate; while it is not the only kind of reason, the applicability of this principle of reason is, so to speak, a *sine qua non* of reason. Given that the agent is of some one kind, then his special circumstances, specific disabilities, *etc.*, come into play. If an American human being has no duties or illnesses, it

110

may be neither reasonable not unreasonable for him to sleep in late on a Sunday morning. A certain kind of knowledge of reason does not explain his now rising at 11.30 a.m.; though the thought that there is food in the refrigerator might. This is part of our general knowledge of our fellow creatures. The examples may be misleadingly obvious. It is often the case that what is wanted is a rather full description of the usual habits of the species; in this way we discover whether they act for communal defence, whether they have elevated sentiments, *etc.* In the case closest to home, what is wanted, if we are ever properly to inventory and align kinds of reason, is an elaborate account of the various areas of human life where the principles in question operate. What I wish to stress is that to speak of a reason is to view an animal's behaviour in the light of our general knowledge of his kind, as it relates to the circumstances in which he is seen to be acting.

The crux here is that reasons come into the picture in connection with one of our ways of *explaining* behaviour, and their relevance is relative to what we know about the animal. Mention of a principle of reason calls attention to a certain familiar pattern of explanation. 'One ought to keep promises' is really very like 'Every effect has a cause'. What must now be stressed is that it is the conceptualizing observer who has the *concept* of reason. It is the conceptualizing observer who, rightly or wrongly, explains a creature's behaviour in this way, in terms of reasons known. The animal himself may quite truly be held to have acted reasonably, although he may not have attained the concept of a reason, *i.e.*, not yet be able to say upon what principle he acted.

The question then arises: What conditions must be met before the observer is able to regard a piece of behaviour as possibly reasonable or unreasonable? In answering, we must hold hard to a ruthlessly third-person, conceptualizing zoologist's view of behaviour. Here almost more than anywhere else we are beguiled into the first-person. But if we find ourselves asking 'Why ought *I* to follow reason?', that is a sure sign we are off the track. Either we shall convert the question to mean 'What's in it for me?', or we shall conclude that one ascertains what he ought to do by balancing reasons. These are just the answers we must fight clear of. Retain, then, the zoologist's perspective, asking in effect, What facts can the animal be said to know, where his knowledge of those facts disposes him to action?

Certain formal conditions must be met. The observer, for one thing, must be able to account for the animal's acquisition of the knowledge. Here the operation of the animal's perceptual apparatus will come into question, as will his ability to acquire skills of various kinds. Thus, while dogs can follow orders, we do not regard them as capable of responding to demands issued from an impersonal,

111

distant source; hence, there is no place for principles of civil law in explanation of canine behaviour. But how, it might be asked, does our zoologist discover which facts the animal is aware of? These are, I suggest, primarily facts to which the animal can be said to respond and (as the zoologist supposes) in such a way as to preserve or ameliorate the condition of the species and the individual members of it, where 'preservation' and 'amelioration' are in the first instance biologically defined. I do not go so far as to say that these are the only kinds of facts properly called 'reasons', but I am not sure that there are any others. The zoologist will be able to discover reasons in the behaviour of his chosen object of investigation as a result of his growing familiarity with the nature of the beast as belonging to a viable, durable species. If he goes on to state the various principles of reason which obtain he will tell us a great deal about the nature of the species. Applying this to the case of the human animal, we have a way of setting out how we regard ourselves, what we implicitly take to be 'The Nature of Man' in some usefully tame sense of that portentous phrase. These are the facts about humankind which are so familiar as to be taken utterly for granted, and against the background of which we view ourselves and our neighbours. We think of a man as an animal having certain appetites, desires and ambitions; he is a creature living with other creatures of the same kind towards whom he has certain sentiments; and he can come to know how others expect him to behave in special circumstances; we think of him as a creature who can convey facts to his fellows by way of speech, facts which he may learn to test and organize; he is capable of becoming explicit about the world at large and about his own behaviour in particular. All the items mentioned at least implicitly foreshadow principles of reason. We could say, your picture of human reason is your picture of Man. Now this picture can be tested, though clearly the tests must be conducted at the highest level of what Aristotle called 'rational activity'. Moralists on one side and moral philosophers on another are constantly engaged in just this kind of testing. It is almost inevitable that their results be somewhat tendentious. I think of the moralizing logician as well as of the down-to-earth egoist, the pharisaical legalist, and the anarchistic sentimentalist. Each of these, with an eye to one face of human nature or another, underscores one or another principle of reason. This is inevitable, because it is extremely hard to see the picture whole—to see in one look and to formulate in brief how we regularly regard the human animal.

But, one may ask, what does this have to do with justification? All you have told us to do is to look at the facts. You have fallen back into the old mistake of confusing what animals do with what they ought to do. To this I can only reply that I have been trying to explain 'ought to do', and my thesis is that this can be done only by reference to what in fact animals of the kind in question regularly do do. However, it is well to recall that we isolate these facts with an eye to how the behaviour of creatures works to preserve and to ameliorate the condition of the species and its members. Among the facts in question are those concerning nutriment, procreation, friend and enemy, the behaviour of one's fellows in certain situations. And here we spy the germ of truth from which have grown so many attempts at egoistic and utilitarian justifications of reason. *General Welfare* and *Private Interest* are not ultimate justifications for agents, but rather natural boundaries within which zoologists, who may be ourselves, find explanations in terms of reason. But we must not try to occupy both positions at once, that of observing zoologist and that of observed rational agent. Thus, as zoologists, we all see, with Hobbes, that the life of our species is more viable and better for all alike, the more we act according to what we believe to be the expectations of others; and we recognize that morality and law rest upon our acting on these beliefs. But as agents, we may feel that this does not tell us why we ought to behave so. We crave for a reason beyond reason, failing to see that we already have all the reason we can have, that what we have noted down as zoological observers is the operation of reason.

This, I think, throws light on the more obscure matter of agents justifying the principles of reason upon which they act, provided that those agents are capable of taking an observer's view of themselves. They come to regard themselves as animals of a certain kind existing in a certain milieu. An important consideration, too often neglected in discussions of the justification of morality, is that all of us know that human beings by and large do regard a good character as something worth having, just as they generally value the possession of goods, agreeable appearance, intelligence, *etc.* As soon as one remarks on the faults of another's character, he demonstrates that he knows that he too would be the better for having a better character. Most, if not all, of us do have an interest in our own character, and would be pleased to be better than we are, provided, of course, that the price is not too high. We know from what we know about people in general that a good character is *a good* for human beings, a natural object of human desire.

I do not want to make excessive claims for this theory according to which we justify a principle of reason by observing that knowledge of reasons falling under the principle could be taken to explain the behaviour of animals of the kind in question, to the extent that such behaviour would conduce to the preservation and amelioration of the

E   113

life of the species and the individual. I think that our notion of reason is in this way tied up with our ways of explaining animate behaviour and with a biologically definable concept of well-being and ameliora- tion. But I allow that this account may completely fail to answer a kind of question which moral philosophers and moralists too have sometimes asked. It is part of our view of man that men should have (possibly idiosyncratic) views of man. But this is not the kind of thing which is easily disclosed to the zoologist. Yet, perhaps, it is the fact which more than any other is stressed by moralists. I am thinking, of course, of what we call 'acting on principle'. The point is that this, when genuine, may excite admiration. Yet nevertheless it seems to me clear that, judged from the outside, it is not always reasonable to act upon one's principles. Yet, we might wonder, ought one ever to sacrifice principle? This im- mediately raises a question as to the correctness of my statement that doing what one ought to do and doing what is most reasonable amount to the same. Thus, for example, most people nowadays would probably agree that Regulus acted in an extraordinarily un- reasonable way, though some would hesitate to aver that he ought not to have returned to Carthage and certain death. Are we, then, to say that sometimes one ought to do what is unreasonable? Hardly. The trouble is that 'ought' must normally go along with what is admirable, or, at least, normally not run counter to what is admirable. This brings us back to the question why we sometimes admire genuine cases of acting on principle, no matter how unreasonable. Now, it is not *always* so. It is common to regard Hitler as a kind of wickedly over-principled man. But the question remains why we should ever *waste* admiration on the unreasonable devotion to reason. I am not sure what the answer is. But surely part of the answer is that when a man does act on principle, this shows that he takes reason very seriously indeed, and that is a disposition which has high biological value for the life of the species. He is acting under his own critical scrutiny, however distorted it may be. He is like, indeed he may even be, a formal logician who says that only this counts as *following*. Now the biological value of this is contingent upon the principles usually having an ameliorative or preservative tendency, as they usually do. Also, the principles in question must themselves be principles which are, as we say, superior to interest. It is just this capacity and willingness to surmount one's own interest which we find admirable. These same observations might be extended to valuable forms of behaviour that should not and could not be 'universalized', including the extraordinarily and genuinely super- erogatory and heroism. These acts serve, at singular points in experience, to secure the preservation or the amelioration of the condition of one's fellows, and are thus the kind of thing which, *could* they be universalized, might well be set down as one of our zoological items. In these cases, indeed, it is quite easy to discern the presence of reason. Anyway, it is part of our picture of Man that he does sometimes act 'on principle', and does brave and glorious deeds for the sake of his fellows. Perhaps *that* is all the principle we need, *viz.* that, when relevant, one ought to act on principle, *ceteris paribus.* That (second-order) principle may have the wanted biological sanction. As to the more general question of how we are to fit in types of exceptional behaviour—behaviour which apparently could not be made a matter of rule—the answer will depend, I suspect, upon achieving some kind of systematic development of a set of 'categories of reason' the force of whose sometimes competitive and sometimes complementary operations we could hope to be able to assess.

10. CONDITIONS OF SUCCESS AND THE IDENTIFICATION OF PURPOSE

[We theoretically define a purpose by specifying tests for establishing the existence and identity of purpose. To establish the existence of purpose we must, at the very least, show that a certain item of behaviour is explained by the animal's awareness of the world. The supplementation of this criterion, to be supplied in no. 12, and the achievement of a criterion of typal identity for purpose follow upon the observation that an act is an item of behaviour that succeeds or fails. There are certain conditions under which an act could not succeed. We call these *necessary conditions of failure of the act.* That such a condition does not obtain, we call a *condition of success of the act.* It is proposed that we may theoretically typally identify the purpose of an act by listing, at whatever length may seem required, types of necessary condition of failure. In the limit, we would finally identify the purpose by listing all the types of conditions of success. We call these *conditions of success for the purpose.* Because this limit can never be reached, it is doubtful that we can ever give a particular identification of a purpose, but must be content with typal identifications only. The conclusion is that there are no particulars, properly speaking, in the domain of purpose. Our procedure for identifying kinds of purpose allows that an animal may have a purpose even though he does not act to attain it.]

We have stipulated that behaviour qualifies as action only if a certain 'mental element' is present. We call that mental element *purpose.* A necessary though not yet sufficient condition for the presence of purpose is that we could explain the occurrence of the movements constituting the behaviour by mention of the fact that

115

the animal is aware of something, where his being so aware implies that he knows or believes certain things. This theme of awareness occasioned a discussion of the notion of self-consciousness and knowledge by reflection, and an investigation of the concept of reason.

Purpose, as here understood, is a technical notion. We first introduced the idea in connection with verbal identifications of action, given in answer to the question, 'What was he (she, it) meaning to do?'; we call these identifications 'specifications of purpose'. But that would be just so much empty verbiage unless we could talk about purpose itself, as in fact we have been doing. 'Purpose' was adopted with the express aim of facilitating the theoretical investigation of our verbal identifications of action. That presupposes that 'purpose' and 'purposes' are meant to be employed to refer to something or other.

How then to provide the wanted explanation sufficient to assure us at least the possibility that there really is purpose in the world? In the usual way, by setting out criteria or tests by application of which we could establish the existence of purpose and the identity of purposes. It would be sufficient if we could but indicate what those tests might be.

As a general rule, we practically discern the presence and the identity of objects in certain preferred situations. Thus we discern the presence of a material body in a region of space at a particular time, and we may identify it as occupying that region at that time. When we proceed to more abstract kinds of thing, existence and identity are generally to be discerned in preferred connection with other types of object or phenomenon or 'medium' in which they are 'situated', 'located' or 'instantiatcd'. Thus we discern the existence and identity of colour in the surfaces of material bodies. This intimates that the tests whose specification would define the objects in question must be taken to apply to the 'media' (places, objects, phenomena) in which they are 'instantiated'. Objects of the kind in question are ones which might possibly be situated or present in the 'instantiating medium'. We establish the existence of such an object by demonstrating its actual presence in such a medium. We establish identity by performing certain additional tests.

Turning to *purpose*, I have already maintained that purpose is most fundamentally instantiated in behaviour. We practically discern the existence and identity of purpose in behaviour. Speaking roughly, we practically ascertain the presence of purpose by observing the operation of the animal's awareness, and, it is to be presumed, we practically identify what purpose from what items of awareness are seen to be operating. Purpose is present in behaviour if and only if that item of behaviour is an act. So we theoretically establish the

116

presence of purpose by showing that an item of behaviour is an act. What we discern in practically ascertaining existence and identity may be taken over and given the additional structure of tests or criteria, by application of which tests we would demonstrate existence and identity.

Using results already arrived at, a necessary condition for the presence of purpose in behaviour is the possibility of supplying an explanation of the movements constituting the item of behaviour in terms of what the animal knows or believes to be the case. If we could supplement this into a sufficient condition, as we shall presently be able to do, that would yield a criterion or test for the existence of purpose.

At the risk of being tedious, let me again, but somewhat differently, say why that is so. A purpose exists if it might possibly be acted with, whether or not it actually is acted with. We show that a purpose might possibly be acted with by showing that it actually is acted with. We show that it actually is acted with by demonstrating the presence of purpose in behaviour. Since what we discern in behaviour that qualifies it as purposive is the possibility of giving an explanation—something verbal—the actual demonstration of the presence of purpose would partly consist in giving such an explanation.

In the balance of this section, I wish to concentrate on the question of theoretically identifying purpose. It is to be expected that, at the level of practical identification, we identify the purpose in an act by noticing what particular items of knowledge and belief would explain the movements. We see that the animal is meaning to drink water only because we see that he thinks that the vessel which he puts his mouth to contains water; we see that he means to sign a contract only because we see that he believes that this is a contract, this an instrument with which to write, *etc.*; we see that he means to make a promise only because we see that he thinks that the object to which he addresses himself is an animal capable of responding to his words. But we still need a test, a criterion, a theoretical delineation of purpose enabling us to select relevant items of knowledge and belief, and by application of which we may justify a particular specification of purpose or verbal identification of action.

I have held that, logically, the primary (though not exclusive) manifestation of purpose is in action, just as colour, logically, is primarily instantiated in material bodies. That suggests that we should try to identify a purpose by reference to certain peculiarities of acts which have that purpose, just as we identify a colour by reference to the wavelengths of light reflected off illuminated bodies which have that colour. Is there any comparable way in which we can manoeuvre with acts, any question we may ask about them, the answer to which would identify purpose?

117

Here we may appeal to an earlier observation about action. An act is an item of behaviour of a kind, items of which kind of behaviour may succeed or fail. Every act either succeeds or fails. It always makes sense to ask about an act whether or not the agent succeeded—attained his purpose—and, derivatively, we may ask whether the act itself succeeded or failed. Just as a body reflects light, so an act is behaviour about which it makes sense to say that the animal tried but failed. One cannot try but fail to stumble into a pitfall, though he might very well make exactly similar movements while trying but failing to test the trap or himself, always provided that he thought there was a trap set in his immediate vicinity. The possibility that an item of behaviour should fail appears to be conjugate with the presence of purpose.

Usually our acts succeed. Why that is so will be discussed in no. 13. When an act does fail, we can usually ask why, and an explanation can be given. Often enough failure results because the state of the world works against our projects and frustrates the attainment of purpose. Thus I may fail in my efforts to kick a field goal because of a strong opposing wind, or I may fail to embark because my car broke down as I was driving to the ship. Such circumstances we may call *conditions of failure of the act*.

Often an agent could succeed in an act in spite of such a condition. When my car breaks down, I might by running or by hailing a taxi manage to get to the ship on time. I might take the wind into account and kick somewhat harder than usual. But there are other conditions of failure which would necessarily preclude success in action. If there were no ship to embark upon, I could not embark; if there were no ball to kick or goal to kick it through, I could not succeed in my act of kicking for a goal. I propose to call such conditions *necessary conditions of failure of the act*. (Such a condition is 'necessary' in contrast with 'contingent' and not in contrast with 'sufficient': the satisfaction of a necessary condition of failure of an act is a sufficient condition for the failure of the act.)

The difference between necessary and contingent conditions of failure may be seen as follows: One may fail in an act for good cause, being alive to the fact in question, and still make the attempt. Setting myself to kick a field goal from sixty yards out, I may be entirely confident that I shall not succeed because the distance is so great, but I still make the try; or I may leave my house only five minutes before embarkation time. But if I knew that the goal posts had fallen or that the ship had sunk, then I could not even try to kick the goal or embark on that ship. Now, necessary conditions of failure of an act are characteristic of the kind of act, given with a specification of purpose, in that such a condition would necessarily result in the failure of *any*

118

act having the same purpose. Necessary conditions of failure for an act of kind K are ones the knowledge of which on the part of an agent A would falsify an observer's statement that A was doing an act of kind K. We may call such conditions of such types *necessary conditions of failure for the purpose.*

From this it follows that among the beliefs that an agent, A, must have in order for an observer truly to assert that A was doing an act of kind K are beliefs that particular necessary conditions of failure for K do not obtain. To be sure, A may so believe and believe wrongly, in which case he may indeed do an act of kind K, which must necessarily fail. But if he does not believe, so to speak, even in the possibility of success, he cannot even be said to try; he cannot have been meaning to do that kind of act. Here then are precisely the beliefs in consideration of which the observer makes his practical identification of the act.

I conclude that we can begin to identify kinds of action by specifying types of necessary condition of failure for purposes of acts, where we must strictly speak of 'types' in order to achieve sufficient generality to ascribe the same purpose to different acts. It is doubtful whether we can ever finally terminate such a list of types of condition. But we may always continue such a list as far as we may think necessary, step by step, giving a narrower and narrower typal identification of the purpose.

This, then, is my proposal: We typally identify a purpose by specifying types of condition under which an act having that purpose must necessarily fail.[1] Examples illustrating the proposal are these: One cannot successfully embark without there being a ship or other vessel, and if we were to explain what it would be to have it as one's purpose to embark, it must be made clear that a vessel is required. One cannot succeed in cooking unless the local temperature is raised above 50° F., and unless there is an object to be cooked. One cannot without a respondent succeed in making a bet. One cannot make what sportswriters call a conversion except in the course of playing a game like rugby or American football.

I stress that the types of conditions which serve to define a kind of purpose are not simply those the obtaining of which would happen to account for the failure of an act's having that purpose, but are the ones the obtaining of which would necessarily preclude success. I might fail to embark because I overslept, but *oversleeping* would not figure in any definition of *embarking*. I conjecture, however, that

[1] Hampshire also makes much of *success* and *failure*. While I cannot but agree with his conclusion, it is arrived at by a route I would never follow; nor would I subscribe to much of the doctrine with which Hampshire embellishes the main idea. See *op. cit.*, *e.g.*, pp. 112f.

whatever might cause an act to fail must also account for the satisfaction of a condition which would necessarily preclude success in the act, *e.g.*, my oversleeping caused me not to be in the presence of the ship at the time of its departure.

That a necessary condition of failure of an act of type P does *not* obtain, we may call a *condition of success of the act*, and, derivatively, a type of condition of success *for P*, where '*P*' schematizes a reference to a purpose. Henceforth I shall usually elliptically speak simply of 'conditions of success for *P*', meaning *types* of condition of success. We would in the limit define a type of purpose by specifying all the types of condition of success. The notion of purpose is thus very like that of real numbers defined as limits of sequences of rational numbers. In fact the limit is never attained by listing, just as we never write down an irrational real number by writing down a sequence of rationals. Nevertheless, we can specify as many types of condition of success as we may care to. This open possibility provides a licence for talking about *all* types of condition of success for an act of type K, at least in certain contexts. In particular we may say that an agent does an act of type K only if he believes that the conditions of all the types which define K are satisfied. We use that formula in the following way. If we come upon a condition whose satisfaction a conceptualizing observer deems necessary for the success of an act of type K, then, if an agent A does not believe that that condition is satisfied, the observer may conclude that A is not doing an act of kind K.

I say that we can probably never give a final listing of the conditions of success defining a type of action. The typal identification of purpose may be more or less full and more or less fine, but never be finally full nor fully fine. Certain conditions must be satisfied if one is to succeed in an act of giving something, *e.g.*, there must exist a recipient, an article presented, *etc*. Now we may wish to identify the act more closely, *e.g.*, as one of giving money or giving a present. We would then identify that purpose by adding conditions, *e.g.*, that there be an occasion for a present. But again we may wish to identify *that* purpose more closely, *e.g.*, by stating that the intended recipient be willing to accept the proffered object.

There is no final elaboration or refinement in the identification of purpose. Our language for identifying behaviour shows, in its development, that we are all the time factoring the conditions and altering the ways in which we parcel them. This has an extremely important consequence for the notion of purpose. Since we cannot list all the types of condition of success which identify a kind of purpose, we must conclude, failing some other way of attaining the limit, that there are no ultimate or atomic particular purposes. Otherwise put, we must never presume to make *particular* identifica-

120

tions of purpose, but must ever rest content with more or less fine typal identifications. In the domain of purpose, there are no ultimate or atomic particulars. We have instead this highly amorphous notion of a limit. Perhaps the continuity of the spectrum, as theoretically conceived, has a similar implication for colour. In the case of the spectrographic analysis of colour, however, we already know how to apply the theory of real numbers to give some structure to this indetermination. Now in practice what fills in for the absence of ultimate particulars in the realm of purpose is our old friend defeasibility. (See pp. 30f.) Certain conditions stand out as conditions which must be met if the purpose is to be attained by action; these satisfied, we are entitled to presume that an act's having that purpose succeeds, although it is always possible to draw attention to some further kind of fact to be cited as a reason for thinking that the act must fail. When all the obvious conditions are met, there is a 'presumption of success', and *success in action* becomes a 'defeasible concept'.

The following three observations are now in order. The first observation anticipates an objection that my procedure is circular, for it would have me identify an act by specifying a purpose itself defined in terms of the conditions of success for an act having that purpose. My response is that in principle we may define a purpose formally by any consistent list of types of condition at all, without having in advance to dignify these with the title of conditions of success. Formally taken, a purpose is theoretically identified by simply writing down a list of types of condition. (Given a sufficiently well-worked-out theory of infinite sets of propositions, a purpose might be defined as a conjunction of the members of such a set or, alternatively, represented by an infinite sequence of numbers which had been individually assigned to particular kinds of condition.) If such a type of condition is found in such a list, *then* it may be called a type of condition of success. We prove the existence of such a list, *i.e.*, of a kind of purpose, by finding an act whose conditions of success are instances of the listed types. But, so far as I can see, there is no consistent list of types of condition which might not define a purpose, just as there appears to be no reason against supposing that any mixture of light waves from the visible spectrum defines a colour.

The second observation is that we typally identify a purpose by specifying types of condition of success. But we may do that without having a particular act in mind. We have, then, an abstracted way of identifying a purpose, independently of any act having that purpose, to be sure, in terms of conditions under which acts having that purpose must fail. This leaves open the possibility of an animal's *having* a purpose, as one may observe, without his having to *act* with that purpose. He may, as we say, 'be inclined' to act from certain beliefs, *viz.*, that certain conditions of success obtain for purpose *P*. But for this possibility of separating purpose and action, the present section would be largely superfluous, for we could by-pass purpose entirely and speak directly of what would make an act fail.

If an agent act with a purpose and his act succeed, I shall say that he *attains* the purpose. However, I wish to use the expression 'attains purpose' more broadly, which brings me to my third observation.

If one attains a purpose by action, there must be some way of telling this. A certain observable state of affairs must eventuate, *e.g.*, the ball fly through the posts, or the man be on the ship. I call that state of affairs the 'measure of success of the act'. Now if an animal has a purpose with which he does *not* act, but if there eventuates a state of affairs which would be the measure of the success of an act having purpose *P*, then too I shall say that the animal attains his purpose. For example, I may attain my purpose of embarking, thanks to the efforts of my friends who transport my drunken, somnolent body to the ship on time. It is important that we may sometimes attain our purposes by inaction and restraint: 'Sit ye down at the doorway of thy house, and thou wilt see them carry by the corpse of thine enemy.'

11. CONDITIONS OF SUCCESS AND CONDITIONS OF DOING

[We typally identify a purpose by specifying types of condition of success. In order that an animal should act with the purpose, whether successfully or not, he must *believe* of every condition of success *C*, that *C* is satisfied. The animal's having such beliefs is a truth-condition for an observer's identification of the act as having the purpose in question. We call such a condition regarding the animal's beliefs a *condition for doing* an act of that kind. Other kinds of condition for doing an act of a certain type are that the animal be awake, have acquired certain capacities, *etc.*]

We now have a criterion for the typal identification of purpose. We identify the purpose, to whatever fineness may be required, by listing, to whatever length may be necessary, types of condition of success, that is, conditions which must be met if an act's having that purpose may succeed.

This method for identifying a purpose may obviously be applied quite independently of whether any animal ever acts with the purpose. It is a method for the theoretical identification of purpose, and not a method for the theoretical identification of action, for which latter it suffices to specify (and not to identify) a purpose.

But it follows from our explication of purpose that there is no purpose which all animals could never act with. We may discern the presence of a certain purpose in an animal's behaviour, and only then may the item of behaviour be identified as an act. What then is the relation of the identification of the behaviour in terms of the agent's purpose to the identification of that purpose? Alternatively, what is the relation between the criteria for the presence of purpose and the criteria for the purpose itself being the kind it is?

One may do an act of a certain kind P even though certain of the conditions of success of certain types, by specification of which P would be identified, do not obtain. Of course, in that case the act must necessarily fail. Thus, I may screw a wire onto an electric fixture meaning to connect up that fixture; but if that wire could not itself be connected to a source of electric power, I shall necessarily fail in what I am meaning to do. Or, I may address words at what I think is a human being, 'Would you please turn on the light?', but if the object is only a wooden statue, I shall necessarily fail in my act of requesting.

These examples all illustrate the connection we are seeking between the criteria for a purpose and the criteria for the presence of that purpose. Though my act would fail if a condition of success did not hold, I could not have been truly said to be doing that kind of act at all unless I thought that the condition of success was satisfied. Unless I thought that the wire could be connected to a source of electric power, I could not be truly said to be connecting the fixture. Similarly for the act of requesting.

Generalizing this, if C is a kind of condition of success whose mention would contribute to the identification of a purpose P, then, should an agent A not believe that any condition of kind C were satisfied, the answer P, given in response to the question, 'What was A meaning to do?' would be a false identification. If C is a defining type of condition for P, then that the animal should believe a condition of type C is a truth-condition for an identification of his behaviour as P. That the agent should believe C is not a condition of success for P; it is a condition for the agent's *either* succeeding *or* failing in an act of kind P. It is a type of condition which must be met before questions of success and failure for acts of type P can arise.

Here, then, is a generalized condition for the presence of purpose P: that the agent should believe that some condition of every type of condition found on a list defining P is satisfied. Since the conditions that the agent must believe in order to be truly said to do an act are conditions of success of the act, we may read the conclusion thus: A purpose P is present in an act A if and only if every condition of success of A is a type of condition of success for P and every type of condition of success for P is instanced as a condition of success of A—briefly, the conditions of success for the act are conditions of success for the purpose, and conversely.

For the sake of a contracting name, I wish to call these conditions on the animal's beliefs *conditions for doing* acts of type P. By extension we may speak of *types of condition for doing for P*. We must not confuse these types of condition for doing for P with the types of condition of success that define P. But among the conditions for doing are the ones we have been discussing, that the animal believe that conditions of success are satisfied.

Here it may be wondered why we ever dallied over conditions of success and did not proceed directly to these other conditions of doing, the satisfaction of which are necessary for the presence of purpose. That would have done for the explanation of the identification of action. But we have introduced the idea of conditions of success, not directly in connection with the identification of action, but to enable us to identify purpose. That achievement at once lends a greater generality to our account and facilitates the discussion of action. But, most important, it permits us to separate purpose from behaviour, and thus warrants our way of talking about action as behaviour with purpose.

We have it, then, that the animal's belief that a condition of success for P is satisfied is a condition for his doing an act with purpose P. I wish now to broaden this notion of condition for doing. I define a condition for doing an act of kind P as any truth-condition for a typal identification of an act as of kind P or as any other condition, the satisfaction of which would be entailed by the satisfaction of such a truth-condition. By extension, we may similarly generalize types of conditions for doing for P. These include all so-called 'presuppositions', *e.g.*, conditions for saying that there was an animal moving, behaving, acting, *etc.* Among these conditions are that the animal be alive and awake; that certain of his perceptual faculties be open and receptive; that the animal have attained a certain level of development, skill, and capacity. Thus a condition for an animal's translating a passage of Greek into English is that he have some capacity for reading Greek. Additionally, the animal must have certain beliefs, most conspicuously that conditions of success for the type of act he does be satisfied.

12. THE RELATION BETWEEN AWARENESS AND PURPOSE, AND THE CRITERION OF EXISTENCE FOR ACTION

[The relation between the existence and the typal identification of action consists in the fact that the awareness, which is a necessary

124

condition of existence, implies certain beliefs, including beliefs that conditions are satisfied, where among the conditions believed are conditions of success for the purpose, by specification of which purpose the act would be identified. With that, we are finally able to formulate a criterion of existence for action. An item of behaviour might be explained by mention of the fact that the agent believes that such and such conditions of success are satisfied. We apply the test by giving such an explanation. This criterion effectively fuses the two necessary conditions of action which were laid down in no. 2. With the relation between the existence and the typal identification of action established, we are able to complete our examination of privileged testimony (no. 8), arriving at the conclusion that the agent's testimony, given in answer to the question of what he is meaning to do, prevails even when the agent does and the observer does not misidentify objects of the agent's awareness.]

We have now laid down a necessary condition for proving the existence of action, *viz.*, that the investigator provide an explanation of the movements constituting an item of behaviour in terms of what the animal is aware of. We have also stated a criterion for the identification of purpose, *viz.*, listing types of condition of success. We have several times noticed that what we have said about the existence of action is not yet sufficient, because there appear to be other types of behaviour which might also be explained by reference to the animal's awareness, *e.g.*, 'mental causation'. It is time to try to remedy that defect in our account. The solution is suggested by the answer to the apparently distinct question, what precisely is the relation between the existence of action and the type of the act? A clue to the relevance of the one matter to the other is supplied by our earlier stated necessary condition for action, that an act be an item of behaviour of kind *K*, where items of *K* might succeed or fail.

Let us then turn to this second question regarding the relation between the existence of action and the typal identity of action. It is sometimes possible to discern and to establish existence, *e.g.*, of a material thing, without there and then also coming into position to discern or to establish what *kind* of thing it is, *e.g.*, what kind of material thing. But that is the exception. Usually when we discern and/or establish existence we put ourselves immediately into position to discern and/or establish what kind of thing. That may be explained by noticing certain general relations which obtain between testing for existence and testing for typal identity. The examination of some of these relations will occupy me in a sequel to this work. For the time being, I wish to consider only the special case of action. What, then, are the relations between the existence and the typification of action? Well, an observer surely may see that an act is being done and not yet see what kind of act is being done. The test for existence must leave room for that possibility. But then again the observer may, in seeing that an act is being done, also see what kind of act is being done. How so?

The observer sees that an act is done only if he sees that the animal is aware of something or other. The observer may also see that the animal acts with a certain purpose. What does the observer see that may at once suffice to inform him that an act is done and what kind of act is done? Pegging it up a notch higher at the level of a theoretical analysis, we ask, what does the observer see that the animal is aware of, our mention of which observed circumstance would contribute to identifying the purpose? Surely not the purpose itself, for, as we have argued (see pp. 77f.), when an animal does an act of kind P he need not be aware that he has purpose P: self-consciousness is not a necessary condition of action. So what is it? Well, we know that awareness always implies items of knowledge or belief. Among the things an animal must know or believe to be said correctly to do an act of type P is that certain necessary conditions of failure do not obtain; otherwise, he must know or believe that conditions of success of every type for P are satisfied. But that describes the items of knowledge or belief in terms of types of condition, *our* mention of which would contribute to the typal identification of the purpose.

Here, too, we may see the relation between *reasons* and *purpose*. If a condition of success for P is satisfied, then the fact that it is satisfied is one of the agent's reasons for doing an act of type P. E.g., if the agent means to kick a ball, and if *this* is a ball, that is a reason for the agent's making propulsive movements with his feet in the direction of *this*; the fact that he knows that *this* is a ball explains his movements.

We must be careful in formulating this result. An agent need not believe that a condition of success which he believes is a condition of success. 'Condition of success' is a term of art, an item in *our* theoretical vocabulary. We are not even entitled to assume that the observer of the agent who reports upon what the agent does is ready to understand what *we* mean by 'condition of success'. Rather, it is this: If an observer O reports that an agent A does P, then what O says, if true, implies that A believes C, where (as *we* can say) C is an instance of a type of condition of success for P. It is supposed that O observes that A believes C, and that O implicitly appreciates that A's act would fail if C did not obtain.

Some may object that it is too much to require that the agent should actually believe that *all* the conditions of success for P are satisfied. Since our stipulation requires only that the agent not believe

126

that any necessary conditions of failure of the act are satisfied, is it not sufficient for him not positively to disbelieve that they are satisfied? Two arguments might be brought against the stronger thesis and, by implication, in favour of the weaker. First, we cannot actually list all the conditions of success: So how can we suppose that the agent actually believes that all are satisfied? We got round this by saying that he does not positively disbelieve. Second, an agent may act in the mere *hope, e.g.*, that this is a cup of coffee. But hope is not positive belief.

To the first objection, I reply, to say that the agent believes that *all* the conditions are met does not mean that he actually entertains a single collective belief that they all together obtain. All that is implied is this: if a certain defining condition *C* for *P* is considered, and if it turns out that the agent does not believe that *C* is satisfied, that is proof that the agent is not doing *P*. Nor is there any problem about the limitless listing of beliefs. Let the reader direct his attention to any object in his immediate vicinity. Is there any place specifiable in advance at which he must stop listing the items of knowledge or belief that are elicited, supported, and conveyed by that awareness? I see that it is a radio; I also see that it is brown, rectangular, has knobs; I believe it has tubes, wires, that it operates on 110–115 V; I think it was manufactured, shipped, *etc.* I therefore find no difficulty in maintaining that the animal must in the intended way positively believe that all the conditions of success are satisfied.

I find the second objection the more challenging one. We have already considered the problem (pp. 50–51). First let it be quite clear that the troublesome kind of example here is that of kicking what I hope is a football or drinking what I hope is a cup of coffee and *not, e.g.*, hoping to kick a football. If I actually put that latter kind of hope into action, then what I should be meaning to do is to kick a football, and if there is no ball to be kicked, I cannot succeed. But it is quite otherwise with (*e.g.*) drinking what I hope is a cup of coffee. I may guzzle the liquid down and my act succeed, though my hopes are disappointed; I might also be pleasantly surprised. My act was one of drinking liquid from a cup—that says what I was meaning to do. To add that I hope it was coffee is to comment on the frame of mind in which I approached the deed. 'With the hope that it is coffee' does not alter the typal identity of the act, but qualifies *how* the act was done.

In fine, I see no impassable objection to this account of the relation between awareness and purpose and so of the relation between the existence of action and the type of an act. We establish the existence of action only by showing that the animal's awareness might explain the movements constituting an item of his behaviour; that awareness might imply beliefs that certain conditions are satisfied, which conditions are among those that we would mention in order to identify the purpose. Seeing that an animal is aware of such and such, we also see that he knows or believes such and such, and we thereby see that he acts with purpose.

In no. 8 I argued that, where an agent has sufficient use of Language and is capable of knowing by reflection what he was meaning to do, his testimony, given in answer to the question what he is meaning to do, tends to prevail over that of an observer, in that any challenge must be either to the agent's veracity or to the correctness of his language. But we deferred discussion of the most interesting kind of case, where the agent does but the observer does not mistake the facts, *e.g.*, misidentify an object of awareness. The observer would identify the act in the light of what he, the observer, thinks the agent is aware of; if we suppose that the observer thinks that the agent is aware of what he, the observer, is aware of, he stands to specify a purpose different from what the agent would specify. Who will be right? Take it that our imagined agent and his observer possess comparable general knowledge and conceptual capacities; suppose a case where there is an object, the agent's present awareness of which accounts for his making the movements he does—let it be a bag of sand. Both parties are equally liable to misidentify the object. Imagine now that the agent takes a good kick at this object. If the agent knew that it was a bag of sand, he might say that he was meaning to kick a bag of sand; if the observer had wrongly identified the object as a football, he might in consequence wrongly identify the act as one of kicking a football. The agent will be right. But reverse the mistake; the agent thinks that the bag of sand is a football, while the observer sees that it is a bag of sand. Again, the agent's testimony will not concur with the observer's report. But, I hold, the observer still stands to misidentify the act, even though what the agent *did* was to kick a bag of sand. The agent certainly was not meaning to kick a bag of sand. The determining consideration here is that the observer practically identifies the act solely in consideration of what he supposes that the agent knows or believes to be the case. Since in our imagined instance, the agent did not think that the object was a bag of sand, he could not either succeed or fail in kicking a bag of sand, even though he kicked a bag of sand. In the realm of belief the believer's testimony must tend to prevail, not because what he tells us about his beliefs must be true, but because any challenge to his testimony impugns either his honesty or his language.

This conforms exactly with our earlier conclusion, that the testimony of a self-conscious agent has privileges. But I repeat that it surely is not true that only the agent can really know. Our analysis begins with an observer's characterization of the behaviour of a non-reflective animal. It goes without question that the observer can see that the agent is aware of such and such and hence believes such and such. The observer, for example, may know that the agent thinks that the bag of sand is a football, and thereby also know that what the agent means to do is kick a football. While the observer is prone to err due to misidentification of an object of awareness either by himself or by the agent, he is not *bound* to be wrong in either instance. On the other hand, it is impossible that the *reflective* agent should make a mistake here, for it is his belief or information that the object is so and so that is at once definitive of the act and is expressed by a candid report.

Here it should be added that at very primitive levels of action, where the agent cannot be said to be aware of anything except an object present, he can neither act with conscious thought of the object nor indeed be said to be moving to be in proximity to or at a distance from a *kind* of object, though of course there is a kind of object towards or from which he is moving. Thus, though it be a football at which the petulant infant is kicking, his act is not one of football kicking, but simply one of kicking at something. But at this stage of behavioural development, there is no room for reflection or testimony, and questions about the privileged status of the agent with respect to his own behaviour cannot arise.

We may now quickly achieve a solution to our second problem of providing a sufficient condition for the existence of action. An item of behaviour is an act only if it might be explained by mention of the agent's knowledge and beliefs. If the movements constituting the item of behaviour are explained by the agent's knowledge or belief that all (of what *we* call) the conditions of success for a purpose P are satisfied, then P is present in the behaviour. An item of behaviour is an act if and only if purpose is present. I conclude that an item of behaviour is an act if and only if the movements constituting the behaviour might be explained by mention of the belief that some conditions of success for some purpose are satisfied. We apply the test by giving such an explanation.

This result tallies with our earlier stipulation that an act is an item of behaviour of type K, where items of K might succeed or fail. That there should be conditions of success or failure for the purpose implied the possibility of success and failure for that kind of action. We have in effect fused the two necessary conditions for the existence of action into a single necessary and sufficient condition.

What chiefly recommends this proposed criterion is that it works, at least as far as I know, and it admits of further testing. It clearly excludes many cases we do not want to let in as action—mental causation, fits of anger, *etc.*—and, provisionally, it appears to exclude all such cases.

But there are two objections to it, which I should like to consider. First, it is crucial to this theory that the conditions, which the agent is held to believe are satisfied, be thought of as conditions of success; but, it may be objected, a condition is simply a condition, and is not marked out by nature as a condition of success. I agree. (See p. 126.) My answer is that it is *our* decision whether the condition, which the conceptualizing observer sees that the animal believes is satisfied, is a condition of success. The possibility of our so regarding the condition is assured by the observer's having language available for the specification of purpose. His choosing to employ it depends upon his taking a certain view of the behaviour of the observed animal. Briefly, if he is willing from what he sees to speak of the animal as being constrained, blocked, frustrated, inhibited, *etc.*, then we may regard some of the conditions, which he takes the agent to believe are satisfied, to be conditions of success.

The second objection is this. If, to see that an act is being done, the observer must see that the animal believes that certain conditions of success are satisfied, then the observer could not see that an act was being done without seeing what kind of act was being done; but that is contrary to fact. The answer is: Mention of the same conditions of success might contribute to the typification of different kinds of purpose. Such purposes may even be, so to speak, opposed. For example, to define the opposed purposes of giving away and taking back an object we would commonly list as conditions of success that there be an object and another person, both suitably identified. Clearly, an observer could see that the agent believes that these conditions are satisfied and that the beliefs might explain his movements, without knowing what *other* conditions the agent believes are satisfied. Hence, an observer may see that an act is done without being yet able to see what kind of act is done. What is of substantive interest in this objection is that it serves to explain why we so often *are* able directly to discern what kind of act is done upon seeing that an act is done.

13. THE PRESUMPTION OF SUCCESS

[We have several times noted that the straight, reportorial use of act-identificatory language usually implies that the act succeeded. That feature of our Language reflects the fact that animals come to do acts by succeeding at them, and we attribute acts to animals largely in consideration of the successful outcomes we observe. Though not all acts succeed, it must be that most acts of most kinds succeed. It is stressed that our account, which insists upon the *possibility* of an identification of action neutral with respect to success and failure, is not meant to supply new ways of talking about animal behaviour, but rather, it is meant to supply ways of analysing extant ways of talking about animal behaviour.]

Success and *failure* are key ideas in this account. Kinds of action are types of behaviour items of which types succeed or fail. Action is behaviour with purpose, and we theoretically identify a purpose by specifying conditions under which an act having that purpose could not succeed. This employment of 'succeed' and 'fail' is familiar, but not the most common. First, our use of 'succeed' and 'fail' in connection with action is actually somewhat brachylogical, if naturally so. Initially it is animals that succeed or fail in their acts, and to speak of the success or failure of the act is at once a compression and a sophistication, albeit innocent. Second, people fail not only in their acts but also in school or life; or their productions may fail, and also their health or their businesses. But I do not think there is any reason to worry about all that, so long as it is also correct to say that they fail in their acts and, derivatively, that their acts fail. We also speak about failure in *activity*, and here, interestingly enough, it is very natural to speak of purpose. For example, one's purpose in playing a game may be to win, or to be a member of a winning (successful) team, or *etc*. This quite common use of 'purpose' differs from the one I have been explaining. But it is confirmatory of my account of purpose as something possibly acted with, that the purposes of activities could also plausibly be explained in terms of what would insure one's success or failure when engaging in those activities. Thus, if one were engaged in playing a game of baseball, he could not win (succeed) if the other team scored more runs than did his own; and if we wished to explain the purpose of winning in baseball, it would be inevitable that our account should imply that one cannot be a member of a winning team if the other team scored more runs than his own. This, I say, is confirmation; but we must still be on guard not to equate purposes like hitting a baseball with purposes like winning at baseball.

Because items of any type of action might succeed or fail, it is important that the typal identification of an act should not prejudge the question. I have been perhaps oppressively anxious to insist upon the point. I reckon this to have been necessary in order to get by an obstacle which our ordinary use of Language might throw in the way of understanding. We have several times observed that the direct employment of most (but not all) act-identifying words or phrases normally implies the success of the act identified. If I say that he was eating, I would normally be taken to imply that he was getting the comestibles down his gullet. Now the attempt to void this implication by affixing a 'trying to' or 'attempting to' or even 'meaning to' will generally carry the contrary implication of failure, equally extraneous to the identification of the act. My way of getting by this obstacle has been to insist that the identification of an act always be thought of as given in answer to a certain question, *viz.* 'What was he (she, it) meaning to do?', where the answer also answers the question, 'What was he (she, it) doing?'. Such an answer typally identifies the act without implying either success or failure. The answer, take note, consists in the utterance of a verb or verb phrase, *e.g.*, 'eat', and is not to include the 'meaning to' prefix, which, if present, would again normally imply failure.

But why should it be? Why should the normal, reportorial use of act-identifying Language imply success? Why must we clutter the context or complicate the utterance with affixes in order to void this implication? Because it must be that most acts of most kinds succeed, and the presumption of success exerts a tremendous pressure on the Language we use to identify action.

To see why this is so, we must consider again the relation between the conceptualizing observer and the putative agent. The observer sees the animal moving; he discerns in the movements the presence of purpose; and he identifies the act from what he sees. Part of what he sees is that the animal believes certain things. But his only clue to that is what he sees happening in the body of the animal and in the circumstances of the deed. In particular, the observer will be inclined to identify behaviour as action if he observes such movements and resulting effects as could be regarded as the outcome of a successful act. For example, conveying comestibles into the mouth. This is especially so when the observed animal is operating at a low level of behavioural sophistication, where there might actually be disputes over whether we should call this (*e.g.*) *calling* or merely *crying*. The point is that whether or not an animal does an act is, at primitive stages of behavioural development, the observer's and not the putative agent's decision; it is a question whether it would be true to say that this is an act of such and such kind; and the argument was that the observer normally must see certain results as eventuating from the animal's movements before he will be ready to say something which implies that the animal is acting. The agent, then, cannot even be said to fail at any kind of act until he has already frequently succeeded in others. Allow now that the animal matriculates into a conceptualizing agent. The answer to the question whether he is acting no longer always depends solely upon the decision of another competent observer. But still a continuing preponderance of successful acts is almost certain. Persistent failure in action would frustrate action, and the type of action in question would, so to speak, fall into disuse, and therewith also would fall into disuse common verbal ways of identifying action. Since that is possible, however unlikely we must grant that other non-purposive behaviour may well then come to fill the gap. The animal would stop looking, and fall back into a state of generalized flutter.

Lest it be thought that this account, which insists upon the possibility of a neutral identification of action, comes into conflict with our ordinary ways of speaking about behaviour, let it be made entirely clear that I am not proposing new ways of talking. My efforts are neither to improve upon common Language nor to correct commonsense, but rather to supply ways of analysing extant ways of talking. All I need presume is the possibility of a neutral identification, and I have no doubts about that. It is important that our Language does have machinery for voiding and for circumventing the usual implication of success. I do not suggest that we really ought always to talk in these prolix terms; even less do I urge that from now on we are not to use (*e.g.*) the word 'eat' so as to imply success unless the contrary be expressly indicated. But if we wish to give a theoretical account of (*e.g.*) *eating*, it is convenient to be able to do so without forever having to dawdle over the threatening possibility of failure; it is, moreover, better to essay the analysis with a vocabulary not including 'eat' and 'try', for in such an account we would not be concerned to say that anyone was eating, but rather to say what eating is. My proposal on that issue is that we proceed by listing conditions of success, *e.g.*, that food be present, that the animal have what we call a mouth, *etc.*, *etc.*

14. COLLATERAL ACTION

[We may use act-identificatory verbs not only to identify what act is done, but also to describe how acts are done. Since one always does what he does in some way, the impression is created that whenever anyone does an act he is doing at least two acts, and possibly many. But that is a mistake, the patency of which shows that we must discover ways of separating what was done from how it was done. That may be achieved by applying our principle for identifying purpose. A specification of purpose identifies what kind of act is done only if the conditions of success for that purpose are conditions of success of the act done; if the purpose-defining conditions of success are not conditions of success of the act done, the specification describes the way in which the act is done. I call the way in which an act is done, when the description exploits act-identificatory Language, a *collateral*

133

act. A collateral act may be thought of as having an 'ultimate purpose' which is the same as the purpose of the act done.]

I now return to a special case of the topic of identifying versus describing action. There are many ways in which an act might be described—as done *quickly, conscientiously, stupidly, by Smith, over the Atlantic, etc.* Anything like a full examination of act-description is beyond the limits of this study. But there is one very common way of describing action which will be constantly intruding itself, a way which we might schematize as: He is --- by (way of) . . . . For example, 'He is paying by signing the bill'. In this case 'paying' goes in place of '---' and 'signing the bill' goes in place of '. . .'. Generally, '---' is filled by an expression which tells us what kind of act was being done, and '. . .' is filled by an act-identificatory expression which in the supposed case is used not to identify but rather to describe how the act is done—if you wish, to say by what 'means' the act is done.

It is well-nigh inevitable that we have this way of describing action. But it is an annoyance when we try to give a theoretical analysis of action, for it creates the illusion that whenever one is doing anything (*e.g.*, paying a bill), he is also independently doing something else (*e.g.*, signing), which is an act by way of which he does what he does. Unless we prepare ourselves to see through this illusion, it will remain a standing threat to our attempts at a coherent theory of action.

Take a case: Suppose a man writes his name on a bill and hands it to a waiter, what is his act? moving his hand, moving the pen, writing his name, signing the bill, or charging the dinner? Is he indeed doing any of these things, or is he doing them all? Is there any *one* act of *one* kind which he may be said to be doing? If not, how many acts then, and of how many kinds? But, if he is doing only one act of one kind, how shall we distinguish that from all the others which seem to rise out of our description? And supposing we can somehow or other isolate *an* act which is being done, how in general are we to describe the relations between *the* act and all the other, so to speak, subsidiary acts?

These questions prefigure the difficulties we are in for if we do not comprehend why act-identificatory language can be used to describe action.

We can be sure that usually there is only one act done, for action is individuated with respect to the actual movements made. We can also be sure that usually there will be one and only one kind of act done, which is (as I shall call it) *The Act*. ('The Act', more exactly, is employed to schematize a singular reference to a particular act which

134

reference also correctly identifies that act.) This is a limiting condition; it must be met if we are to speak about acts at all. That it is satisfied is shown by the fact that there will always be somewhere that a list like *moving, writing, signing, charging* terminates. (Perhaps at the end of the list another kind of explanation will take over, but that in no way embarrasses the point.) What the list finally stops with fixes what kind of act was done. Let it be the charging of the meal; then The Act is one of charging a meal; 'charge a meal' specifies the purpose of and identifies the act.

Occasionally, one may act with more than a single purpose, and a single act be of several heterogeneous kinds. The list may fork and have a double termination. Thus, by selling shares one may at once be taking profits and switching his holdings out of an unpromising issue. He both gets the money and switches his holdings. But this kind of case is the exception. It is not, at any rate, the result of mistakenly treating how one acted as another act by which he did the act. That is the mistake we must fortify ourselves against.

But is it a mistake? One might protest, 'Doesn't he, in charging the meal, also sign the bill?'. Surely he does sign the bill, for the bill is signed by him.'

The answer is twofold. First, it is essential when doing an act that one shall make movements; but these movements do not define what kind of an act he was doing. But certainly these movements occurred, and were essential to *that particular* act. Similarly, 'signing the bill', while it does much more than give a bare physical description of the movements, tells us that the agent's movements were made in the light of certain information or beliefs about the situation before him, and had certain results. But, though essential to the particular act, 'signing the bill' does not yet say what kind of act was done. (That the movements made and the *way* in which the act is done bear a similar relation to act-identification can be seen from the fact that we can always speak of the movements one makes in doing an act as movements that he *might* have acted to make. But it is clear that when we speak of the movements we do not always imply that the agent was acting to make those movements; similarly, where the way in which he acted was, so to speak, an act he might have done, we do not mean that he acted to do the act in that way.) Second, one might very well put his name down on the bill and still fail to get the meal charged, perhaps, *e.g.*, because the management refuses him credit. His act, in this case, is just as fully frustrated as it would have been had he not been able to sign his name. And, moreover, he would not have been frustrated if, finding his pen dry, he was nonetheless able to get the meal charged by giving a familiar signal to his usual waiter. If one acts to attain the purpose of charging the meal, then his signing

135

does not matter, but his charging does. The Act separates from the way the act is done when we consider what would necessarily cause it to fail.

Now why *should* we have any occasion at all for using act-identificatory phrases for describing action? Would it not be better to adopt a neutral, physical mode of description? Well, we are usually unable easily to give a bare physical description of the required kind, and when we can, we do so most commonly with words borrowed from the act-identificatory stock, *e.g.*, 'kicking movements'. We learn to refer to animal movement against a background of circumstances, the knowledge of which by an animal would be definitive of action. But suppose that a bare physical description be given, as it were kinematically, it is still important that we see the animal as an agent. That is, we must see his movements as issuing from his awareness of his surroundings and situation and his knowledge of or beliefs about these. Now an agent does his act in one way rather than another in order to protect or enhance his chances of success, exploiting his knowledge of the facts of the case, or, anyway, acting on what he believes to be the facts of the case. One may wish to describe the act by drawing attention to what the agent knows or believes to be the case. But this is just what the use of act-identificatory Language does. So, if we wish to draw attention to the agent's knowledge or belief that is operating subsidiary to the task at hand, it is natural to do so at least partly by the use of act-identificatory locutions. To put the point otherwise, that we see the agent to be moving in the light of certain items of knowledge or belief enables us to tell what kind of act the animal is doing; but other items of knowledge or belief may also be relevant to our explanation of his movements, and presumably that is what is conveyed by the act-descriptive use of act-identificatory language. We describe an act with an act-identificatory locution *L* only if we take it that the movements constituting the act might be explained by the agent's knowledge or belief that certain conditions are satisfied, where those are among the conditions that would be listed to identify a purpose, which would be specified by the use of *L*.

Faced with an actual episode which the observer correctly identifies as such and such kind of act, we see that he might, lacking certain information about the beliefs and/or knowledge of the agent, have identified it otherwise. He might have ended the list *moving his hand, moving the pen, . . . charging the meal* prematurely; *e.g.*, not knowing that the paper was a bill, the observer would also not have known that the agent knew or believed it was a bill, and he might have identified the act as one of handing a signed paper to the waiter. He might, that is, have identified the act in the light of those presumed

136

items of the agent's information or belief which in fact account for his doing the act in this way rather than that.

It remains to say how we are to draw the distinction between the identification and the description of the act. Which locutions specify the purpose of the act? Now if the observer makes a mistake on this, he need not have been wrong about the identity of the agent, the shape of the movements, or the character of the circumstances. All that remains is the purpose. That suggests that we can always find an answer by making direct appeal to our principle that purpose may itself be identified by listing conditions of success. In the kind of case under examination, act-identifying and act-describing locutions both could be employed to specify purpose. We would identify these respective purposes by listing conditions of success. If failure of any of the conditions of success for a purpose P would not necessarily result in the failure of the act done, then the act was not done with purpose P. So we decide whether a locution L describes or identifies an act A by asking whether any of the conditions of success definitive of the purpose signified by L are *not* conditions of success of A. If the quest is successful, we show that L does not identify but only describes A. Thus, in our previous example, we saw that the man could have charged the meal even had the only available pen run dry, though then perhaps he could not have signed his name to the bill; having a usable pen or other writing instrument was not a condition of success for his act; his act was therefore not one of signing a bill. On the other hand, had the management not been willing to extend him credit, his act would have failed necessarily; of course, his act might still have been one of charging a meal provided that he thought that the management was willing to extend him credit.

Since questions regarding both what an agent does and how he acts can arise in connection with any act, we must always be ready to draw the distinction; to facilitate that I shall now introduce a bit of technical jargon.

If an agent A does an act of kind I, a correct description of which is D, I shall, to facilitate presentation, say that A was D-ing *collaterally* to his act of I-ing. I shall also say that the act of D-ing was collateral to the act of I-ing. Thus, I say that the act of signing the bill was collateral to the act of charging the meal.

Now there is danger lurking in this last formulation. It strongly suggests that there were indeed two acts being done. But the suggestion is gratuitous, for we have brought in this technical idea of a collateral act just to fix the distinction between what is done and how it is done. A collateral act is not an act separate and distinct from that within which it is collateral. What are separate and distinct are the identification and the description, together with the explanatory items of knowledge and belief on which they are founded. A collateral act is no more the kind of act done than the roof or the walls of a house are what one lives in, though roofs and walls are kinds of architectural structures. If the threat of 'collateral *act*' becomes too pressing we may always retire to the formulation, 'He was *D*-ing collaterally to *I*-ing'.

Let us now extend the idea of a collateral act somewhat. It *might* have been that what our agent was doing was signing a paper and not charging the meal. In that case, moving the pen across the paper might have stood collateral to signing the bill. But 'moving the pen across the paper' is also act-identificatory, and, even in the case where the agent was charging the meal, conveys that he was acting in the light of information or belief about the situation. For this reason I shall also say that *moving the pen across the paper* is collateral to the kind of act actually done, *viz.*, *charging the meal*, and also collateral to the collateral act of signing the bill. Within any act there will usually be a nested set of subsidiary collateral acts, where *collateral to* is a transitive, irreflexive, asymmetrical relation. The series thus generated terminates in The Act done, and all the other members are descriptive features of the act. The situation may be more complicated. It is sometimes useful to view an act as breaking up into stages; and it may be that those features of the act which we fix as a collateral act attach to only one stage. For example, he charges the meal by signing the bill and *by subsequently* handing it to the waiter. Here *signing the bill* and *handing it to the waiter* have no collateral relation to each other. In principle there may be any number of such nested sets of non-overlapping collateral acts within a given act. We must resist regarding The Act as the last link of a chain; it is, so to speak, the full chain, coincident with the first and coterminous with the last nested set of collateral acts. The Act is therefore not a consequence of, or in any other way essentially subsequent to, its collateral acts.

Acts of any *kind* may be done collaterally to an act of some kind. That is, any act-identificatory expression may be used act-descriptively. This is to claim no more than that the information or beliefs which are definitive of doing a kind of act may be subsidiary to doing another kind of act. One would be puzzled about this only if he thought that there must in the nature of the case be some kind of act which is intrinsically non-collateral; but the only candidate for that office would be the living of life itself, which, of course, is no kind of act at all, nor even a kind of activity. On the other side, acts of any kind may be ones to which other kinds are done collaterally. Now, to be sure, there are kinds of actions which are more 'natural' than others; *i.e.*, there are purposes with whose specification we should not be surprised to finish when we are concerned to identify what kind of act was done, and other purposes which would be rather unexpected: eating is not generally done for a further purpose, but it may be; contrariwise, one does not usually just write down his name on a piece of paper, though one may.

The agent, whether he be eating or merely writing his name, will, of course, have reason or mistaken reason for doing the deed he does. What I am calling *The Act* is what one 'just wants to do' and, in my view, there is nothing that some kind of animal may not in some circumstances 'just want to do'[1], though, whatever one does, he has beliefs which, if true, are of his reasons for doing that act.

We have given a systematic way of deciding whether a locution is employed to identify or to describe an act, in terms of the conditions of success of the act. This test enables us to say how distinct items of knowledge and belief contribute to animal behaviour. Here two questions arise. First, is there always some starting place for spelling out a nested set of collateral acts? Is the series limited, as it were, from below by an element of the series? Second, is there always an act immediately collateral to The Act with no other collateral act between; more generally, are our sets of collateral acts discrete or compact? These questions taken together inquire in effect whether there is always a unique canonical way of setting out act-theoretical descriptions of action.

My view with respect to the first question is that the list begins at the place where behaviour becomes action, that is, where we reach a place where animals of the kind in question in circumstances of the kind in question, could not conceivably be thought to behave with purpose; roughly, that is, where the animal's presumed knowledge and beliefs about the world do not explain the movements. For example, in the usual case, the moving of one's tendons or the blinking of one's eyes is not an act collateral to whatever it is that one is doing. Now the tests we employ to distinguish action from other lower-order varieties of behaviour and animal movement generally are open. So, too, is the proposed answer. The test is applied against the observer's presumed knowledge of the species, and the answer we get is relative to that knowledge. Someone with a mite of physiological learning could very well be thought to be moving his tendons, *e.g.*, by writing his name on a piece of paper. But this openness does not destroy the test, it means only that any proposed starting point is subject to revision in the light of what the observer may discover about the beliefs of his supposed agent.

---

[1] I doubt that any kind of *object* can be wanted just in itself; what I hold is that success in any kind of doing can be wanted in itself, *e.g.*, acquiring an undesirable object.

In answer to the second question—is there always an act immediately collateral to The Act done, no matter what kind of act The Act is—yes and no! Yes, in that any given analysis of an act will be against a background of investigation that will identify the act as of a kind to which acts of other kinds are regularly collateral. For example, repeating a sentence is regularly immediately collateral to doing what I shall call a Language act. On the other hand, we might have analysed the act against another kind of background, in which case we might have placed another act of another kind as immediately collateral to The Act; e.g., we could have said that the immediately collateral act was one of setting up sound vibrations in the air, as indeed the agent might have been doing were he making every effort to say his piece in a phonetically impeccable way. It has already been pointed out that, if the agent is engaged in a definite sphere of activity, that will bear heavily on how we would analyse his act into a nest of collateral acts.

The Act and acts collateral thereto are the same act. In referring to the act as a collateral act, we mean to refer to it as it would be properly described. Now a collateral description of an act *A* of type *I* is given in consideration of the agent's making certain movements in connection with certain elements of the circumstances, where the movements are among those that constitute the act. Those very same movements and elements of the circumstances possibly supplemented might be similarly involved and considered in the course of identifying the act as *I*. In view of this, it seems to me appropriate to describe a collateral act as *part of* The Act. Thus the collateral act of signing a bill is part of The Act of charging the meal.

Allowing this as a way of talking, we must take care not to suppose that what we could call the purpose of the collateral act, *i.e.*, the purpose associated with the collateral description of the act, is a part of the purpose of The Act, *i.e.*, of the purpose of the act. It may be that one's purpose is to write a letter to John, and we might want to say that writing a letter is *part of* that purpose. This kind of partial purpose—to be contrasted with the case where the agent has more than a single 'whole purpose'—is never the purpose of a collateral act. A 'partial purpose' is simply a purpose less definitely specified, and the purpose of the collateral act is no less definite intrinsically than is the purpose of The Act, though, of course, both may be openly specified.

The sense of any locution which might be used to identify an act, *i.e.*, to specify the purpose of an act, could be explained by listing conditions of success for the purpose. Now the sense remains exactly the same when the locution is employed to describe how an act is done. In such a case, I want to say that the purpose in question is the

140

immediate purpose of the collateral act. I shall also want to call the purpose of the act the *ultimate purpose* of each and every collateral act and of The Act together. From this it is clear that whenever I speak of 'ultimate purpose' I am talking about the purpose as the purpose of the particular act in question; and when I speak of 'immediate purpose' I am talking about something which could be the purpose of some act, but which is not the purpose of the act in question.

Now, if one succeeds in an act, it is to be assumed that he would have attained each immediate purpose of the act, had it been the purpose of the act. If I succeed in charging a meal by signing a bill, then I must have got the bill signed. But the reverse relation does not hold. If I get the bill signed in the course of trying to charge the meal, I need not succeed in charging the meal.

But the agent might have attained the purpose of an act differently than he did, not requiring that he have attained the immediate purposes of the collateral acts which were parts of The Act he did. Thus, while he killed her with a gun, he might have done it with a knife, where getting her dead is the common ultimate purpose of the two ranges of imagined possible collateral acts.

Summing up these relations, while the attainment of the immediate purposes of collateral acts subserves and is (at least usually) necessary for the success of The Act and for the attainment of the ultimate purpose of the act, the attainment of the ultimate purpose is neither necessary nor sufficient for the attainment of an immediate purpose itself, which could be the ultimate purpose of another act.

15. HYBRID ACTION

[Given a scheme for identifying acts and for describing them as done in certain ways, it may be that we would wish, somewhat misleadingly, to say that it is part of an agent's purpose to do an act of kind *I* in a certain way *D*. His purpose is not simply to do *I*, but rather to do *I*-by-*D*. In such cases we say that his purpose is a *hybrid* of the *Original Purpose*, *I*, and the *Original Way*, *D*. Action with such a purpose, we call *hybrid action*.]

The purpose of an act may be more and less complicated, and in various ways. But there is one kind of complication which it will pay us to notice explicitly, for it will be indispensable for the analysis of action and especially of the use of Language. The purpose of an act might, in a variety of ways, be of such a kind that its attainment would imply the attainment of what could have been the purpose of some other act, where that other purpose is in a certain sense

141

'part of' the purpose presently sought. Thus, it may be one's purpose to play a particular piece of music on the piano. It is then part of the agent's purpose that music should be made present in his immediate surroundings, and his act surely would be deemed unsuccessful if nothing of that kind issued from his manipulations. Yet it is certainly not his purpose simply to make music present. He could not succeed by playing a record of the piece on the gramophone, or by switching on the radio, or by transporting himself to a concert hall. That music should be made present is only a *part of* his purpose.

Take now another example. In playing golf, one will have occasion to make certain kinds of shot, *e.g.*, approaches. One may make such a shot in various ways, *i.e.*, by way of various lines of collateral action. Thus, one may make an approach to the green by making a nine-iron shot; he hits the nine-iron shot collaterally to approaching the green. Let us now change our venue to the practice range, where it is presumed that the imagined agent is trying to improve at making certain shots. Here it may be his purpose, not just to approach to the practice green, but rather to make a nine-iron approach to the practice green.

In such examples as the last, it is natural to say that one part of the agent's purpose is to make a nine-iron shot, and another part of his purpose is to get the ball onto the green.

Though we may discern 'parts' in both kinds of purpose—playing a piece on the piano and hitting a practice shot—they differ in one important respect. Whereas it may be one's purpose simply to make music present, where that could be done in a number of ways—by going to a concert or by switching on the radio or by playing the piano—as we usually regard ourselves and our fellow men, we do not naturally and easily think of acts having such purposes as being somehow more primitive than and prior to acts of playing the piano, going to a concert, *etc.* Rather the reverse. It would normally be a distortion to describe the piano playing as collateral to making music present. But in the golfing case, we do naturally and easily think of the act of approaching as a more primitive kind of act than that of approaching with a nine-iron. Agents would never do acts of the latter kind unless some agents sometimes played golf.

We might describe the latter kind of case by saying that what would normally have been regarded as the immediate purpose of a collateral act is now regarded as part of the ultimate purpose. The immediate purpose of the collateral act is absorbed into the ultimate purpose. Again, it becomes part of the agent's purpose to do the act in a certain way. But all these attempted descriptions are importantly inaccurate. We shall have to refine them. Still, we sometimes do think of acts in the way I have been indicating. It will be well to have a special name to facilitate our dealings with such acts. I shall call them *hybrid acts*.

A hybrid act pretty clearly is an act of a certain kind. The identification of the act implies that it is a hybrid. There is, therefore, a characteristic sort of purpose associated with hybrid action which we may call *hybrid purpose*. A hybrid act is an act with a hybrid purpose. How then to give a more exact account of hybrid purpose?

We noticed that a hybrid purpose has as one of its 'parts' another familiar kind of purpose which would commonly be specified to identify action. Had the actual situation been more normal, it would have been natural to identify the act as I and then describe it as being done by way of a collateral act D. But, the situation is not entirely normal. The act is done against a somewhat abnormal background of interest, activity, and achievement. We now see that it is part of the agent's purpose that he should be D-ing as well as I-ing. He is not I-ing by D-ing; rather, he is D-I-ing. This well illustrates what is always true, that behaviour is identified relative to the observer's understanding and knowledge. A physical transaction seen to be an act is not essentially hybrid or non-hybrid. It is to be identified as a hybrid only in consideration of another possible identification, only within a familiar scheme of identification. All this must come out in our definition of a hybrid purpose, and can be made to do so if we define hybrid purpose in such a way that the purpose would be identified expressly in terms of its 'parts'.

Now it is clear that if one's act is D-I-ing rather than simply I-ing, he could not have attained his purpose by D'-I-ing ($D' \neq D$). He would necessarily fail if anything kept him from D-ing. Now I schematizes a kind of purpose, to be identified by listing conditions of success. D is brought in to schematize what normally would have been a specification of the purpose of a collateral act now regarded as part of the ultimate purpose. But any such term also could be used to specify *a* purpose, to be defined by listing conditions of success, the failure of any of which would result in the failure to attain the hybrid purpose.

With that, we may now give our definition. A purpose H is a hybrid if and only if there are two purposes I and D, defined by conditions $C_{I_1}, \ldots, C_{I_n}, \ldots$ and $C_{D_1}, \ldots, C_{D_p}, \ldots$, respectively, where I is a purpose familiarly known to the observer as one which is commonly acted with, and D is familiar to the observer as a common way of doing acts of type I, and the conditions of success for H are $C_{I_1}, \ldots, C_{I_n}, \ldots, C_{D_1}, \ldots, C_{D_p}, \ldots$. In brief, every condition of success for I or D is a condition of success for H, and no condition of success for H is not a condition of success for either I or D.

143

If H be such a hybrid, I say that H is a hybrid of D into I. I call I the *Original Purpose* of H, and D the *Original Way* of H, *i.e.*, the Original Purpose is what would have been specified by the normal identification, and the Original Way is what would have been given as a normal description, where both are now 'parts' of the purpose. The Original Purpose and the Original Way can be separated by listing conditions of success. Thus, a condition of success for approaching is that there should be a green; a condition for hitting a nine-iron shot is that the player have a nine-iron; and both together are conditions of success for making a nine-iron approach.

We now define a *hybrid act* as an act with a hybrid purpose; since we identify an act by specifying the purpose, every hybrid purpose determines a type of hybrid action.

About hybrid acts we must observe the following. First, we cannot analyse a hybrid as an act which simply has a *double* purpose, the Original Purpose plus doing the collateral act, which is the Original Way. It is not that I want to hit the ball to the green *and* to hit the ball with a nine-iron; I want to hit a nine-iron shot to the green.

Second, hybrid purposes too may be attained by way of variant collateral acts, the mention of which does not identify The Act. For example, wishing to hit a nine-iron approach, I may do so by taking a full or a half swing. While it is thus always possible and necessary to distinguish collateral acts from The Act, it is sometimes easy to err in the separation, and that is particularly true in the case of hybrids. We must take care when dealing with hybrid acts not to misallocate certain features of the purpose as elements of the immediate purpose of some collateral act.

Finally, hybridization regularly occurs in certain special ways. Thus, acts of deception and jest, which are kinds of acts, are often conveniently analysed as hybrids. Or, one may do an act I, and he may do it in the right or the polite way D; but, again, it may be part of his purpose to do it in the right or the polite way—this last would yield a hybrid of D into I. Or, an agent may in French try to say something; or he may try to say it in French, and that would be a hybrid. The notion of hybrid is especially useful when dealing with Language, where 'style' and 'effect' are often what the speaker or the writer most desires. Because of such manifold applications, it is useful to have this notion in our armoury of technical apparatus.

16. MEANS AND ENDS

[A number of different conceptions of means and ends are distinguished, of which the most important are (1) the means is a collateral act by way of which The Act, which is the end, is done; (2) the means

144

is The Act done, and the end is the circumstances whose realization would make the act successful; (3) the means is a stage which must be got through before some other stage, which is the immediate end, can be reached; (4) the means is The Act done, and the end is the reason for which the act is done, or the fulfilment of a principle of reason for doing such acts.]

Our discussion of collateral action affords convenient entrance to the topic of Means and Ends, a subject whose complexity is as little recognized as its presence is inevitable in a general study of behaviour. This is an area in which philosophy has had an effect on common-sense, but not without confusing it. Here, as so often, we find philosophers employing a number of different, if related, conceptions which are easily confounded. Our immediate task is to sort these out, with an eye to seeing how they relate, not for the sake of any direct application, but to protect us from serious misunderstanding at later stages of our course. A little clarification may also contribute to the cause of good sense in daily life. Some philosophical *pictures* of means and ends play almost no role, if any, in life; but some matter a lot. Though frequently overlooked, the differences between those which do perform is marked in our Language. Thus one kind of relation of means to ends is signalized by the use of two present participles, *e.g.*, 'He was *charging* the meal by (means of) *signing* the bill'. In other cases, the end is set off by the use of an infinitive, *e.g.*, 'He was clearing the ground in order better *to plant* the garden'. In still other cases it would be best to use a 'that'-clause describing either a state of the world that would eventuate from the agent's act or indicating for what kind of a reason the agent did the deed. To illustrate the first case, 'He jumped that he might be out of the way of the car'; and, the second case, 'He jumped that he might avoid being hit by the car'. I do not for a minute think that these grammatical differences are of crystalline clarity or hardness. But they do suggest distinctions which it would be well to try to make explicit.

It is clear that we shall here be trafficking in *kinds* of action. I remind the reader that I sometimes speak of 'The Act', meaning an act of the *kind* the supposed agent is doing. 'The Act' compresses a supposed singular reference and a supposed typal identification; 'the act', by contrast, simply means 'the act done'.

Perhaps the most natural sort of situation for describing M as a means to an end E is the case of the two present participles, in which M is a *way* of doing an act of kind E. Giving M describes *how* The Act E was done; and giving E says *what kind* of act was done. Again, E is The Act done and M is collateral to E. Thus, signing the bill is one's means of charging the meal, which is one's end. Let us call that the *collateral act conception of means and ends*.

F   145

This case in fact divides. M may, on the one hand, be a way of doing E or, on the other hand, a way of doing E *successfully*. The end in the second case is *successfully doing*. One may protest at this for being logical conjuring, and quite correctly argue that there is no difference between the two cases so far as the agent is concerned, for in doing anything one acts, so to speak, for success. We would separate the two cases only to dissolve the idea of doing an act. But if, as we should, we hold hard to a third-person's (observer's) account of what occurred, the difference is plain to see, and may be given explicit expression. Thus, 'He charg*ed* the meal by signing the bill' leaves no question but that he succeeded, while 'He was charg*ing* the meal by signing the bill' does allow room for failure. The difference, therefore, seems real if somewhat unimportant. It certainly has no application to cases of deliberation over how to do an act.

A second major kind of relation of means to ends is that in which M is The Act done and E is the state of affairs whose realization would constitute the success of M. Thus, my act of putting a golf ball towards a hole is M, and that the ball should plop into the hole is E. In this kind of case, M is The Act and E identifies a state of affairs, the bringing about of which would render M successful. It is natural to fix M with a present participial form and E with a 'that'-clause. To give it a name let us call this the *success conception of means and ends*. Some might regard this notion of means and ends as spurious. In our verbal presentation, what follows the 'that'-clause surely identifies nothing beyond The Act itself, serving merely to make the identification more specific. E is little more than a further addition to M. We may always alter 'He does M that E' to 'He did M-E', *e.g.*, 'He was putting the ball at the hole'. Yet the form of speech 'M that E' occurs, if infrequently, and might by some philosophers be thought to express a relation of means to ends. For that reason we should be ready to recognize the case and say what it is. The form of description in question is expectedly more natural when the success of the act is shown by an event or happening subsequent to that happening which is the act. For this reason examples of the success conception of means and ends might easily be miscast as cases of our next type, the staging conception of means and ends. However, it must be insisted that we describe the event as an *end* ('E') only if it comes about as a result of action. Anyway, 'E' does not really schematize a reference to an event, but rather a possible description of events. If the act should fail and an event of type E not occur, it was still one's end to bring about an event of type E. What befuddles the matter is that we are identifying action in Language used to describe events which, in this kind of case, would, if they occurred, be separable from the supposed act.

146

A third familiar picture of means and ends is that in which M is one stage and E a subsequent stage in a programme of action, where reaching E is conditional upon having reached M. Imagine a man who wants to qualify for a job for which he must show a knowledge of German; he may take courses in German, during which he may be expected to pass examinations, which are stages on his way towards passing the course; but he may stage himself to take an examination by studying the night before. We may call this the *staging conception of means and ends*. It is the staging *picture* that leaps to mind, for it is a natural one, though I do not normally feel easy in describing actual cases which the picture fits in the language of 'means and ends'. And the idea is far from homogeneous, there being any number of different sorts of cases which the picture might be made to fit. Either or both M or E can be an act or a successful act; or a state of affairs which would result from a successful act; but it is not perfectly clear that particular acts need figure at all. Cases may be mixed. Thus a student may retire (act) early (how) as a means of being fresh (in a certain state) the next morning as a means of passing (succeeding) an exam (activity) as a means of being passed in the course (happening). All that is required is that E or an associated state of affairs be temporally subsequent to or thought to be consequent on M or an associated state of affairs; E, of course, need not be ultimate, and there may be some further E' to which it is M'. The programme of action so staged will usually not itself be a single act. If it ever is, and if the various stages are all describable in act-identificatory Language, then this chain of stages may be regarded as collectively collateral to The Act done, and the stages are all collateral means to that end. Here we would analyse a single act into an order of temporal stages each of which is fixed in act-identificatory Language. Thus, *putting* paper into the typewriter, *turning* the paper on the roller, *adjusting* the alignment, *etc.*, are all in turn done collaterally to The Act of *typing* a name on a letter, and success in each collateral act might be counted a means of coming to be able successfully to do the next collateral act.

A further general kind of case is that in which the act done is the means, and specification of the end indicates that the agent has a certain kind of *reason* for doing the act. Thus M might be an act of executing the prime minister, and E might be to expedite social reform, or to consolidate power, or to fulfil an assassin's contract. Strictly, specification of the end does not itself indicate the reason, which might be that the prime minister is an obstacle to social progress, or that the prime minister is a rallying point for the opposition, or that I have contracted to assassinate him. In giving E we specify, rather, a principle under which facts of certain kinds will count as reasons. So, in mentioning E as an end we are saying that

147

the agent's act *M* was done with a certain principle of reason. We may call this the *reason conception of means and ends*.

There are a number of hybrid cases, some of which we have already mentioned. An especially interesting kind of case is that in which *M* is the act done and *E* is a state of affairs which would mark the success of *M*, where the bringing about of *E* would require *no* explanation, the principle of reason being obvious. Thus, *M* might be an act of eating; if the agent were asked why he was eating, he might say, 'I'm only eating'.

There are still other models of means and ends, over which we need not dally long. First, we may take as the means the tools, implements, or sundry apparatus employed in doing an act, *E*. Second, we sometimes picture the end as the very object whose possession by the agent is the proof of his success in an act, which is the means.

My aim here has been to untangle a net so that it should not later catch us up and impede our progress. But there is an immediate lesson which is obvious. The fashionable formulas concerning means and ends which have been purveyed by philosophers and moralists are as equivocal as is the idea of means and ends itself. There are several ways in which it might be held that we cannot reason about ends, but only about means; several senses in which one cannot will the end without willing the means; and it is not obvious that these will all be equally true or false; indeed to the contrary.

17. ENDS AS REASONS: THE PRINCIPLE OF THE END

[One must have reasons, good or bad, for doing an act; but one may also have reasons for doing the act in a certain *way*, *i.e.*, by way of such and such kind of collateral act. In the latter connection, we may also mention facts, the knowledge of which might explain movements. Sometimes a description of an act specifying a collateral act might provoke a request for a reason. We may sometimes meet the request by saying *what* the agent was doing, *i.e.*, by specifying the purpose of the act. We may allow that this would count as a kind of reason, though not in the earlier explained sense of 'reason'. We denominate the general principle for this kind of reason the *Principle of the End*. Philosophers appear to have held, wrongly, that the Principle of the End is the only genuine principle of reason for action, a mistake which is abetted by certain common ways of thinking and talking about behaviour and action.]

In our earlier examination of reason we noted, but did not discuss, the distinction between reasons for doing an act and reasons for doing it in a certain way, *i.e.*, by way of a certain line of collateral action.

There certainly are both of these kinds of reason, and similar formulas apply to them. Reasons generally are facts, awareness of which facts might explain movements. Pre-eminent among the reasons for doing an act are that the conditions of success of the purpose be satisfied. Now a locution employed to mention a collateral act also specifies a purpose, to be defined by listing conditions of success. The correctness of a description of the act as done in a certain collateral way turns upon whether the agent actually believed that the conditions which define the immediate purpose of the collateral act were satisfied, and that these beliefs might explain his movements. From this it follows that reasons for doing an act in a certain way are also conditions of success, not for the ultimate but for the immediate purpose of the collateral act. Reasons of both kinds are alike facts, the knowledge of which would explain movements made. In short, we may found an explanation either of what an animal did or of how he did it on his presumed knowledge or beliefs—with respect to certain reasons or mistaken reasons. But for all that, they are different kinds of reasons. We commonly draw a distinction between whether what an agent did was reasonable and whether he did it in a reasonable way. People sometimes say, whether shamelessly or as a joke, that the wrongdoer's only mistake was in getting caught—the strangeness of which underscores the difference I have in mind.

Reasons commonly are elicited in answer to the question 'Why?'. I might identify an act, and you ask me why the agent did that, and my answer would give a reason for the act. What I initially said might, however, have also described how the act was done. Now, in answer to the question 'Why?' I might give an answer as before, mentioning a fact presumably known to the agent, thus indirectly explaining why he did what he did in the way he did: 'Why is he cleaning the rug by beating it?'; 'Because he has a beater but no vacuum'. But it may also be that my report does not enable my interlocutor to know *what* the agent did. Then I may indeed answer the question 'Why?' by saying *what* the agent did: 'Why is he pounding a nail in there?'; 'To make a hole in the screen'. I scarcely need argue that explanations-what are common: I explain noise coming from the box by saying what it is— a radio. But clearly enough that answer when given in connection with action does not specify a reason, as we have already seen; what it gives rather is the purpose of The Act.

Despite the difference between specifying reasons for and purposes of acts, it is still convenient to bring the latter kind of answer to the question 'Why?' under the umbrella of 'reason'. In the first place, the answer indirectly constitutes an explanation of the movements: he was moving so (indicated by our description of how he did whatever act he did) because he had such and such a purpose. But, second

149

and more important, a given way of doing an act is the more *reasonably* done the more effectively that line of collateral action conduces to the success of The Act done. The Act, the end in one sense of 'end', sets a kind of standard for the means in one sense of 'means'. The reason, if we may extend that idea, for doing things in one way rather than in another is to compass a successful conclusion for what one is doing. This can always be made specific by saying *what* the agent is doing—that is, by identifying the act. Let us say that such 'reasons' fall under *the Principle of the End*.

The Principle of the End, strictly taken, is not a principle of reason in the sense earlier introduced. This principle can never supply reasons for doing what is done, for the principle operates precisely by bringing to the forefront of attention what is being done, no matter the reason. Again, if asked to account for my behaviour, I may say that I am lecturing; that is, say what I am doing; or, I may say that this is the way I make my living. The first answer tells what I am doing, and the second why I am doing it. Let us, for the sake of contrast, call the latter *a principle of the act*.[1]

Though the distinction between principles of the act and the Principle of the End is easily drawn, it has nevertheless often been missed by philosophers, and even somewhat blatantly denied. Anscombe slides over the distinction (see pp. 65f.), and it appears that Aristotle also does, and indeed rather more deliberately, when he holds that we can reason about means alone (see *Nic. Eth. III*, 1112b.). But the most flagrant if most gallant attempt to suppress the obvious was Hume's provocative declaration that Reason is and should be the slave of the passions. The suggestion here is that somehow what we choose to do is always simply a result of personal impulse, a kind of blind manifestation of animal *connatus*. But of course, being more or less ignorant about the locale of action, we can cut more and less effective channels to the desired debouchment of our fervour. It is hard to state the thesis coherently and completely, but, perhaps partly because it never has been properly stated, it can be a very persuasive

---

[1] Part of what Kant may have been lamely and confusedly getting at in his distinction between categorical and hypothetical imperatives is just this distinction between reasons for doing an act and the Principle of the End. Of course, not all reasons for doing what one does must or should be *moral* reasons. An imperative need not, as Kant suggests, be moral in order to be 'categorical' in this sense; though one *could* argue that moral reasons are superior to all others and ought to prevail when relevant. Baier says useful things about Kant's distinction between categorical and hypothetical imperatives (*op. cit.*, Chap. 11, 2.1.).

The general distinction between the two kinds of reason, interestingly enough, is echoed in the Spanish use of 'para' and 'por'. To say 'para que' I act is to say what I am doing, while that 'por que' I act is my reason for doing whatever I do.

doctrine indeed. We are predisposed to accept this travesty of good sense for the following reasons.

First, the Principle of the End as a deliberative principle comes into operation only on the presumption that the agent has already decided what he means to do. At that point, there is no longer scope for him to deliberate about 'ends', and to consider reasons for acting as he does.

Second, we think of reason as theoretical reason only, as reason for believing. Hume has the merit of being explicit about this, though he speaks no less falsely for all that. Since it is held that reason is not to be discerned in action, an agent's reasons can only be a kind of adventitious accessory to action. That is, it is never that one acts on knowledge of the facts, though one might bring his knowledge of cause and effect more or less effectively to bear on the course of his attempts at success. But, I have urged, one cannot be said to act unless he is aware of his surroundings, and therefore one acts only on his knowledge or beliefs about the world. Reason, far from being adventitious to action, is essential to it.

Third, Hume's arguments witness a distinct predilection for one reason conception of means and ends—for one particular principle of reason. Hume tells us that it is not contrary to reason for one to prefer his own lesser good to his greater (*Treatise*, Selby-Bigge ed., p. 416). Normally that *would* be unreasonable, as Hume's choice of it as an example well shows. He also holds that one might prefer the destruction of the whole world to suffering a scratched finger (*loc. cit.*). That too would be contrary to reason. In both instances Hume is invoking the (genuine) principle of personal preference (significantly also called 'desire' and 'passion'); but in both cases he illicitly accords it a status it does not deserve, making it superior even to other forms of personal interest. The effect of this is to force all other considerations into a position subsidiary to the principle of preference; if having what one prefers is then regarded as the inevitable End, all other principles of reason, including egoistic principles, are brought under the principle of preference. Now that an agent prefers such and such is indeed a reason for his acting to acquire it or to bring it about: preference is a principle of reason. Sometimes there may be no other reason; but then again there may be. If we regard preference as a dominating consideration, as Hume appears to do, then that one kind of reason becomes the inevitable End of action. All other kinds of facts in the knowledge of which agents act are subordinated to facts which fall under the principle of preference, stated as End. Now agents rarely dare to *justify* their deeds by invoking the principle of preference—for that principle is characteristically operative where questions of justification do not arise; so, where

PART TWO: BEHAVIOUR AND ACTION

questions of justification must be answered, agents will regularly cite other kinds of reasons. Now if we regard reasoning as like justification (as many appear to do), we shall, by pursuing the above line of analysis, be led to conclude that agents reason only about means and not about ends: for if the only kind of reasons agents can allow themselves to submit have been antecedently forced under a spurious Principle of the End, we shall indeed be constrained to hold that agents can deliberate over and provide justification of only the means and not the end.

Fourth, we saw that reasons may always be stated in terms of what the agent 'wants to do'; Hume makes just the mistake commented upon earlier of taking this as the sign of desire, ultimately incapable of support by reason. (Something of the same is intimated by the word 'prefer': preferences not only supply reasons but may be supported by reasons.) But, again, what one wants to do, when filled out, would itself be a principle of reason, and it may be filled out in many ways.

Fifth, when we describe an act as done in a certain way we are drawing attention to what the agent knew or believed to be the case. Take it that he knew, then the facts, which are his reasons for doing such and such in this way, *might* have been reasons for his doing something else. I see that this is food before me. That food is before me may be a reason. If what I am doing is paying my respects by eating another Christmas dinner, then the reason is that I am showing my respect; eating what I see to be food, then, falls under the Principle of the End. But it may be simply that I am hungry. The facts in the knowledge of which one may act are not, in themselves and in complete isolation from the possibility of action, to be regarded as reasons, let alone as reasons of one kind or the other. Everything depends upon how the behaviour is to be identified. But now, it is not always immediately clear how behaviour is to be identified. And it may be that what is said to be an animal's reason for doing an act in a certain way is really his reason for doing what he is doing; or *vice versa*. But it is impossible that this should always be the case, for we introduce act-identificatory Language in connection with episodes where there can be no question that it is the agent's awareness of these facts that explains why he is doing *what* he is doing.

Another, sixth, factor tending to efface the distinction between the Principle of the End and various principles of reason is that we have many words in vernacular usage, whose employment at once implies a specification of purpose (the End) and a statement of reason, *e.g.*, our earlier example of 'answering a letter' which tells us that what the agent is doing is writing a letter for the reason that he owes a letter.

Finally, observe that by supposing that reasons bear exclusively on the choice of means, and by thus bringing the whole domain of reason under the Principle of the End, we *seem* at once to provide sense for an answer to the question over the justification of reason*s* in terms of a reason, while cleanly avoiding the difficult and possibly meaningless question over the justification of reason itself. One justifies his reason, according to this analysis, by saying what he means to do; and what he means to do is simply sheer *connatus*, brute unreasoned fact. I hope already to have shown that something more can be said about justifying reason. But even if it were not so, that would lend small support to investing the Principle of the End as the only ultimate reason. It looks ultimate solely because it is not a proper principle of *reason* at all. The Principle of the End is a principle of explanation by appeal to which we account for an animal's behaviour by saying *what* he means to do.

18. WHAT MAKES AN ACT SUCCEED

[Acts may succeed or fail. We identify the purpose of an act by specifying conditions which would preclude success, conditions which would necessarily make the act fail. There is, in general, no comparable specification of conditions which would make the act succeed, both because success in action is defeasible and because it is often measured by some ensuing effect or resulting production. These two explanations are connected: when the desired effect or production is not forthcoming, we naturally inquire what caused the act to fail. The conditions which explain the failure of the act may then come to be regarded as defining necessary conditions of failure for that type of action. That circumstances which would necessarily preclude success do *not* obtain are conditions of success, and they may be specified in any number, and may be classified in various ways, in particular according to whether or not they have to do with the states, dispositions, *etc.*, of the agent, or with the state of the world apart from the agent.]

An act of any kind may succeed or fail. We have observed that acts usually succeed, and that this is reflected in the Language we use to identify action. But in our theoretical account we have given more importance to failure, for it has been held that the purpose by specification of which an act is identified is itself identified by listing conditions under which acts having that purpose must fail.

But why not come straight at the matter, one may demand, and say right out what will make the act succeed? Because it is not possible, in general, to say 'what will make the act succeed'. That is so for two connected reasons, one of which we have already noticed.

153

That reason is that success in action, like many other ideas that apply to animal behaviour, is *defeasible*. We know that certain conditions make success impossible. Observing such conditions, we take it that the act fails. But supposing that such conditions do not actually obtain, we are normally entitled to presume that the act succeeds. Since most types of action are not especially difficult and since the agent is often in good position to observe the satisfaction of conditions of failure, and could then not so much as attempt the type of act in question, it happens that normally (not always) there is a *prima facie* or presumptive case in favour of success. But a presumption may always be questioned. A challenge to the supposed success of an act may always be issued, even long after the deed is done, where all that limits the form of such challenges is that they might, in principle, be met. This possibility of reiterated challenges to the presumed success of action engenders a progressive widening of our conceptions of types of action, for, by drawing attention to new features, *etc.*, which we say must or cannot be present, and by dividing and amalgamating conditions of failure, we introduce new kinds of purpose and so new kinds of action into our thinking. We have cited several examples of this, and they can easily be multiplied.

The second reason why we cannot say in general what will make an act succeed is that success is usually measured, externally and independently of the act, by some tangible resulting product or ensuing effect, *e.g.*, the table made or the lady's buying the table. While the desired product or effect could not be brought about if any essential condition of success should fail, that the conditions are met does not in itself bring about the desired product or effect. The fish just might not be biting. But even if they are, the angler still must cast his line. It is a mistake, as Wittgenstein once pointed out, to think that if only nothing keeps me from walking, I shall walk.[1] The act succeeds only if the agent succeeds, and if there is anything which makes the act succeed it can only be the deed itself.

It might be suggested that what ultimately makes the act succeed is the attempt, and that therefore one of the essential conditions of success is that the agent must *try*. But that won't do at all. Suppose the contrary, that *trying* is one of the conditions of success; that trying at least is something that the agent must do if his act is to succeed. Trying, we know, is always trying to do something. Put misleadingly, what one tries is to attain a purpose *P*. Mention of *P* is essential to the specification of the try. What one tries to do is an act of a kind at

---

[1] *Philos. Investig.*, part I, no. 183. 'But here we must be on our guard against thinking that there is some totality of conditions corresponding to the nature of each case (*e.g.*, for a person's walking) so that, as it were, he could not but walk if they were all fulfilled.'

which he may fail. Now the listing of conditions of success, supposed now to include that the agent try to attain *P*, would tell us not only what would make the act succeed, but would also serve to identify the purpose of the act. But clearly 'try to *P*' must mention the purpose *P*, and so cannot be among the conditions we are seeking. Trying is not a condition of success, it is rather a condition of *doing* (see p. 124), for it is the very doing of the act itself.

A more workable suggestion would be that an act succeeds if and only if, on the presumed success of an immediately collateral act, all essential conditions of success obtain, and the essential conditions of success are . . . . The mention of a collateral act assures us that the animal is really doing an act. While this explanation has possibilities as an account of 'what makes the act succeed', it does not seem to me to get away from the objections already registered against the likelihood of finding a general, workable formula answering the question. It would demand that we explain what is meant by the 'presumed success of a collateral act', and it would not by itself efface the defeasibility of success in action.

The two considerations we have mentioned, that success is defeasible and that it is often measured by some product or effect, are related. If the desired product or effect is not forthcoming, a *prima facie* case is created for saying that some essential condition is not met. It is rather as when a distribution of coin tosses is not 'normal'; we look for an explanation of the abnormal distribution in the one case and of failure in the other. In discovering such explanations of failure, we might then also come to divide and ramify the conditions which define the purpose. There is a tendency to make more and more of these features which might cause an act to fail into items whose presence would, even from the outset, be deemed to preclude success. Conditions which explain failure come to be regarded as defining, necessary conditions of failure. If one *knows* that there are no fish in the pond, he cannot be said to fish. That he *believes* there are fish in the pond is a condition for *doing* such an act. It is natural to regard *what* is believed as a defining condition of success (see p. 123). So we *might* stipulate that, since one can only fish for fish, if there are no fish one cannot succeed in fishing, whatever he might know or not know about the pond. There is no place at which developments of this kind must terminate. What sets it all in motion is the actual failure of action, and what makes it possible is the defeasibility of *success*. It would be a kind of madness to insist that we be hamstrung in advance by some sacrosanct listed set of conditions of success.

It is, in brief, an important feature of our conception of what I call 'action' that alterations in the identification of action should come about naturally and almost automatically in the normal course of affairs. So much is this so that we can only arbitrarily draw the line between alterations in identifications of action and increasing specificity in our understanding and definitions of such identifications. (It is again like drawing a line between two bands of colour. See p. 121.) Both kinds of change result from the knowledge that hitherto unconsidered conditions may matter.

So far I have concentrated on acts of a kind whose success is measured by a resulting product or ensuing effect. What I maintain holds equally if less obviously for those other types of act whose success is measured by the movements of the agent's body, e.g., jumping over a bar or wiggling one's ears. Here too one may fail, and not all the conditions of failure can be listed at any single sitting. Moreover, conditions which account for failure may or may not come to be included among the essential necessary conditions of failure. Take high-jumping; one succeeds only if he throws himself over a bar without displacing it. But the bar may fall by cause of the reverberation from a nearby explosion. If this happened very often, we might make it a condition of success or even a condition of doing such acts that no such explosions be taking place. Again, international committees have stipulated that a runner cannot succeed in an attempt to break the world-record in the 100-yard dash if he is favoured by an assisting wind in excess of 4·473 miles per hour.

All I have been holding is that we cannot find a *general* rule stating what makes an act succeed. I have argued for that by drawing attention to the way in which hitherto unremarked conditions may obtrude themselves upon our attention. Occasionally it *is* possible to say what will make a kind of act succeed, but only if we can avoid any detailed consideration of particular conditions. Later (Part III, no. 13) I shall introduce the notion of a *rule for succeeding*. By conforming to a rule for succeeding an agent will succeed, *provided* that all conditions of success, whatever they may be, are satisfied. For such kinds of action we could say that conforming to the rule makes the act succeed. Usually, however, we have no such formula available. We can determine the success of action only by attention to the resulting products or effects or to the shape of the movements made. These products, *etc.*, may then be consulted for information regarding conditions of success.

Suppose, now, that we can recognize the product, effect, or movement, should it be forthcoming. How do we know what conditions must be fulfilled if the act is to succeed? Alternatively, how do we know what would necessarily preclude success? These conditions will all concern 'elements' of the act other than elements of purpose; the purpose must be 'fixed' if the question is to be asked, and we define the purpose by a specification of those conditions. These conditions will, in brief, concern the agent, his movements, and his situation and circumstances. Of these, the movements are usually, but not always, the least important. In general, the conditions are 'what is given' and the movements are what the agent adds. It is this fact that makes attempts to define types of action as patterns of conditioned response so unsatisfactory, for such efforts generally stress the agent's movements and play down his circumstances and states, where the emphasis should be reversed. Take a couple of examples: one cannot successfully kick a football unless there is a football present; in this case, a further condition is that there must be nothing which would block the movement of both of the agent's legs. In order successfully to *take a gift* there must be another party proffering an object, and the agent must believe that the other wishes him to have the object.

Trying to fix this in a general formula, we would come up with something like the following: There must be a competent agent, making suitable movements upon an appropriate occasion. That may seem disappointingly empty. But I do not think anything better can be achieved for purposes of general theory. This play on 'competent, suitable, and appropriate' does still have the merit of reminding us that not any old thing is competent, suitable, or appropriate, and of guiding our analysis of particular cases in a useful direction.

The occasion, we say, must be appropriate. That means that the circumstances must be such as to insure that the act will not fail for certain reasons traceable to what happens around and about the agent. Thus to cast for fish requires that one move or be moved in or near the water, and if one lives in a houseboat he need transport himself no farther. But there are further conditions: The angler must have apparatus suitable for landing the fish, and must, in any case, make motions in the direction of the water. (If the waves, uncalled upon, throw fish into his boat, that is not fishing.)

Take as another example a putative instance of ballroom dancing; make it a case of dipping in a waltz. To succeed in such an act, one must make certain kinds of movements on certain kinds of occasion, certain other conditions being fulfilled, where 'certain' does not imply that we can list or otherwise categorically limit those conditions in advance. One must move like a dancer. But that is not enough. Were I now to stand, lifting my arm at the side from the elbow, balancing now on my left and now on my right leg, executing a series of curious manoeuvres, terminating in a dipping movement, some might guess that I was practising dancing or impersonating a dancer. But no one would think that I was dipping in a waltz. How could I be with neither music nor a partner? The occasion is not appropriate.

Focusing attention on the various elements in this manner reminds

157

us that acts fail and necessarily fail for specific reasons, as they cannot be said to succeed for specific reasons. The conditions may be immensely variable. Success may (or may not) depend on the identity, history, situation, and knowledge of the agent; the existence or the presence of a respondent; the disposition of certain properties; a background of custom, law, and the like. Consider that in certain cultures only a judge duly invested can pronounce criminal sentence, and he must do so in a courtroom, and there must be an accused and an ostensible violation of law. If any of these conditions are not satisfied, the sentence may be voided, the verdict quashed, and the act deemed not to have succeeded as a sentence. (This kind of case, resembling that of scoring in officiated games, is interesting because the act is 'deemed' to have succeeded so long as the act was done and the presumption of success remains intact. Once the sentence has been delivered, it cannot be held to have failed until it has actually been nullified by another judicial act. Perhaps, then, that is *the* condition of failure? Not necessarily, because the nullification may also be quashed. At all events we cannot give an advance list of all possible grounds for nullification.) Again, the success of the act may depend on some previous act's having been successful, *e.g.*, one may repay a debt only if he has previously succeeded in borrowing. Still again, certain acts may presuppose the possibility of doing other acts upon which they are, so to speak, parasitical. Thus practising doing something presumes that the agent be aware that someone might not merely practise doing the act but actually do an act of the kind practised. One cannot simply practise; he must practise something. In practising, the agent acts as if he were doing an act of the practised kind. Notice, moreover, that we could distinguish the practising of a kind of act from an act of the kind practised by observing that the one type of action requires the fulfilment of certain conditions which the other does not, and this quite apart from the one condition that an agent can practise only when aware that there is another kind of act that he is practising doing. Thus, to baptize requires the presence of a live body, while to practise baptizing does not.

For certain purposes it is useful to divide these various conditions into two categories, which may overlap. On the one hand, certain conditions concern the agent particularly—his state of body and mind, situation in the world, acquisitions and endowments. It may be, for instance, that he must be a citizen or member of a union or elected, or that he not be deaf and that he have learned to multiply, or that he believe or know certain special things. Other conditions concern the state of the world apart from the agent, *e.g.*, that a ball be present, or a jury have been called. We may respectively call these *conditions of the agent* and *conditions of the world*.

158

ACHIEVEMENTS, EFFECTS, AND PRODUCTS

19. ACHIEVEMENTS, EFFECTS, AND PRODUCTS: ENDOTYCHISTIC, EFFECTIVE, AND PRODUCTIVE ACTION

[The thesis is advanced that all acts, if successful, lead either to what are here called *achievements, effects*, or *products*. An achievement is moving oneself in a certain way; an effect is an alteration of something in the world; a product is an object whose existence and identity depend upon a producing act. These ideas are explained in reference to action, and the existence of the movement, the effect, or product, as the case may be, is the *measure* of an act's success. Products are divided into two general classes: those which are individuated in space and time and those which are not, the former being called 'material products' and the latter 'non-material products' or (alternatively) 'upshots'.

The thesis that the measure of the success of any act is an achievement, an effect, a product, or a combination of these, if true, leads to the conclusion that purposes may be correspondingly categorized, thereby yielding a possible exhaustive set of typifications of action according to the measure of success. Such presumptive types of action are respectively denominated *endotychistic, effective*, and *productive*.]

I have been speaking in such a way as to suggest that the measure of success of an act is to be found in the production of some one or more product or effect. I have also allowed that there are acts which succeed only if the agent manages on some occasion to get through certain desired movements. In the latter kind of case I call the act an *achievement*; if an act of the kind in question is successful, it is an achievement. (Clearly, this is not the ordinary sense of 'achievement'.)

I wish now to make this more explicit, and to set forth the thesis that all successful acts have either products or effects, or are themselves achievements. This, if true, would afford us, not strictly a classification, but a finite and exhaustive set of independently definable typifications of action according to what measures their success. That could come about only if a given purpose when attained would always be attained by an achievement, an effect, or a product. That is just what we would expect. Indeed, the utility of being able to say that the act is of one kind or another is that it might show the way to discovering conditions which are definitive of purpose. Thus, to have an effect, there must be something on which the effect is had. Failing that, the act cannot succeed. To produce a certain kind of product, I may need certain materials like wax and wire. To jump a creek (*viz.*, to move in a certain way relative to something else), there must be a creek to jump.

159

We must now say more particularly how this distinction between achievements, effects, and products is to be drawn. What is essential to the notion of an achievement is the following: Since the purpose is simply to make certain movements with respect to certain objects, we can, from a full identification-cum-description of the act done, conclude whether the act succeeded or failed. We wish now to define the corresponding kind of purpose, but so as to avoid difficulties due to the possibility of an act's having several purposes not all of which are of this kind. So, I say, a purpose is to attain an achievement if and only if we could conclude from a description of the circumstances of and the movements constituting that act whether it succeeded or failed. A successful act that has such a purpose I call an achievement. We shall find ourselves often wishing to talk about such acts without prejudging the question whether they succeed or fail. Unfortunately, I cannot find any suitable English word for that purpose. I have, therefore, to coin a term, and shall call such acts and their purposes *endotychistic*. [1]

Examples of endotychistic purposes are wiggling one's ears, jumping a fence, writing one's name, looking to see a bird, and going to bed.

An act will be said to have an effect if the agent by his movements in some way alters other objects which exist apart from him and may be identified independently of his act. According to this explanation, the agent has an effect on *other things*. The effect may be such as to alter the physical conditions, dispositions, attitudes, beliefs, of other objects which may or may not themselves be animals. The purpose of an act is *effective* if and only if an act having that purpose would succeed only if the agent's movements would bring about an effect. Acts having such a purpose are also to be denominated effective acts. An effective act, if successful brings about an effect.

Effects are not definitionally dependent upon action, in that an effect which might have been brought about by action might also have occurred without the intervention of animal agency. The burning down of a house may mark the success of the arsonist's act, but it might also have been due to lightning or spontaneous combustion. Interestingly, the possibility that an effect may come about without animal agency carries over to the case of what I shall call conventional effects. Property rights are most typically created by acts of exchange or appropriation; but they also may be founded on the fact of mere possession over a period of time. Similar observations hold for the state of matrimony and the possession of civil authority and rights of citizenship.

---

[1] Later, I shall call endotychistic Language acts *calculative acts*.

ACHIEVEMENTS, EFFECTS, AND PRODUCTS

Some might protest that an achievement (in the sense introduced above) is itself an effect, an effect which the agent has upon his total self. The need for 'total' shows what is wrong with that suggestion. While it is quite clear that the agent may have an effect on some particular part of his body, his fingernails or his hair, the 'whole self' is different. Observe that if it is one's purpose (*e.g.*) to clip his nails, a full identification of the act requires mention of the nails; but in looking to see a bird or in going to bed one does not alter or put away any part of the body, nor is it like directing the attention of another to a bird or putting another to bed.[2] Again, it is one's movements which are causally responsible for the effect one may have on another; but they can scarcely be held to be causally responsible for the movements one attempts to make.

We come now to *products*, a somewhat difficult idea. A product is something which is produced by an act or a number of acts. It is something whose existence and identity in some way or other depends upon acts of the kinds in question, whereas an effect is upon an independently existing and identifiable something. How then to clarify 'in some way or other'? I wish to allow that some products may be produced many times by many acts, as when we reassemble a dismantled television set, or when the composer rewrites the lost sonata. Furthermore, the product may be identified independently of a particular act or connection of acts. But the point is this: A product, in contrast with just any old thing, must have been produced by some agent or agents acting sometime, and it is an *essential* fact about it that it should be partially identified by the kinds of acts which produced it. For example, if we know that something is a table (and not just something that could be used as a table) or music (and not just sound, *e.g.* wind in the trees), we then and there know that it must have been produced by acts of carpentry or acts of playing music. A product, then, is an object brought into existence by an act or a number of acts, where that remains an essential fact about the object even when it is regarded apart from any particular act. (Strictly, products often issue, not from particular acts, but from *activities*, which may involve many people's co-operating. This is a messy complication, but does not endanger the distinctions I am attempting to make. I am committed to saying *only* that some acts produce products and all products issue from some act or acts.) It follows from what I have said that a product, unlike an effect, cannot be produced except by animal agency.

[2] The point I am trying to make is rather like one that Hampshire notices (*op. cit.*, p. 8): while the various members of the body might be regarded as like instruments which may be alternative one to another, the whole body cannot be so regarded.

Products, like effects, are of many kinds. It is not in order here to go into details regarding these various kinds, except to remark one important if obvious division. Certain kinds of products are individuated in space and time, and others are not. Thus, a table maximally occupies a single, connected region of space at a given time. A performance of a play—not to be confused with the play performed—occupies a single connected region of time at a given place. Such objects are either put together once and for all, or must be destroyed or dismantled before they may be reproduced. I call such products *material products*. But there also are products which are not individuated in space and time. Examples are Beethoven's 5th Symphony, the American Constitution, The United States Steel Co., and the statement that $-1 = e^{\pi i}$. Such objects can be reproduced without first having to be destroyed; *e.g.*, it is quite conceivable that Beethoven should have written out the 5th Symphony several times over. These I call *non-material products* or, alternatively, *upshots*.

Upshots, if you wish, are 'abstract objects'. But they are not 'universals'. A universal is something under which particulars might fall, but, while 'non-material products' may be reproduced, what is then produced is not an instance but the product itself. Universals are entirely atemporal. Upshots, on the other hand, come into existence at some time or over a stretch of time, though they may then persist for evermore. Universals, *e.g.*, the colour yellow, are not 'produced', as products must be. Finally, I would observe, upshots are singular things, regularly (though not invariably) referred to with proper names, and that is not the case with universals. 'Beethoven's 5th' and 'The French Defence' sound much more like proper names than does (*e.g.*) 'blue'. A non-material product is contrived; it is a complex thing set together in no *a priori* order; and the expression by which we identify it may, as proper names characteristically do, convey a sense of this logically disorganized complexity. [3]

While upshots are not universals, there is a sense in which they may be said to have instances. There may be *performances* of Beethoven's 5th, *numbers*, *editions* and *copies* (all different) of *The San Francisco Chronicle*, and *assertions* of statements, to select but a small number of different kinds of case. Adopting a useful word from the vocabulary of the theatre, let us call these *productions* of the upshot. A production may itself be the result of an act, in which case it is a product, a *material* product. In the more familiar sense of 'instance' a production is always an instance of a universal; *e.g.*, it is an instance of *production of Beethoven's 5th* or *Copy of the American Constitution*. It is essential that upshots may have productions, and

[3] See J. Searle, 'Proper Names', *Mind*, 1958, pp. 166–73. Also, Wittgenstein's *Investigations*, part I, no. 79, and my *Modes of Referring*, pp. 56–62.

indeed they often are identified for the particulars they are, *in* particular productions, much as those particular products, which are the productions, are themselves primarily identified in the regions of space and time they may occupy. Characteristically, an upshot is not reproduced in its productions, nor need it be produced in a production at all. Surely there are pieces of music which have never been played. Still, it is conceivable that one might produce a musical composition by playing it off on the piano. [4]

I am aware that many will resist the whole idea of an upshot, some on the spurious grounds of nominalistic distrust or compunction, and others on the more substantial ground that the upshot can be nothing more than a successful production. It might also be held that I am making symphonies and promises look much more like tables and chairs than they really are. I shall return to this objection later when we come to the important case of conventional upshots (pp. 313f.). For the moment, I wish simply to deny that the upshot is no more than a production. It cannot be true, because, first, an upshot may have many productions or none at all; and second, I may refer to a symphony or a promise without hearing the symphony played or the promise made, as when I say that Hayden's Toy Symphony is by Leopold Mozart or that John kept the promise. I also deny the charge that I am too closely assimilating symphonies and promises to chairs. I have supplied an independent characterization of *product, material product,* and *non-material product* (upshot); it simply remains to determine whether tables and symphonies are products and, if so, of what kinds. But this account also enables me to begin to say how symphonies differ from tables, and we shall later also be able to say how promises differ from symphonies.

Allowed my generalized notion of a product, I wish now to say that a purpose is *productive* if and only if an act's having that purpose would succeed only if the movements constituting the act would lead to or contribute to bringing a product into existence. An act is productive if it has a productive purpose.

My general thesis is that every act is either endotychistic, effective, or productive. An act must be one of these, but it may be any or all of them. The latter possibilities result from two facts. First, a given

[4] I am indebted to Mr. Charles Caton for first drawing my attention in a generalized way to upshots. See also Professor Nowell-Smith's contest question, 'Is *Paradise Lost* a general name, proper name or what?', with contributions by P. Swiggart and T. Hunt, *Analysis,* 1958, pp. 1–7. R. Meager ('Tragedy', *Proc. Arist. Soc. Supp. Vol.,* 1960, pp. 165–86, esp. p. 167) also intimates the distinction between material and non-material products in her explanations of our different attitudes towards the originals of paintings and manuscripts of musical scores. Paintings and statues are material products, whereas pieces of music and works of literature are upshots.

act may have several purposes of different kinds. Second, an act might be productive and, hence, such as to succeed only if it contributes to bringing a product into existence, and yet do that by way of bringing about an effect: an act of knocking a table leg into a table top has an effect on both pieces together, but also contributes to bringing a table into existence.

In dealing with products, effects, and achievements, we have been investigating indirectly and in a general way by what criteria the success or failure of an act is to be measured. Before quitting this topic, two further isolated observations. First, an act may *more or less* succeed, and for two reasons. In the first place, the agent may (though in general he will not) have several purposes, some of which he attains and some not. But, also, any single product or effect one produces may be only more or less perfect, and success is proportionate.

The second isolated fact is that one may fail or succeed, as the case may be, without anyone, including himself, ever finding out. Of course, there must be some way by which someone *could* find out, but the search may not be essayed, nor, if it is, need it turn out successfully.

20. KNOWLEDGE OF SUCCESS, WITH REMARKS ON THE CONCEPT OF LIKING[1]

[Though an animal must be aware of something in order truly to be said to act, he need not be aware that his act succeeds or fails. But provided that he has attained sufficient behavioural sophistication, he will usually also have that knowledge. By way of contributing to the ancient search for a definition of *pleasure*, the idea of *liking* is provisionally explained, first, in terms of appreciative awareness, and then in terms of an analogical extension upon the idea of being aware of success in acting: an animal likes something if it is a fact that he is

[1] In revising this section, I have profited from discussions with Mr. D. L. Perry, and from reading an unpublished work of his on the concept of Pleasure. There is a large and growing contemporary literature on the topic of pleasure, including writings by Anscombe, Baier, Bedford, Gallop, Mauser, Nowell-Smith, Ossowska, Penelhum, Thalberg, B. A. O. Williams, and others. I confine explicit reference to the near-classical discussions of Ryle (Chap. IV of *Dilemmas* and 'Pleasure', *Proc. Arist. Soc.*, *Supp. Vol.*, 1954) and to a paper by W. B. Gallie ('Pleasure', *Proc. Arist. Soc.*, *Supp. Vol.*, 1954). My own account resembles those of Aristotle (*Nichomachean Ethics*, esp. 1175a–20, and *De Anima*, 431a–8), Hobbes (*The English Works of Thomas Hobbes*, ed. Sir Wm. Molesworth, Vol. III, p. 42), Spinoza (*Ethics*, Part III, Def. II), but esp. Kant (*Critique of Practical Reason and Other Works in Moral Philosophy*, trans. L. W. Beck, p. 124 n.). Gallie says some things which suggest a similar account. See *op. cit.*, p. 160.

aware of it as one he now reacts to as he would to the attainment of some purpose.]

We have defined action and purpose so as to imply that one does an act only if he is aware of something. But his act may raise all sorts of questions to which he may not know the answers. That is so even if the creature has sufficient Language to know that he is doing what he is doing. In particular, and as we observed at the end of the last section, he may not know nor be able to come to know by mere reflection whether he succeeded or failed, although, having sufficient Language, he can know by mere reflection what it *would be* to succeed or fail. The ensuing result may be beyond his immediate reach in both space and time. An agent, in short, may do an act and so 'know what he's about', and perhaps he may more fully even know what he is doing, but still not know whether his act succeeds or fails.

It is nonetheless true that most acts are such that if the agent has sufficient capacity in the use of Language, he can know that he succeeds or fails, and possibly (beforehand) know that he will succeed. As to what he *has* done: if the results of the act are within his purview, he can directly become aware of those results and, having Language, by reflection come to explicit knowledge that his act was successful. Most acts issue in movements, products, or effects which are indeed within the agent's field of observation. As to knowledge of success of acts contemplated: most acts do succeed, because we usually first come to have the kind of purpose which typifies the act on occasions where success is assured. I cannot doubt that I shall succeed in rising from my chair, as I shall presently do, because I first came to do such acts when there was no possibility of my failing to bring off the deed. While only an agent with Language has full theoretical knowledge of what his purposes are, ability often to be *unaware* of the outcome of his acts is also the privilege of Language, which alone enables him to act to attain purposes whose results are not within his immediate purview, and even to *know* in the fullest sense that he will fail, *e.g.*, my kicking for an 80-yard goal. Since the object of desire cannot be directly presented, we need some verbal way of bringing it to the agent's attention.

Knowledge of success or failure in action relates to a concept on which centres one of the classical problems of philosophy, a problem which has traditionally been presented under the title of 'Pleasure'. The problem, vaguely put, is to give an analysis of the concept of pleasure. The claims which have been made on behalf of pleasure in Ethics as an ultimate criterion of value lend importance to the problem. We shall not bother about that, but seek merely to throw light on the question of what pleasure may be, whatever its value. Unfortunately, the question as we have stated it is so extremely vague as to be almost without sense, and attempts to make it more definite lead us into a labyrinth. Presumably the problem has to do with the use of the word 'pleasure' and cognates, and equivalent expressions in other languages. The first difficulty is that 'pleasure' is obviously employed in many related ways, not all of which are equally important for the problem. The most central uses, I believe, are those in which an animal is said to get, take, or gain pleasure and that in which we say that the animal is pleased, or that something pleases someone. But 'pleasure' is used, differently in the singular and the plural, in ways roughly equivalent to one's choice (*e.g.*, 'The King's pleasure'), to signalize the sources of one's pleasure ('My pleasures are few'), or as a moralizing term to mark possibly vicious and voluptuous self-indulgence ('a life of pleasure'). There are doubtless other easily identifiable uses of the noun. Apart from straightforwardly signalizing the getting of pleasure (*e.g.*, 'I was pleased that he was able to come'), 'pleasure' and its cognates are employed derivatively, I believe: (1) to indicate that a certain kind of reason is being given ('Why is he reading Prescott?'; 'Because he enjoys [takes pleasure in] reading history'); (2) as a device for terminating questions about reasons and motives ('Why is he saying such stupid things?'; 'Just to irritate her'; 'But why does he so much want to irritate her?'; 'Well, he just gets pleasure from (enjoys) doing that sort of thing'); (3) as a motive-fixing epithet ('He was doing it only to please himself [not, *e.g.*, to help the cause]'; 'For his own sweet pleasure'). Presumably 'pleasure' as a topic-fixing abstract noun covers all these different uses. But, though related, they do not all come to quite the same, and we may easily and unconsciously fall into error as we move from one use to another.

The second difficulty is that 'pleasure' in 'gets pleasure', say, is not the only word that figures in the picture. A short list would include cognate adjectives, 'pleasant', 'pleasing', 'pleasurable', all of which are somewhat different in force. To these we must add 'enjoy' and its cognates, 'glad' and 'agreeable', 'satisfying' and its cognates, 'gratifying' and its cognates, 'delight' and its cognates, 'approve' and its cognates, and many others. (I exclude such items as *joy, happiness, thrill,* and *rapture.*) It would be important to determine and to come to understand the different ways in which the included words contribute to different idioms (*e.g.*, 'take pleasure in', 'gain pleasure from', 'get pleasure out of', *etc.*). What matters for now is that these terms, different as they may be, fix concepts which are closely related to an alleged central concept of pleasure. It is no accident that pleasing things often please (not always), that we easily move from talking about what we enjoy to what pleases us, *etc.* This raises the question whether there is indeed this alleged central concept of pleasure. It is

166

notable that no one of the terms we mentioned seems to cover the whole field.[2] So perhaps there is no such field.

I think there is the field, though I doubt that there is a single, completely central concept of pleasure. I also think that there is a factor common to all these apparently near-central concepts which seem to cluster together. I believe that this common factor is approximately fixed by a common use of the word 'like'. This is highly conjectural, and I have no argument, except to consider examples.

If it can truly be said of me that I enjoy playing golf, watching football, the taste of mushrooms, or thinking about philosophy, it follows that I *like* to play golf, watching football, the taste of mushrooms, and to think about philosophy. If it pleases me to hear nice things said about myself, it follows that I like to hear nice things said about myself. If I am gratified at a promotion, find the evening pleasurable, or I'm glad to hear the news, then all of these things are to my liking. 'It was an agreeable conversation, and I liked it very much'. I can see and say that something is pleasant or pleasing, without being pleased by it, in which case it's not necessarily to my liking, but I certainly do imply that it's the kind of thing which is apt to be to someone's liking.

Borrowing and adapting results from Perry, I would venture to define pleasure in the sense of *being pleased about* as a liking for something which is a matter of recent knowledge or belief and of personal interest to the animal in question and which implies that the animal believes the matter to be a positive good.

Enjoyment is a kind of liking for some actual object for what it is in itself, where the object in question involves either the subject's behaviour, experience, or thought, or is an occurrent transaction in the world of which the subject is immediately aware.[3]

---

[2] I was once inclined to favour 'gratification', and at another time 'appreciation' as a title. But these are scarcely any better than any others. However we answer the questions, the traditional problem of pleasure, like that of excuses, seems to be an outstanding candidate for Austinian analysis (see, *e.g.*, 'A Plea for Excuses', J. L. Austin, *Philosophical Papers*). Here we have a tremendous diversity of related conceptual phenomena, reflecting characteristic discriminations in human concern, and for which we could hope to find a number of fairly general, distinguishing principles, marked by the occurrence of certain words and affixes. One is mistakenly apt to think that it is all very vague, uncertain, *etc.* (see, *e.g.*, Gallie, *op. cit.*, pp. 154f.). To the contrary, it is all too exact. What is vague and uncertain is our understanding.

[3] A note on some *differentiae*. Something is *pleasant* if it is regarded as an object from which an observer is apt to *get* pleasure.

Something is *pleasing* if it is regarded as an object which is apt to *give* pleasure to someone.

A pleasant face is one which it is nice to look upon; a pleasing face is one which makes itself nice to look upon.

I wish now to try to put my finger on and to isolate the conjectured common factor of liking.

My efforts follow the suggestion of Aristotle, that we might be able to explain pleasure (liking) in connection with the analysis of behaviour. Aristotle tells us that pleasure is the completion of activity. I think that that can be jiggled into a nearly correct analysis of *liking*, where I say 'nearly' because I admit in advance the possibility of counter-examples which I am not able to deal with in a satisfactory way.

The question is, What does 'completion of activity' mean?. There are two difficulties here.

First, Aristotle's use of the word '*energia*' (activity) is obviously extremely wide. If pleasure is the completion of activity, then, since we can get pleasure from behaviour, sensation, the having or the acquisition of knowledge, bare physical movement, or merely doing nothing, presumably any of these things may qualify as activity. And perhaps they do. But we don't know all that is included here. We need something more specific. I propose to utilize precisely the notion of *action* as we have defined it.

Second, Aristotle is not constant in what he appears to mean by *completion* of activity.[4] Sometimes he appears to mean simply movement with purpose, *i.e.*, action. At other places he appears to mean *successful action*—what completes the activity is success. But clearly neither of these will do for the analysis of pleasure or liking. If completing action is pleasure, then what completes the act is not just getting through, for the act could have disastrous results. Nor is it yet enough that the act succeeds, for clearly the agent will not be pleased unless he knows or at least believes that the act succeeds. So let us take that as our interpretation. What completes the act is the knowledge or at least the belief that the act succeeds. Knowledge or

[4] See D. W. Hamlyn, 'Behavior', *Philos*, 1953, esp. pp. 60–64.

Something is *pleasurable* only if it is enjoyable; *i.e.*, it must be an activity, *etc.*, immediately experienced and not known by report.

The *pleasure of* (*e.g.*, seeing Venice again, vanquishing a foe) is something the animal likes and which globally occupies his activity, attention, *etc.* The *pleasures of* (*e.g.*, hiking, vanquishing a foe) are not (*e.g.*) the hike itself, but incidental attendants thereto which one likes.

One is *gratified* at something only if it is not something which he would be entitled entirely to expect. One is *satisfied* with something only if it meets or fulfills something, a wish, demand, purpose, *etc.*

Something is *agreeable* to an animal only if both the thing and the animal make a contribution to the animal's liking the thing. It suggests active participation on the part of both the thing and the animal.

And so on.

belief of success in one's own action is one species of what we mean by *liking*. More narrowly described, it is a kind of *satisfaction*. [5]

It is clear that this is not yet sufficient as a *general* characterization of liking. The object of liking need not be one's own behaviour. One may enjoy or get pleasure from good news or the autumn sun. But it surely does give a clue. If the analysis is right for the case of action, then it follows that liking is not to be classified with physical stimulation, though physical stimulation may be one object of liking. If it is to be classified under traditional categories, then *liking* will be better cast as a kind of cognition. But this must be carefully qualified. First, the liking is not itself the agent's being aware of or knowing or believing such and such, but is rather the *fact* that the agent knows or believes such and such. Whether the agent is right or wrong, he likes what he likes. Second, the knowledge (if knowledge) is not necessarily full-fledged theoretical knowledge-that, for we can truly speak of creatures without Language liking this or that. It is in the nature of awareness, as that idea was earlier explained in connection with our attempts to pin down purpose. The creature is aware of something if a Language-using animal who acted in or was affected in an analogous way could come to know something, or would be held to have knowledge or belief about that something.

My provisional conclusion is that liking is the fact (state, circumstance) that an animal knows or believes something or other. It remains now to try to be more specific about the 'something or other'. I have suggested that what an animal likes is somehow connected with action; his liking is to be equated with the fact (state, circumstance) that he knows or believes that his act succeeded. How now to generalize this special case?

We would do so by putting some appropriate constraint upon the nature of the awareness or belief. Now normally, when one succeeds in an act, he would regard that as a good thing. Only if there were other attendant circumstances, consequences, *etc.*, which he did not or was not able to take into account would that not be so. Confining attention, therefore, to the act itself, the agent likes what he did, if he is *appreciatively aware* of the result. Generalizing, he likes what he did if and only if he appreciatively thinks that the result was as he wished. I propose, therefore, as a more general thesis, that liking is the fact of appreciative awareness or belief.

Liking essentially involves the agent's supposed good or evil, as an observer would view it. When we say that an animal likes something,

---

[5] So pleasures can be false after all? No, for the act is no less 'complete' because the belief is false. On the other hand, perhaps the agent ought not to be satisfied if he mistakenly believes that his act was successful.

we take it that he believes himself to have received something that he values. Probably the most fundamental objects of liking are the possession of objects, experience, sensation, and the satiation of appetites. At higher levels of development, success in action becomes such an object of personal value, that of course being our model case. My conclusion is once again anticipated by Aristotle, who said, 'To feel pleasure or pain is to act with the sensitive mean towards what is good or bad as such' (*De Anima*, 431a–8).

That an object be of value to an animal does not imply that it is valuable, *tout court*. People often value things which they may even know are of no positive value, objectively regarded. Still it is reasonable to suppose that the notion of objective value presupposes that some things are valuable to particular animals. Conspicuous among these objects of personal value are what we previously called 'natural goods' (see p. 74). As a consequence of this, we see that hedonism, as an explanation of the difference between good and evil, is a theory which reverses the truth. We define *liking*, hence pleasure, in terms of what is regarded as good or evil, and not conversely. If, however, we take hedonism as the doctrine that sensation is the basic object of liking, then it may indeed be true.

This idea of appreciative awareness or belief is rather tricky, and easily subject to misinterpretation. An animal is appreciatively aware of an object if he is aware of it as he would be aware of something which the conceptualizing observer could say is a natural good for the animal. The animal *A* is appreciatively aware of an object only if an observer could discern that *A*'s behaviour is analogous to what he would observe when *A* acquires a natural good. Now, it is not implied that the subject animal is aware of two things—the object and its value for him. He is aware of the object only. But the manner in which his awareness shows itself in his behaviour entitles the observer to describe that awareness as evaluative or appreciative awareness. Appreciative awareness is the most elementary practical counterpart to theoretical knowledge of personal good.

As a first formulation of what we mean by 'liking', I would therefore propose:

A likes *O* if and only if *A*'s behaviour shows that he is aware of *O* or shows that he believes that *O* exists in the same way as he would be aware of receiving an object which an observer would be entitled to say is a natural good for *A*.

A's liking O is the fact that *A* likes *O*.

This account of appreciative awareness in terms of behavioural responses which resemble the acquisition of natural goods strongly suggests the possibility of analogically extending the model case of the fact of being aware of one's own success in action into a general explanation of liking. It is clear that liking is not always a matter of the fact that an agent believes that he attained a purpose. Many, if not most, of our pleasures come unsought. But still we have explained liking in terms of what an observer would see in an animal's behaviour. And clearly enough the acquisition of a natural good could constitute the attainment of a purpose.

Therefore, as an alternative explication, I propose: *A likes O* if and only if he reacts to *O* as he would to the attainment of some purpose. 'Reacts as he would to the attainment of some purpose' is suggested by 'behaviourally shows awareness or belief that he has acquired a natural good', and is put forward as an analysis of 'appreciative awareness or belief'.

If the supposed animal has sufficient use of Language, we can make it more concrete: *A* likes *O* if and only if he believes that *O* exists or that *O* is the case and he regards *O* as something which he now believes it would have been a purpose of his to bring into existence or to bring about had the thought occurred to him that that would have been possible. One likes the warm sunshine if he is aware of the warmth of the sun as something which he would if he could have acted to move himself into, had he known (as he now does) of its nearby presence.

Against this account it might be urged that there are many things that people like or would like which no one could conceive of as being anyone's purpose to bring about, *e.g.*, gardens in the Antarctic or a stellar explosion. But I think I have protected myself with the use of the conditional mood. One need not, as it seems to me, envisage himself or anyone else's acting to bring about *O* in order for us to say that he reacts to it as he would to the bringing about of something. I admit to having heavily analogized the idea of a natural good. But it is not entirely clear that the objection is true whether or not decisive. One could appeal to the possibility of supernatural agency to give sense to 'attainment of purpose' in our explication. Disallowing that, we still must make a distinction between what we *can* envisage could be done by action (*e.g.*, landing on the moon as against causing a stellar explosion) and what we *could* envisage could be done by action (two millennia ago no one could have said, 'I can envisage that we could effect a landing *on* the moon by our own action'; today I think we can say, 'We could envisage someone's causing a stellar explosion'). So long as we could (present tense) envisage that such and such could be brought about by action, then we can think of it as possibly counting as the attainment of a purpose.

I am not entirely satisfied with this defence of my explication of *liking*. I offer it as an account which might be true and which, at a minimum, it seems to me, comes very close to being true.

21. TOWARDS A FORMAL THEORY OF ACTION: THE ELEMENTS OF ACTION

[To facilitate a formal statement of criteria for action, our theory of action is re-formed as a theory for the analysis of acts into elements. These elements are of four kinds: the agent, identified in some standard way; elements of the occasion; elements of movement; and beliefs that conditions of success of the act are satisfied, which beliefs are elements of the presence of the purpose of the act. Elements of all these kinds must be shown to be present in order to prove that an act exists. Specification of elements of movement serves to individuate an act, and we re-identify an act by establishing that these elements are the same. Specification of elements of the presence of the purpose fix the typal identifications of the act. Certain other act-characterizations may also be introduced in terms of these different elements. Special warnings are posted against equating act-elements, especially elements of movement, with acts of which they might be elements.]

A well-formed theory of action must either straightforwardly state suitable tests or criteria for establishing the existence, identity, and both typal and descriptive characteristics of acts, or be so formulated as to imply what these criteria would be. [1]

Foreshadowings of such test formulations are discernible in the preceding material. But I have not yet attempted a formal statement, nor could I have without an account of testing. Now, quite often we can formulate a theory in terms of basic elements, which would imply the desiderated formulations of the tests. I propose now to give just such a formulation of our theory of action. I am well aware that there are risks attaching to the construction of such theories, but I hope to be wary enough to escape misdirection.

Elements are always introduced for purposes of theoretical analysis of complexes into elements. Therefore, what is to count both as an element and as a complex is always decided in consideration of a background of theory, perhaps implicit, against which analyses are conducted. Indeed, the use of some theories is hardly more than the employment of some scheme of analysis into elements, and we begin to make the theory explicit by saying what the elements are and how they combine. The theory enables us to articulate gross phenomena into their elements and, by attention to possible combinations of elements, we can then specify the criteria for that type of phenomenon. In order to understand the operations of such theories we must be consistently clear that the complementary notions of complex and element are co-determining, and that the definitions of both are

---

[1] A formal statement of a theory of theories of this kind, including a theory of testing, will be developed in a sequel to this volume.

relative to the theory. The elements of one theory (*e.g.*, the ions of chemistry) might be the complexes of another (Quantum Mechanics). The same gross phenomena, as known to commonsense, might be variously restructured as complexes according to different theories.

There are many familiar examples of such theories. The prime instances are classical theories of chemistry according to which material substances are variously analysed into ions or bonded elements in conformity with rules of valence. Contemporary Quantum Mechanics, as I understand, would analyse chemical elements and other phenomena too into assorted particles consisting in turn of elements of mass, charge, spin, parity determination, *etc.* Still again, classical geometry affords various ways of analysing configurations into points. Plato in *The Theaetetus* and *The Sophist* used the analysis of words into letters as an analogy for explaining Language;[2] phonemic analysis of utterances into elements of sound is a contemporary counterpart which is actually extended as morphemic and sememic analyses for the very phenomena which Plato was concerned to elucidate.

Elements, I say, are introduced for the analysis of gross phenomena which are thereby restructured as complexes. Elements are elements and complexes complexes only within a theory. In applying such a theory we must not think of the elements as small-scale instances of complexes into which we resolve the phenomena by use of the theory. Ions are not small molecules, sounds not small words, points not small intervals, and, similarly, as I shall insist, movements are not small acts. Moreover, an element cannot be isolated as an element except as the element of a complex. A mistaken tendency to attempt just that abets conceptual difficulties over (*e.g.*) ions and mathematical points. It is of the essence of a mathematical point that you cannot (*e.g.*) measure it as you measure intervals, if only because a theoretical account of measurement makes essential appeal to bounding points; similarly, we cannot accumulate collections of ions in the same ways we accumulate collections of molecules. Now we may switch our interest, and, taking the elements as gross phenomena, submit them to analysis as complexes of elements: *e.g.*, points are analysed as ordered triples of numbers. But in doing that the governing criteria would alter. Quantum analysis, I take it, is not simply a more refined chemical analysis, and phonemic analysis is certainly not a more refined morphemic analysis.

Let us now turn to action. An act exists if and only if an animal behaves with purpose. An act is an item of purposive (animal) be-

---

[2] See *Theaetetus*, 201D–208B, and G. Ryle, 'Letters and Syllables in Plato', *Phil. Rev.*, 1960, pp. 431–51.

haviour. An item of behaviour is a sequence of movements in and/or of an animal occurring at a certain place over a certain stretch of time, *i.e.*, on a certain occasion. We individuate, reidentify, and typally identify the act solely by mention of the identity of the animal, of how he moved on what occasion with what purposes. Here, then, are four basic categories of the elements of action: elements of the agent, elements of movement, elements of occasion (situation, space and time), and elements of a present purpose. Elements of each of these kinds must be co-ordinately present if an act is to exist.

Now, movement, purposes, *etc.*, are disparate items. We must, at this level of analysis, take care not to assimilate them one to another, or to reduce them to one. They all are essential, and some of each of them must be present if we are correctly to say that an act was done.

Consistent with what was said about the relation of elements and complexes in general, we must also take care not to suppose that acts are elements of action or conversely. There is scarcely any danger that this would happen for the elements of agent, occasion, and purpose.

But one might hesitate over movements. After all, can't any movement be an act? That depends on the intended force of 'can'. Notice first that a movement taken as gross phenomenon need not be an act or an element of an act. It may, for instance, be reflexive, or perhaps part of a pattern of 'undirected behaviour'. But suppose it now is regarded as an element of an act. It is clear that an act may be constituted of a number of movements, no one of which could be called the act; *e.g.*, in returning the book to the shelf I take a number of steps and stretch my arm in a characteristic way. No one of these movements is returning the book to the shelf. But, one might query, are not all these movements at least collateral acts? No, but we are inclined to think so because we are accustomed to describe movements as if they were elements of some act; that is, we picture the movement as it would be made in the course of doing an act. There is a kind of motion which we might describe as pounding movement, but that description leads us to think of *someone* pounding *with and at something*. That would be a kind of act. But now consider the pounding movement detached from hammer and nail, with nothing to take their places; it no longer seems so full-blooded an act. If we surround the pounding movement with an agent, a purpose, and an appropriate occasion affording a target, a weapon, and so on, it becomes an act or collateral act of pounding; but not until then.

Now, while a movement is not necessarily an act, and never so when it is an element of an act, there is one important sense in which movements of any kind can be made as acts. Any animal movement is such that one might deliberately try to make just that movement.

Thus, if something frustrates the upward movement of the arm which would be an element contributing to my present act of wood-chopping, I may try to lift the arm, then the elbow, *etc.* Such acts are of the type we called endotychistic. But even here the movement is not the act. Only if I harness the movement together with an agent, a purpose, and imbed it in an occasion do I get an act, as we did above; but then the act is not merely the movement.

Let us now say something about each of the four kinds of element in turn. Of these, the agent is the most singular and, for present purposes, the least problematical. Our common ways of thinking about agents, and in particular about human agents, do not naturally generate any canonical scheme for resolution into elements. Certain factors are especially prominent—type, age, sex, ancestry, office—and we could take these as types of elements of the agent. But except where that is necessary or convenient, let us simply take the agent, identified when possible by name, as a single, somewhat singular element of the act. (By stipulating that the agent be identified by name, we receive many of the advantages of a formal resolution into elements without suffering the imposition of arbitrary stringencies. We could not correctly use a name unless we knew something or other about the animal, where no *a priori* restrictions can be placed on what counts as relevant information, and where different people using the same name in the same sense may have different information about the animal. See note no. 3, on p. 162.)

Elements of movement may always ultimately be specified kinematically. Such elements may be of arbitrary finite size in space and time. We then have an advance possibility of any number of different resolutions of an act into elements of movement. The choice depends upon considerations of relevance and in part upon the co-ordinate elements of purpose. We observed in no. 1 that the identification of an item of behaviour, given by the specification of purpose in the case of action, implies a certain kind of partitioning of the constituting movement into a sequence of movements.

Elements of the occasion are specified partly in geometric terms, including a decomposition of a connected region of space and time into elementary intervals, and partly by identifying what is to be found around and about the agent, *e.g.*, the presence of a hammer in the agent's hand or of a person within earshot. What we said concerning the infinite divisibility of the movements, and the advance possibility of alternative resolutions into elements goes equally for the occasion.

The elements of purpose or, more accurately, of the presence of purpose, are the most interesting and characteristic for the analysis of action. We identify a purpose by listing conditions under which an

175

act having that purpose could not succeed, alternatively, by listing conditions of success (see no. 10). A certain purpose is present only if the agent believes these conditions are satisfied (see no. 12, p. 126). The elements of the presence of purpose, therefore, are beliefs that certain conditions are satisfied. We may generalize this to include not only all the beliefs that the conditions defining the purpose of the act are satisfied, but also other beliefs that conditions defining the collateral acts are satisfied.

We cannot put advance, a priori limits on such a list of beliefs. It is at bottom a matter of deciding which of these beliefs might relevantly be cited to explain the movements. The ultimate and collateral purposes of an act are also 'infinitely divisible'.

I stated earlier that the determination of the elements of movement and occasion depends in part upon the co-ordinate determination of elements of purpose. That comes about as follows: Among the beliefs that are elements of the presence of the purpose are beliefs that certain movements are or will be made, and that the occasion has certain features. These beliefs have limits within which they would be verified or falsified, and they thus partially determine what may be an element of movement or occasion. E.g., in meaning to throw a ball one believes that part of the arm will move, but not necessarily that certain tendons in the arm will move. This yields a rough lower bound on the size of relevant movements. But we also know that the conditions of success of the purpose are relative to the elements of movement, because we select only beliefs which we judge might explain *these* movements. The co-ordinate determination of elements is the rough equivalent of positive and negative valence in the theory of inorganic chemical analysis.

The 'infinite divisibility' of the elements of movement, occasion, and purpose does not imply that an analysis of an act into elements can never be given, but only that the analysis is always given against a background which determines what is appropriate and relevant and how much refinement is needed. One will always know in advance whether specification of the occasion will require that we isolate other particular elements within it, e.g., other animals. But 'infinite divisibility' also makes possible alternative analyses by the theorist of the same episode, as indeed we have learned to expect in the case of action, and also permits the free introduction of new types of action by the imagined observer (see pp. 120f.). To illustrate, in analysing acts of carpentry, say for further purposes of inculcating the techniques of using a saw, I should never have occasion to mention the movements of tendons; but such might have to be mentioned were I, while instructing medical students, conducting a physiological examination of the same act. And we have seen how, moving our eye from movement to a combination of the purpose with the occasion, we are able to introduce new kinds of acts by dividing the conditions of success, *e.g.*, as we distinguish giving gifts from giving merely things.

We may now schematize criteria for action: To demonstrate that an act *exists* we establish that elements of all four kinds are present together. There must be an animal moving in specifiable circumstances with a purpose. We *individuate* an act, *i.e.*, apply an individuating test, by specifying the elements of movement constituting the act, as these are determined by the observer.

We earlier observed that the individuation of an item of behaviour, hence of an act, is relative to a typal identification. It is necessary to take this into account to resolve possible cases of concurrent action: the movements of a single animal's occurring over a single stretch of time may sometimes constitute two distinct items of behaviour (see no. 1). Applying our earlier stipulations to the case of action, which is identified by specification of purpose, I conclude: The same movement may be resolved into two acts provided (1) the movement may be decomposed into two sequences of movements which are connected only through the body of the agent; and (2) we must be able independently to specify two distinct purposes having no collateral relation to each other associated respectively with the two sequences of movements. Thus the man, who while shifting the gears of his automobile also addresses a remark to his wife, is possibly doing two acts. This kind of case is to be contrasted with those in which the agent seeks to attain one purpose collaterally to attaining another, and in which he does a single act to attain two independent purposes (*e.g.*, says two distinct things to two different people by uttering the same words). The significance of this is that it shows that the individuation of action is relative to a presumed identification as well as to a kinematical description. It remains that we individuate an act with respect to a particular sequence of movements.

Different observers may individuate acts from different places, hence raising questions whether one or more acts were individuated. We demonstrate *identity* by establishing that the two individuations include the same elements of movement which occur in the body of the (same) animal.

We demonstrate the *type* of the act by establishing the presence of elements of the presence of purpose which are also beliefs that conditions of success for the act are satisfied.

We may also define further (but not all) characteristics of action in terms of tests for the presence of elements. Any single element might occur in any number of acts, and to establish the presence of such an element would be to demonstrate a common, differentiating descriptive feature. Thus, we have John's acts, wood-chopping acts, acts involving arm movements, and acts done in such and such place. In fine, by availing ourselves of the notion of an element, we have a systematic way of characterizing and classifying acts. Not all descriptive features of acts are generally of this kind, *e.g.*, the success or failure of the act. We might want to call features of action which can thus be explained in terms of elements *primary* features of action.

The theory of act elements is also useful for defining other technical notions employed in this work. Thus we might want to define a collateral-act description *D* of an act *A* as follows: The definition of *D* would include reference to some but not all elements of the purpose of *A*.

A hypothetically conceived 'complete description' or 'analysis' of an act would consist of a complete specification of all the elements determined relative to some true report. Of course, such a 'complete analysis' can never be achieved with finality. The elements of an act may be only incompletely implied by the report even relative to the observer's current competence and concerns. Questions may remain open, to be closed only by filling in details regarding the movements, the circumstances, or the beliefs of the agent.

Circumspection must always be exercised in placing these details. It may be that the usual way of stating 'what happened' may leave an ambiguity. Suppose I say, 'She hit him on the nose'. I may be taken to mean that she aimed for and hit him on his nose; details respecting where she hit him then indirectly serve to identify her purpose further. In hitting him, she thought of his nose. On the other hand, I may be taken to mean that she simply meant to hit him, neither meaning nor not meaning to hit his nose. In that case the 'on the nose' adds to the description of the movements, but in no way further determines the purpose. While we can always give a more or less full description of the actual physical transaction—the movements and their effects—it is important to see that this sometimes may involve a description of an act of a different kind as 'kinds' are determined by specification of purpose. The additional elements the presence of which is implied by the fuller description, 'on the nose', may thus be either elements of the presence of purpose, movement, or both, and complete identification of the act requires that we say which.

These remarks provoke a reminder regarding the relations and differences between movements and action. I may describe the same *movements* more or less completely by saying, 'She hit him' or 'She hit him on the nose'; but, though the movements be the same, the acts (if acts) therewith also identified might be different in kind. She could, after all, succeed in her efforts to hit him, and yet fail to hit his nose, notwithstanding the actual fact that when she hit him she hit him and upon his nose.

To conclude on this matter, I maintain a point first made on p. 176: it is not that the same elements may occur under two headings—a movement is never an element of the presence of purpose—but rather, an observer's report that a certain act occurred may be so condensed as to leave it unclear to us what elements contributed to the act and in what manner.

22. WHAT AN ACT SHOWS

[We must take care not to equate an act with any of its elements, features and parts, conditions of success, success or failure, products or effects, reasons. Items of any or all of these kinds might be mentioned in or follow from a description-cum-identification of the act. That these factors are present is what is *shown* by the act. The idea of showing will be especially useful when we later come to analyse acts of assertion.]

I have been at some pains to separate out certain elements and features and parts of acts. Let us now be entirely clear that none of these factors are themselves kinds of action, and that it would be a mistake to equate an act with an item of any of these kinds that might be mentioned in the course of identifying and/or describing an act. In particular, we must not confuse the act with its successful (if successful) outcome, or with the products or effect which may result, or with the agent's reasons. Again, we should not confuse the success of the act with any of the conditions for success, although, if the act be successful, we know that all such conditions are fulfilled.

What an observer can see in an act is what the act *shows*. That an act was done and what its elements are, and even, perhaps, whether the act succeeded or failed, are among what the act *shows*. Were I to *observe* an agent's acting, and were I then to make an accurate and true report of what I saw, I would, quite apart from whatever thoughts on the matter the agent might himself have, give a statement of what was shown by the act. It is not excluded that the agent himself be an observer, sometimes but not invariably a privileged one. The observer, even when he is the agent, might of course make a mistake in his report, but this mistake could be corrected only in consideration of the report of some other observer who was there to see what was shown by the act. It is important that not all that is shown is equally patent; e.g., a purpose is often (but not always) more difficult to ascertain than is the identity of the agent. Uncertainty or error as to what is shown by the act may be over the typal or particular identity, or the 'success value' of the act. All that 'shows' in the act would follow from a true, full description-cum-identification of the act.

Much of what has recently been discussed under such rubrics as 'contextual implication' and 'presupposition' would be shown in the intended sense. ('Presupposition' has generally meant *condition of success for a Language act*.)[1] The language of 'implication' is both appropriate and misleading here. It is appropriate because, operating with observers' reports, statements of the 'implications' would 'follow from' in the more regular sense of being entailed by the full description-cum-identification. To speak of 'implications' is misleading because it suggests that an agent who is simply doing an act, thus 'implying' what is 'shown', is already operating at the level of a conceptualizing observer when patently he may not be, and that his act is a report on itself. This can be mystifying because it suggests that acting is itself always a kind of saying.

'Showing' is most apt where what is shown is something about the agent. In the course of doing what he does, the agent exhibits himself as being of a certain kind, in a certain state, having certain mannerisms, *etc*. Thus in eating I may show my bad table manners. Most interestingly, one may exhibit or show those conditions of success we earlier called 'the conditions of the agent', *e.g.*, certain beliefs about the world.

Showing in this technical sense of 'show' is not a kind of action. The agent 'shows' what is shown by the act. In another, probably more usual sense of 'show' or 'exhibit', one surely may also act with the purpose of exhibiting himself, *e.g.*, exhibiting his knowledge. Exhibiting acts proper, that is, acts in which the agent means to exhibit something about himself, are of an interesting kind, to be investigated in a sequel to this volume.

This idea of what acts show will take on considerable importance later when we come to consider assertions or acts of expressing belief. If one succeeds in assertion, he asserts that something is the case. But what he asserts to be the case must never be confounded with what he shows to be the case just in asserting and possibly succeeding. That is, there are acts which not only show such and such to be the case, *e.g.*, that so and so believes and asserted something, but whose very purpose is shown to be to assert that such and such other is the case. I have taken this chance to speak generally of what

---

[1] See P. H. Nowell-Smith, *Ethics*, Chap. 6, [2]; also *Proc. Arist. Soc. Supp. Vol.*, 1962, pp. 1–18; P. F. Strawson, *Introduction to Logic* [Chap. 6, III. 7]; I. Hungerland, 'Contextual Implication', *Inquiry*, 1960, pp. 211–58, and esp. J. L. Austin on A_2-conditions and 'presuppositions' in Lectures III and IV of *How to do Things with Words*. I also especially think of the distinction which Wittgenstein draws between saying and showing in the *Tractatus*.

(any) act shows, that we might later more easily grasp this particular distinction between what is shown and what is asserted in an assertion, as a kind of special case.

23. EXPLAINING ACTION, WITH SPECIAL REFERENCE TO MOTIVES

[Animal behaviour may be explained in various ways, by reference to various kinds of what we may call explanatory factors, of which *awareness of reasons* is one type, others being *causes, dispositions, opportunities, emotional agitations, etc.* Mention of an explanatory factor explains when that factor is the completing element showing the phenomenon in question to be an instance of a familiar pattern. Mention of what we call 'motives' may also explain behaviour. Motives should not be confused with purposes or with any particular kind of purpose-explanatory factor such as awareness of reason and disposition. Mention of a motive draws attention rather to the pattern of explanation itself, possibly thereby implying the presence of dispositions, awareness of reasons, *etc.* An important difference between factor explanations and pattern explanations, motive explanations being included among the latter, is that with the former we fit the *explicandum* into the pattern by associating with elements of the phenomenon strands of the pattern, and with the latter we fit the pattern onto the *explicandum*, thereby possibly being enabled to discover explanatory factors in the phenomenon. Motive patterns pertain to commonsense, and are not the result of scientific discovery. A motive pattern serves primarily to explain acts, and acts done by agents who could conceal their purposes. The mention of a motive usually but not invariably implies an appraisal of the agent and/or of his deed. Motive explanations may be likened to certain types of explanation of historical, political and social phenomena.]

To conclude this part, I wish to say something in general about the explanation of action, the possibility of which has been presupposed by the whole of the foregoing analysis, and about motive explanations of action in particular. Both *behaviour* and *action* were explicated relative to an imagined observer's explanation of animal movement. Specifically, *action* was so defined as to imply that the animal's movements might have been explained by reference to his awareness of reasons. An investigation of *reason* was thereby indirectly brought within a larger arena, that of explaining behaviour generally. Reasons are facts, the knowledge of which might explain. But clearly reasons are not the only kind of item we might have occasion to mention in the course of explaining action. Others are *causes, dispositions, emotions, opportunities, upbringing, social circumstances, etc.* Each of these is best understood in contrast with the others, which it may

complement or be alternative to. I shall call them *explanatory factors.*
This idea of an explanatory factor is a technical one, requiring explication. Partly for that purpose, I beg the reader's indulgence to dwell in a general way upon this topic of explanation.

Explanations are of many kinds. I shall mostly consider only explanations 'why' or 'how-come', and not explanations 'who', 'what', 'how', *etc.* Even so circumscribed, 'explanation' has at least three related applications. First, we use 'explanation' generically to to cover *acts of explaining.* Here I shall simply speak of 'explaining'. Second, we may speak of what is brought forth by such an act if it is successful: we may thus speak of *his* explanation, which *I* now reproduce. Finally, 'the explanation' may be a feature of the world which would be correctly invoked to explain such and such phenomenon, *e.g.*, the presence of such and such a disposition is the explanation. I choose to employ 'explanation' only in the second application. An explanation is therefore something produced or brought forth by a successful act of explaining. It is the measure of success of such an act.

Acts of explaining resemble acts of instructing and acts of persuading. In all such acts, success is achieved only if such and such is brought about by way of the agent's saying something. Thus, I successfully instruct only if I bring another to understand and possibly to believe such and such; but it is also necessary that he be brought to understand, not, *e.g.*, by my edging him into a position to see for himself, but rather by my telling him. But my telling him is itself not sufficient, for I may very well succeed in saying my piece and yet fail to impart understanding. It is much the same with persuading, only here I succeed only if I bring another to do something by telling him something. So, too, with explaining. Explaining is a creature of Language; success in such an act requires a conceptual structuring of the world. Explaining things is a privilege of our imagined conceptualizing observer, upon whom this analysis has centred. But explaining is not merely a matter of Language, for my act of explaining succeeds only if something comes about by way of my saying something. The proof of this is that my Language act, say, an assertion, might succeed and yet I speak falsely; but in that case my act of explaining must fail. Again, it may be that nothing calls for explanation, but I may still state the facts. Briefly, an act of explaining fails unless such and such is brought about by way of the use of Language. [1]

---

[1] An act of explaining is not an act of producing an explanation by way of a collateral act of saying something. It is rather a hybrid, whose Original Way is some kind of saying and whose Original Purpose is the bringing of a problematic phenomenon into a familiar pattern.

What now is the 'such and such brought forth'? Understanding perhaps. But for whom, and whereby, and is the achievement of understanding peculiar to explanation? Often explanation consists of a mere drawing of attention to what is already known; at other times it may involve the discovery of hitherto hidden facts. Again, *I* may fail to understand, and yet the explanation be impeccable. Still again, one may understand a gesture without having it explained. The imparting of understanding to someone is neither a sufficient nor necessary measure for the success of an act of explaining. A clue to a possible useful general formula is that one may succeed in explaining by the mere mention of a *single* circumstance. If it be objected that that cannot be, because there are always any number of other conditions which must be met before the indicated factor could operate in the expected way, we must respond that that would make explaining an impossible idea. What the reaction does suggest is that the mention of a single fact may suffice only because it brings the problematic phenomenon into a familiar pattern of conditions which we are entitled to assume are met. The suggestion is that an explanation is called for when the phenomenon at question for one reason or another seems problematic, which I think we may always attribute to the phenomenon appearing for some reason in some way *unfamiliar*. The act of explaining is successful only if it truly brings the phenomenon into a familiar pattern. Explaining is always a matter of utilizing available knowledge.

Familiarity is, of course, relative to where one stands. Nothing in daily life could be more familiar to us than gravitation, yet it ceases to be when we move into a scientific sphere and consider how it relates to the Laws of Motion; hence, Einstein's explanation of the equivalance of inertial and gravitational mass. Though I am not entirely confident that this general formula invoking familiarity will stand, I can offer no better. Let me then tentatively lay it down that an act of explaining succeeds only if a problematic phenomenon is brought within a familiar pattern. If the act succeeds, *an* explanation is produced. The pattern is itself a connection of various different *kinds* of factor, where by italicizing 'kinds' I mean to indicate that the pattern is not itself a phenomenon within which the factors may be present. But if elements corresponding to any one of these kinds of factors are present in the phenomenon, mention of factors of other kinds might serve to explain. Thus, the presence of a wild bush in the garden may be explained by mention of the state of the soil, the humidity, the strong winds which spread seeds, the plot of parent bushes down the hill, the aesthetic predilections or botanical madness of the householder, *etc.* That mention of any of these might settle the question presumes a familiarity with the ways of plants, how they grow and what they grow from, and whether or not they would be cultivated or destroyed by human beings. I am not supposing that all or even any such patterns can be spelled out finally and in full detail. Explanatory patterns are often commonsense types, and like commonsense types in general are manifested, so to speak, grossly by the particular kind of connection of events and circumstances, which may be 'analysed' in a number of alternative ways. However, the pattern can be seen in things, and becomes familiar. If, as we know, plants exist within this nexus of events, circumstances, dispositions, etc., then, if we see that such elements are present, no explanation is called for. But if one of the elements is not evident, we might explain by mentioning it specifically.

Along one line of division there are two different but closely related kinds of act of explaining which produce distinct kinds of explanation. Let us, for convenience, fix our attention on the case of explaining human behaviour. We earlier defined reasons as 'facts, knowledge of which might explain'. So we might have occasion to mention knowledge of a reason to explain behaviour. But that is not the only kind of item which we might mention to explain behaviour. Others we saw are *causes, dispositions, emotions, opportunities, upbringing, social circumstance*. A *cause*, in a philosopher's sense, might, for example, be defined as an *occurrence* or *happening* which might explain a subsequent occurrence or happening. Causes, unlike reasons, operate, not by being known, but by *occurring* or *happening*. Causes, knowledge of reasons, etc., are all of them what I have called 'explanatory factors'. An explanatory factor is an item of a quite specific kind which might be present in the phenomenon to be explained, mention of whose presence might explain and, in particular, explain an act done. Now an explanatory factor of any kind might be present and still not explain, either because nothing happened as a result of the presence of the factor, or because what happened wants no explaining anyway, or because the explanation is to be found elsewhere, possibly *via* the mention of some other explanatory factor. Still, by calling these facts, occurrences, circumstances, 'causes', etc., we view them as items of a kind, mention of which might (but need not) explain phenomena of the kind in question. [2]

---

[2] There is *something* right in Hume's doctrine that causal relations do not obtain between 'real existences', but consist in a 'determination of the mind' (*Treatise*, pp. 165f.). What Hume says would be true if we replaced 'cause' by 'explanation' (which is what he sometimes means) and take 'determination of the mind' to mean something like 'conceptualizing thought'. As it is, the sense of 'cause' is relative to forms of explanation, although we must allow that particular causes may occur without there being call to mention them for purposes of giving

Suppose now that we observe this phenomenon, and discern in it certain features or connections, *e.g.*, causes, dispositions, the phenomenon is then explained by fitting it into a familiar pattern by finding strands in the pattern corresponding to the features or connections that were seen in the phenomenon; the phenomenon is explained by mention of the features in question to which the strands in the pattern are taken to correspond. The important point is that the phenomenon is taken and matched against the pattern by finding in the pattern correspondents to the observed causes, dispositions, *etc.*, in the phenomenon. We may, of course, observe these causes, dispositions, *etc.*, without proceeding to find correspondents in the explanatory pattern, and indeed without attempting any kind of explanation at all. But when we do in fact attempt an explanation we purport to indicate that a factor in the phenomenon does indeed have a correspondent in the pattern, and thus we fit the phenomenon into a familiar pattern.

Putting this together with what was said before, we may lay it down that such an act succeeds only if the agent shows the phenomenon to manifest a familiar pattern by way of indicating that such and such factor is present in the phenomenon, which factor corresponds to one of the strands (one of the types of factor) in the pattern. If the act succeeds, I call what is thereby produced a *factor explanation*. Alternatively, we could call this a *determining explanation*, for the indicated factor is mentioned as one of the items which determine the phenomenon to be as it is.

The second kind of case is this: Again there is a phenomenon to be explained and a pattern to which appeal is made. But now we regard the *explicandum* not with an eye to finding in it some hitherto unremarked factor corresponding to a strand in the pattern. We may even be quite unprepared to find the pattern manifested or to see any factor to which the strands of the pattern correspond. But then we might explain by saying that this indeed is the pattern. Thus Newton explained the movements of the planets by regarding them as gravitating bodies; or we explain thermal phenomena by interpreting them according to a statistical dynamical pattern; or we explain the behaviour of ants by seeing it as manifesting a pattern of social living.

How, one might ask, can this kind of case differ from the other? In both instances a correspondence between the *explicandum* and the explanatory pattern is essential. And in both cases there must be a

---

explanations. *Causes* are, if you will, happenings in the world selected and identified relative to a general 'determination of the mind' to impose causal explanations, *i.e.*, explanations in terms of antecedent happenings.

constituting correspondence between the elements of the *explicandum* and the strands of the pattern. The difference lies in the direction from which the correspondence is sought. We explain by mention of an explanatory factor by taking the *phenomenon* in question and fitting it *into* a familiar pattern, by finding a strand to correspond to the indicated factor. On the other hand, we explain by mention of an explanatory pattern when we take the *pattern* and fit it *onto* the *explicandum*. If we succeed in this, we then may come to see in the phenomenon factors corresponding to the strands in the pattern. Explaining by mention of a pattern, so to say, *interprets* the phenomenon as, *e.g.*, dynamical or social. The interpretation is tested by looking for and finding suitable features of the phenomenon corresponding to strands in the pattern. If a pattern is thus established, it may thenceforth be appealed to with some confidence in the giving of future explanations for phenomena of this kind. The difference between the two kinds of explaining is seen in the fact that where we may observe an explanatory factor to be operating we may but need not then go on to explain the phenomenon in question; on the other hand, assignment of an explanatory pattern already and of itself constitutes an attempt to explain. I call what is produced by a successful act of explaining of this second kind a *pattern explanation*. We might alternatively call it an *interpretative explanation*. While both kinds of explanation essentially involve both factors and patterns, there remains a difference between them which I hope to have made clear.[3]

We instanced a number of kinds of explanatory factor which could be mentioned to explain animal action. *Motives* were perhaps conspicuous by their absence from the list. But surely among the many types of explanation of action which in daily life we might have occasion to volunteer are ones that mention *motives*. Perhaps

[3] Analogues to pattern explanations may be found outside the sphere of explaining itself. An interesting instance is what is sometimes called 'critical judgment' in respect to works of art. (See A. Isenberg, 'Critical Communication', *Phil. Rev.*, 1949. The following suggestion is, I believe, very like that of Isenberg.) Here too, as in pattern explainings, I can proceed only when face to face with a challenging instance or if I can imagine myself in such circumstances. In both instances something is said and we may thereby apparently be brought to see the phenomenon in a certain way. In both cases it is entirely natural to speak of 'interpretation' and of 'coming to see'. In both cases our efforts are tested, not by a simple checking of the facts, but rather by our success in finding in the example at hand decent correspondents for the strands in a pattern. In both cases success gives promise of a deeper understanding of similar phenomena. If success is substantial and successive, the judgment may be canonized into a system; *e.g.*, we may come in a systematic way to consider works of art in their historical settings or as 'solutions to problems'. Such relatively mechanical investigations are analogous to factor explanations.

no other topic which owes its contemporary resuscitation to Ryle's *Concept of Mind* has received more attention of late, and for no other has so disparate a variety of suggested analyses been put forward.[4] Because the topic of motives obviously pertains to our programme and because it is intrinsically interesting, I wish to devote the balance of this part to an analysis of motive explanations.[5]

A short list of motives is *sympathy, passion, sentiment, revenge, gratitude, loyalty, hate, jealousy, ambition, envy, pity, despair, curiosity, vanity, fear, shame, greed, love.* We also speak of generous, treacherous, selfish, disinterested, good, and bad, political motives. A listing such as this is our only control, for we want to understand motives in a literal sense of 'motives' and not in some perhaps interesting philosophical use of the term. This investigation, if it be successful, is a terminating project. I am not concerned with motives because they have any further interest for or use in philosophical theory. Here it would be well to post a warning that the terms listed and their cognates may be used to fix what are not motives. One may have a jealous disposition and may or may not act from the motive of jealousy. And there we find another useful verbal lead, that motives are characteristically (though not inevitably) acted 'from' or 'out of'. Another similar lead is that motives are sometimes signalized by the use of 'want' with a direct object, often shielded with the presence of 'just' or 'only': 'He only wants money', 'He just wants deliverance from turmoil'. The above list of motives could be greatly expanded. But these items illustrate well enough what has made it hard to find a good answer to the question what kind of thing is a motive. Motives at least sometimes have something to do with the explanation of human behaviour. Yet it is not immediately obvious what kind of

[4] In addition to Chap. IV of *Concept of Mind*, see, for example, R. S. Peters, *The Concept of Motivation*, Chaps. 1 and 2; a symposium in *Proc. Arist. Soc. Supp.*, 1952, entitled 'Motives and Causes' with contributions by Peters, D. J. McCracken, and J. O. Urmson; A. R. White, 'The Language of Motives', *Mind*, 1958, pp. 258–63; Anscombe, *op. cit.*, nos. 12–14; N. S. Sutherland, 'Motives as Explanations', *Mind*, 1959, pp. 145–59; A. I. Melden, *op. cit.*, chap. 2. The most notable contribution, in my opinion, is chap. 4 of A. Kenny's *Action, Emotion and Will*. I find Kenny's book generally more congenial than anything else recently published in philosophy of mind. Regrettably, I did not read the book until my own had already long been in press.
[5] It has lately become common, first among psychologists and then, at their lead, among ordinary folk as well, to speak a great deal of 'motivation'. Like so many technical words which are taken over into the vernacular, it has become something of an incantation, and a very dull piece of equipment. However, the word can be used carefully, and when so taken seems to mean something like *strength of purpose* or *dominating inclination* or possibly that particular *bent of interest* mention of which will explain one's engaging in a certain activity. Motivation, however explicated, is not my present concern.

explanatory consideration a motive might be. Our list, abbreviated as it must be, illustrates a formidable variety.

Philosophers who have discussed motives regularly have made one or both of two mistakes. First, they are prone to identify the motive with what I have called the purpose; *i.e.*, they suppose that we specify motives in order to say what was done. Sometimes this is called 'purpose' and sometimes 'intention'. What makes this plausible, as we shall see, is first, that motives primarily explain action, *i.e.*, *purposive behaviour*, and second, that giving motive explanations does imply that there could have been some question about what was being done. Consequently, motive explanations tend to focus on purpose, as wanting explanation.

The second mistake is to equate motives with one or other of the various explanatory factors we have mentioned, *e.g.*, awareness of reasons, dispositions, emotions. Now to say that one acts from this motive or that may certainly suggest or even imply that this or that kind of explanatory factor was operating. Thus to impute revenge as a motive implies that one was acting for one kind of putative reason, and gratitude for another, and both imply that something happened or was believed to have happened in the past, a cause, which provoked revenge or gratitude; jealousy suggests the presence, if not the operation, of a jealous *disposition*; *lust* implies the consciousness of an exciting object, which tends to trigger one's sexual dispositions. Philosophers by fastening on one kind of motive rather than another have been able to make a plausible case for their favourite factors. What is of substantive interest is that assignment of motives should suggest or imply the presence of these other explanatory factors.

Most frequently, if implicitly, motives have been miscast as reasons.[6] This is partly because reasons or imagined reasons always figure when an act is done, and mention of motives, we remarked, explains acts done. But, also, many words are used *both* to impute motives and to formulate principles of reason, *e.g.*, 'gratitude'. It is noteworthy, too, that principles of reason, which may figure as major premises of practical syllogisms, may often be formulated in the language of 'to want'. Thus, 'He wants water; that is water— glug!'. But this formula, when suitably protected by qualifiers like 'just' and 'only', may also be employed to impute or dismiss a motive implying or suggesting awareness of a certain kind of reason, *e.g.*, 'He just wanted to avenge the murder of his brother', 'He only wanted to help'. Still there is a difference. But hate, while a motive, neither implies nor suggests kinds of reason, real or imagined,

---

[6] The classical discussion of motives tends in that direction, as does Peters in his recent book. I confess to much the same misconstruction in a paper called 'The Sense of Duty', *Phil. Quart.*, 1957.

though, of course, usually one harbours hate for some reason, real or imagined. Traditionally what has usually happened is that motives have been equated with reasons of interest, as against reasons of law or morality. Others have suggested that motives are always emotional agitations, an idea strongly suggested by the word 'passion' so fashionable in an earlier epoch. Ryle's oft-refuted analysis of motives as *dispositions* is another case, no more one-sided than the others, and having the merit of being explicit.

This tendency to place motives as various kinds of explanatory factor, any of which may be suggested or implied by the assignment of some motive, strongly suggests that there really is no single, unified idea of motive; that there is no such *a* concept, and that we have been made victims of verbal illusion in thinking that there is. Motives may then simply be that which *moves to action*, and that can be any kind of thing depending upon what kind of explanation is wanted. Thus some suggest that motives are reasons which excite to action, reasons which are the agent's reasons, especially reasons of interest. [7]

But that surely will not do. We are quite able to distinguish motives from having reasons, dispositions, *etc.* I am quite sure, for instance, from talking with Spaniards, that our use of the term differs from the Spanish 'motivo' in just that way.

Yet there is something in the idea that a motive is what *moves one to act*. Disregarding 'motives for believing', I am inclined to think that motives cannot be assigned unless some act was done wanting explanation. But it would follow from this that motives, far from being any kind of explanatory factor whatsoever, are not explanatory factors at all, for such factors may be present even though they explain nothing.

I offer this in the face of the police inspector's search for *a* motive. There, too, something has happened, and he thinks it may have been done by N.N., but to make the charge stick he must present a reasonable case. He presumes that what was done is to be explained by finding a motive by finding a man who has a motive. We still have before us phenomena whose explanation is presumed to be that someone acted in a way that wanted explanation. The police inspector himself is in an importantly different position. What *he* is after is the culprit, not the explanation. But his guiding presumption is that a deed was done which must be somehow or other explicable; and he reasons that N.N. might have done it from this motive. The inspector operates within the limits of the explicable.

[7] Frankena, in his previously cited 'Obligation and Motivation in Recent Moral Philosophy', seems to doubly misidentify motives with reasons of interest and with reasons that move to action.

One might still protest that the inspector will find that many people 'had' a motive, where it is presumed that only one of them did the deed; so after all a motive can be present even though no deed was done, contrary to what I maintain. Now here we have to be careful about our language. We can say that someone has or had a reason, even though mention of the reason would not explain the act, *e.g.*, in case the man was not aware of the reason. To explain the deed in terms of reasons we must be able to say that the reason was *his* reason. *Awareness* of the reason is the explanatory factor. Something similar holds for motives. We can say of someone that he has or had a motive without thereby ascribing the motive to him, for which latter purpose we would have to say, 'His motive was *M*'. Holding that in mind, my reply to the objection is as follows: After we solve the crime, it is possible for us to say with respect to someone who we know did not do the deed that his reason for doing it would have been *R*; but it is not correct for us to say of him who we know did not do the deed, 'His motive for doing it would have been *M*'. The phrase, 'His motive was *M*' turns attention away from those who we know are innocent and onto the guilty party. The importance of this is that the awareness of reason, an explanatory factor, may have been present whether or not it explains; but, as I have argued, the motive is not an element or feature of the phenomenon at all; it is the explanatory pattern through which we regard the phenomenon.

Another important fact about motives is that they do not appear to have temporal spread. To be sure, one acts from a motive at given times. But now one may act from a certain motive only once in his life. Are we then to say that the motive came into existence or occurred only at that time, or are we to say that the motive existed prior to and/or after the act? Either alternative sounds queer. It would be equally queer to ask about the temporal duration of a motive, even if the man happened often to act from the motive in question. But if motives were explanatory factors, it should not sound at all queer, for the supposed factor would presumably be present in the phenomena at or over the indicated times.

Another argument against treating motives as explanatory factors is this. While we may speak of the particular reason*s*, cause*s*, disposition*s*, which explain an act, motives, *when made specific*, are always singular. We speak of the motive. That implies that there is no room for either agent or observer to balance motives, as we may balance various explanatory factors present, only one of which need be operative. Motives, like breeds of dogs, may indeed be 'mixed', but the constituting factors, however conflicting, are still concurrent.

We have been barking up the wrong tree after the wrong cat. We are looking for a kind of explanatory factor. What we want is not that,

190

but the idea of a certain kind of explanation of acts. That can be no other than what I earlier called a pattern explanation. Consequently, motive explanations are not factor explanations, but rather pattern explanations. To explain a deed by mention of a motive is to *interpret it* according to a certain pattern. It is much as if we might explain some opaque physical phenomenon by appeal to the Laws of Motion taken collectively, or when we explain the behaviour of ants as analogous to the social behaviour of mammals. Motive explanations are all of this kind. For what it is worth, such is strongly intimated by the sense of 'motif', certainly an etymological cousin of 'motive'.

So my thesis is that motive explanations are of the second kind we discussed, the kind we called 'pattern explanations'. We fit the pattern onto the deed rather than fitting the deed into the pattern. We 'interpret' the deed according to the pattern. This explains why assigning a motive must count as an attempt, at least, at an explanation; for what we are operating with is an explanatory pattern itself. On the other hand, we may want to assign an explanatory factor without wanting to give an explanation, for in this case what we are operating with is the act; of course we may go on and fit the act into some pattern, being guided by the explanatory factor which we discover to be present, for which we wish to find the corresponding strand in the pattern. The police inspector who was looking for a motive and found a number of candidates is rather like the scientist who is looking for general hypotheses, patterns of explanation which he may fit onto the facts. [8]

Motives, then, are not pieces, parts, or factors possibly present in

---

[8] An interesting possible counter-example was suggested by Mr. Jackson of the University of Melbourne. In *The Republic* (IV, 439), Socrates recounts the story of Leontius, son of Aglion, who was drawn against his will to gaze upon the bodies of some executed prisoners, to argue for the view that anger and appetite are distinct parts of the soul. Leontius was, as we might describe it, drawn by 'morbid curiosity' to feast his eyes upon the sordid scene. What is operating here is some kind of compulsion, and a compulsion surely is a kind of explanatory factor. But at the same time, curiosity is a motive. Well, that does not matter, for, as we shall see more fully later, the very same words may be used to signalize both motives and explanatory factors. What makes the case an interesting one is that 'morbid curiosity', like terms for motives, indicates the concurrent operation of a number of factors, *e.g.*, that an object capable of exciting curiosity was present, that Leontius had an interest in the morbid, *etc.* But surely morbid curiosity is an explanatory factor. So a complex of factors may be a complex factor. Why then not simply regard motives as complex explanatory factors? In answer to this I could only review the *differentiae*: Leontius might have been morbidly curious and yet have refrained from turning his head, *etc.* The factor of morbid curiosity would not explain that deed, for now he is supposed to have done what he did in despite of the factor. Interestingly, we might explain his turning away, as he is now imagined to have done, by citing the *motive* of morbid curiosity.

191

problematical phenomena. For this reason, motives do not determine, compel, constrain, give impetus to, or even motivate, action, as may awareness of reason, disposition, neurological disorder, *etc.*

The one necessary qualification, so far as I can presently see, to this account of motives is that motive patterns may consist of something more than explanatory strands. His diffident *manner* or sheepish *look* may also matter, when it comes to supporting the claim that he acted from shame. But explanation is also offered. I shall in what follows consider only the explanatory strands of the larger motive pattern. [9]

Of course, there are relations between motive and factor explanations of behaviour. Every motive pattern, if it is to serve the purposes of explanation at all, must be a connection of various strands—types of explanatory factor—which could be made to correspond to explanatory factors. Hence, the assignment of motives often implies or suggests the presence of such factors; but, as we have seen, these implications and suggestions will differ from case to case. Interestingly enough, it might sometimes be true to say of someone (*e.g.*) that his motive for leaving was jealousy, despite the fact that the act was done for the reason that only in this way could the agent avoid the actualization of his jealous *disposition*; that is, the explanation was not the jealous disposition, because it was not actualized; by citing jealousy as a *motive*, we see the act as manifesting a pattern the suggested strands of which are awareness of reason, disposition, and perhaps other things as well, such as the immediate effects of the presence of the beloved. (See also the discussion of 'morbid curiosity' in note 8 above.) These patterns, though they may be discussed abstractly, are not present (if they be 'present' at all) apart from manifesting cases which want explanation. This is a direct corollary of the fact that motives are patterns, not explanatory factors. To assign a motive *is* to offer an explanation. These interpretive, explanatory schemes are open and, like most 'patterns', hard to pin

[9] Here it is worth pointing out that the cognates of 'intend', in their literal senses, are indeed quite like 'motive', and quite unlike (*e.g.*) 'purpose'. Examples are, 'He took it intending to put it back', 'He proposed with the very best intentions', 'He did it intentionally'. In all such cases, the point of the supposed remark is not so much to say what the imagined agent was doing, what his purpose or 'end' was, as to say in what manner, in what frame of mind, *etc.*, he was doing it. More specifically, to raise questions about the intentions of an act is to regard that act as having wider connections with the circumstances of the agent—his situation and orientation, and the sequels he envisages—and to inquire how the agent viewed the act in relation to his circumstances. Remarks concerning intentions thus, in a certain sense, 'interpret' the act from the agent's point of view. Such interpretation differs from the ascription of motives chiefly in that it does not necessarily bring in anything by way of *explaining* why the act was done. Also, the interpretation is given from the agent's point of view: the agent must know his intentions in a way in which he need not know his motives.

down, which accounts for the quickness with which disputes may arise regarding someone's motive, and also goes some way towards explaining why the fine ability to discern and identify motive is so rare a gift, however much it might be cultivated. The skill required is more like what is needed for inventing scientific theories than for solving scientific problems. And, like motives, rival theories are characteristically debated, sometimes acrimoniously, while solutions to problems are usually cut and dried. We could with reservations say that mentioning a motive is to put forward a *theory* regarding someone's behaviour. The theory is tested by seeing whether we can indeed find factors corresponding to various strands of the pattern.

We have been likening the assignment of motives to the use of scientific theories. But clearly motives are in some respects very unlike scientific theories. Patterns of scientific explanation are few and seldom compete; and when they do compete it is at those junctures of crisis where professionals must decide which theory to adopt, the loser losing all status as an explanation. But patterns for explaining human behaviour are legion, and they do in fact frequently compete; moreover, upon resolving such issues, there is no cause for utterly and eternally banishing any of the less likely patterns proposed for the immediate case. The actions of our fellows are of such enveloping interest to us that we early become familiar with many different syndromes, as it were, which may seem to differ only slightly and uncertainly but importantly, as when we wonder whether a man was acting from jealousy or pride. It is a matter of 'interpretive sensibility', a faculty with which we are not equally endowed, however much it may and possibly ought to be cultivated.

These last remarks indicate that not any old explanatory pattern is a motive, *e.g.*, not that structured by the Laws of Motion. There also appear to be other kinds of pattern explanation for animal behaviour, familiar enough to commonsense and hence not initially scientific in character, and yet different from motives. Such are found, I believe, in our common appeals to *habit* and *instinct*. Thus, asked why he did it, I may say 'Just habit', and therewith incidentally reject any further probing of motives, *etc.* So the old question returns: What is common to motives? The answer to this, I submit, is that motives are called in only to explain behaviour which is presumed to have reached a certain level of sophistication, and that the explanation itself must not be at too high a level of sophistication. There is also usually to be found in motive explanations an intimation of an evaluation either of the deed or of the agent, hence the naturalness of the word 'impute'. Let us then ask ourselves:

(1) What is it that might be explained by assignment of motives,

193

and what conditions must be met before something can be *possibly* so explained?

(2) At what level of experience do we learn about motives? More specifically, are the explanatory patterns in question technical or commonsensical, scientific or everyday? I have already substantially prejudged this question.

(3) Does the assignment of motives always involve an evaluation of something or other, and, if so, of what?

(4) Finally, are motive explanations in some important sense *unique, sui generis*, or is it possible to find elsewhere analogues rather better than those already suggested, and which assemble into a similarly amorphous family?

I shall now propose answers to these questions, answers developed in the light of my list of examples of motives. In answer to the first question, I submit that what may be explained by mention of a motive, at least in the first instance, is *an act done;* that is, actual animal behaviour of the acting kind. Mention of the motive explains the act by *explaining why the agent should have the purpose*, specification of which would identify the act. I furthermore conjecture that the motive pattern explains the presence of the purpose by drawing attention, among other things, to what the agent believes or knows and/or to considerations which would account for this knowledge or belief. That, if done, goes some way towards explaining why we are so apt to confuse motives with reasons. Anyway, motives, by explaining why the animal should have a certain purpose, *ipso facto* explain the animal's doing a certain kind of deed. But we do not speak of motives in connection with just any kind of act. We do not commonly impute motives to brutes or to infants. Nor indeed is there sense in requesting the motive in my act of drawing the curtain, say upon waking in the morning, though an explanation may very well be wanted. Here motives differ importantly from *habit* and *instinct*. It appears, for one thing, that acts which might be explained by reference to motives are acts which cannot be done by agents who have not attained a certain level of sophistication. In particular, a motive can be meaningfully assigned only if (but not always *if*) the agent is an animal whom we regard as capable of dissembling his purpose, and also, to take care of the curtain-drawing case, the act must be of a kind that we expect might be dissembled in circumstances such as these. This is confirmed by the very rare instances in which we may assign motives to, say, dogs: I return from work and observe that my dog wants, with her joyful tail, to draw me away from the room in which she did the damage; discerning this, I may also want to say that she is acting from motives of fear or shame or simply

194

guile. It is not that the agent must actually be currently veiling his purpose, but he must be capable of so doing. Moreover, frequently when motives are assigned the implication is either that the agent is not really doing what he appears to be doing or that he really is doing what he appears to be doing, despite doubts which may have arisen on that score. It may also be that we may know very well what he was doing, and wonder why. But even then we must regard his deed as one, the purpose of which, as we suppose, he was capable of dissembling. In any case, the act done must be one which needs explanation; and the explanation will account for the agent's having a certain purpose. What creates the need for an explanation may be just that we are, for one reason or another, unclear what it is that the agent is doing; or sometimes we wonder why he should have done so odious or so exemplary a deed.

When a specification of a motive is requested for an act done by a known agent, it must be that the motive is not entirely obvious. Motives must be found and may be *discovered*. Indeed, even the agent himself may not know and have to be told. This again would show that, while motives imply purposes, motives themselves are not those purposes. The agent who acts from vanity may full well know what he was meaning to do and yet, notoriously in the case of vanity, not know from what motive he acts.

My thesis is, then, that motive explanations always imply an assignment of purpose, because in the first instance they explain the act by explaining why the agent should have that purpose. The purpose is the key to the application of the pattern. But the purpose is itself not the pattern, not the motive, although one might easily equate these two distinct kinds of things. I may know what another is doing, and yet still wonder why. *What* he does is slay his wife's imagined paramour; vanity, not jealousy, she tells me, was the motive.

Mention of motives, I hold, *in the first instance* explains acts done. But there are further, derivative kinds of application. First, it seems to make sense to speak about 'motives for believing'; *e.g.*, from vanity a person may believe that another has aided him and deserves gratitude. I shall not discuss motives for believing except to aver that they are to be explicated in terms of motives for doing. The second derivative application of 'motive' is that of 'unconscious' motives for doing. If an agent is an animal of a kind capable of acting to attain a certain purpose which he might have dissembled, but even knowing that he has not so acted, we may still impute to him a motive which would interpret his behaviour as directed towards what would be the attainment of the purpose in question. Thus a man, without even intending to, may never fail to make insulting remarks to a certain party. He does not even know that he is being insulting;

in fact we know that *he* is not insulting the other, however insulting his words may be; we volunteer as an explanation his pique at a slight long ago received from the second party; we explain his insulting remarks by way of drawing attention to a pattern of behaviour which would nicely accommodate the giving of insults. We say that he unconsciously acted from motives of pique. We treat the agent as if he had such a purpose; and we do that by drawing attention to a pattern of events, circumstances, *etc.*, which would account for the presence of that purpose. This extension, which is rather like the extension of scientific theories to new kinds of phenomena, is easily made partly because we allow that an agent may not know the motive from which he actually acts. Here we really have at hand the possibility of 'unconscious motive'. It is just such a term that Freud needed, as against 'unconscious reason', when he set out to trace the etiology of compulsive, obsessive, and hysterical behaviour; here the "purpose" is also "unconscious". Only he pushed the idea further than we usually do, purporting to find motive-like patterns including as strands kinds of episode in the long-forgotten past.

The answer to my second question has been foreshadowed: Motive explanations are given at the level of *commonsense*. The patterns in question are not founded upon the discovery of recondite kinds of fact, nor are they structured mathematically or according to a neat schema like the periodic table of the chemical elements. The facts at issue are familiar to every normal adult. While motives are only words for the quite young, still it is not very late in life that we begin to learn about avarice, jealousy, hate, *etc.* The patterns to which we draw attention by mentioning motives are familiar not just to the specialist or to the erudite, but, in some measure, to Everyman, to all who have reached years of discernment.

I believe it would be possible to give a very full catalogue of motives by combing a vernacular dictionary. (Not complete, because we also place motives with phrases.) That could not be done for explanations that depend upon the discovery of new facts or result from the construction of scientific theories. It is interesting that those parts of scientific psychology which are beyond dispute seldom show much concern with motives. To the extent that psychology is indeed a science, it seeks and achieves alternative kinds of explanations. Motives are a topic for writers, moralists, and diplomats. Still, while motives are commonsensical, a fine sensitivity to motives and ability to formulate them accurately are rare, and show an imaginative intelligence of the highest order, rather like diagnostic skill in medical practice. Working with motives is, if you wish, an art.

I cannot resist a speculative and possibly irresponsible aside on the psychoanalytic use of 'motive'. Above all else Freud was a moralist.

He is historically important because of the impact he has had on commonsense. Nothing is a better index to this fact than his translator's use of 'motive' and 'unconscious motive', for motives are among the ideas of the market place. What makes one dissatisfied and sceptical of his accounts as originally presented is the suggestion that psychoanalysis is a new kind of *science*. But we do not know what to make of this. In reading Freud, almost everyone feels that he immediately understands; here is something we can all see before us every day of the week. We are shown and soon become able to identify something fairly prevalent in the behaviour of our fellows; Freud with the use of 'motive' brings these phenomena into the ambit of commonsense explanations. But this apparently commonsense-like explanation is directed at phenomena which we feel might be better accounted for by an investigation of conditioning patterns. Apart from therapy, the field of application of the theory—the etiology of neurotic behaviour—is not one in which commonsense feels most at home. Also, by the reticulation of a rather elaborate theory, Freud undercuts the idea of motives as familiar patterns which anyone might learn about in the course of growing up, without need of special training. Now I am told that what has happened is that Freud's *theory* no longer much matters, but the psychoanalytic syndromes to which he drew our attention have become a part of commonsense, at least in societies where fashions of thought are easily diffused. Whatever our would-be psychoanalytic scientists may think about it, 'neurosis' is no longer a technical term.

Putting together the facts that motives are adduced to explain certain kinds of acts done by certain types of animals and in a commonsense way, we may now be a bit more explicit about the various strands which are pulled together into motive patterns. They will be kinds of cause, disposition, agitation, reason, *etc.*, recognition of instances of which in animal behaviour is part of the work-a-day knowledge of the adult human. They will be dispositions which are, so to speak, inherent in our idea of human nature, of the species, such as dispositions to return evil for evil received, to seek positions of advantage over one's fellows, or to help them when in need, or to allot oneself a special position in the world. Or they will be dispositions which set one personality off from another, such as relative sensitivity to slights and criticisms. Or perhaps certain kinds of *deeds*, such as insulting, which we cannot learn to recognize without learning that they *cause* people to respond in various ways. In assigning a motive we explain an act by regarding it through a grid of these various familiar kinds of factor. Other kinds of cause, disposition, *etc.*, *e.g.*, neurological ones, are not strands of such a *motif*. It is natural, then, that many terms for motives should be the same as or

197

substantive cognates of terms which are also used to describe people as having these dispositions, being affected in these ways, or being in these states. Thus 'love', 'hate', 'ambition' and 'ambitious', 'generosity' and 'generous', 'jealousy' and 'jealous'.

Our answers to the first two questions, regarding the subject of motive explanations and the level of explanation, together show how we might distinguish motives from such other commonsense patterns for explaining behaviour as *habit* and *instinct*. While both habit and instinct might be invoked to explain action, and action of almost any kind, they are not restricted to action and even less to any kind of action, as are motive explanations. Both habit and instinct may be used to explain the most obvious kinds of deeds done by the least sophisticated of animals, and even perhaps lower forms of behaviour (the instinctive blink of an eye or habitual clumsiness). A second point of difference is this: while motives, as we say, may involve a great variety of different kinds of factor, the mention of habit or instinct draws attention to certain special kinds of factor, *e.g.*, present stimuli and inherited organic mechanisms for instinct and past experience for habit. Habit and instinct are fairly stereotyped patterns, like blank schedules, to be filled in with attention to the case at hand. Habit and instinct are, to be sure, patterns familiar to commonsense, and nowadays not much cherished by working psychologists or physiologists. Yet, probably because they are so stereotyped, they are the originals, as it were, upon which more recondite, scientific-like patterns of explanation are modelled—from instincts to basic drives, from habits to conditioning bonds. This, then, is a third point of difference from motives: habit and instinct stand closer than do motives to scientific patterns of explanation. This obviously ties up with the inclination that most of us sometimes have to suppose that instinct and/or habit may qualify as explanations of behaviour *überhaupt*, as no one could suppose for (*e.g.*) vanity, jealousy, or curiosity. Habit and instinct, even as known to commonsense, already take on part of the character of a favoured scientific 'model'.

We come now to the third question, whether the assignment of a motive always implies an evaluation. Usually, it seems, motives are bad. But is it always so, as I have heard some say? No. One may have 'good' or 'generous' or 'honourable' motives. It is interesting, though, that we often have to make these up with the word 'motives'. *The* motive is not made specific. But need we evaluate the agent at all? Well, 'curiosity' I take to be a motive-fixing term, and its meaning does not always imply an evaluation of the agent. But, it may be replied, we should assign this or any other *motive* only if something fortunate or unfortunate, commendable or reprehensible occurred. The act or its result must be viewed as being agreeable to or ob-

198

noxious to someone. We typically seek motives for crimes or for what seems rather too commendable. If one takes poison, we ask for a motive, and are told 'curiosity' or 'spite'.

But surely there is nothing either criminal or commendatory in a bricklayer's attending a lecture on the evolution of the Gothic alphabet, however unusual and inexplicable it may at first seem; yet we discover as an explanation that his only motive was *curiosity*. I tentatively conclude that the assignment of motive is not universally even implicitly evaluative of anything.

Still something will call for an explanation; something wants interpretation. Since we are always comparing our fellows to each other and to ourselves, what *requires* explanation will often be something suspiciously praiseworthy or obviously obnoxious in the deed explained or its results, or something wicked or unwontedly saintly in the agent. Most motive words seize on this, and their use tends to lend an appraisive coloration, or to invite questions about good and evil.

Finally, we must consider whether motive explanations are *sui generis*. In a sense they obviously are not. Motives, we saw, are patterns of explanation, not explanatory factors. They compare with those patterns of explanation that are structured by the Laws of Motion or those statistical patterns which are the Mendelian Theory. Most if not all scientific *theories*, as contrasted with generalizations, conjectures, *etc.*, are patterns of explanation. But it remains that they are scientific, while motives are not. Connected with this, a theory imposes a single, systematic pattern upon a given range of phenomena, and success in making the imposition work is a measure of progress; motives, though they all concern human behaviour, are manifold, and we can argue about which one best fits a given case. To find a parallel to motives we must look to the field of human affairs, with its great variety, the field most of us are tilling most of the time, facing situations the understanding of which cannot wait upon the scientific testing of some favoured explanatory scheme. Such are the fields of politics, history, and social affairs. In all of these we are early taught to recognize numbers of familiar patterns including elements of economic and administrative organization, class and national aspiration, distribution of population and resources, and facts about human nature too, including facts about the motives from which men act. Here too it is a fine art to discern the pattern in particular episodes and to say why one sees it so; here too there may be disputed cases, as the writings of historians well show. Multiplicity is the keynote, as with human nature, where no single pattern, *e.g.*, egoism or benevolence, will do; we know in advance that attempts, such as those of Marx and Toynbee, to impose favoured

199

unitary, monolithic patterns are doomed to failure; but just such patterns are exactly what we hope to achieve in science. And here too one wishes to resist the idea that science could conceivably supplant commonsense, without wishing to deny that scientific knowledge can be used to advantage.

In summary, then, my views are these: Motives are commonsense, explanatory patterns of various kinds of factor, where, in the straightest case, mention of a motive is put forward to account for an act done, by way of accounting for the agent's having the purpose in question; such explanations are apposite only when we regard the agent as capable of dissembling his purpose. The assignment of a motive commonly but not invariably implies an evaluation of the agent or of his act. Motive explanations of human behaviour may be likened to certain kinds of historical explanations of political and social circumstances.

Part Three

THE STRATIFICATION OF BEHAVIOUR WITH SPECIAL ATTENTION TO CONFORMATIVE BEHAVIOUR

---

1. THE CONCEPTUAL STRATIFICATION OF BEHAVIOUR

[We have defined *behaviour* as a kind of *animal* movement, and action as a kind of behaviour. In this part we shall extend this programme of definition by specific differences first to define what I call *proficient behaviour*, or behaviour involving *skill*, as a kind of action, and then to define what I call *conformative behaviour*, or *rule-considering behaviour*, as a kind of proficient behaviour. Subsequently the *use of Language* will be defined as a kind of *conventional behaviour*, which is itself a kind of conformative behaviour. This progressive partitioning of behaviour by specific differences will be effected with regard to the situation of an imagined conceptualizing observer of animal movement. Species are to be detached from their respective genera by drawing attention to conditions which must be met if the supposed observer may truly assert that an act of a certain kind, falling within the species in question, is done by the imagined agent. These are what we earlier called *conditions for doing*. Because this is an attempt to produce explanations of certain kinds of (verbal) characterization of behaviour; the result might be styled a conceptual stratification of behaviour.]

In Part II, we were centrally concerned to elaborate an explanation of *action*. Briefly stated, our conclusions were that *action* is to be

201

defined as a kind of behaviour involving the factor of purpose. Purpose is present in behaviour if and only if the movements constituting the behaviour might be explained by the animal's knowledge or belief that certain (what we would call) conditions of success are satisfied. What the animal knows or believes—or, in Aristotle's words, 'perceives, conceives, or imagines'—are reasons or mistaken reasons for the act.

Behaviour, which is the genus of action, was in its prior turn defined as a species of animal movement, for which (as the observer sees) the animal *might* (but need not) be *held responsible*. The movements for which the animal might be held responsible are ones such that there is a presumption, founded on our common knowledge about the type of the animal in question, that creatures of this kind, if trained and disposed in advance, could, when placed in circumstances of the kind in question, by exercise of sufficient attention and expenditure of energy, have arrested or inhibited movements of the kind in question, on occasions like those in question. The definition makes an essential appeal to the observer's knowledge about the species, complemented by whatever special facts he may know about the particular animal, especially as regards prior training and immediate preparation.

The ultimate genus is *animal movement*. No attempt was made to define either 'animal' or 'movement', although it is always presumed that the animal in question is a particular creature of a particular type and that its movements may in the limiting refinement be described kinematically. Usually no more is required than that the observer should be able to see the creature stirring and then be able to describe these movements in some one or other familiar way, often, as we have noted, in language borrowed from our act-identificatory stock.

We have been engaged in a programme of definition *per genus et differentiam*, where the ultimate genus is animal movement. In this part I extend this programme of the partitioning of animal behaviour by specific difference. I shall first review the ancient distinction between practical and theoretical knowledge. Using that as a foundation, I shall then proceed, somewhat diffidently, to define two important kinds of action, one of which includes the other as a species. These are, respectively, action which necessarily manifests skill or knowing-how-to, which I call *proficient behaviour*, and action which is done either in conformity with or in violation of rules, which I call *conformative behaviour*. The former includes the latter as a species. In Part IV I go on to define *conventional behaviour* as a kind of conformative behaviour, and in Part V the *use of Language* will be defined as a species of conventional behaviour. In a sequel to this volume one of my tasks will be to show how the use of Language may itself be partitioned into kinds, some of which include others. These natural though not inevitable strata correspond roughly to familiar psychological categories. My use of 'behaviour' is a rough equivalent of the psychologist's use of the same word. My 'action' covers the range of phenomena which psychologists study under perception. Proficient behaviour is learned behaviour, conformative behaviour is social behaviour; and the 'use of Language' speaks for itself as covering a topic which has recently excited interest among psychologists.[1]

Although there be this rough correspondence between my strata and the psychologist's familiar classifications, the aims and methods of this study are importantly different from those of psychology, for reasons set forth in Part I, no. 3. The psychologist, chiefly the Learning Theorist, is concerned to explain behaviour in terms of 'models' which, as it were, depict condition-and-response bonding mechanisms. In practice he tends to concentrate on the movements of the animal imagined to be under observation and upon the special items in the immediate surroundings of the animal which provoke a response. Now there are many other conditions which might come into play—the existence of a community, for example. The psychologist's inclination to push everything else into the movements as made in response to certain specific elements in the immediate vicinity of the animal leads to 'models' which become more and more difficult to articulate and less and less fruitful in application as we move from the salivation of Pavlov's dog to discussions of theoretical physics. The movements of the tongue and larynx are almost adventitious to the use of Language. Allowing that behaviour, or at least all behaviour which must be learned, is 'conditioned', to account for the inculcation of such behaviour will in general require attention to much more than

[1] A lattice might prove useful to the reader:

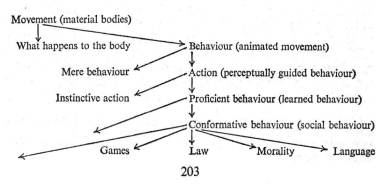

animal movement made in response to immediate stimuli. Now, unlike the psychologist, I am not beholden to any 'model' or kind of model, and have no hesitation over appealing to any kind of 'condition' you please. Here then is one difference, but a rather superficial one.

The really important difference is that, while the psychologist supposes that he means to explain the facts of the observed animate world, the 'theoretical position' here assumed is the quite different one of 'conceptual epiphenomenalism'. The aim is to expose putatively fundamental cruces in our (for the most part) common ways of thinking and talking about animal behaviour. To this end, we concentrate attention upon an imagined conceptualizing observer of behaviour, and therefore upon our own selves who have acquired a quite high level of behavioural sophistication. We ask after what is importantly implicit in the observer's reports upon behaviour. The programme of definitions is designed to display an increasing behavioural sophistication in the imagined observed animal, by considering what the observer must take note of in the movements, situation, and circumstances of the observed creature in order to be warranted in his reports. It is the conceptualizing observer who is the direct subject of investigation. Caution must be exercised not to suppose that the imagined observed animal also be able always to take note of the facts which warrant the report. The observed animal could do that only were he performing at the same level of behavioural sophistication as our conceptualizing observer, implying a capacity for reflection on the part of the observed animal, which is not generally required for action (see Part II, no. 8), that capacity being a *special* feature of what I call *conventional behaviour* (see Part IV, nos. 3, 5).

The facts which warrant the observer's report may be brought under the umbrella title of *conditions*. Our analysis would proceed by specifying conditions characteristic of the behavioural type or stratum under investigation, where these are conditions of the movements, situation, and circumstances of the observed animal. Confining ourselves to types of action, as we shall henceforward do, it would suffice to consider only types of condition of success. This follows from our principle that we identify a type of action by specifying a purpose, where the purpose itself is identified by specifying conditions of success. It is presumed that each such type of action is first found on some lowest stratum.[2] We might then

---

[2] The implicit qualification is required by the fact that acts of the same type may be done in more and less sophisticated ways, *e.g.*, eating and eating with knife and fork. The latter would count as proficient behaviour, though not so for all acts of eating.

characterize the stratum by specifying *kinds* of condition of success definitive of all kinds of action which first appear at that stratum. I shall not eschew this method, but nor shall I confine myself to it. A more general and more familiar method is to ask after the 'truth-conditions' of the imagined observer's report. We do not ask merely under what conditions the act must fail, but rather what conditions must be met for the act *either* to succeed *or* to fail, *i.e.*, under what conditions such and such a kind of act was done at all. These are what we called *conditions for doing* the act. Included here is the condition that the agent believes that all the conditions of success of his act are satisfied. The method of conditions of doing therefore implicitly has all the advantages of the method of conditions of success. But the method of conditions of doing is obviously much stronger and also of wider application, for it can be used to elicit explanations not only for types of action but for non-purposive behaviour as well; *i.e.*, we say what conditions must be satisfied for the observer to give any kind of true behavioural report on the movements of the supposed animal. Behavioural strata are defined by specifying kinds of condition for behaviour at that stratum. Any true behavioural report which implies that the item of behaviour in question is at a certain level of behaviour will also imply that conditions of every kind definitive of that level are satisfied. Thus, 'connecting an electric circuit' is an identification of action at the level of proficient behaviour, and a report given in these terms will imply (*inter alia*) that the observed animal be in possession of certain equipment and have acquired certain skills including the ability to connect electric circuits. These conditions must be satisfied if the imagined agent is even so much as to fail in an act of connecting an electric circuit. The one condition, that the agent have a specific capacity or ability, is both characteristic of and peculiar to proficient behaviour; the other, that the agent have suitable equipment available, is typically, though not inevitably, implied by reports of proficient behaviour.

It is evident that the kinds of condition we may have to mention for purposes of characterizing a behavioural stratum are various. They may be both conditions of the agent and conditions of the world, and may have to do with beliefs, social circumstances, age, education, capacities, *etc.*, of the agent as well as the existence or presence of environmental props, respondents, equipment, social institutions, *etc.*

Because these conditions are conditions of truth for an imagined observer's report, and are to be sought and listed for purposes of classifying that report, the ensuing stratification is in the first instance a theoretical system for categorizing our (common) ways of thinking

and talking about behaviour. We thus might denominate what results
a *conceptual stratification of behaviour.*

2. PRACTICAL AND THEORETICAL KNOWLEDGE, WITH SPECIAL ATTENTION TO PARTICULAR IDENTIFICATION

[We have in this work already made use of the traditional distinction
between practical and theoretical knowledge, which is important
throughout philosophy. One has theoretical knowledge only if he has
retained information previously acquired and is capable of giving
verbal expression to that information. Practical knowledge is
genetically prior in order of acquisition to theoretical knowledge.
But the ascription of practical knowledge to an animal by a conceptualizing observer is made on analogy with the theoretical
knowledge which the observer must have. Practical knowledge, which
does not require the capability of giving verbal expression to information acquired, is to be explained by analysis of the observer's
analogical ascriptions. More specifically, the idea of practical knowledge is explained on analogy with the perceptual acquisition of
information. The distinction between theoretical and practical knowledge is applied to the special but interesting case of the identification
of particulars. Our analysis, when applied to the case of action, yields
the conclusion that the (particular) identification of an act can never
be merely practical.]

In our explanation of *action* we found it necessary to appeal to the
idea of awareness, and therewith also to the ancient distinction
between practical and theoretical knowledge. This distinction is
among the most recurrent, hence essential as well as venerable, in the
whole of philosophy. It insinuates itself, sometimes, alas, invisibly
into every corner but especially into classical discussions of the
origins of our ideas and of our knowledge, and is neglected with
peril. Attention to it will enable us to see how some philosophers
have gone seriously wrong. As an example, I have already mentioned
Hampshire (see pp. 79f.), who, while doubtless alive to the distinction,
fails to hold the line, and seems usually to suppose that an agent must
theoretically know facts which he may be aware of only in the practical
sense. The paradoxical air of Hume's theory about reason and the
passions is, as we saw, partly due to his insistence that knowledge be
theoretical. We are perhaps most in need of the distinction where it is
important to distinguish an agent's behaviour from an observer's
theoretical account: the observer, to give his account, must have
theoretical knowledge of what the agent may know only in the
practical sense. Where the observed behaviour presupposes Lan-

guage, the distinction includes the cardinal one which Moore so correctly and usefully drew between knowing the meaning of a word and knowing its analysis. Locke's polemic against innate ideas has a similarly salutary effect of not allowing us (as Leibniz seemed to want to do) to regard theoretical principles about the use of Language, so-called 'maxims' like the Law of Identity, as being on a genetic and logical par with statements about (*e.g.*) sticks and stones. It is possible to interpret what Kant called the 'transcendental' as a body of putative theoretical knowledge concerning our practical capacities to engage in theoretical activities. At all events, the distinction is inescapable in any discussion of behaviour; we have encountered it already, and shall be forever stumbling across it as we go on. But now this distinction between practical and theoretical knowledge, though philosophically pervasive, is technical, only implicitly familiar to commonsense, and not visible in the vernacular. It is easily overlooked in the conduct of theorizing, and hard to make out even when its presence is felt. I therefore deem it advisable to supply some further explanation of the distinction, that we may have it sufficiently well under control to need suffer no compunctions from its use.

An observer says that another animal knows such and such. The report will have different implications depending among other things upon the character of the observed animal and the 'such and such'. We may equally say that Jones knows that there are mountains between Denver and Salt Lake City or that Fido knows that food is cooking in the patio. But the implications of the two reports are different. The observer implies that John has learned something in the past, which he could now tell us if we asked him. But Fido, we take it, shows all by his wagglings here and now. John may express his knowledge in speech, Fido only in (other) behaviour. John has *got* it and could be brought to say it; Fido simply sniffs it. John's knowledge is *theoretical*, Fido's only *practical*. But what precisely is the difference?

It is *not* that the word 'know' is ambiguously employed by our imagined observer. Nor is it even that we are being confronted by two different *kinds* of knowledge. The observer in both instances tells us that the observed animal *knows that* something is the case. He might equally unambiguously have told us that both observed animals knew (were familiar with) some object or other, Denver or his master, Hume's *Treatise* or the garbageman. The distinction between theoretical and practical knowledge in particular is not the distinction between *knowing-that* (propositional knowledge) and *knowing-how-to* (proficiency or skill). Like any other kind of action, proficient action implies at least practical knowledge on the part of the supposed agent; we shall see that proficient behaviour always implies the possession of a rather superior kind of practical knowledge, which is conclusive against equating practical knowledge with proficiency. The distinction between practical and theoretical knowledge is, rather, a distinction between different *grades* or *levels* of propositional knowledge, now taken also to embrace knowledge of particulars. (One of our results will be to show, contrary to what some have thought, that knowledge-*that* is presupposed by knowledge of particulars on the levels of *both* practical and theoretical knowledge.)

But what is this distinction in 'grade'? Our drawing out of the different implications of 'John knows' and 'Fido knows' clearly reveals that the distinction is one phase of the difference between behaviour which does and does not presume the use of Language. Only when we ascribe knowledge to conceptualizing creatures do we imply that their knowledge is theoretical. Theoretical knowledge is a possession which presumes a capacity to say what one knows. One need not express his (theoretical) knowledge, but he could. For this reason, it might seem that discussion of the distinction should wait until after we have explained the use of Language. But that would be inadvisable if not impossible. From here on out, we shall have frequent occasion to characterize behaviour by saying that the observed animal must have practical knowledge of . . .. But 'practical knowledge', I shall presently argue, may be understood only on analogy with 'theoretical knowledge'. The observer to make his report must in general have 'theoretical knowledge' of what the observed in general has only 'practical knowledge' of. Understanding the distinction is needed for protecting the more primitive personality of the observed against the impositions of the observer.

So, again, what is the difference? That is, what differences exist between those ascriptions of knowledge to creatures by a conceptualizing observer that *we*, for purposes of our analysis, would wish to distinguish as ascriptions of practical and theoretical knowledge? Our examples make clear that one who has theoretical knowledge has 'got it' and can say it; but one who has merely practical knowledge may neither have got it nor be able to say it. The 'it' in question is an item of information. The 'have got it' means to remember the information. To 'be able to say it' means to be able to give express conventional formulation to the fact, the general knowledge of which constitutes the information in question.

It will pay to dwell on this at some length. I use 'information' to cover only what is actually the case. If I pass on information that my department is to be reorganized I imply that it is actually the case that the department will be reorganized. So if we explain theoretical knowledge as the retention of information acquired, it is implied that we cannot be truly said to know theoretically what is not the case. To speak of something as information also implies that the something in question has become known to someone at some time. Information, to be sure, may be lost, but only if previously acquired. It might now seem that any attempt to explain theoretical knowledge in terms of actual information must be circular. The charge would, I allow, be well founded if we were trying to give some general explanation of the idea of (human) knowledge, which could perhaps be described as a fund of accumulated information. But we are not doing that. We are trying to explain observers' ascriptions of (theoretical) knowledge to creatures. What is implied by such reports is that *what* the observer says the creature knows is an item of information, *i.e.*, something known to someone sometime, usually of course to the observer himself.

To say that the animal has 'got' the information, or that he remembers it, implies that he *acquired* the information on some one or several occasions and has *retained* it. Animals acquire information always on particular occasions if in many different ways. It is always implied that, upon the occasion or occasions of acquisition, the animal was awake and alive to the world. He must have been perceptually sensitive in specific ways, having suitable sense organs, operating and properly trained upon the world. He will commonly also need various capacities and skills special to the kind of information acquired and to the way in which the information is acquired. Consider the last first: To acquire information from a book one must generally know how to read. About the former: To acquire information (*e.g.*) that a certain light bulb is burned out, one must know how to switch on lights, not necessarily this light but lights sometime, somewhere. Combining the two considerations, to acquire information that a certain piano is out of tune by hearing the piano implies that the animal have certain acoustical acuities. Thus, while having (theoretical) knowledge is not itself a kind of capacity or skill,[1] it will certainly imply that the subject animal should have capacities including intellectual capacities, of various kinds.

Turning to the retention or memory of information, it is required that the information could be made to recur to the animal sometime after he has acquired it. In general, he need not remember when or how he acquired the information. Nor, in general, need the information recur to the animal at any particular time after acquisition—we do not always 'realize' what we know. Nor, again, need the animal by his own efforts in general be able to bring the information to mind in order that we be able to say that he remembers. In general all that is

[1] As some have held. See J. Hartland-Swann, *An Analysis of Knowing*, Chap. IV.

required is that it be possible that the information be brought to his mind, *e.g.*, by putting him into familiar circumstances, by giving him certain tests, recalling certain facts to his attention.

Finally, let us consider the requirement that the animal who has theoretical knowledge must be able to give express conventional formulation to the information in question. Pre-eminently, what is wanted here is capacity in the use of Language, among other skills. It is not universally required that the animal be able to say *that* he knows what he knows (he may not have the use of 'know' or any equivalent word), only that he be able to say that which (as the observer sees) he knows. The capacity in question includes, and indeed is to be defined by the capacity or knowledge how to verify and/or falsify the propositions which result from formulating the information. That in its turn implies that the animal was capable of having acquired the information in question as a result of making (what *we* could call) a deliberate test. Of course, he need not, and perhaps in fact could not, have actually acquired the information in that way: he might simply have seen it or have read it. Finally, I hold, to be able to formulate the information implies that the animal could by his own efforts *bring* the information in question to mind, whether or not he ever does.

The ability to give expression to what one knows is not independent of the acquisition and retention of information. A test that an animal acquires or retains information is that he should report what he learns or remembers. It follows that giving a verbal report of information is also a criterion or test for the possession of theoretical knowledge. We *prove* that an animal has theoretical knowledge by eliciting such a report. Of course, an animal may have theoretical knowledge, as the observer very well may know, and still no proof be forthcoming.

My view is that ascriptions of theoretical knowledge require, whereas ascriptions of practical knowledge do not require, that the observed animal should remember and be able to give express formulation to information. In the course of explaining this, I have begun (but only begun) to give an analysis of theoretical knowledge. But now we must face the inevitable question over the *common* character of theoretical and practical knowledge which justifies the common (non-ambiguous) use of 'know'.

I take it as given that we regularly do correctly and truly apply terms of cognition to creatures who do not remember what they know and who are certainly not capable of giving verbal expression to what we say they know. Dogs as well as infants are regularly and truly said to 'be aware of' smells, to 'know that' food is cooking, to 'think that' they will get some, or to 'be conscious of' the presence of danger. (I have chosen types of example where the animal neither

PRACTICAL AND THEORETICAL KNOWLEDGE

remembers nor is able to say what he knows. Clearly animals sometimes do remember, though they could not say what they know—as
when we say that the dog knows where he buried his bone. Also an
animal may be able to say what he now sees, hence practically knows,
though he does not remember.)

If only we could put our finger on this 'common factor' it would
seem very natural to regard theoretical knowledge as practical knowledge *plus* something else. Theoretical knowledge appears to have
features not needed for practical knowledge, *e.g.*, the animal's
capacity to give verbal expression to what he knows—what we might
call 'reflective self-consciousness'. Furthermore, it is clear that
practical knowledge is prior to theoretical knowledge in order of
genetic development. Infants know things only in the practical sense,
whereas adults know (perhaps different) things in both the practical
and theoretical senses. Before the observer can truly ascribe theoretical knowledge to an animal, it must be possible to ascribe items of
practical knowledge to that animal, but not conversely. Theoretical
knowledge is a later acquisition, a condition for which is the possession of some, not necessarily the same, items of practical knowledge. This is a simple consequence of the fact that the development of
memory and the acquisition of the use of Language both presuppose
quantities of awareness. That is the origin of the idea that we should
explain theoretical knowledge as practical knowledge *plus*, indeed
perhaps as a kind of elaborate augmentation of practical knowledge.

I do not deny it could be done. But I certainly do not believe that
we need thus to duplicate the genetic order in our order of explanation. Nor do I think that it could be done easily. As regards the last,
evidently we must first isolate the 'common factor'. Here it is not at
all obvious how to proceed. Moreover, doubts can be raised over the
existence of a common factor. Our explanation would appear to
imply that theoretical knowledge is a kind of memory. But many of
our examples of practical knowledge are not memory.

It is more important to understand why we do not need to follow
the genetic order, for that will bring us close to a resolution of the
question of the relation between practical and theoretical knowledge
and also possibly enable us to put a finger on the common factor.
We are asking what it is for an *observer* to ascribe knowledge, where
the nature of the ascription either implies that it is practical or that it
is theoretical knowledge. Knowledge, for our purposes, is an
observer's concept. We want to understand what it is to *say* that Fido
knows where his dish is. Now it is clear that an observer cannot
ascribe any specified and particularized item of knowledge[2] to an

[2] By which I mean knowledge of a mentioned matter of fact, *e.g.*, knowledge
that John is in the kitchen, as against knowledge of *who* is in the kitchen.

211

animal unless he, the observer, could have theoretical knowledge of the same fact. The argument is simply this. The ascription of such knowledge, whether practical or theoretical, involves the equivalent of a 'that' clause which the observer takes to be true. But if one is capable of thus formulating a 'that' clause which he takes to be true, he must be capable of having theoretical knowledge: the observer's use of 'know' is gained in connection with what he, as viewed by another observer, theoretically knows.[3] We are, therefore, not compelled to explain theoretical knowledge in terms of practical knowledge. Since we are, in effect, 'given' that the imagined observer has theoretical knowledge, we may, as we have done, inquire how his ascriptions of the two kinds of knowledge differ. We might then exploit some previously given account of theoretical knowledge to explain practical knowledge. We have already given such an account of theoretical knowledge, not complete, to be sure, but perhaps sufficient for the project we envisage.

It is reasonable to assume that the observer ascribes practical knowledge as something the possession of which is *analogous to* theoretical knowledge he must have. We would then explain practical knowledge in terms of theoretical knowledge by drawing out the analogy. Rather than explain theoretical knowledge as an enlargement upon practical knowledge, we explain practical knowledge as an attenuation of theoretical knowledge. And that is exactly what I propose. The 'common factor' may come out by subtraction.

Taking 'aware of' as a compendious summary of all cognitive terms as used to ascribe practical knowledge, my submission is that *our use* of 'aware of' is to be explained on analogy with *our use* of 'know', which it thus presupposes. While the acquisition of practical knowledge and the exercise of practical intelligence are indispensable preliminaries to having theoretical knowledge, our *concepts of*, what we mean by practical knowledge and intelligence, are derivative from their theoretical counterparts.

What now of this analogy? How is it to be made out? Ascriptions of practical knowledge are often provoked by observations that the subject animal is reacting in a 'biologically intelligent' way to his immediate surroundings. He goes there because he sees food. We say that he knows that there is food in the dish. We also observe that he has a nose for smelling and eyes for seeing and that these are indispensable to his behaving as he does. The possession by the animal of perceptual acuities and of organs of perception is not a matter of

---

[3] This argument I confidently believe is sound, but far from complete for avoiding entanglements in a network of surrounding issues, the connections of which are intricate and the correct unravelling of which would require extreme delicacy. For further arguments, see J. O. Urmson's 'Recognition', *Proc. Arist. Soc.*, 1956.

analogy. Dogs have eyes and ears in as full-formed a way as do human beings. The possession of perceptual apparatus affords the non-analogical basis upon which we analogically ascribe knowledge to animals. More specifically, practical knowledge may be ascribed to creatures who are in a position to receive those facts by a perception, which for a creature having theoretical knowledge would have verified the information in question. The animal must be perceptually sensitive, open, and directed in comparable ways. All that need be different is that the perception not occur as the upshot of an actual verification test. The explanation of it not so resulting may be simply that the creature may not know such tests, or it may be that he was not capable of making such a test. The analogy is secured by the mere occurrence of a perception. Positively, all depends upon how we establish that animals are perceptually sensitive, open, and directed in 'comparable ways'. No hard and fast rules can be set down regulating the comparison. The principal clues will be biological and physical ones, e.g., that the animal seeks the object, that light or sound or scent is present, etc.[4] More may be needed, for we must assume that the creature have reached a level of development, including the acquisition of various skills, comparable to those which are implied for one to have the ability to verify the statement in question, though not necessarily including that skill itself. And here again 'comparable' appears upon the scene.

'Comparable' may stir suspicion. It should not; it merely echoes our appeal to analogy. However, if a stiffer sounding formulation is wanted, we may say practical knowledge is sometimes ascribed on analogy with the *acquisition of information by direct perceptual verification*. That, I believe, is the most primitive case. This kind of practical knowledge differs from theoretical knowledge in that no memory of information previously acquired is demanded or even permitted. Such practical knowledge shares no 'common factor' with theoretical knowledge. But it may share any number of common factors with the perceptual acquisition of theoretical knowledge.[5]

---

[4] Hampshire (*op. cit.*, p. 45) holds that only agents can be held to perceive. That is not true, for the infant who blinks and is then said to 'have seen light' is not an agent. Yet it may be true that only animals whom we regard as *potential* agents may be said to perceive, and the reason for that could be that our criteria are largely biological. In particular, perception occurs chiefly in connection with an animal's approaching to or moving away from an object, which he 'perceives', and such movement is behaviour of the action kind.

[5] It would be wrong to maintain that all theoretical knowledge could be acquired perceptually, for that would exclude mathematical knowledge. But that does not matter for present purposes. There is no distinction between practical and theoretical mathematical knowledge. Only creatures capable of having theoretical knowledge know mathematical truths and if they know them at all they know

The chief difference is that the fact of this acquisition is verified, not by the animal's perceptual report, but by his non-verbal behaviour. He may have the theoretical knowledge without actually giving it express formulation, but the formulation would be the proof.

So far I have considered only practical knowledge that is *perceptual*, and which has no factor in common with its theoretical model. Can we extend this account to cover practical *memory-knowledge*? If *A*'s report of what he remembers is proof of what he theoretically knows, something analogous would be wanted for the proof of practical memory-knowledge. Here we can say no more than that he behaves as would a man who could and would say what he knows. The behaviour manifests approaches and retreats which the observer can understand only as conditioned by the prior acquisition of information. Needless to say, our willingness to allow that a creature has practical knowledge which is non-perceptual, that is, practical memory-knowledge, depends upon our view of the animal, his kind, *etc.* It is, again, a zoological question, to be answered *pari passu* with our reasonable judgments regarding how far his behaviour is analogous to our own.

Practical memory-knowledge does have a factor in common with theoretical knowledge, *viz.*, memory of information acquired.[6]

One who is capable of theoretical knowledge of a fact, *F*, may still have only practical knowledge of *F*. We meet with all sorts of things in our daily experience which make their mark, but which we are not conscious of, *e.g.*, when walking down a corridor we unconsciously avoid physical encounter with other objects, and thereby show our

---

[6] It is clear that my efforts have not been to explain, psychologically or otherwise, the development of knowledge and intellectual capacity. I do not derogate such projects, though what I attempt is of a quite different order. In particular, Piaget's discussion (*e.g.*, *Judgment and Reason in the Child*, Chap. V, § 2) of the attainment of conscious thought out of behaviour by way of a reproductive shift from the plane of action to that of Language, prompted by the necessity of social communication, and leading ultimately to the animal's reflection on his own behaviour, seems entirely consistent with my analysis of the relation between practical and theoretical knowledge. I certainly do not object to his 'law of shifting' (*décalage*) according to which theory recapitulates practice; though I am not too clear what it all comes to. It is not in conflict with the principle that our *concept* of practical knowledge recapitulates our *concept* of theoretical knowledge. What I do boggle at are his claims for some kind of preconceptual egocentric, autistic, infantile 'thought'. I think that my method of analysis would obviate the need for that.

---

them theoretically (not necessarily by having proved them). My submission is that so far as there is a distinction between practical and theoretical knowledge, theoretical knowledge may be acquired by direct perception and practical knowledge is ascribed as something analogous to the acquisition of theoretical knowledge by a successful verification test.

awareness of their presence. However, one who has sufficient Language may, on reflection, come to know the facts theoretically. It is important that practical knowledge neither is nor ever can be entirely superseded by theoretical knowledge. To have theoretical knowledge of one fact will involve practical knowledge of other facts. Now those facts, too, can be known theoretically, but such express theoretical knowledge will carry with it further practical knowledge, *e.g.*, of the rules of some tongue by recourse to which the animal would express his knowledge. Practical knowledge, which is the first kind of knowledge a creature has, is knowledge which others ascribe to animals in consideration of how they behave with respect to their environment; and its primary and regular manifestation is in behaviour, pre-eminently in action.

There are various kinds of knowledge, cross-classifications if you wish, of both practical and theoretical knowledge. We have already remarked on the distinction between knowing facts and knowing objects. There is also a distinction between perception of a fact and memory of it, which, at the practical level, turns out to be a distinction between kinds of knowledge. (I do not believe that there is a kind of perceptual, theoretical knowledge; perception is one way by which theoretical knowledge is *acquired*; it is not itself a kind of knowledge.) We may also classify knowledge according to the forms of the propositions in which it would be formulated, *e.g.*, singular subject-predicate knowledge, knowledge of identity, existence.

I cannot go into all this. But I should like to say a bit about practical and theoretical *identification*.

This is an important case for philosophy because there is a traditional if implicitly held doctrine according to which all other knowledge is based upon the acquisition of the practical knowledge of the identity of particulars. It is the doctrine of classical empiricism, recently refurbished as Russell's theory of Knowledge by Acquaintance and Knowledge by Description. I think it is mistaken. Our investigation of knowledge of identity will touch upon the distinction between knowledge of facts and knowledge of particulars and the distinction between practical perceptual and memory-knowledge, and will thereby begin to show how the empiricist view is in error. At all events, the distinction between theoretical and practical identification is an especially important one for our purposes and will be encountered constantly in the sequel, often only implicitly. I shall be somewhat careless about it, and it is partly to ease my conscience for this laxity that I wish to examine the distinction, which we must at any rate understand.

The philosophical use of the concept of *identification* is often hampered by a double equivocation which cuts across both the

215

practical and the theoretical varieties. There is, in the first place, the distinction we have already met between *particular* identification and *typal* identification. Theoretical particular identification is a matter of saying or implying *which one*; theoretical typal indentification is a matter of saying *what kind*. Though these two types of identification are distinct and can be defined independently, in actual practice they are usually complementary. Usually (not always) particular identification presumes a prior determination of type. Thus we identify which *radio* or *animal*, and often we cannot settle the question which one without a determination of type (see pp. 42f.). Another point is this: Both particular and typal identification presuppose that we have individuated an object. And both kinds of identification attach to the object given as a whole (see pp. 44f.). An object thus individuated always has a variety of subsidiary features. As a rule, mention of some of these would contribute to fixing the theoretical particular identification of the thing, while mention of others would contribute to fixing the theoretical typal identification of the thing. For example, we individuate an object—let it be a lion—in 'space and time'. And we say which object it is by saying where it is when. None of this says anything about what kind of object it is. Particular position in space and time is no part of the definition of the lion if only because it is that which distinguishes one lion from another. On the other hand, the object will certainly have other non-individuating features from which we select in order to explain what a lion is. The relation between particular and typal identification is difficult to elucidate because the notion of typal identification is itself so difficult. I am able to say no more about it at this point than I was in Part II, no. 4. So let us simply note the fact that particular identification should not be confused with typal identification, and let it go at that.

I shall, then, confine myself to particular identification, which is itself of two kinds. Let me first illustrate and explain both varieties of *theoretical* particular identification, later extending the distinction by analogy to practical identification, a procedure recommended by our general analysis of the relations between theoretical and practical knowledge.

'Identify' can, in the first place, mean 'make a true statement of identity': *e.g.*, 'The first guest to arrive was John', 'cos $\pi/2 = \sin \pi$', 'That is the man'. Such statements contain two references which are held to determine one and the same object.

One may, in the second place, be said to have identified an object if he has simply made a statement about that object, not necessarily a statement of identity, if that statement includes at least one suitable or 'identifying' reference. Thus, if I say 'John killed her', I may be said to have identified the killer.

The connection between the two occurrences of 'identify' are, first, that a statement of identity must itself include at least one suitable or 'identifying' reference, and second, that the second kind of identification, when realized in an act of making a statement, will always imply the possibility of making a true statement of identity, *e.g.*, 'John is the killer'.

Not all references are identifying. 'A man' in 'A man whom I saw enter the study killed her' does not necessarily identify, for just what we may want to know is who was the man who entered the study. Also, the simple unqualified uses of 'this' and 'that' never afford identifying references. What then makes a reference 'suitable' or 'identifying'? An identifying reference is one which would occur in a statement made in answer to a question 'Which?' or 'Who?'. It would, moreover, have to belong to a fairly well organized family of possible answering references, which are or tend to be mutually alternative and exclusive. That is brought about by conveying the reference *via* a kind of expression whose use is appropriate both to the kind of object (*e.g.*, a *person* or a *number*) and to the circumstances. An example of a family of expressions especially appropriate to people are their names, Christian plus surnames; and a family of expressions especially appropriate to natural numbers are the numerals. The employment of such expressions would usually yield identifying references. But we can also secure identifications by using other numerical expressions when talking about numbers, or by using numerals when dealing with almost any kind of thing which has been ordered. Definite descriptions of a variety of kinds may also be used to identify, *e.g.*, 'The first man to the left'. For every type of object there is a preferred kind of reference, which I call 'locating reference'. Such references refer to objects in such a way that they *must* individuate, for example by way of the specification of sets of characteristics, features, or circumstances which no two objects can possibly share. Material objects are located by specification of the largest region of space they completely occupy at a given time. Natural numbers are located by way of numerical references, which, of course, are not descriptions. Locating references are identifying, and other identifying references give verbal indications possibly leading to an individuation.

It is the second observation—that an identifying reference presupposes a true statement of identity whereas non-identifying references do not—that is crucial. This point may be formulated as follows: The occurrence of an identifying reference in the product of some Language act indicates that a condition of success for that act is that the speaker could successfully apply a test to verify a statement of identity involving that reference. Thus the success of an assertion that my dog is dumb implies the possibility of testing a statement of identity involving a reference to *my dog*, *e.g.*, the statement that my dog is Chula. That is not so for non-identifying references. We may consider two kinds of example, what we may call 'demonstrative references' and 'indefinite references'.

A demonstrative reference is characteristically conveyed by use of a demonstrative pronoun, *e.g.*, 'This'. If I point to a book and say, 'This is overdue at the library', I do not identify the book I refer to. Indeed, tyros in the use of Language may get a grasp on the very same use of 'This' without as yet being so much as able to understand the question 'same or different?' (see my 'The Temporal Order', *Phil. Quart.*, 1960, pp. 32–43). Demonstrative references do better than identify. The successful employment of 'This', in the intended sense, depends upon the actual presence of the object referred to in a location, which location therefore need not be verbally specified or indicated in the reference. We might call demonstrative reference 'references in location'. Such references clearly do not form a 'family'. Nor do they imply that the speaker could successfully apply a re-identification test. Such a test, if successful, would bring the object into a specified location, but a demonstrative reference to the object depends upon its actually being in the location. This observation connects with what we earlier noted about the first kind of particular identification: A statement of identity must contain at least one identifying reference; hence, it cannot contain two demonstrative references. That is what we find: there is no sense to the questions 'Is this = this?' or 'Is this = that?' for the answer in both cases would be settled by the question itself. Now we may raise a question about the identity of an object referred to in location, to be answered by a statement of the form 'This = R', where 'R' schematizes an identifying non-demonstrative reference. That statement would be verified by bringing the object from the location specified by 'R' into the location which must be occupied by the referent if the current employment of 'This' is to succeed. [7]

---

[7] Not all occurrences of 'this' in referring expressions are non-identifying. Thus, pointing to two objects, I may ask whether *this colour* is the same as *that colour*. The question makes sense and may be answered. Moreover, I identify (second sense) the colours, respectively, as the colour *of this object* and the colour *of that object*. I might more accurately have formulated the same question, 'Is the colour of this object the same as the colour of that object?'. Here 'this' and 'that' are used to refer to the objects which have the colours and are indeed employed to convey demonstrative, non-identifying references: it makes no sense to ask whether this object is the same as that object, for understanding of the reference depends upon an understanding that the objects are different. Briefly, 'This colour' is short for 'The colour of this', in which latter 'this' conveys a demonstrative, non-identifying reference.

Indefinite references, a second important kind of non-identifying reference, are characteristically conveyed by use of an indefinite article. Compare 'The dog is in the garden again' and 'A dog is in the garden again'. The references to the dog in both cases are singular references, and the successful verification of either statement implies that the other could be verified: the two supposed statements would presumably be equivalent in truth-value, but they are not identical. The difference is that the speaker, in making the first statement, implies that he knows *which* dog; success in the assertion of the statement therefore implies that a (non-trivial) statement of identity involving the same reference could be successfully verified. Not so for the second example. Otherwise put, the possibility of the speaker's establishing the identity of the dog is a condition of success for making the first statement but not for the second. That condition satisfied, the two statements are true and false together. [8]

We have, then, two kinds of theoretical identifications and two kinds of theoretical knowledge of identity: that which is shown by the making of a true statement of identity, and that which is shown by the occurrence of an identifying reference in any other kind of true statement.

We turn now to 'practical identification'. It occurs primarily when the object identified is present with the animal whose reactions to certain features of the object warrant the observer's saying that the animal becomes aware of the identity of the object. That is the perceptual case, and is the only one I consider. As with all practical knowledge, we must be able to frame a counterpart report that would be made by the animal, had he enough Language. That report either is or implies a statement of identity. One of the references of the statement would be a demonstrative reference conveyed by the animal's saying something like 'This' or 'That'. That sort of reference, we just saw, certainly cannot be the required identifying reference.

Holding this in mind, we must now look for practical analogues to our two kinds of particular identification, statement of identity identification and identifying reference identification. Analogous to the case where one makes a statement of identity is that in which one

---

[8] I do not pretend that this constitutes an adequate account of this very difficult distinction between identifying and non-identifying references. I shall return to it in a sequel to this volume. Needless to say, the distinction is a highly technical one, but for all that it is one which I think would prove useful throughout philosophy, not only in logic and metaphysics. In an interesting paper on the philosophy of law, J. Z. Krasnowiecki ('A Logical Problem in the Law of Mistake as to Person', *Phil. Quart.*, 1960, pp. 313–21) observes in effect that some apparent paradoxes in the law of mistake could be avoided by allowing for identifying references other than personal name references. He also makes use of a doctrine of the primacy of non-identifying demonstrative references in location.

recognizes an object. Recognition implies prior familiarity. The counterpart statement is one in which the animal would if he could say that the object presently on view—'This'—is such and such; his perception of the object might have been the result of a successful attempt to verify the identity of the object. What he identifies the object as, would be indicated by the identifying reference. In the typical, though not inevitable, case, that reference will indicate a time and place of previous awareness, *e.g.*, 'That's the man I saw last night at The Dunes'.

There is also a practical counterpart to the second kind of identification, in which the statement in question, while not a statement of identity, implies that the subject knows some statement of identity including the indicated identifying reference. One may identify a symphony even if he cannot be said to recognize it, not having heard it before. Another kind of case which will be especially interesting to us is where what the animal identifies is what another animal wishes to say.

With diffidence, I now hazard the opinion that to say of an animal that he has made a practical identification of this second kind always implies that he has the use of Language. Our examples suggest this: To identify the symphony which he has never heard the listener must still be able to give its composer and number, or perhaps opus number or name ('Eroica'); to identify the statement he must be able to make the statement himself. The argument is as follows: Counterpart to the practical identification is a report, 'This is ϕ', where neither 'this' nor 'ϕ' fixes a particular identifying reference; but there must also be an implied statement of identity, 'This $= R$', where 'R' must identify. Now 'R' cannot identify by reference to time and place of some previous awareness, for the practical identification here, by assumption, is not a case of recognition. What kind of identification is it, then? Well, the animal's response to the object as a single, identifiable thing must in no way be conditioned by his familiarity with it; its identification must in no way be dependent upon its presence to him, now or before; the animal must know what it is, as it were, in the abstract, *e.g.*, by its name, or by its permanent relations to other things, which seems to me to imply that he could frame the corresponding identifying reference to the object. If what I say is right, then recognition, or the first kind of practical (particular) identification, turns out to be logically a more rudimentary skill than is the ability to make the second kind of practical (particular) identifications. This accords well with the idea that one first identifies an object by virtue of prior familiarity with it. The result also, in an interesting way, corroborates the result of an independent investigation I have made into the relation between knowledge of facts and knowledge of things. It seems to me that theoretical knowledge of things, *e.g.*, of persons, books, and places, implies that the knower has knowledge of certain facts about those things, where the converse dependence does not hold. A parallel conclusion has now been established in the domain of practical knowledge, where we might at first have been inclined to think that knowledge of things would have to be primary to knowledge of facts. [9]

We have been chiefly concerned to elucidate the concept of action. It will be interesting to consider, as a special case, the practical identification of acts. A 'complete description' of an act, we saw, calls for descriptions of the movements and circumstances, and specification of the agent and his purposes. Knowing the transaction to be an act, we would theoretically individuate it by specification of the movements, locating it as an episode, a happening, in space and time. Turning to practical identification, we must imagine ourselves face to face with the act. Now, since the act occurs over just that stretch of time during which it may be observed, there is no question of prior familiarity. Therefore, one cannot 'recognize' particular acts. (One might, of course, recognize elements of the act, the place, the agent, the purpose, *etc.*, but no one of these is the act.) I conclude that one could make only second-sort practical, particular identifications of acts, which, if I was right above, implies that the animal making the practical identification must have the use of Language. He must, that is, be capable of moving from the practical identification to the theoretical one. But let us now consider the practical identification, which, it would seem, must at any rate be possible. What would such a (second-sort) practical identification of an act be ? Well, if one makes a practical identification of an act, usually everything is on view except the purpose; that is, usually everything but the purpose is conveyed by the 'This'; the purpose is thus usually what the animal would put into words when making the corresponding report, 'This is *R*'. That would be comforting corroboration of the theory of no. 4 of Part II, *if* we were here talking about typal identification. But we are not; we are talking about *particular* identification. The conclusion

---

[9] Versions of Russell's doctrine of Knowledge by Acquaintance and Knowledge by Description seem to hold this. It is part of what I earlier called the empiricist theory. Russell likens Knowledge by Acquaintance to what would be expressed by use of verbs like 'connaître' or 'kennen', as contrasted with 'savoir' or 'wissen'. 'Connaître' is indeed typically used to ascribe knowledge of things. Now it is a cardinal feature of Russell's theory that Knowledge by Description (*savoir*) is dependent upon and logically subsequent to Knowledge by Acquaintance (*connaître*), which yields a conclusion directly contrary to the one I have drawn. The trouble is, of course, that Russell means by 'Knowledge by Acquaintance' many different things, presumably including the barest, non-theoretical, perceptual exposures to the world.

which I am forced to draw is that at least one of the identifications must be explicitly theoretical. Mere practical identification of action is not possible. The earlier conclusion was that a practical identification might be possible, but only for one capable of making a theoretical identification; the present conclusion is a much stronger one, that a practical identification is in no case even possible. It is not that one must actually make the report; he may only 'think it', but at least that is required. Extending this, I conclude that the only possible kind of statement of identity about acts must involve acts already done and mentioned by or thought of by two distinct people, preferably observers of the episode. One of the parties must, moreover, make his (second-type referential) identification explicit before the question of same or different can arise for the other party, or for anyone else. If my reasoning is correct, we have reached very strong conclusions regarding the character of particular identifications of action. One might still be able to make practical *typal* identifications of action, and doubtless such are made by all of us all the time when we observe, unreflectively, what our fellows are doing around us.[10]

3. PROFICIENT BEHAVIOUR

[Acts of certain kinds manifest accomplishment, skill, proficiency, or what Ryle has called 'knowledge-how' (to). I call this *proficient behaviour*. The idea of proficient behaviour, though completely familiar in daily life, is hard to explain. It is not to be confused either with practical knowledge or with capacity. Part of the difficulty is that skill must be acquired as a disposition, and may be acquired in varying degrees; and agents may show varying degrees of skill in performance. It is observed that one totally without such a skill could not so much as attempt an act requiring that skill, *e.g.*, reading a passage of Greek, and so could neither succeed nor fail in such an act. As a provisional, rough demarcation of proficient behaviour, it is suggested that the (contingent) explanation of the failure of such action is always to be traced to the agent's being in special respects ignorant, obliviscent, awkward or otherwise physically inept, or without suitable apparatus; no other similarly general conditions are discovered. Taking a lead from that and capitalizing on a suggestion from Learning Theory, it is finally proposed that a type of action K is proficient action only if a condition for *doing K* is that the agent be able to succeed at an act of another type K', whose measure of success is that the agent come to believe a fact of type F which is a condition of success for K. Proficient behaviour is action of a kind

---

[10] Mr. J. Bennett's recently published *Rationality* suggests that much more could and must be said about Practical Knowledge and Reason than I have succeeded in doing.

which requires that the agent be able to put himself into position to get a reason for acting. It is argued that this definition accounts for the characteristic features of proficient behaviour.]

There are kinds of action which one must 'know-how to' do. Such behaviour must, in different degrees, manifest accomplishment, skill, proficiency, ability, where, of course, there are many kinds of skill, proficiency, and ability. Examples are using a knife and fork, playing the piano, reading Greek, tying one's shoes, integrating partial differential equations, playing tennis, saying 'I love you' in Bantu, connecting electric circuits, repairing plumbing, typing. Such types of action I call *proficient behaviour*.

There is no type of action, instances of which may not manifest skill or proficiency, but only some kinds of action invariably require skill or proficiency in some measure. Eating, kicking, and scratching do not generally require skill. The dog simply chews the bone, laps the milk, or scratches his ear. For all that, one may more or less skilfully eat an orange with a knife and fork or hot dogs at a baseball game. But, one *could not* play the opening passage of a piece of music on the piano (in contrast with merely thumping the piano) unless, in some measure, he *knew how to* play the piano; one could not translate a passage of Greek prose unless he knew how to read Greek. Here the requirement for proficiency is a veritable part of our very idea of the type of action, and should follow from any adequate theoretical account of the purpose. It is only such types of action that I call proficient. (I say that the agent must have some proficiency to do a proficient act. Of course, he need not have sufficient proficiency to succeed. Interestingly, he may succeed even though he does not have sufficient proficiency, as when a student makes a lucky guess in his efforts to render a passage of Greek. But even to do that, he must have *some* skill in reading Greek.)

Scarcely anything could be more familiar than this idea of proficient behaviour. Luckily, it is duly marked in the vernacular by our everyday employment of 'know how to'. For that reason, I need not explain it. I could simply eschew the fancy tag 'proficient behaviour' and fall back on 'know how to' where and when I cared to. Perhaps I could also take the easy way and forego an attempt at an 'analysis'. But I choose to try. *Knowing how to* is an important idea 'in life'. Since Ryle's *Concept of Mind*, it has become evident that it is also a powerful, if questionable, piece of philosophical equipment. It would be desirable to have an explanation, *if* we could. It is much the same as with the cognate 'knowing that'.

Unfortunately, it proves very difficult to find that explanation. Proficient action is an enormous field of varied terrain, which it is hard to survey transpicuously. Easy confidence that one has got it all while not including too much would be rash. The kinds of factor which may be present are extremely multifarious, as my examples were calculated to show. Moreover, skill, usually if not always, may be had in greater or less degree, and this kind of gradation is always troublesome, if only because it makes it hard to draw a line between a little and none at all. A further complication is that skill and proficiency are manifested not in behaviour alone. One may be said to *know-how to recognize* poison oak. However, I shall here consider proficiency only as directly manifested in behaviour, partly because I feel sure that this must be the fundamental case in terms of which the others are to be explained, and also because it is the only case which directly matters for present purposes. I will not be completely satisfied with my results. This is the weakest link in my chain of definitions. Happily, it will bear less strain than the others, because we have recourse to the vernacular usage of 'know how to'.

Philosophers have spent little effort upon the analysis of *knowing how to*. But one gets the suggestion from some writings that the authors would be inclined to equate proficient behaviour with either *being able to* or with what I have been calling 'practical knowledge'. The first identification clearly will not do, for there is no kind of action which one might be said to be unable (and so, able) to do, quite apart from one's degree of proficiency. 'Unable to do' is in fact ambiguous: it might mean 'unable to succeed at' or it might mean 'unable to attempt'. For the first, an act is essentially something which might fail; and whatever would necessitate failure would render the agent unable to succeed; so there is no kind of act at which one might not be unable to succeed. Similarly, for the second, to be said to do (attempt) an act, the agent must at a minimum be *aware* of something; failing that he is unable to do the act regardless of questions of constraint, *etc.*

It is the first kind of *being unable, being unable to succeed*, which is most naturally equated with want of skill. Being able to (succeed) often does require a measure of skill. But, interestingly, being able to *fail*, e.g., at reading a passage of Greek, also requires *some* proficiency in Greek. The conclusion is that having skill is sometimes not necessary and is never sufficient to be able to (succeed). Equating skill with being able to encourages a mistake (which I confess to have once laboured under) that skill, in the relevant sense, is knowing how to succeed. We now see why that is wrong. A reverse error has also been made. One could plausibly argue that having skill is having a disposition; one is then inclined to suppose that 'being able to' is always simply a matter of having acquired certain dispositions. We also see why that is wrong.

I come now to the second faulty equation, of knowing how to with the traditional idea of practical knowledge. All proficient behaviour does, of course, manifest practical knowledge, just because it is action, and all action manifests practical knowledge. But surely not all action also manifests skill or proficiency, and we, therefore, should not equate proficient behaviour with behaviour manifesting practical knowledge. What obscures this is, first, that *theoretical* knowledge, on analogy with which practical knowledge is explained, does require skill in the use of Language. Second, many kinds of practical knowledge do require that one could do acts manifesting know-how, *e.g.*, counting.

Proficient behaviour would seem to be co-extensive with *learned* behaviour, in our everyday non-technical sense of 'learn',[1] in contrast with what is 'instinctive' or 'innate' to the species. Proficiencies and skills, as a matter of empirical, natural fact, must be 'acquired'. That is an important clue, lending substance to our presumption that here indeed is something real and palpable. But the conjectured equation of proficient behaviour with types of action that agents must learn to do contributes very little to the search for an analysis. *Learning* is quite as problematical as *knowing how to*. We have simply shifted the question terminologically into one regarding the nature of learned behaviour.

It will pay to note with comments some facts about proficient behaviour with the hope that this will show the way to a general characterization. The first observation is that the possession of skill, proficiency, or 'know-how' is a *condition for doing* proficient acts, and not merely a condition of success. I could neither succeed nor fail at reading passages of Greek because I have no Greek. I could not so much as try to connect an electric circuit if I had utterly no knowledge of how it might be done. My skill might be greater or less, but it could not be nil. The possession of skill is then a condition for the animal's either succeeding or failing in proficient action. Alternatively, it is a truth-condition for the observer's report that the animal did such an act at all.

A possible counter-example[2] is the case of spelling a difficult word. This is unquestionably an example of proficient behaviour. Yet here one's failure is evidence that one does not know how to spell the word; the possession of that skill, therefore, cannot be a condition of failure. The contestant in the spelling bee fails *because* he does not know how to spell the word. The argument may be generalized to all kinds of endotychistic, proficient behaviour. The measure of success

---

[1] As against that of 'learning theory', which comprehends any and every kind of 'conditioned behaviour'.

[2] Pointed out to me by Professor Marcus Singer.

is the making of certain movements, which also proves the presence of skill; failure is always evidence and sometimes proof of the absence of skill. The reply is that one could not fail at spelling 'Macuilxochitl' unless he knew how to spell, could succeed at spelling other words; one could not fail at integrating a complicated differential equation without knowing how to integrate simple ones. So *some* skill in the *type* of action is wanted, and that is all the observation demands.[3]

The second general fact about proficient behaviour, already noted several times in passing, is that the requisite skill may be greater and less. Thus, one may be better or worse at reading Greek or playing tennis. Yet it is not clear what this means. Apparently the degree of one's skill is partly shown by his success at doing acts which manifest that skill. But no amount of skill is enough to assure success. Degree of skill is then *shown* by success, but it is not to be defined by success. It is also shown in the animal's quickness, accuracy, style, and, I think, above all, in his adaptability to different and unusual circumstances.

It would appear, then, that the explanation of any type of proficient behaviour must imply that an agent's doing such an act would manifest greater or less skill. But there is no hope of exploiting this in reverse to achieve a definition of proficient behaviour. *How well* one performs does not contribute to the identification of what he is doing. The features of his act that we might report in our assessment of skill are all items of act-description, not identification. It even appears

---

[3] What is the *first* word the animal spelled? That is exactly like Wittgenstein's question about *reading* (*Phil. Invest.*, Part 1, no. 157). The answer is: the question makes no sense. But, one may protest, it must make sense. The skill started somewhere and was presumably shown by some successful act of spelling. Well, that is like insisting on an answer to the question at what precise point did the car start averaging 30 miles an hour. There is no answer, because to get an answer we need to consider a stretch of performance, possibly a very short one. But what was happening over that stretch of time when the animal was learning to spell? The animal was surely sometimes succeeding in his efforts to spell, in which case he must have had the skill, but we could not say he had the skill until after he had correctly spelled a number of words. Well, the driver cannot average a certain speed unless he also moves at certain speeds at certain times, but *moving at a speed at a time* is a different idea from *averaging* a speed over a time. So too, the acts which prove the capacity to spell are not all full blown acts of spelling, but perhaps acts of imitating, or of trying to get others to approve of one's efforts. These attempts may *result* in one's correctly spelling a word, which is taken by the observer to show that the agent is capable of correctly spelling the word. Although the agent, as viewed by the observer, was not actually meaning to spell that word, nevertheless he spelled it. He knows how to spell *that* word, even though he has not actually made a full attempt at spelling it. Of course, the observer knows that all this comes about in the course of someone's teaching the agent to spell. To have spelled a word proves a capacity for spelling only in such circumstances, which must include other attempts of the same general kinds.

that one who could not perform at all might still be said to know-how-to, though there might be no answer to the question of *how well* he knew how to. Consider the aging arthritic former football player who was once selected All-American on account of his superb ability at blocking. He knows how to block if anyone does; he coaches it at the university. But his arthritis makes it out of the question to ask *how well* he blocks. (It is not that our former All-American simply knows how it is done—he knows how to do it. If we allow that knowing how something is done is sufficient for knowing how to do it, then all the more clearly one may have skills of no degree at all.) In brief, we cannot explain what it is to have skill in terms of performance. But our account of the performance type will imply that the agent has skill, in turn implying that he had it in some degree.

This conclusion is to be welcomed. It releases us from the hopeless task of separating knowing-how-to a little, from knowing-how-to not at all. Our explanation of skill need not effect the separation; on the other hand, our explanation of proficient behaviour should imply the possibility of a gradation of degrees of skill, and that fact at once is a constraint upon the explanation and a useful pointer to finding it. We may expect that among the factors contributing to the explanation of proficient behaviour must be some which are themselves susceptible to gradation, *e.g.*, things which people may have more and less of, like knowledge, dexterity, co-ordination, and equipment.

Earlier we noted that knowing-how-to is not the same as being able to. But I believe that they are close enough to reflect illumination onto one another. I would like now to pursue this idea, using as best I can points made or suggested in Austin's celebrated analysis of *can* and *could* ('Ifs and Cans', in *Philosophical Papers*). In the course of showing both that *could* is not to be analysed as invariably conditional and that it does not always require supplementation with a conditional clause, Austin reveals an answer to why we might be tempted to the contrary opinions. The chief point, if I catch him, is that failure to do an act may be explained as due to the absence of *opportunity*, *will*, or *capacity*, and perhaps other factors as well. One's failure to act might be explained as due to want of will, opportunity, capacity, *etc*. To say that one did not act may, therefore, indirectly raise questions whether these conditions—one or the other of them—were fulfilled, and that might be expressly indicated with a conditional clause: he would have (He would have, *if* he had the opportunity, wanted to, had the ability, *etc*.). Now we may also wish to deny or to affirm that he could have even if he did not. Clearly, want of will would not figure. Whether he could have or not must be decided independently of whether he cared to. Austin's suggestion is that the non-conditional use of 'could' is to report that the imagined agent had opportunity and capacity, *etc.* That is the 'all-out sense' of 'could'. But we also commonly use 'could' to report that the animal had the opportunity, whether or not he had the capacity ('He could have shot before the time ran out') or to report that he had the capacity whether he had the opportunity or not ('He could have sunk it from the middle of the floor'). There is also the suggestion that success was in the offing had the agent actually acted. We are, therefore, often licensed to conclude from the fact that he could have that he would have (succeeded), *if* he had tried (chosen, *etc.*).

But that is at most a conclusion, not an analysis. Similarly, one's failure *in* acting might be explained by want of capacity. We might still truly report that he could have in the sense of having had the opportunity. This again might imply that he would have (succeeded), *if* he had had the capacity. This makes for a compelling but false picture of human action: that an act successfully done simply consists of attempt plus capacity plus opportunity plus . . . If the act is not done or is unsuccessful, then one of the essential factors must be absent, which seems to imply the conclusion that if that factor (with all others) had been present, the act would have been successfully done. I have argued against this picture (see Part II, no. 18). It may be added that an agent might successfully do something that he was trying to do, *e.g.*, hit the bullseye with the arrow, even though he lacked the necessary capacity, his error in shooting being offset by the wind. The presence of some of these act factors is neither necessary nor sufficient for successful actions. What does follow is that we might *explain* failure to act or failure in acting by reference to such considerations. And if one does do an act, there is a *presumption* that all the factors are present. Observation of these facts contributes to our understanding of action.

This analysis clearly cannot be directly applied to our problem of explicating proficient action. First, we are now concerned, not with action in general, but with something more special. Second, since we are asking what it is to do a certain kind of act, we presume that such an act was done, whether or not successfully, and the presumption is that the agent had both opportunity and will. These factors cannot figure in the picture we wish to draw. The factor of capacity is part of what we want to explain, so we cannot simply appeal to it as understood. Anyway, an understanding of capacity would not be enough, for two reasons. First, success in non-proficient action also presumptively requires capacity, *e.g.*, the dog must be able to move his tongue to lap the milk. Second, proficiency or skill is always only part of the capacity presumptively required for success in proficient actions, a part *some* measure of which, we have noticed, must always be present

228

for success *or* failure. The athlete may know how to high-jump, but may still not have the capacity to get over seven feet.

But Austin's analysis is useful for suggesting a parallel strategy. It may be that we can delimit proficient behaviour as behaviour which characteristically fails for certain reasons. These would not be types of necessary conditions of failure for proficient action, but types of conditions which presumptively explain the failure of proficient acts. Such a delimitation *might* give a lead to finding characteristic kinds of defining conditions of success.

Clearly, it will not suffice to say that failure will be explained by lack of skill. First, one needs some skill even to fail in proficient action. Second, part of what we want to explain is what it is to have or lack skill. Thus, skill is a disposition, the presence of which is tested for by consideration of how well the supposed agent does proficient acts.

We need something of a different kind and more specific. Since skill may be had in varying degrees, and since a proficient act must manifest a certain degree of skill, it is natural to expect that at least some of the characteristic causes of failure could be in greater and less degree. Suppose, then, that an agent attempt such an act—to read a passage of Greek, play the piano, tie his shoe, use a fork, integrate a differential equation, play tennis, type, connect a circuit—what would lead to failure, in possibly greater or less degree? So far as I can see, any or all of the following, and only these, all of which may be in varying degrees. Ignorance of fact (He doesn't know certain Greek words, or he doesn't know which wire comes directly from the switch-box); lapse of memory (He forgets a formula, a word, a wiring diagram); physical ineptitude (numbness in the hand, all thumbs on the shoestring, insufficient strength to lift down the lexicon, lame legs, stutter); or want of suitable operative equipment (screwdriver, dictionary, tennis racquet).

These are not necessary conditions of failure. One may translate Greek even without a dictionary. But he may yet fail even if all necessary conditions of success are satisfied, for want of a dictionary. There are circumstances which would presumptively explain failure, although no condition necessarily resulting in failure obtains. Similar circumstances might also account for the failure of non-proficient acts, *e.g.*, jumping a creek. I seek no more than a delimitation, an 'upper-bound', and what I submit is that the mentioned kinds of condition are characteristic causes of failure for proficient behaviour. Roughly and provisionally, then, proficient behaviour is action which might in varying degrees fail for these reasons: because the agent was ignorant, obliviscent, or in want of physical ability or suitable equipment. Reversing it: the agent has acquired some degree of skill only if he could attempt acts which would fail on account of want of knowledge, memory, physical aptitude, or suitable equipment.

This delimitation is clearly unsatisfactory as a definition of proficient behaviour. It is only an 'upper-bound' and is plainly *ad hoc*; but it is suggestive. It suggests, for example, that a condition of success for certain types of proficient behaviour would be that the agent should realize certain things, which he may remember or look up in a book, or that the agent should have physically altered something, say by brute strength or by use of suitable equipment. Is there any way that we may generalize upon this?

Psychologists have recently come to give importance to what they call scanning, searching or exploration (see Mowrer, *op. cit.*, Chap. 5, Part V, pp. 180–83). They intimate that searching is present in all behaviour. That would be true if they meant only that *perception* is always present in action (as they sometimes appear to mean). But, taking 'sensory search' to identify a kind of action (as the psychologists also sometimes do), it is clearly wrong to demand that it be an indispensable factor in all kinds of action. More to the point, the psychologist also intimates that *searching* has something to do with *skill* (*loc. cit.*, p. 183). It tabs very well with our rough demarcation of proficient behaviour, which may now be taken to read that want of knowledge, strength, equipment, *etc.*, would make it difficult to effect a successful search possibly required for success in proficient action.

Now this is a figurative employment of 'search'. I think the idea is that the agent should put himself into position to gain information. If he is doing a proficient act, then, to succeed, he must adjust himself to the world in order to gain reasons for doing the act as he does it, *e.g.*, look up a word in a dictionary, find the fork, trace a wire, look to see where middle C is on the piano, *etc.* The agent must act to gain belief. We might provisionally stipulate that a type of action K is a type of proficient action only if a condition for doing an act of kind K is that the agent should do another act of kind K' which would bring him to have a belief that would explain his doing an act of kind K.

That demands too much. One may simply see a signpost, and read it. Again, one may simply say something. Both of these types of action—reading and saying—require proficiency. But they may surely be done without active preliminaries, in a manner quite as direct as scratching one's head. Still one could not say anything if he could not conceive of being corrected in his choice of word; one could not read the sign if he could not spell or by other means render the written word. In both cases the agent must be somehow capable of getting the information upon which the success of his performance depends. It must be that the agent in such proficient action *could* gain information by taking active measures to that end.

PROFICIENT BEHAVIOUR

Assembling all this, and putting it into the terminology we have been using, I would define proficient action as follows: *K* is a type of *proficient behaviour* if and only if (1) *K* is a type of action, where (2) a condition for doing *K* is that the agent should be able to succeed at an act of another type *K'* whose measure of success is that the agent should come to believe a fact of type *F*, where *F* is a condition of success for *K*. Making use of zoölogical categories, we can say that proficient behaviour *K* is necessarily based on a capacity for some kind of (lower-order) *investigative* behaviour *K'* [4].

Glossing all this: (1) It would be false to say that *A* did an act of type *K* unless it were true to say that he could succeed at acts of some type *K'*. (2) The proof that *A* could succeed at acts of type *K'* is that he has succeeded at them. (3) What *A* in fact believes as a result of doing a *K'* in a particular instance may be false, in which case his act of type *K* will fail. But he must be capable of getting (true) beliefs of *facts* of type *F* in order to do acts of type *K*. (4) There may be various kinds of *K'*'s underlying a given *K*. (5) *A may* come to believe *F* without doing any *K'*; but he *could* come to believe *F* by doing a *K'*.

In support of this definition, I now argue that it accommodates, though it does not always imply, all the characteristic features of proficient behaviour that we have noticed.

First, proficient behaviour is not 'instinctive' behaviour, because it is not something one does without preparation, but only in dependence upon other things which he may do without preparation. Proficient behaviour is a level of behavioural sophistication, the attainment of which requires that one have *learned* to seek out and to profit from information naturally to be gained at a lower level of behaviour.

Second, one acquires skill and hence capacity for proficient behaviour only by doing other kinds of acts. But success in a lower-level act is not proof of skill unless the observer is entitled to conclude that the lower-level action is also a foundation for something else, implying that the agent could succeed at other lower-level acts in similar circumstances. That is why a skill is a disposition, acquired only over a stretch of time.

Third, we see why possession of the skill is a condition for doing. We say that one does a proficient act only if he could come to have a belief as a result of doing another kind of act. A condition of proficient act is that he have the belief and know, in the practical sense,

---

[4] See John Paul Scott, *Animal Behaviour*, pp. 18ff. All nine types of behaviour proposed by Scott as possibly exhaustive (ingestive, shelter-seeking, agonistic, sexual, epimeletic, et-epimeletic, eliminative, allelomimetic, and investigative) first appear below the level of proficient behaviour.

231

how he could confirm it; he would achieve confirmation by succeeding in a lower-level act. But that would also prove that he was capable of acquiring the skill, at least in some measure. (If one looks and finds a word in a dictionary or a wire in a switchbox, that proves that he has at least some skill in reading or in wiring circuits.)

Fourth, we see why the failure of proficient action might be accounted for by want of effective knowledge, physical aptitude, equipment. The belief, which is a condition for the proficient act, is one that the agent could have come to have as a result of another act and then retained. Hence, special knowledge and memory are natural concomitants of successful proficient action. One could have come to the belief by independent action, requiring physical capacity and perhaps the use of equipment. The definition of proficient behaviour does not immediately tell us why ignorance, obliviscence, physical ineptness and want of equipment should be the only contingent explanations of failure (if they are). But perhaps that too can be made to look plausible. Every type of action, I hold, is either productive, effective, or endotychistic (see Part II, no. 19). Now it is reasonable to assume that productive action is a species of proficient action. To the extent that failure at proficient action is due to failure in the underlying kind of action, we may always trace it back to failure in either effective or endotychistic action. But non-proficient endotychistic action normally fails on account of physical incapacity. Failure in effective action is also often due to physical ineptness but also sometimes to want of effective equipment. Knowledge and memory figure for reasons already mentioned: among the beliefs which explain the proficient act are ones which could be garnered and retained; these, if true, are of facts possibly known and remembered. One can succeed at proficient action in spite of want of dexterity, equipment, and specific items of knowledge. That is because one may come to the belief which explains one's act by different kinds of lower-level action, or by none at all. But the relevance of these factors of knowledge, dexterity, etc., is to be traced to the demand that the agent could repair to a lower level of behaviour for the sake of information.

Finally, our definition of proficient behaviour reveals why skill may be manifested in greater and less degree. To the extent that the definition really does account for the relevance of the graduated factors of knowledge, memory, aptitude, and equipment, that is already explained (see p. 229). But it is confirmed by the consideration that the beliefs in question may be numerous, relating not only to what is done but also possibly to how it is done, and possibly arising in more and less efficient ways out of lower-level acts. One shows his skill at carpentry by the quickness with which he is able to pick and choose materials, adjust them to one another, etc., as well as by the force

232

with which he drives a nail. Selecting and adjusting materials is a deliberate exercise of acquired knowledge.

Practically every type of action we shall encounter from here on will be a species of proficient behaviour. The use of Language, in particular, is something we acquire or learn as a proficiency. Now it is evident that there are different levels of proficient action. It is important to be keyed to this, especially when talking about the use of Language. The analysis of types of action, including the use of Language, requires quantities of theoretical and Language skills. A frequent cause of conceptual confusion, especially in philosophy, is our failure to separate the subject skill from the analytic skills to which it is submitted. Capacity in any use of Language is an absolute precondition for putting forward an analysis of that use of Language. But a skill in a use of Language surely does not assure a comparable analytic proficiency—otherwise the whole programme would end before it began. Ancillary to this we must not fuse one's knowing how to say something with his knowledge *that* (1) he is saying it (2) by use of certain expressions (3) in conformity with certain rules, or (4) that what he says has such and such a character. All of this last presupposes that one has also gained a variety of analytic skills including high capacity in the use of Language.

4. CONFORMATIVE BEHAVIOUR AND THE IDEA OF A PRACTICE

[The recently fashionable use of 'rule' in philosophy is obviously a technical one which has never been properly explained. In the balance of this part an effort will be made to give that explanation. Rules in the intended sense figure when a certain kind of proficient behaviour is being done, which species of proficient behaviour is called *conformative behaviour*. One cannot be said to be doing an act which is of this kind unless he is acting in consideration of a rule. Such acts are usually done when one is engaged in certain activities or general areas of behaviour which are defined as involving rules or kinds of rules. These areas of behaviour are here called *practices*, where particular rules may or may not serve to define a practice. We must then distinguish conformative behaviour from the operating rules, and both the behaviour and the rules from the practice. But the plan is to explain what rules are by explaining what it is to act in consideration of a rule, and by separating kinds of rules we shall be classifying kinds of practice. The keys to this analysis are that in conforming to a rule one acts with a certain *kind of reason* or mistaken reason which itself might be explained in terms of what others would be *entitled to expect*, where the existence of these expectations and of the rules supplies a standard for assessing the correctness of the behaviour.]

The idea of a *rule* has long been a favourite of philosophers, but especially in recent years, when the express and conscientious appeal to rules has become a fashion if not something of a movement. It is a focal point in the theories of a number of writers on moral and legal philosophy.[1] Most important of all, it has become a major instrument in the philosophy of Language, where it has been used to explain the practice of using Language and the very nature of conceptualization itself; in particular, it has been employed to get away from the sometimes compelling thought that Language could and perhaps must be something private to whomever it is we suppose to be using Language.[2] The counter-argument is that Language exists only in the midst of rules, and rules operate paradigmatically and always possibly within a public arena. This represents an enormous expansion upon one theme in Locke's doctrine of nominal essence, *e.g.*, that to be able meaningfully to say that an animal is a dog depends upon our having imposed certain rules on the employment of 'dog'. The chief actor in this story undoubtedly is Wittgenstein, and that we should be brought to a deliberate consideration of a use of 'rule' which may possibly be a sheer invention testifies to his enormous influence on current philosophical thought.

Additional to these special uses of some concept of rule, some have gone so far as to aver that all acts are 'applications of rules', and that all reasons are rules.[3] One need not acquiesce in so exaggerated if expected opinion to appreciate that these movements in various parts of philosophy with the idea of *rule* represent a more than incidental extension upon some more ordinary use of 'rule'. It is not entirely clear to me that we very often speak of either moral rules or language rules outside of theoretical discussions of morality and Language. The very force of these philosophical analyses of morality and Language seems almost to depend upon that. While we may speak

[1] See, for example, S. Toulmin, *The Place of Reason in Ethics*; K. Baier, *The Moral Point of View*; H. L. A. Hart, *The Concept of Law*; J. D. Mabbatt, 'Moral Rules', *Proc. Brit. Ac.*, 1953, pp. 97–118; J. O. Urmson, 'The Interpretation of the Moral Philosophy of J. S. Mill', *Phil. Quart.*, 1953, pp. 33–39; J. Rawls, 'Two Concepts of Rules', *Phil. Rev.*, 1955, pp. 3–32; J. J. C. Smart, 'Extreme and Restricted Utilitarianism', *Phil. Quart.*, 1956, pp. 334–54; H. J. McClosky, 'An Examination of Restricted Utilitarianism', *Phil. Rev.*, 1957, pp. 466–85, B. J. Diggs, 'Rules and Utilitarianism', *Am. Phil. Quart.*, 1964, pp. 32–44; and my own 'Moral Rules and Moral Maxims', *Ethics*, 1957.

[2] The 'privacy' theory derives from Russell and Wittgenstein, and achieves what is probably its most compelling formulation in Schlick's lectures 'Form and Content' in *Gesammelte Aufsätze*, pp. 152–249. The counter-argument makes up a major part of Wittgenstein's *Investigations*. But see also A. J. Ayer's and R. Rhees' Symposium contributions, *Proc. Arist. Soc. Supp.*, 1954, pp. 63–94.

[3] See P. Winch, *op. cit.*, esp. pp. 49 *et seq.* I agree with most of what Winch says regarding rules—that they are primarily social, need not be formulated as rules, are of many kinds. But he certainly overstates his claims on behalf of rules in any understandable sense of 'rule'.

about rules of judicial procedure, it would be strange to call a parking regulation a rule; while we might naturally speak about the rules of German grammar, it is far from natural sense to speak about the rules for the use of 'darstellen' or 'Regel'. In American English we frequently speak of *the* 'rules', *e.g.*, of baseball or chess; but examples of particular rules of baseball or chess seem to be rare, cases being the rule of *en passant* in chess and the infield fly rule in baseball; we do not speak of the rule for the Knight's move or the rule that a runner is 'out' if touched with the ball when not standing on a base. Yet statements concerning the Knight's move and how a runner is put out surely are part of the rule*s* of chess and baseball, respectively. Now the philosopher wants to call all these items rules, whether they be taken singly or together, and that is proof that his use is a technical one. The big question is whether this is coherent.

Interestingly enough, no one to my knowledge actually has considered and formulated in so many words what he takes the ordinary use of 'rule' to be. Nor can I claim to be able to offer a completely satisfactory definition. [4]

More distressingly, it is not very clear what this technical, philosophical usage of 'rule' is. This poses a double threat to any explanation given in terms of *rule*; it may actually be an utterly incoherent account, which fact may be hidden behind the ordinary use of 'rule'; or it may devolve into something completely trivial, there being a rule if only one says so. In fact, there seem to be a number of different kinds of case covered by the philosopher's use of 'rule', which, taken together, comprise some rather startling differences. Additional to rules in the ordinary sense are sometimes included here what are commonly called 'regulations', 'instructions', 'recipes', 'directions', 'guide-lines', 'prescriptions', 'demands', 'precepts', 'laws', 'licenses', 'enactments', 'statutes', 'precedents', 'ordinances', 'principles', 'maxims', 'canons', 'rubrics', 'codes', 'standards', 'fashions', 'modes', 'observances', 'procedures', and 'practices'. Again, these terms all have their own quite special forces, though I cannot claim to know how to say what they are. [5] For what they are worth, allow me to make some observations about some of these ideas.

---

[4] See pp. 236f. below. Philosophers commonly begin by dismissing certain 'senses' of 'rule', which they take to be obviously irrelevant, *e.g.*, 'rule of thumb'. Nothing in my view could be better calculated to conceal the facts, and to seduce one into thinking that he means something when he does not. Precisely what is wanted is an examination of what is meant by *political rule*, what it is to *rule in* and *rule out*, and *rule upon*, and to *give* and to *appeal to rulings*. There is also something significant in the various senses of the noun 'ruler'. I think it is important that particular rules are given *names*.

[5] Some of these items are linguistic, *e.g.*, rules literally taken, and others not; some are kinds of behaviour or activity viewed in a certain way; others are what

235

A *regulation* is a general order taken to be issued by a properly installed authority by which agents engaged in transactions of a fairly recurrent or continuously operating and ongoing kind are to govern themselves. Thus, regulations for the conduct of trade, or the taking of examinations, or smoking. Regulations regularize kinds of behaviour which existed before. They keep us within channels. Because the behaviour in question must already exist, regulations cannot 'constitute' the practice; that is, failure to comply with a regulation is not evidence that one is not really engaged in the regulated practice (*e.g.*, importing goods), but may be cause for the assignment of penalties, recognition of which latter is part of 'playing the game'.

Rules in the literal sense of 'rule' resemble regulations. A particular rule (not a system of rules) is something which must be issued, and issued linguistically, *e.g.*, in a proclamation; and it is issued not to originate a practice, but only after a practice has been going on for some time, to govern cases of highly specific kinds, which one expects to recur fairly frequently. But rules, unlike regulations, are characteristically issued to govern official rulings concerning special kinds of incident which may arise in the course of the activity. Rules, in contrast to regulations, are administered and are issued to guide and govern the behaviour of *administrators*—officials in games, customs inspectors, official boards—and not directly the behaviour of those over whom the administrators administer. Hence importers may be held liable to conform to regulations for the governance of trade, and customs inspectors administer rules for the governance of trade. We can expect such a distinction wherever there is a sharp division between those who participate in a practice and those who administer, govern, or officiate it. This feature of rules literally taken is strongly suggested by the cognate verb 'rule'.

Principles, as etymology tells us, are first *truths*. They need not be stated, but when stated, they serve to make explicit the nature of that which they are principles of, in particular, kinds of activities. For one to doubt the principles of (*e.g.*) economics or civil law would be evidence that he did not know what economics or civil law is; similarly, to know a man's principles is to know what kind of man he is, though here we must add that a person has a principle only if he has *made* it a principle, *viz.*, adopted a policy of according a dominating or "first" role to certain types of consideration. Leaving theory for practice, when one behaves in such a way that certain principles are not true of him, that is evidence that he is not engaged in an activity of which these are the principles.

---

we might 'appeal to', 'consider', or 'balance' when engaged in some activity or other; some are discovered, others imposed; some are specific to institutions, or to communities, others not.

Maxims are second truths, *viz.*, consequences of or glosses upon principles. Thus it is a principle of American football that one ought to call plays which are best calculated to score or which will put one into the best possible position to score; it is a maxim that the ball should be worked towards the centre of the field when one cannot hope to score by running or passing but can hope to score by kicking. Again, it may be a principle that men should have regular habits and make the best use of their time, as a gloss on which one might proclaim the maxim early to bed and early to rise makes a man healthy, wealthy and wise.

Practices are spheres of activity as engaged in in certain customary ways. A practice is one community's manner of engaging in a certain activity. Thus we speak of British legal practice or Arab military practice. It is essential that when engaged in the kind of activity in question one should sometimes do acts which are examples of what I call 'conformative behaviour'. That is, rules, in the yet to be explained sense of 'rule', operate.

Is there something common to rules, regulations, principles, *etc.*— if not a central core of meaning, then at least a general area which either includes or borders upon these different ideas? I believe that there is. But no vernacular word has yet been cast for this common something. The situation is like what we found with purpose, and the explanation both here and there is that the idea comes to the surface only when we enter into a theoretical investigation of behaviour, as in fact we seldom have occasion to do; our ordinary ways of talking about behaviour are already so multifarious, precise, and specific as not to require theoretical refinement or to suggest general patterns. I agree with Wittgenstein that this still unexplained idea of rule is essentially involved in certain kinds of behaviour and especially in the use of Language. My efforts throughout the balance of this part are meant to explain what I take this area to be. The argument, though I hope it will have general applicability, is implicitly directed towards the case of Language rules.

This area, as I have styled it, which includes or borders upon these various ideas, is an area of *behaviour*; it might better be described as a *level* of animal behaviour. In particular it is a species of proficient behaviour. Behaviour of the kind in question on the part of an animal requires that he should *know how to* conform to rules. I stress in advance that this form of behaviour is one for which the question may arise whether the *agent* acted in conformity with or in violation of some rule; it is not sufficient that a question may arise whether the *behaviour* conformed to a rule. The latter circumstance could come to pass even though the agent were utterly oblivious of the rule, in which event his behaviour would not be of the kind we wish to define.

We are after a rather sophisticated kind of proficient behaviour, in which the 'mental element' is relatively more conspicuous than the 'physical element'. To give it a name I shall call it *conformative behaviour*. Our account of this form of behaviour must tell what is presumed if an agent's deed is to be of this kind. The general presumption is that the agent should believe that there be (what *we* can call) a rule to which he might conform. Conformative behaviour is of a kind which requires that the agent have a certain kind of reason or mistaken reason, which we can schematize as 'That's the rule'. In clarifying the force of this general presumption we shall be giving the desired explanation of 'rule' in the indicated general sense. The analysis will be quite in line with our idea that forms of action may be defined by mention of characteristic beliefs.

'Conformative behaviour' is a technical phrase, and some preliminary elucidations of how I propose to use it are in order. 'Conformative' is meant to cover both compliances and violations. When performing a conformative act one is not necessarily acting to conform to a rule; he may also be acting in violation of a rule. All that is required is that he be acting with the belief: That's the rule. To mark the distinction between generalized compliance and violation, I shall speak of 'acting in conformity with' and 'acting in violation of'; I shall also speak of 'conform*ing*' and 'non-conform*ing*' behaviour as two all-inclusive types of conformative behaviour.

Conformative behaviour does not require that there actually be a rule so long as the agent *thinks* there is. But this matters little, for it may be argued that if the agent thinks there is a rule, then there is *a* rule. Our chief task in the remainder of this part is to define the nature of the belief: That's the rule.

My last preliminary gloss on 'conformative' has been anticipated. It is not enough that the agent's *behaviour happens to be* in conformity with or in violation of a rule for it to be conformative behaviour. It is essential that we be able to say that he is *acting in* conformity with or in violation of the rule. In the rare instance where the agent acts to violate (to conform to) the rule where in fact his behaviour does (does not) conform, then his deed is still an item of non-conforming (conforming) conformative behaviour.

Conformative behaviour is of many kinds, and is found in a great variety of circumstances. It is seen in our respect for law and in our morality, in how we deal with strangers, and in how we speak and write, in the games we play, in calculating, spelling, eating, housebuilding, scheduling of events, and operating of instruments, and in getting one's self ready to meet the day. Almost any kind of behaviour may be made subject to rule or (better) may be replaced by conformative behaviour, as long as a rule is supplied. I shall here adopt the word 'practice' to refer to something which essentially involves some kind of conformative behaviour. Thus I shall speak about Language, law, and morality as *practices*. This is not an ordinary sense of 'practice', though it does come rather close to one of these. The difference is that while I speak of Law as a practice, we would more ordinarily speak about legal practice*s*. To make room for this, I shall allow for different versions or manners of a practice.

Practices typically are kinds of *activity*, e.g., playing games. But they also may be cross selections from the *activities* of life, as is the case with law, morality and Language. In all cases I shall speak of one's *engaging in a practice*.

Now to engage in a practice requires that one might sometimes be held to act in conformity with or in violation of a rule. Certain of one's acts must qualify as conformative behaviour. Engaging in a practice therefore requires that rules be thought to be in force. The supposed rules provide a standard against which the agent's behaviour may be assessed, possibly by himself. I shall speak of these rules as *underlying* the practice.

The practice is not the rules which underlie the practice, as some writers seem to suggest. Indeed, there may be alternative rules which underlie a single practice. Thus part of the traditional practice of courtship in western countries was that proceedings may issue in a proposal of marriage by the man to the woman. That one should make the proposal requires conformity to rule, and in particular that one use Language. In order to use Language one must follow the rules of some language—German, French, Spanish, or English. But which tongue is employed and so which particular rule or rules are conformed to is a matter of indifference to our general description of the practice, though it may have considerable bearing on the agent's success.

To be sure, practices are sometimes, as I shall put it, 'constituted' by particular rules. Thus the practice of speaking English, to be contrasted with the practice of making proposals, is (perhaps) constituted by the rules of English. But not *all* practices are so constituted; neither the practice of using Language nor the practice of acting decently toward one's fellows is constituted by the underlying rules. All that is generally required is that some rules be in force, whether or not they constitute the practice, or, to reverse the order, whether or not there be alternative rules underlying a single practice.

In what follows I shall indirectly be trying to say what it is to engage in a practice, my study being directed towards the study of the practice of using Language. This will be a by-product of my direct efforts to say what it is to do a conformative act.

Since I wish a *general* characterization of *conformative behaviour*, I

239

must try to avoid concentrating on special types to the neglect of others. Initially I shall take care to include types of conformative behaviour where the operating rules may or may not need to be formulated, where the rules may be open or closed in their sway, where they are 'constitutive' or 'non-constitutive' of a practice, where they limit, prescribe, license, and create new forms of behaviour. To see what will thus be covered, I deem it advisable in due time to draw out a number of these distinctions between kinds of conformative behaviour.

The points of reference by which I shall guide my efforts to discover what is peculiar to and distinctive in conformative behaviour are these: (1) If one does such an act, it is always meaningful to ask whether he behaved correctly or incorrectly; (2) when one does such an act, he is acting with a certain kind of reason or mistaken reason, which we may schematize as 'That's the rule'; finally, (3) standardly, the agent's reason will be or imply that certain others would be entitled to expect him to act as he does. The rule will come out as that which one is aware of as a reason; and the rule, in standard cases, is to be explained in terms of *warranted expectation*.

5. SOME GUIDING DISTINCTIONS

[Both to avoid confusion and to attain generality a number of distinctions are indicated, which are to be explored further in later sections. First, we must distinguish conformative behaviour from behaviour which happens to conform to rules. Second, we must distinguish the rules which underlie a practice from generalizations about the practice. Third, we must distinguish rules from the formulations of rules. Within the realm of rules, in the fourth place, we distinguish rules which must be formulated in advance from rules which need not be. Fifth, we distinguish rules from the practices which those rules underlie. Sixth, we distinguish rules which do from rules which do not *constitute* practices. Seventh, rules which control already extant modes of behaviour are distinguished from rules by conforming to which agents are enabled to engage in new kinds of behaviour; these are, respectively, called *restrictive* and *enabling* rules. Each of these types may be further broken up. Thus restrictive rules may be inhibitions or licenses or prescriptions. Finally, certain rules are such that conformity to them is sufficient to assure success in conformative action, provided that all conditions of success are satisfied: these are called *rules for succeeding*.]

Success in our project of demarcating the general area of conformative behaviour depends palpably on distinguishing rules from what are not rules and upon exercising care not to adopt only one pattern of rules to the exclusion of all others. To these ends it will pay us to direct attention to a number of distinctions, all of which are to be more fully examined in later sections, which are at once important and easily passed over in the course of theorizing.

The first distinction has already been anticipated. It is the distinction between acts which happen to conform to rules and full-blooded conformative acts. A rule may be in force within a certain community and provide a standard against which members of the community assess each other's behaviour. Now there may be persons, whether or not members of the community, whose behaviour is submitted to this kind of assessment but who are as yet totally ignorant of the existence of the rule. As viewed by others, their behaviour may be held to conform, or fail to conform, as the case may be. But it will still be incorrect to characterize their behaviour as conformative to that rule. For that to be possible, the agent must himself either conform to or act in violation of the rule. A condition for that is his believing that a rule exists. Of course one may be brought to an awareness of a rule by having his more primitive, non-conformative behaviour assessed in respect of a rule by his fellow men. But here we want to consider only that kind of behaviour which is realized after the transition has been effected.

Second, we must never confuse a rule which underlies a practice with *generalizations* about that practice. Generalizations can be made about all kinds of behaviour, conformative and non-conformative, and blindness to the distinction could very well frustrate our efforts to sequester conformative behaviour.

Third, we must not confuse the rule in conformity with which one may act with a *formulation* or *statement* of that rule. We are apt to miss this distinction because certain practices are necessarily instituted by formulated rules, *e.g.*, *playing chess*. But even in this kind of case, the rule one follows is not itself the formulation, but is, rather, what is formulated.

This shows that we must distinguish, fourth, rules that must be formulated in advance from rules that need not be. The former I shall call statutory. Neither morals nor Language, the elucidation of which inspires an appeal to the idea of *rule*, typically depend upon formulated rules. But the idea that a proper rule exists only by being formulated intrudes itself constantly here, leading either to over-formalistic conceptions of morality and Language or to the sceptical conclusion that the kinds of reason to be found in these areas are figments or frauds.[1]

[1] This may be part of what provoked P. Ziff to declare that the appeal to rules for the understanding of Language is irrelevant and obfuscating, and that we

Fifth, we must not confuse practices which require rules with the rules which underlie those practices. That there is a distinction here is most obviously seen in the fact that alternative rules may underlie the same practice; *e.g.*, there are alternative ways of saying that women are wonderful. But even when the rules are essential to the practice, one *engages in* the practice by sometimes *conforming to* the rules, which shows that the rules and the practice are not the same.

We must, in the sixth place, distinguish rules which are and rules which are not essential to a practice. I shall call these *constitutive* and *non-constitutive* rules, respectively.[2] Rules of the former kind, of which the rules of chess and the rules of English are perhaps examples, are ones such that an unwillingness on the part of the agent to conform to the rules would be proof that he was not engaged in the practice. On the other hand, one may refuse to conform to non-constitutive rules, and still be engaged in the practice, as one may refuse to speak English and yet use Language. This distinction is made the more difficult by the fact that some rules may concurrently be non-constitutive of one practice and constitutive of a subsidiary practice. Thus, as we have just seen, the same rules may be constitutive of English and non-constitutive of the use of Language.

Seventh, we must distinguish rules conformity to which serves to alter and control already extant modes of behaviour from rules conformity to which enlarges the scope of human action and enables agents to engage in new kinds of behaviour. These I respectively call *restrictive* and *enabling* rules. Restrictive rules are of many kinds, *e.g.*, prohibitions, prescriptions (which we might lump together and call 'injunctions'), and licenses. Enabling rules are also of many kinds. [Obvious question: Are all constitutive rules also enabling rules? The answer will be found in no. 12.]

Finally, some but not all rules are such that conformity to them is sufficient to assure success in particular acts, provided that all the defining conditions of success are satisfied. For such kinds of behaviour we can actually say what will make the act succeed, *viz.*, *conforming to the rules*. Examples of such rules, which I call *rules for succeeding*, are rules for making arithmetical calculations, also possibly rules for getting from one place to another, *e.g.*, as embodied in maps,

---

[2] 'Constitutive' is an item in a body of terminology for talking about rules dating from at least the time of Kant. It is a natural term, but, alas, almost everyone employs it differently. What Kant seemed to mean by 'constitutive rule' (in contrast to 'regulative rule') is, I think, closely approximated by what I shall mean by 'enabling rule'.

---

must in this area speak rather about regularities and deviations therefrom (*Semantic Analysis*, no. 34). I concede that Ziff's irascible protests have force, failing an effective elucidation of *rule*.

and rules of Language. Not all rules are of this kind. One does not succeed in getting into a certain chess position by following the rules of chess, for one's opponent may interpose resistance. Contrary to first appearances, not all rules for succeeding are enabling rules, *e.g.*, not the rules for getting from one place to another which are embodied in a map. Knowledge of the rules facilitates the journey, but it might have been successfully brought off without recourse to the rules.

6. RULE AND GENERALIZATION[1]

[Rules should not be confused with generalizations, a mistake which we may be tempted into by the fact that rules must be learned, by thinking that rules must be formulated, and by the fact that conforming to rules creates behavioural regularities about which generalizations may be made. The distinction between *rule* and *generalization* is drawn out in a number of contrasts, all of which point to the essential difference, that generalizations are produced by way of the use of Language, whereas rules need not be.]

In America it is a rule of morality, one pretty widely adhered to, to refrain from saying things which might be taken to show disrespect towards the religion of those present. An example of a rule for the English language and so a rule for the use of Language is that the spoken counterpart of 'I' is a first-person singular personal pronoun; that is, 'I' may be used by a speaker to refer to himself as the speaker, or to bring himself, as speaker, into what is said. These are rules, I say, not indeed in the literal sense of 'rule', but in the sense that one may either conform to or act in violation of them and his behaviour be accordingly judged as correct or incorrect.

Now, when faced with such examples of rules, some might be likely to answer: 'Ah yes, quite accurate descriptions of the customs and speech habits of Americans, fairly reliable sociological generalizations; but do understand, these are not rules at all; they simply report on social regularities.' Curious that in offering such a reply one would be likely to presume the truth of the second alleged generalization in summarizing the evidence in its favour ('*I* have discovered that most Americans sometimes refer to themselves with the spoken counterpart of "I"'). Curious too to note how very bad these would be as generalizations, if we were right in so regarding them. In the first

---

[1] In this section 'generalization' covers both universal statements ('All the books on that shelf are hard-back') and open generalizations not susceptible to final verification ('All dogs die before 50'). Only the former are susceptible both to full verification and to full falsification, though generalizations of both kinds have truth-value.

place, the scope of the generalization is not at all clear. Apparently these are not universal statements about the behaviour of all Americans: but then we are entitled to some explicit specification of their limitations, some indication of their statistical width. Also, there might be alternative ways of referring to oneself as a speaker, which surely would have to be taken account of by any proper generalization about such behaviour. The fact is that what are formulated in these two examples are not meant to be generalizations; and, while they are not rules in the literal sense, they do expressly formulate that to which one might conform when talking about himself or when engaged in conversation. What are thus formulated are good examples of rules in the sense of 'rule' we hope to make explicit.

There are at least three reasons why people are apt to think that these are generalizations. First, the practices in question are certainly not ones which are created by the express formulation of rules. What is formulated, therefore, cannot be what creates the practice. That, if it be anything at all, is what one may consult in order to discover what conformity to the rule would require. The formulations we gave are reports upon existing practices. But now rules in the literal sense of 'rule' are indeed produced by formulations, which may in turn engender practices. In view of these two facts—that there are no rules in the literal sense at hand and that what is formulated as the rule is a report upon existing practice—it may seem but a short step to go on to say that what is formulated is really a generalization about the practice in question, and that there is no rule but only a regularity in the offing. The trouble with that is that just some such formulation might be given in the course of correcting someone's behaviour or in teaching him to speak. The formulation may be given as instructions regarding how one is to behave, *viz.*, to conform to the rule which is . . . . Here, surely, what we have in hand is not simply a generalization about how people do behave; it is *something like* a rule, in the literal sense. It is, if you wish, a standard of behaviour.

Second, it might be argued that we learn to conform by generalizing upon the behaviour of our fellows, as it were 'inductively'. That is altogether wrong. While we may well allow that conformative behaviour involves *learning*, surely not all learning is *induction* in any of the many senses that could reasonably be given to that unhappy term. Making inductions is only *one* of the things we learn to do; it is one quite particular kind of proficient behaviour; and, moreover, I should guess, a kind of conformative behaviour, where the practice involves rules of evidence, truth, *etc.* Learning, in short, is not necessarily making generalizations upon the facts; one may, after all, learn from a single instance, whereas to make a generalization would require that we consider a range of cases. But even if one did learn to conform to the rule by making generalizations on the behaviour of his fellows, and it may sometimes be so, the generalization is itself not what one learns to conform to, but rather it tells him what the rule is.

That brings me to the third reason we may confuse rules and generalizations. It surely is true that conformity to rule on the part of the members of a community usually lends a certain regularity to their behaviour, and so creates the possibility of making generalizations regarding how they behave. Thus we may make generalizations regarding the speech habits of Americans, *viz.*, we say that such and such a community follows such and such Language rules, as we might say that upper-class Indians speak English. But if this is to be the generalization, then it is quite clear that we are declaring on what rules operate in this community; it should be made explicit that what we are generalizing upon is conformative behaviour, implying a sharp distinction between the rule and the generalization. While we may discover what rules govern a certain practice by making generalizations upon human behaviour, that presumes that there are rules to be found. It remains that we may generalize upon behaviour of any and all kinds, but not any and all kinds of behaviour are conformative. Regularity of behaviour is not enough to make a rule. The regularity must, in ways yet to be explained, be *due to* the rule. The point might be put by saying that animals do not conform to generalizations as they do conform to rules; and that the possibility of generalizing on their behaviour does not efface the distinction between the rules and the generalization. In support of the point we can invoke the distinction between conformative behaviour and behaviour which happens to conform. For, if it be insisted that whenever an animal's behaviour is regular he is 'following a generalization', it would be necessary to notice that we might turn up a generalization to the effect that an animal's behaviour conforms to a rule, although it would still be wrong to say that he, the animal, conforms to the rule. To conform to a rule is to act with a certain kind of reason ('That's the rule'), while one's behaviour may conform even though he have no such reason. Indeed, behaviour may conform to a regularity and be utterly without purpose, and hence not qualify as action at all. In this latter case we would do better to say of the animal that he was behaving as if he were following a rule; but that is not to say that he is following the rule and still less is it to say that he is following a generalization which summarizes his behaviour.

Many writers have correctly observed that rules characteristically provide standards guiding the choice of behaviour and against which behaviour may be assessed, as brought out in our inclinations to cite rules as justifications for our behaviour or as grounds for the evaluation of behaviour (see, *e.g.*, H. L. A. Hart, *op. cit.*, pp. 136f.). But

245

surely one does not feel he ought to scratch with his right hand just because most people happen to. Regularity is not enough to make what we want to call a rule, hence what we want to call rules are not simply regularities. At every point the distinction between the rule and the generalization obtrudes itself as inevitable.

Conformity to rules doubtless regularizes behaviour and hence provides ground for making a generalization. Allow that, for rules must be *general*. But a rule is general in a quite different way from that in which a generalization is general. Consider the difference between the rule that '?' may be used to show that a question is being asked and the generalization that '?' is used in such and such communities to terminate written sentences which the writers of those sentences would regard as having the interrogative form, or to mark the desire to place a question, or as an abbreviatory device signifying a doubtful or problematic situation, or . . . . The generalization is general in that it must hold over a range of phenomena, the limits of which ought to be expressly shown in the generalization itself. The rule is not general in that way at all. The formulation of the rule makes no attempt either to give all the uses of '?', or to give all the ways of indicating that one is asking a question. The rule gives those who know it *one* way of doing the latter job, and the formulation of the rule says what that way is. The rule is general in the sense that a proper formulation would leave certain things open and *unspecified*. It may in fact be that the rule operates only once, but it cannot in itself say that or how often it will operate; the formulation may tell us under what kinds of condition the rule is to be in force, and the rule is general just because and only because that statement must be about *kinds* of condition and so be left open. On the other hand, a generalization is the better the more closed it is.

If the distinction between rules and generalizations needs further support, we may find it by noting some of the ways in which the two ideas characteristically connect with other ideas.

Rules regulate or govern behaviour, while generalizations describe it. Rules 'apply', while generalizations 'hold'. One conforms to or acts in violation of a rule, but not a generalization. Generalizations are true or false; not so rules. That which runs counter to an acceptable rule is wrong or incorrect, while that which runs counter to a true generalization simply is not the case or, if we take as our instance a singular statement, that statement is false. Rules are applicable or inapplicable; not so generalizations, though the *mention* of either a rule or a generalization may be relevant or irrelevant. We may (though we need not always) adopt rules; we establish generalizations. Rules may be rejected; generalizations refuted. Rules may be deliberately changed, even if I cannot change them; not so with generalizations;

for, where rules may sometimes be enacted and made effective, generalizations must wait patiently to be discovered and established. An unthought or unformulated generalization is a contradiction in terms; rules, on the other hand, may never be thought of, simply followed, and seldom achieve complete formulation. We are taught *how to* behave in compliance with rules; we are instructed *that* such and such generalizations hold. Nor, as some suppose, do we always or even usually learn to conform to rules by making generalizations. Finally, as we just saw, rules may apply over a generality of cases, but the scope of application is usually unstated and much may be left undetermined, and this is not in itself a flaw in the rule; generalizations can be more and less extensive, but the conditions, limitations, and qualifications should be clear.

The conclusion which emerges from all this is that generalizations are creatures of the use of Language, while rules are not. Rules are patterns of behaviour to which one may be expected to conform; they are facts, and reasons for action. While certain of these patterns presume Language and indeed are created by express formulations, not all rules are of this kind. Those rules which do presume Language, when taken as reasons, should not be confused with the Language they presume; no more than should a corporation be confused with the articles of incorporation.

The argument of this section is not meant as an analysis of either 'rule' or 'generalization'. It is meant rather as a kind of prophylactic against blindness to the distinction between rule (in our still unexplained sense of 'rule') and generalization, which even a cursory examination of philosophical literature will reveal to be widespread. There is much work to be done to elucidate and harden the distinction; but the preparatory moves we have made in that direction should keep us out of the more treacherous and dangerous pitfalls which lie before those who fail to see that rules are not and cannot by themselves count as general statements of fact.

7. RULE AND COMMUNITY

[The idea that conformative behaviour presumes a community is defended on the grounds that private rules, which are quite possible, must be capable of becoming community rules, and that practices underlain by private rules come into being only by superseding and/or as extensions of practices underlain by community rules.]

Philosophers sometimes find themselves appealing to the idea of a rule when they wish to argue that the facts under investigation are very much out in the open. The one most responsible for the popularity of this move is Wittgenstein, who was particularly exercised to establish, first, that Language, far from being necessarily private (as he himself at an earlier period seems to have held), must be based on possibly public conventions, and, second, that our criteria for private experience are themselves public. The argument is that a rule is something shared by the members of a community; so, if the phenomena in question essentially involve rules, they must be in certain respects accessible to public observation.

As against this it might be argued that private rules—ciphers or the most secret principles of the heart—are quite easily installed and not hard to find.[1] This is quite true, but does not threaten the thesis that there must be *something* essentially out in the open in practices and their underlying rules. Significantly, we can decipher ciphers, and penetrate even to the most hidden principles. But the possibility of private rules does show that the claims for the public character of rules must be carefully framed. I propose to do that by arguing that private rules both borrow from and presume public practices.

I hold that any private rule might be made public and could then conceivably become a rule for some community. In a formulation of the rule all reference to particular agents may be deleted, and it then becomes conceivable that any number of agents might on any number of occasions conform to or act in violation of the rule, there being public tests for deciding, tests prefigured in the formulation of the rule. So, even private rules are public in that they *might* become the property of others. These others, if properly instructed and sufficiently apt, will then be in as good a position as any one agent, A, to ascertain and declare whether A's behaviour did or did not conform to the rule. All one need know is what the behaviour was—and that might be a matter of public record—and what enactments or precedents cover the matter—and these might be the possible subject of public instruction. It is, of course, not required that the rule itself be canonized by explicit publication: a body of precedent is often enough. What is ruled out is any essential element of intrinsic inaccessibility. The two essential assumptions in this argument are (1) the possibility of deleting reference to particular agents in the formulation of a rule while still retaining the formulation of a rule; (2) the fact that rules are manifested in behaviour, and behaviour can be observed by others and, as it were, deciphered.

I wish to claim more than that any rule may become public. Community rules are primary to private rules in that one could not engage in a practice which involved possible conformity to private rules were he not able to conform to community rules. This condition granted, private practices may then come to supersede or stand in for equiva-

[1] The issues are nicely contrasted in the symposium contributions of Ayer and Rhees.

lent public practices, or they may be extensions upon them. Thus, by adopting a cipher, one may put a private orthography in place of a standard one. Or a naturalist may invent a private nomenclature in which to set down his discoveries. But in the first case, our imagined agent must first have learned spelling in some other way; and, in the second, the naturalist must first have learned to speak about kinds of creatures known to others. While this seems to me true without question, the only argument I can find in support of it is the following: In order for one to follow a private rule it is necessary that he *conceive* the rule and expressly adopt it, though of course without having to publicize his intent. When following the rule, his reason will always be of the form, 'This is the rule (which I have adopted)'. The agent must find the rule in this way because he does not have the alternative of seeing it in the presumed expectations of others. But now no one could come to follow such a rule unless he could see rules in the presumed expectations of others. This follows from the fact that no one could conceive and *adopt* a rule without having the use of Language, which presumes familiarity with rules. This argument, be it noted, does not imply that all idiosyncratic behaviour presumes community rules. Such behaviour need not be rule-conforming, even when we can discover a rule in the behaviour. The argument applies only to the case where one acts to conform to or in conscious violation of an idiosyncratic rule. Finally, to quiet the objections of those who can conceive any possibility and of those who suspect *a priori* pedagogy, yes, someone might be born into the world capable of following private rules, but only if he could also follow community rules; but ability to conform to or act in violation of community rules does not imply that one could follow private rules.

'Community', like 'normal', is a dangerously open term. All of us belong to any number of different communities—church and state, club and family, *etc.* This is revealed in the multitude of practices in which we regularly engage. But this poses a threat to the coherence of our account. We must not stumble into the mistake of wishing to define the community by reference to its practices and rules, while relating rules to the community. That would be a vicious circle. We must always allow that there could be clear tests, independent of conformity to the underlying rule, for discovering who belongs to the community. And of course there always are. We can discover where one was born, raised, educated, *etc.*, and from such facts as these we are entitled to assume that he belongs to a community whose members might be expected to conform to these or those rules. [2]

[2] It is much as with words and their senses. We often identify words by coming to understand what is meant by them, just as we often may see to what community someone belongs by observing how he behaves. Nonetheless there must be

249

8. RULES ARE REASONS

[We have held that rules are reasons for acting. The existence of a rule is a condition of success for conformative purposes, and we identify an item of conformative behaviour by cause of the fact that the agent believes that a rule exists. The belief may be schematized as 'That's the rule'. The fact in question is a reason in the light of a principle of reason specific to the practice in question, *e.g.*, 'One ought not to steal'. The principle is not always 'One ought to avoid the consequences of an infraction or breach'. Nor, in general, is the principle, 'One ought to act to conform to rule'. Not just any fact is or could be a rule, nor indeed is every reason a rule. In the next section we shall try to define those facts which are rules.]

Our guiding thought has been that a rule, or, more exactly, the existence of a rule, is a reason for acting. That at once accounts for the influence of rules upon behaviour and serves to distinguish conformative behaviour from behaviour which happens to conform. The influence of rules is accounted for because a reason by definition is a fact, believing which might explain behaviour. It distinguishes conformative behaviour from behaviour which happens to conform, because the former requires, while the latter does not, that the agent should act with a reason of the form 'That's the rule'.

This conception of rules swings the analysis of conformative behaviour into line with our general theory of action. We are to define purposes by listing conditions of success. The existence of a rule is a condition of success for conformative behaviour. A purpose is conformative if and only if one condition of success for that purpose is of the form 'That's the rule'. We practically identify a conformative act by seeing that such a purpose is present, *i.e.*, in part by observing that the agent (truly or falsely) believes 'That's the rule'. He acts with a reason or mistaken reason of that form.

In performing a conformative act the agent does not necessarily act *for* the reason 'That's the rule'. That is so only when he acts to conform to the rule. But he may act in violation of the rule. In neither case can he be oblivious of the existence of a (supposed) rule. But in the latter case he is either indifferent to or wilfully resists the rule, whereas in the conforming case he, as it were, 'accepts' the rule. The condition, generally stated, for conformative behaviour is that the agent acts *in* the belief 'That's the rule'.

Let us now consider only the case of true belief where it is a fact that there is a rule. A fact is a reason only in consideration of some

independent criteria for identifying words and independent criteria for ascertaining the membership of communities.

principle of reason, which is, for the observer, a principle of explanation and, for the deliberative agent, a principle of deliberation. In consideration of what kinds of principle are rules reasons? One is apt to jump for a unifying answer of a Kantian kind. The principle, it might be urged, can only be 'One ought to act to conform to rule'. That would be mistaken. I do not deny that that is sometimes the principle in consideration of which a fact of the form 'That's the rule' gives reason for acting. But surely conformative behaviour is not always so abstractedly second-order and oppressively conscientious; not even the silliest sissy does the 'right thing' always only 'not to be a bad boy'. Sometimes the principle of the act is only (*e.g.*) that it would be wrong to steal, or that one can allude to dogs by uttering the word 'chien', or that we are playing chess.

Another, opposite-tending unifying answer is that the principle is always 'One ought to act to avoid the penalties or discomforts which may ensue upon an infraction or breach of the rule'. Again I do not hold that rules are *never* reasons in consideration of this principle. But surely it cannot be the only rule-making principle. Not all conformative acts are so calculatedly callous. Even the most villainous juvenile delinquent will habitually wear his clothes in the fashion of his peers and speak in the argot of his block, quite without cynical calculations of consequences. It is true that most community rules have their 'sanctions', however indefinite, unspecific, and unforeseeable. We may in considerable degree distinguish kinds of rule in terms of how these sanctions work. Thus, while the 'sanctions of morality' are characteristically unspecified and unspecifiable except in such vague terms as 'public opinion' and may never be borne, the 'sanctions of the law' are characteristically annexed to the very formulation of the law and officially enforced—there would be no law unless it were generally felt that wilful offenders would be compelled to comply. It may also be true that we are brought to the level of conformative behaviour by being made to feel the advantages of conforming and the disadvantages of non-compliance. But for all that, upon acquiring 'the exercise of reason' one may (*e.g.*) refrain from taking what belongs to another neither because he fears punishment nor out of a suspicious compunction, but simply because he knows that it is (legally or morally) wrong to steal. [1]

I submit that the principles in consideration of which a rule is a reason are multifarious and specific to particular practices. They are of many types—legal, moral, linguistic, *etc.*, *etc.* They may be as

---

[1] For discussion of these see Hart, *op. cit.*, pp. 88f., 98f., and my own 'The Sense of Duty', *Phil. Quart.*, 1957, pp. 116–125, and 'Moral Rules and Moral Maxims', *Ethics*, 1957, pp. 269–285.

specific as, 'One ought to keep promises' or 'One may use a first-person singular pronoun to refer to himself', or as general as 'One ought to behave decently, speak grammatically, obey the law' (under which would fall such reasons as 'I promised to write the letter', '"I"' is an English first-person singular pronoun', and 'That's a red light').

All this shows that we still need a general characterization of rules. The formulation of a principle in consideration of which a rule is a reason will not always be explicitly of the form 'It's a rule that . . .'. We need a criterion for determining that the principle is implicitly of that form, *e.g.*, that it's a rule that 'One ought to keep promises'. We need a characterization of which facts are rules. In the next section we shall try to arrive at that criterion for or definition of rules.

Certain writings give us the feeling that the author would suppose that all reasons or good reasons are rules, excepting possibly those which fall under the Principle of the End. Kant is an example, as also are those writers who have suggested that we can define 'ought' and elucidate the distinction between right and wrong in terms of rules (see Part II, no. 9, pp. 106f.). I have held that these ideas of 'ought', *etc.*, are invoked to assert that the preponderance of reasons of whatever kind is on one side or the other. It is clear, I hope, that these intimations that all reasons are rules are mistaken, howbeit encouraged by the fact that we do not generally formulate principles of reason so as to indicate expressly whether or not they be principles in consideration of which rules are reasons.

9. RULES ARE SYSTEMS OF EXPECTATION

[Community rules are systems of expectation. An agent conforms to such a rule if he acts for the reason that the members of the community are entitled to expect him so to act. Efforts are made to explain and generalize this formula, resulting in the conclusion that behaviour is conformative only if the agent acts *in* the belief that there are or were creatures belonging to a specific community, who, were they present, would believe that he would act *from* the belief that they expect him to do such and such kind of act. In the absence of clear counter-examples, this is taken as a sufficient condition for proficient behaviour being conformative-to-community-rule behaviour. This criterion for conformative behaviour is extended to the case of private rules by the stipulation that, were those rules made public, they would create a system of expectation. More exactly, one's behaviour is conformative to private rule only if he acts in the belief that he has determined to act in a way, the making public of which would give others, were they present, reason to believe that he would act from the belief that they expect him to do such and such.]

In the last two sections it was held that rules are reasons and that community rules are primary; summarily, one conforms to a rule when his reason for so acting is that there is a rule present in the presumed expectations of others regarding his behaviour. This seems to me to strike very close to the heart of the matter and may, when filled in, supply the answer to our question what a rule is.

Confining ourselves to community rule, the idea is this: One follows a rule if he conforms to what he sees are the legitimate expectations of others; and the existence of a rule is, moreover, what entitles the others to their expectations, thus rendering them 'legitimate'. A community rule exists if the members of a community regulate their affairs according to what other members of the community would legitimately expect them to do. The rule is at once the expectations one conforms to and what legitimizes or warrants those expectations. The rule is, as it were, a system of community, mutual expectation. When one conforms to a rule he acts in the knowledge or belief that others would expect him so to behave. That the others are entitled to those expectations is his reason. Of course one may act in violation of such rules; but even there too one must believe that others have legitimate expectations. If one has no thoughts about what is expected of him, then he can neither conform to nor act in violation of the rule.

Take some examples: I conform to the Moslem rule of entering a mosque without shoes; in order to conform to this rule, or even to act in violation of it, I must suppose that Moslem native onlookers would expect me so to behave and that they are entitled to that expectation by a Moslem rule of behaviour. Or, I appear before an audience of Mexicans; I try to speak Spanish because I know that Mexicans are entitled to expect those who would speak to them when assembled together in Mexico to employ the Castilian tongue. Again, a law is passed by act of the legislature that all automobiles must display evidence that they are properly registered and licensed; this act creates and warrants a general expectation on the part of all those who live in the state in question that owners of automobiles will register and obtain licences for their vehicles and display evidence of having done so. By way of contrast, one complies with a *request* when he acts to satisfy what he takes to be the *wishes*, not the warranted expectations, of another.[1]

---

[1] For more of this kind of contrast see J. F. G. van Loon, 'Rules and Commands', *Mind*, 1958, pp. 514–521. Much of what I have said above borrows from this excellent article. Van Loon is especially concerned to draw a distinction between rules, which 'provide a basis for legitimate expectation of some addressees

However right, all this is vague. Who are the 'others'; and, more precisely, what 'entitles' them to their expectations; and what if none of them are present, can I not still conform to the rule? To resolve these questions, I should now like, somewhat slowly and I fear tediously, to ferret out what I think is an essential condition for an act to be an instance of conformative behaviour. I shall simply assume that one must *know how to* conform, *viz.* that we are concerned with a species of proficient behaviour. The guiding presumption, already stated, is that one conforms to a rule when he acts with a certain kind of reason, which could be schematized as 'That's the rule'. Conformative behaviour must be taken to manifest a characteristic kind of (at least) practical awareness. Suppose one tries to conform, he may still fail in his act because he lacks that knowledge, either through ignorance or obliviscence. But even then, if one is to do an act of the conformative kind, he must *believe* that the rule is such. What I shall now try to do is to state what kind of belief this is.

Let us begin by taking what is surely the most fundamental and persistently the most common case, that of rules of community, with the additional conditions (1) that some of the members of that community are *present*, where (2) the agent acts to *conform*, and (3) the agent and his observers may be taken to *know* all that is relevant to be known about the situation. These conditions—of *present informed community* with the agent acting in *full knowledge* to *conform*—will then be progressively relaxed.

A community, we saw, must be constituted independently of the various rules which hold within it, *e.g.*, by birth, education, election, convention. A rule for that community would be formulated by specifying the manner in which the various members of the community regulate their behaviour as members of the community, in respect of certain practices. There are all sorts of such manners or patterns of behaviour: some of them are reciprocal, some special to certain offices, *etc.* One conforms to a rule only if he adopts a manner of behaviour appropriate to him as a member of the community, in his special roles, capacities, and circumstances.

Now, in order that one should behave 'as a member of the community' the following formal conditions must hold. *First*, one must have a practical knowledge of the manner in which he is to behave, and so be able to know whether or not he is conforming.

---

concerning the conduct of some other addressees in relation to the conduct of the former', and commands, in following which one conforms to the will of another. There are various points of contrast. For example, commands must be expressed, whereas rules need not be. Even where rules follow upon the issuance of a command, or where the rule provides a legitimate basis for command, as in the Military, the contrast between rule and command stands.

Second, it is implied and known by the agent that all the other members of the community should have a similar practical knowledge about the manner in which they are to behave.

Third, the agent knows that other members of the community will, as does he, believe that all others whom they take to be members of the community will have comparable knowledge.

In short, we have a community in which each member is presumed to know how he is to behave and to believe that all others have knowledge comparable to his own.

These conditions do not yet create a 'system of expectations', because it is not required that anyone should know how anyone else is to behave. It is only infrequently the case that everyone will know in what manner anyone is to behave. However, anyone *A* may expect that someone *B* will know in what manner he, *A*, is to behave and since some *C* knows that *A* knows this, *C* will expect *A* to behave in the prescribed manner, to conform to the expectations of some *B*.

So let us begin there. By seeing me in these circumstances, others in the community will, by recognizing me as a member of the community, be given reason to expect that I will behave in such and such a manner. But that is not yet enough, for, as we saw, I myself must know in what manner I am to behave. The satisfaction of this condition is implied by a further, stronger one: that I act with the knowledge that I am expected to behave in the prescribed manner. But that is still not enough. Action may conform to a rule, even when the agent does not himself conform to the rule. The latter is what is wanted. It is not only that *my behaviour* must conform, as I may know it does, but *I* must conform. We can put this by saying that I must act, not merely *with* but *from* the knowledge that this is expected of me.

More is needed. I may know that I am expected to make a fool of myself, and, being a buffoon, I act accordingly. Here there is no rule operating; there is no question of correct or incorrect; it is simply that I am a conscientious fool. What is required is that the others be entitled to their expectations. Moreover, what entitles those expectations cannot be just any old thing; it must be based on their knowledge that I am a member of the community. Going back to condition no. 3 on p. 254, and holding to the simplest case of knowledge, they must know that I know in what manner I am to behave, and their expectations that I shall so behave are based thereupon, and not upon some other special knowledge about me, *e.g.*, that I am a fool or an inveterate rule breaker. So, it follows that if I am to conform to a rule I must take it that the others know that I act from the knowledge that they expect me so to behave.

I am deliberately no longer speaking about what the others are

255

entitled to expect; nor am I even saying that their expectations must be based on knowledge that I am a member of the community. Some might object that the others could have this knowledge about what knowledge I will act on, even though their resulting expectations are not 'entitled'. I cannot prove that this is impossible. But nor am I sure that it is possible. The others may, for instance, know that I will act from the knowledge that they expect me to act foolishly. But that very strongly intimates, if it does not indeed imply, that I am, by profession, if you wish, by rule, a buffoon, rather like the king's jester. So, pending good counter-examples, I shall leave it as stated. The others know that I will act in the knowledge that they expect me so to act.

But now that must be *my reason* for so acting. Still holding to the case of knowledge, we may recast that as *I act from the knowledge that others know that I will act from the knowledge that they expect me so to behave.* There, then, is our first major result.

Now we must begin to relax the conditions. I may be wrong about what others expect me to do. And they may be wrong about me, and I am now alive to that possibility. That means that we must systematically delete 'know' and 'knowledge' in favour of 'believe' and 'belief'. The condition then becomes *I act from the belief that others believe that I will act from the belief that they expect me so to behave.*

That covers the case of conforming to rule. But I might also act in violation of what I take to be the rule. In this latter kind of case I am not acting for the reason or the mistaken reason that others are entitled to expect me so to behave; *i.e.,* I do not act *from* the belief. But it is not that I simply act *with* the belief either, this belief being merely incidental to my deed. I am, rather, acting *in* the belief (with the reason). So the condition, now changed to the third-person form, becomes as follows: *The agent does act A in the belief or with the reason that others believe that he will act from the belief that they expect him to do an act of kind K, where the kind of act A may or may not be the same as K.*[2] So framed, this covers both conforming and non-conforming behaviour.

This is a necessary condition for one's behaviour being conformative, on the condition that the rule is a community rule and that one is acting in the presence of members of the community. Let us now relax that second restriction, for of course one may speak his own language or hold to the moral rules of his tribe, even when he knows that no members of his language community or tribe are present. They may even all have expired. To make room for this, we must now change the condition to *the agent does act A in the belief or with the*

---

[2] The formulation is inescapably heavy-handed, for it is clear that we must make reference to types or kinds of act.

reason that there are or were creatures belonging to a specifiable community who, were they present, would believe that he would act from the belief that they expected him to do act of kind K where, again, the kind of A may or may not be the same as K.

That, I submit, is a necessary condition for one's acting in conformity with or in violation of a community rule. Is it also a sufficient condition? I do not know. But my conjecture is that it is. The idea, I repeat, is that one conforms when he acts with the reason or mistaken reason that others are entitled to expect him to act so. The rub is the 'entitled', or, in our occasional formulation, 'legitimate' or 'warranted'. And I urge that what 'entitles' this expectation is my communicants' knowledge that I am a member of the community. But is it not possible that they should believe that I shall act from the belief that they expect me so to act even when it is not true that I am a member of the community? And if I believe that, I cannot believe that their expectations are entitled. So my behaviour is not conformative. I have already allowed that this *may* be possible. Suppose I have a French name. Some visiting Frenchmen may, on this account, come to believe that I will act from the belief that they expect me to speak French; but I cannot speak French, even though I know they expect me to. I would comply if I could. I see that they believe that I shall act out of respect for their expectations. But I cannot. This works on my behaviour. The ungrammatical English I loudly assume is surely not spoken in violation of the rules of French. But if I am really acting *in* the belief that they believe that I will try to speak French, then surely I must either disdain them or make some effort to get through to them. *Disdain* would be contrary to 'correct practice' —a kind of bad manners. I do then act in conformity with or in violation of *a* rule, to be sure not a rule of French, but a rule of some kind; and my behaviour would indeed seem to qualify as *conformative.*

This is but one kind of example. I cannot be sure that it is typical. But pending counter-examples, I shall adopt the stated condition as my definition of conformative behaviour with respect to community rule: *The agent does act A in the belief or with the reason that there are or were others belonging to a specifiable community who, were they present, would believe that he would act from the belief that they would expect him to do act of kind K, where the type A may or may not differ from K.*

Supposing I am right about behaviour conformative to community rule, we still have to deal with the case of behaviour conformative to private rule. In the next to last section it was argued, first, that it was essential that a private rule could become a community rule and, second, it was held that for one to conform to or act in violation of

257

private rules presumes prior familiarity on his part with community rules. Private practices—including private languages, moral codes, superstitions, and religious observances—are of a kind borrowed from community practices, perhaps with extensions. In support of this it was argued, in the third place, that private rules, unlike community rules, must be *expressly adopted* by the agent. When the agent conforms to the rule, he acts for the reason: This is the rule (which I have adopted). He has expressly made an advance determination to act in a certain way.

There would seem to be two ways by which we might extend our formula to handle private rules. First, and ideally, we could use the second fact just mentioned, that private rules presume community rules and in ways which would be explained by the conditions we have enumerated about expectation. That is, we would make precise the idea of acting to attain a purpose that one could not act to attain unless he had learned to act to attain similar purposes by way of conforming to community rule. Though I am sure that there must be a formula which would work here, I cannot find it. The second option is to utilize the fact that private rules might become community rules. In pursuing this line, we must take care to keep our attention on the agent; that is, we must say what it is for *him* to conform to a rule which could become a community rule. Here we must use the third fact, alluded to above, that the agent have expressly adopted the rule. This implies that he could formulate the rule, and hence that the belief on which he acts is *theoretical*. He may then be able to think of the rule in highly explicit terms, and, by thinking of the rule, imagine it to be made a community rule *via* a suitable formulation. Now when he conforms to the rule his reason will be that he has *determined* to do so, where it is not implied that others have made a similar determination. In short, he acts for the reason that he has determined to act in a certain way, and others might expect him so to act if the rule were made public. His reason is not a system of expectations, but the existence of a determination of mind. The fact that he has determined to act so, be it noted, separates things which he does idiosyncratically 'as a rule' from his *conforming* to private rule; e.g., it separates his mannerisms from his superstitions and principles. Some may now object that this appeal to the highly problematical idea of a determination of mind is inadmissible because the notion is already loaded with rules. I confess to having no effective analysis of determining to act (it is not merely deciding). But even without that, it is clear, first, that this is a familiar idea and, second, one not limited in its application to private conformative behaviour—an agent may publicly state his determination to do what he does. Determining to act in a certain way probably also presumes a background of practice, hence rules. This, if true, but confirms what I have held regarding the dependence of private rules upon public conformative behaviour.

Drawing the strands together, I propose the following: *An agent conforms to or acts in violation of a private rule only if he does an act A in the belief that he has determined to act in a certain manner, which determination he may publicly declare, thus giving others reason to believe that he would act from the belief that they expected him to do an act of kind K, where the kind of A may or may not be the same as K.* This formulation also covers those cases where an agent has expressly acknowledged the rules he intends to follow.

10. FURTHER OBSERVATIONS ON CONFORMATIVE BEHAVIOUR, RULES, AND PRACTICES

[Because rules are or may become systems of expectation which give positive reasons for acting in certain ways, their operation tends to *regularize* behaviour. The existence of a system of expectation, the rule, provides an observer of behaviour with a standard or gauge against which to measure that behaviour. This goes even when the behaviour is itself not conformative behaviour, perhaps because the agent is not yet alive to the rule. However, it is important that the existence of this standard may also become a reason for an animal's acting in one way or another, and it thereby becomes a standard of correctness, a fact to which one may appeal when correcting or assessing the behaviour of an animal. When an agent acts with the belief that a rule exists, he is alive to the possibility that his behaviour may be gauged against the standard of the rule, and he is practically aware that what he does is accordingly susceptible to correction. The operation of rules, then, creates the possibility of correcting behaviour, and when one acts in conformity with or in violation of a rule he must have a practical awareness of this possibility. This gives support to a conjecture that capacity for conformative behaviour is a sufficient condition for an agent to be able to be aware of facts *as* reasons. The regularizing tendency of rules plus the fact that they afford ground for the objective determination of correctness confirm the thought that rules will govern, will give reason for behaving, in any number of possible cases, though not in just any case at all. What calls a rule into operation will be the nature of the circumstances at hand. The effect of these observations is to support our earlier conclusion that rules are most typically and fundamentally rules of community. The fact that these observations cohere very well indeed with the account of the last section lends additional plausibility to that account.]

We have, subject to provisos and pending the discovery of good counter-examples, arrived at something like a definition of a rule, in the philosopher's rather special use of 'rule'. Roughly, a rule is a system of expectations or (in the case of private rules) a conscious determination to act, the declaration of which would create a system of expectations, which, when called into operation by relevant circumstances, gives reason to act in certain ways. This result should not obscure the manifest differences among kinds of rule, a matter into which we shall subsequently inquire. There are a number of other pervasive features of conformative behaviour, and in this section I should like to draw attention to and explain the most immediately obvious of these. They are facts we may observe without mention of a theory such as that set out in the last section. But just for that reason the successful attempt to show that they are concinnous with such an account would weigh heavily in favour of that account. While I could not claim that these results necessarily follow from the condition arrived at in the last section, these characteristic features of conformative behaviour do seem to cohere very well with that result, and thus tend to confirm it. [1]

First, the operation of rule has a tendency to *regularize* behaviour, and rules will most naturally enter into our lives when there is call for or advantage to be had from the regularization of behaviour. I do not say that all rules *regulate*, nor do I hold that only rules *regularize*. 'Regularize' means little more than 'such as to cause to be in accord with expectations'. Now rules usually exist only when people regularly act for the reason that such and such is the rule; and if the rule is a system of expectations, then acting for that reason will bring one to conform to expectations. Hence one will be brought to act in accord with expectations; hence the regularizing tendency of rules. Because the existence of a rule gives the agent a special kind of reason to act, it also gives the observer reason to believe that the agent will act so.

Rules will naturally be found operating within those areas of behaviour where conflict might be dangerous or co-operation advantageous or where 'understanding' is a condition for amelioration or where one's behaviour directly impinges upon the welfare of others. Regularization, it should be noted, does not necessarily entail

---

[1] Hart, in the *Concept of Law* (see pp. 54ff.), contrasts rules with habits by observing that rules (1) provide standards of criticism; (2) give reasons for criticism; and (3) have an 'internal aspect', which I read to be a way of saying that rules are *regulative*. I agree with all this, though I would not give the first two observations a fundamental place in my exposition. They are, in my view, derivative, common, but not invariable features of rules. Also, I regard rules as primarily operative in actual behaviour, whereas Hart stresses their second-order aspect as standards of assessment. I emphasize their character as reasons for doing, while he emphasizes their character as reasons for saying (judging).

uniformity. The rule may tend to assign special competences to special offices; this is one version of the principle of the gains of specialization. All that is required is that the existence of a rule not only gives reason for acting in certain ways, but also reason for believing that others will act in certain ways.

The second general fact which we should notice is that rules provide a basis for correcting behaviour, and thus for estimating it as right or wrong. Rules, like all kinds of reasons, give grounds for appraisal as right or wrong, that special kind of right and wrong which we speak of as 'correct' and 'incorrect'. It will pay us to see how this fact fits in to our general account. If one is expected to behave in certain ways, then it is always possible to determine whether his behaviour was or was not in accord with those expectations. When those expectations are 'entitled', then they supply a standard or gauge on the behaviour in question. In this special case, where the existence of the gauge is possibly also a reason, it is natural to frame the result of applying the gauge in the language of 'right' and 'wrong'. To say that a fact is a reason is to imply that it ought to affect one's behaviour, other things being equal. One is to be brought to act for this reason, and to that end his behaviour will be 'corrected' in consideration of the rule. Community rules thus occasion distinctions between correct and incorrect behaviour. This carries over in ways not hard to trace into the domain of private rules. Holding to the simpler case of community rules, what we have said goes even when the agent is not alive to the demands of the rule, when he is not yet capable of knowing or believing that he has this reason for behaving so, and therefore has not attained the level of conformative behaviour. We still measure his actions against the standard of a rule. It is by bringing him to recognize these expectations as reasons that we inculcate conformative proficiencies.

The description of conformative behaviour as proficient behaviour which is inculcated by bringing the animal to respond to correction lends credibility to an interesting conjecture. A condition for action is that the animal be able to be aware of facts which are reasons, but agents need not in general be able to be aware of facts *as* reasons. My conjecture is that a sufficient condition for an agent to be able to be aware of facts *as* reasons is that he have attained the level of conformative behaviour. This is suggested by the following. First, a conformative agent is a proficient agent, hence an agent who can look for facts which are reasons. That suggests that the agent must already be behaviourally keyed to *select* facts which have special relations to his behaviour. Particularly, he must be able to look for rules in the behaviour of his fellow men, and then recognize that he has found them. Second, a conformative agent must be responsive to corrections given in consideration of a rule—it is, I suppose, mainly in that way that he knows whether or not he had found the fact. But for the agent to respond to the correcting as a correction strongly suggests that he must be aware of the indicated fact as a reason for acting, which is the substance of our conjecture.

The conformative agent need not have theoretical knowledge of facts as reasons. A necessary condition for that is that the agent have also attained the use of Language, which is but one species of conformative behaviour. While the conformative agent must be responsive to correction, he need not have the equivalent of the use of the word 'correct'. That acquired, he comes into position to measure his own behaviour and that of other agents *theoretically* and *expressly* against the standard of a rule. (Only when he has reached this stage, I have argued, can he act in conformity with or in violation of private rules.) We teach him the use of 'correct' in order to give him a theoretical lever on conformative behaviour, his own and others. We, then, who are presently engaged in theorizing about what it means to say that rules exist and are operating, if you wish, in the theory of our student's behaviour, will do well to observe that the equivalent of 'correct' is an indispensable tool for talking about conformative behaviour.

Our conclusion has been that the existence of rules, and of the practices which they underlie, tends to regularize behaviour and to create the possibility of correcting behaviour. Both of these facts point to the further conclusion that a rule must possibly operate in any number of cases. A rule may in fact be conformed to or violated but once or twice or never at all. (These possibilities probably pertain only to rules which come into existence only by being formulated: *e.g.*, regulations governing the evacuation of the civilian population in case of nuclear attack.) It is essential that sensitivity to rules can be inculcated; in the course of such inculcation others may come to have expectations regarding the agent's behaviour. The initiate must, by the way, get the idea that others will expect him to act in this manner when in situations comparable to the one in which he finds himself. To this end, the rule must not appear to be an expedient contrived for the moment.

But while a rule must be such as to operate in an open, possible multiplicity of cases, it does not operate in just any case at all. One does not make arithmetical calculations according to Emily Post, or play baseball in English. It is always the particular circumstances in question which bring the rule into force. The circumstances contribute to creating the particular expectations which, according to rule, give one reason to act.

What I have been observing in this section has been noticed by almost everyone who has discussed rules, in the heretofore unexplained philosopher's sense of 'rule' under examination. Rules regularize and create the possibility of correcting behaviour on any number of occasions and supply objective tests for the assessment of behaviour. All of this supports my assumption that rules will most typically pertain to communities and be publicly accessible. We have effectively enhanced the plausibility of our general explanation of conformative behaviour by arguing that these rather more readily accepted results about rules follow naturally, if not yet necessarily, from that explanation.

11. RESTRICTIONS AND ENABLING RULES

[Rules are divided into two exclusive kinds: those which operate to modify independently existing forms of behaviour and activity, and those which create new forms of behaviour and activity. The first are called *restrictions* and the latter *enabling rules*. Restrictions may be of various kinds, broad categories of which are injunctions (including prescriptions and prohibitions) and licences. The existence of practices underlain by enabling rules may occasion further restrictions. It is conjectured that capacity for conformative behaviour underlain by enabling rules is sufficient for an agent to be capable of self-consciousness.]

It is now time to define a number of distinctions between kinds of rule. In drawing out these distinctions I shall, in every case, have community rules first in mind, for these are at once more typical than and fundamental to private rules. We may immediately divide rules and the practices they underlie into those that do and those that do not regularize forms of behaviour or activity which exist independently of and antecedently to the operation of the rule. People may and do eat, sleep, converse with their fellows, engage in trade, aid or damage others, all in utter ignorance of and totally without benefit of etiquette, manners, or morality, or of rules and regulations for the licensing or regulation of trade. But familiarity with (*e.g.*) the rules of morality commonly alters the manner in which an agent does such acts or pursues such activities. A person is taught to believe that others expect him to eat his victuals so, and accordingly he does; or, in the presence of women, he refrains from expressing his thoughts in physiological terms. In short, he modifies the *manner* in which he eats, converses, engages in trade, by doing what he does in conformity with what he takes to be the expectations of others. We could call the resulting rules with the corresponding practices *modificatory*. But I think a better term is 'restrictive', for this word, if somewhat misleadingly, suggests that independently identifiable behaviour is being channelled, regularized, and confined. Let us then call such rules *restrictions*.

Obviously there are any number of kinds of restriction. The details must be left to the philosophers of law, morals, and society. I would, however, point out one very large division. Conformity to the rule may, on the one hand, require an agent to act or to forbear from acting in certain ways. In order to conform to the rule—to act for that reason—he is (*e.g.*) to mean to say things that will flatter the lady and to forbear from saying things that will shock her. Borrowing a term of law, we may call these *injunctions*, which is meant to include all manner of prescription and prohibition, certain kinds of direction and instruction, and much else besides.

In contrast with these injunctive restrictions, a rule may *permit* or give one licence to engage in activities or do deeds not open to all. The behaviour is still of a kind which could be done without benefit of rules; but the tendency of the rule is to restrict that behaviour to certain specially designated agents. These agents are, by the rule, not required but *permitted* to behave so; the rules *license* them, and we may call these rules *licences*. There is, perhaps, something illusory in the distinction between licences and injunctions, for the same rule which licenses your behaviour may be injunctive upon mine. But still not all injunctions are licences. More importantly, those rules which may operate in both ways do, nonetheless, operate in two ways, and with respect to different people. [1]

Not all rules are restrictions. Making moves in a game of chess and playing chess generally depend upon the existence of rules; similarly with arithmetical calculation. But in these cases conformity to rules does not modify independently existing forms of behaviour; the rules, rather, open up entirely new locales of action and activity to those capable of mastering them. They enable us to act in new ways otherwise beyond our power. They enhance our potentialities by cutting new tools for new jobs which we could otherwise not undertake or even so much as hope to undertake. To give them a name, let us call these *enabling rules*. Enabling rules should not be confused with licences. Licences, we saw, permit agents access to lines of action which they are otherwise enjoined from entering upon. Enabling rules do not merely permit such access, but veritably create the lines of action, which anyone capable of learning the rules may enter upon, though he may, thereby, come under both injunctive and licensing restrictions in respect of the behaviour created by the

---

[1] We are here confronted with the problem of the definition of rights, and with the question of the relation between rights and duties. These matters are not within my province.

enabling rule. One may do what he would naturally do but without proper licence, and his deed would then be in *violation of* a restriction; but one cannot act in violation of an enabling rule unless he sometimes shows that he meant to conform to that rule or, at least, another rule underlying the same practice. Enabling rules do not only serve as a standard for correcting behaviour, but create the form of behaviour itself. They make it possible to do what is forbidden, and do not merely make certain doings forbidden. It is not to be counted as a move in violation of the rules of chess when the child pushes the horse straight ahead, for he makes no *move* at all. When an *agent* does not act in violation of a licence unknown to him, his *deed* may truly be said to be in violation of the rule; but where the rule is an enabling rule, the agent must know of the existence of that rule if even his deed is to be held to be in violation, for if he is unfamiliar with the rule his act is simply not of a kind which that rule may license or enjoin. Rules, we saw, are reasons for acting. Enabling rules are reasons which are either of the form 'I am engaged in this activity (*e.g.*, chess)' or are reasons which fall under the Principle of the End; *viz.*, mention of the rule identifies what one is doing.

Conformity to enabling rules enables one to enter into new kinds of behaviour, and by coming to learn enabling rules in the first place one attains a somewhat higher level of behaviour than he previously occupied.

These remarks suggest an interesting possibility. Our general theory of action requires that an animal who is doing an act must have a purpose and have a reason. The general theory does not require that an agent should be aware of the purpose he has, *i.e.*, be self-conscious, or that he be aware of his reason *as* a reason. In no. 10, I argued that a capacity for conformative behaviour is sufficient for an agent to be able to be aware of a fact as a reason. The interesting possibility to which I just alluded is that a capacity for conformative behaviour underlain by enabling rules is sufficient for an agent to be capable of self-consciousness. The argument is that one learns the rules which he must be capable of being aware of *as* reasons and thereby but only thereby learns to engage in a new form of activity, which he must be capable of identifying. The agent does something which he could not do except by conforming to rules that are defined as rules underlying this practice; and, so it may seem, when he conforms to such rules, which he is capable of recognizing as such, he must know what he is doing in at least the practical sense; for the rules can be identified as such only by appreciating that they create a certain practice. In learning the behaviour one learns what it is. This account seems to fit most examples of conformative behaviour underlain by enabling rules. Surely the chess player could not make a move unless he were capable of knowing what move he was making; similarly for the baseball batter, and the man who makes a promise. But there also seem to be counter-examples. As a child I learned to speak English; speaking English is a practice underlain by enabling rules, *i.e.*, the conventions of English; but surely it was a long time before I was capable of knowing that I was speaking *English*, though I was capable of knowing (in the practical sense) (*e.g.*) that I was asking for food. Admittedly, the counter-example is suspicious. 'In English' applies in the supposed kind of example as a description of *how* the agent does what he does, which is, *e.g.*, asking for food, of which latter he surely is aware. But, since I surely was engaged in speaking English, the counter-example shows that an agent in conforming to enabling rules underlying a practice is not necessarily capable of knowing that he is engaged in *that* practice. It sought to show only that the agent must be capable of knowing that he is doing a certain kind of act pertaining to some form of activity, *e.g.*, asking for food, and is therefore capable of knowing what he is doing, *i.e.*, is self-conscious. The argument depends upon the consideration that the agent knows that the rules create some practice which he is learning, for he learns the rules as rules but only as rules for the practice; but the same rules may underlie a number of practices, but he need not know for each such practice that the rules in question underlie that practice. To suppose the contrary would yield a distorted description of the native learning of English. Pulling all this together I would conjecture the following: If an agent is capable of engaging in a practice underlain by enabling rules he must be capable of knowing that he is engaged in some practice underlain by those rules, and, *a fortiori* be sometimes capable of knowing what he is doing when engaged in the activity, *i.e.*, be capable of self-consciousness. Needless to say, the condition that an agent can conform to enabling rules is not sufficient for him to be capable of having reflective ('non-observational') knowledge, which is also a sufficient condition for self-consciousness (see Part II, no. 8). We shall discover that a sufficient condition for reflective knowledge is that the agent have attained the level of conformative behaviour and be capable of referring to himself as an agent.

I have in this section been exercised to draw a distinction between restrictions and enabling rules. May the same rule not be both a restriction and an enabling rule? No. However, while the distinction between enabling rule and restriction is definitionally relative to a particular practice, what may appear the same rule could be restrictive relative to one practice (*e.g.*, socializing) and enabling to another (being courtly). Here we may speak of *converting* a restriction into an enabling rule. Also, a form of behaviour created by enabling rules may itself become subject to restrictions, *e.g.*, rules of good sportsmanship. Too, there may be difficult questions whether a rule is enabling or restriction. Some would argue, for instance, that property legally conceived is created as well as protected by civil enactments, and that property rights therefore exist only within a practice underlain by enabling rules; others argue that rights to the enjoyment of property exist prior to enactment of civil law, which, among other things, is a contrivance designed to protect those antecedent rights. (See, *e.g.*, Locke's *Second Treatise.*) To resolve the matter, we might need to appeal to the familiar if problematic distinction between 'natural' and 'legal' property. The real issue, of course, is the larger one over the relations between law and morality. Suffice it to observe, for present purposes, that it is not always obvious whether a (primary) law of the land creates a restriction or an enabling rule, but the question should nevertheless always be decidable.

12. CONSTITUTIVE AND NON-CONSTITUTIVE RULES [1]

[Enabling rules underlie the practices they create. In some cases the particular rules are definitive of the practice and admit no alternatives; in other cases alternatives are possible. The former are called *constitutive* and the latter *non-constitutive* rules. One's refusal to conform to a constitutive rule would imply that he was not engaged in the corresponding practice; not so with non-constitutive rules. Contrary to first appearances, it is suggested that the distinction between constitutive and non-constitutive rules may be extended from enabling rules to restrictions.]

There are kinds of behaviour, then, which one cannot attempt unless he knows how to conform to some enabling rule or other. Here, as elsewhere, we may speak of the rules underlying the practice. It is important to realize that there are different kinds of enabling rule, and that they do not all underlie their corresponding practices in the same ways.

One obvious difference which obtrudes itself is this: Sometimes the practice may be separated from the particular rules which underlie it, and sometimes it cannot. Thus (subject to certain qualifications) one cannot play chess except by acting to follow the rules of chess; one cannot multiply except by acting to conform to the rules

---

[1] 'Constitutive' has been used by a number of philosophers, notably Kant (for a contemporary instance, see M. Black, 'Notes on the Meaning of "Rule"', *Theoria*, 1958, especially pp. 117f.), in part to signalize the distinction between enabling rules and restrictions and also in part to mark the distinction to be developed in this section. These are different distinctions, however easily they may be confused.

of multiplication; and one cannot speak English except by acting to conform to the rules of English; finally, one cannot play football without following the rules of football. On the other hand, even those who know English may use Language, *e.g.*, request directions, without following the rules of English—they may speak in Hindi or French. Similarly, there are different rules for summing infinite sequences, with sometimes identical and sometimes different results. I call the first kind of rule *constitutive* and the second *non-constitutive*.

Plainly the application of this distinction is relative to the practice. The same rules may be constitutive for the practice of speaking English and non-constitutive for the practice of using Language. The idea is that certain practices require us to follow certain rules, while others do not. The crux here is the possibility of *alternatives*. I know that the rules of English are not constitutive for the use of Language, for I can imagine rules for other tongues; I know that certain dialing procedures enable me to bring TV programmes into the immediate environment, but these procedures are not constitutive for this practice, for I know that the same programme may enter on more than one waveband. Similarly with telling time, as those will know who have seen clocks which run in reverse.

The examples we have considered are all such that one cannot engage in the practice unless he follows *some* rule, where there may or may not be alternatives. What is peculiar about practices underlain by constitutive rules is that one must follow particular rules. But it is not entirely easy to make clear this notion of 'having to conform to a particular set of rules'. In the first place, one may make a mistake, and perhaps thus fail to conform. But he is still engaged in the practice, though he may incur penalties or fail in his efforts. But more seriously yet, one may act in direct violation of the rules, and still be said to be engaged in the practice. I may cheat at chess, or play dirty football. It is important, of course, that if the rules in question were non-constitutive, then this behaviour would not necessarily count as an infraction as it must do in the case of constitutive rules.

What then is the criterion of a constitutive rule? A sufficient but not yet necessary condition for a rule's being constitutive is that the agent's express and honest *declaration* of intention not to conform to the rule would strictly imply that he did not intend to do the kind of act in question. While some qualifications may be in order where the underlying enabling rules are numerous and complex, as they are for tongues like English, the principle is clear. To the extent that I refuse to conform to the rules of English, I am not speaking English. (The qualification is that I may speak what I wish to become English, and my efforts not be disqualified in advance.)

A conditionally necessary condition for a rule's being constitutive is that *if* one could respond to verbal correction, then, if he did not acknowledge proper correction, he would be held not to be engaged in the activity.

Now this condition is expressly contingent upon the imagined agent's having enough Language to respond in the required way; and the first condition is only sufficient chiefly because it is restricted to those who have enough Language to make the required declaration. Conformity to rule does not necessarily presume so much Language on the part of agents, as is proven by the simple consideration that one may still be incapable of making such declarations, although he had acquired some Language and had begun to learn to follow the rules constitutive of his mother tongue.

For the agent who has enough Language to declare whether or not he wishes to engage in a practice, if he is engaging in that practice, it is essential that he not give others reason to think that he means them to know that he is not engaging in the practice. For example, if he be capable of making such declarations, he should not have declared his unwillingness to 'play the game'. For less sophisticated agents, our only clue is their actual behaviour. But we know that this cannot be conclusive. Considering all these possibilities, I would, at this point, submit as a weak necessary and sufficient condition for an enabling rule's being constitutive that failure of the agent's behaviour to conform must, *pending explanations to the contrary*, be taken as relevant *evidence* for the conclusion that he is not engaged in the practice in question. Otherwise, we take it that he *would* acknowledge his errors, *if he could.*

Can this be strengthened? It suggests that we might modify as follows the first sufficient condition for constitutive rules which we gave: If the agent *would* if asked declare an intention not to conform to the rule, then he is not engaged in the practice. It is worth trying to rework this idea, with an eye to converting it into a necessary as well as sufficient condition. The condition, as stated, is already both necessary and sufficient, on condition that the agent be able to *enter into* a practice, say by adopting it. The only other reason why one, whose behaviour can be said not to conform to the practice, might be held not to be engaged in such a practice is that he has not *learned it*. With this in mind, I venture to conclude that an enabling rule is constitutive of a practice if and only if failure of an agent's behaviour to conform to the rule implies either that he would acknowledge correction or that he has not learned the practice in question.

I have, in effect been trying to explain what it is for there to be no possible alternative rules. It remains to say something about non-constitutive rules, which may have alternatives. There are at least two kinds of 'alternative', one of which is irrelevant. The irrelevant case is that in which there are alternative completions for what is left open. We decide to play cards, and we know of certain rules implicit in our deck of fifty-two cards; but how we fill this out, with the rules of poker or the rules of bridge, remains to be decided. Here we are faced with a choice, not between alternative rules for the same practice, but between alternative practices. The case that does matter is that in which we are faced with alternative *ways* of engaging in some one practice: alternative ways of speaking, telling time, summing a series, or bringing a TV programme into a room. Now in each of these cases we see that, while the rules are not constitutive of the practice in question—using Language, telling time, *etc.*—they are constitutive of another subsidiary practice—speaking English, getting station KTVU into the room, telling time by a standard clock. This suggests that acts done in conformity with non-constitutive, enabling rules will always be done by way of collateral acts done in conformity with constitutive rules. This conclusion, venturesome and tentative as it is, suggests another. Practices underlain by constitutive rules could be but not necessarily will be imbedded in practices of which the same rules are non-constitutive. This is *not* a result of the fact that any kind of act might be collateral to some other, for in the general case the one act may be an example of conformative behaviour and the 'some other' not be; it is rather a conjecture that practices may be systematically generalized. That conjecture, I submit, lies behind the idea that different people are capable of attaining the same levels of behaviour.

So far I have tried to draw out a distinction between those enabling rules which do and those which do not admit of alternatives in respect to given practices; and I have endeavoured to explain this sense of 'alternative'. I have deliberately confined the examination to enabling rules. But the question arises whether one could not extend the distinction between constitutive and non-constitutive rules to restrictions, and thus secure a general bifurcation.

At first glance there would not seem to be such a contrast available in the realm of restrictions. Or, if you wish, *all* restrictions may appear to be non-constitutive rules. One might reason: restrictions modify independently identifiable kinds of behaviour; so none of these rules can be constitutive. If the rule only modifies behaviour, how can it be constitutive of it? In answer, it might be argued that rules, if they constitute, constitute *practices*; and there is no *a priori* reason why we cannot describe a modification of some given form of behaviour as a practice; indeed, that seems even ordinary.

But can we find constitutive restrictions? I believe so. A group of companions may formalize their familiarity into a club, the activities of which are then constituted by the rules of the club. If one proclaim his intention not to conform, he is out of the club; it is no longer one of his activities. Again, certain rules constitute the procedures according to which cases are to be conducted before courts of justice. If these rules are not held by, that constitutes ground for mistrial.

In these examples, given forms of behaviour—consorting with one's fellows or requesting a decision regarding reparations—are modified, but in fairly standardized ways calling for the use of terms like 'club', 'procedures for . . .', which terms imply a certain set formalization possibly not admitting of alternatives.

I conclude that all rules are either constitutive or non-constitutive, and that this distinction cuts across that other distinction between enabling rules and restrictions.

13. RULES FOR SUCCEEDING

[Conformity to rule by itself usually does not assure success in action. But there are kinds of practice where it does, provided that all the defining conditions of success are satisfied. I call the underlying rules *rules for succeeding*. Rules for succeeding may be either constitutive or non-constitutive. There remains a question whether rules for succeeding must always be enabling rules; it appears that they need not be.]

An agent may act to conform to a rule, and his behaviour actually so conform, and he yet not succeed in his act. This is especially evident in the case of restrictions, where conformity to rule modifies only the manner in which one proceeds. While 'correct' behaviour may indeed enhance one's chances of success, it does not assure it. I may fail to get the fish into my mouth, however impeccable be my use of the fish knife; I may fail to placate the policeman, however respectful I am of his authority.

The situation is not relevantly different for certain types of enabling rules. The rules of baseball enable me to take my turn at bat, conforming to the rules, placing myself correctly in the batter's box, *etc., etc.* I may still fail to get a hit, which was what I was trying to do. Again, the rules for selecting channels enable the would-be viewer to make a certain TV programme visible in the room, and yet he may fail to bring in the correct programme even though he selects the correct channel. This may seem a straightforward corollary of our principle that we cannot in general say what will make an act succeed (Part II, no. 18). However, there seem to be cases where this principle is overridden. Suppose I wish to say something, *e.g.*, that

271

the cat is on the mat, it appears that I shall succeed in saying it simply by saying it, *e.g.*, by uttering, 'The cat is on the mat'. Again, I make a calculation simply and just by calculating in conformity with the rules. It thus appears that there are kinds of rules, conformity to which assures success.

But let us take another look. Surely one may fail to make a calculation if the figures he makes keep altering madly in the course of the calculating. One may fail to state that the cat is on the mat, even though he conscientiously conforms to the rules of English, if what the speaker takes to be a mat is no mat at all. In both instances, a certain condition of success is not satisfied. Nor can we in these cases any more than in any other pretend to be able to give a terminated, ultimate list of conditions of success.

Yet the cases of batting a baseball and saying something are notably different. The difference is that *if* all the defining conditions of success for saying something are satisfied, *then* the speaker will succeed in saying what he means to say simply by conforming to the conventions of some one language or other. Otherwise, if no necessary condition of failure obtains, conformity to rule is sufficient to assure success. Although we cannot list a totality of conditions of success, it is assumed that we can spot any particular one.

Here, then, we have a formal way of getting round the difficulty of saying what will make the act succeed. Conformity to rule makes the act succeed, *provided* that all the conditions of success for the purpose of the act are satisfied. But this device is available only for certain kinds of conformative acts performed in the course of engaging in certain kinds of practice. The underlying rules have a special character relevant to the practice. I shall call these *rules for succeeding*.

So far all our examples of rules for succeeding are enabling rules. Are there any rules for succeeding which are restrictions? I am not sure, but I suspect that there are.

A curious possible instance is the one mentioned earlier of a person's getting to where he wants to go by following a map. Though there is some question whether this really counts as conforming to a rule, I believe it does, although the rule in question is probably a private rule, however public the map itself may be. Let us assume that the map is correct and accurate, so that following it does assure success, provided that the destination town has not been obliterated, that the roads are open, *etc.*, *etc.* Now what kind of rule is this? Is this an enabling rule or a restriction? Since, in following the map, the traveller goes from one place to another, a procedure which in itself does not require that he follow a rule, it seems to be a restriction. (One may, of course, simply be meaning to follow a map, just as one may be simply meaning to be polite or to speak French, no matter what he does politely or what he says in French. In these cases the manner of performance, as it were, is peeled away from the apparent deed, and becomes the deed itself. One acts to be polite or to speak French or to follow the map. The rules embodied in the map are indeed enabling rules relative to the practice of map-following. But they are not enabling with respect to travelling. In the proposed example it would be wrong to hold that the traveller is simply map-following, and not travelling from one place to another.) In our example, the traveller succeeds by following the map, provided that certain conditions are satisfied. It would appear that some private restrictions are rules for succeeding. Some doubt is thrown on this conclusion, however, by the consideration that the conditions are not all of them conditions of success for travelling from one place to another; *e.g.*, if the road is out, one might still fly. Still, it could be answered, the behaviour in question is really that of travelling from one place to another by road, and the rules embodied in a map are indeed restrictions relative to the practice. Frankly, I am not able to decide. I do not understand the example as well as I would like. But I am inclined to take it as a genuine example of a restriction that is a rule for succeeding.

14. STATUTORY AND NON-STATUTORY RULES

[Some rules and the corresponding practices come into force only upon promulgation, enactment, publication, or such other express formulation. What is so formulated we call a *statute*, and the rule and practice thus created we call *statutory*. Rules and regulations in the literal sense are types of statute; another interesting possible type of example is a promise. Not all rules in the sense we have defined are statutory, though any rule could gain formulation and codification after the fact. Statutory rules allow for an appeal to the originating statute when questions of correct or incorrect behaviour arise. For non-statutory practices, the usual appeal is to precedent.]

Rules in the most literal, English sense of 'rule' must be promulgated, enacted, posted, published, or otherwise formulated and made public. These promulgations, *etc.*, are not rules in the sense of no. 9. But such promulgations, *etc.*, may and frequently do serve to create systems of expectation, which are rules in our sense. If a rule could not come into existence unless it were promulgated, *etc.*, I shall call it a *statutory rule*. Practices underlain by such rules I call *statutory practices*. A statute, generally conceived, is then any product of the use of Language the publication of which might suffice to create a statutory rule. A statute thus explained, is *not* a generalization or other such statement regarding the character or requirements of an already existing rule. Such statements, to be discussed in the next section, we shall call 'codifications of rules'.

Examples of statutes are the rules of chess and games generally, ordinances, and statutes in the literal sense, resolutions, treaties, and possibly promises. The rules are (*e.g.*) that one is allowed two free throws for a foul suffered in the act of shooting, that one is not to park in the red, *etc.*; and the practices are those of playing basketball, parking a car, *etc.*

Promises are interesting, if only uncertainly possible, examples of statutes. Promises are products of the use of Language, the publication of which creates expectations. But they are at best surprising candidates as statutes, and their qualifications are doubtful. First, it would appear that the expectations in question are confined to the keeping of the promise and are not left open in the way that rule expectations characteristically are. Second, one might protest that there is no sense in speaking of the *practice* of keeping a particular promise. Finally, it would certainly stretch things to hold that promises made between private parties create *systems* of expectation. On the other side, one might, first, allow that not all promises create rules; only some do. That conceded, it would then appear that there are certainly kinds of promises which do create rules in our sense, *e.g.*, those made by public officials. The advocate of the claims of (some) promises to the status of statutes could furthermore argue (1) even private individuals sometimes make *general* promises; (2) rules *need* not always underlie practices; and (3) promises create something like systems of expectations, insofar as we can indicate a community, namely, all those who are party to the promise or who are within earshot of the making of the promise, who would be entitled to expect the promiser to do as promised. I tentatively conclude that at least *some* promises are statutes.

Part of what makes one doubt that promises could be statutes is the fact that *a* rule, in my sense of rule, must already be in force in order for the promise to create a rule, the rule, namely, that promises ought to be kept. This points to what I think is generally true, that the use of statutes to create rules always presumes the operation of some other rule, which may or may not itself be statutory. (The rule that one should keep promises, if not actually statutory, can be inculcated only by being formulated, for no one could learn the force of (*e.g.*) 'I promise' without coming to theoretical knowledge of the rule that promises are to be kept.)

The implications of this are twofold. First, some statutes are not rules in the literal sense of 'rule', but other kinds of Language products. Second, some rules (in my sense) are not statutory. The argu-

274

ment for this last conclusion is simply that the rules by virtue of which the publication of statutes creates rules cannot all be statutory, without an infinite regress of statute promulgations. This result, though perfectly obvious, is still of some importance, because there seem to have been those who have wanted to deny it. It is obvious because, apart from the abstract regress argument, any number of examples can be found. Rules for Language and good manners, for instance, far from being necessarily brought into existence by statutory formulations, are very hard to formulate even after the fact. Still, the existence of non-statutory rules may seem sheer anarchy to some of our most conscientious theoreticians, who may feel that a proper rule must be formulated.

As antidote to this, I stress the opposite side. Not all rules are statutory; *viz.*, not all systems of expectation need be brought about by promulgation, stipulation, *etc.* This does not deny that any rule may be formulated, in the sense of possibly being made explicit to whatever degree of accuracy and generality may be desired or required. I am not saying that rules are ineffable. Rather this, that rules and the practices they underlie are not in general dependent upon the use of Language. It is interesting to observe that what we have called *private* rules are indeed Language-dependent, and are created, if not by being formulated, then, anyway, by being thought.

Statutory rules are such that questions which an observer may have raised concerning the correctness of the agent's behaviour may possibly be settled by consulting the originating statute, which statute should state or indicate where the rule will operate and what conformity requires or permits. We may call this *appealing to the statute*. Even in the case of statutory practices, appealing to the statute may not be enough to settle every case. We may have to probe the 'intent' of the promulgator, or consider previous applications.

When the issue is over a possible infraction of a non-statutory rule, the usual procedure is to appeal to actual precedent or to clear cases as imaginatively conceived. Sometimes a well-wrought statement of the rule is useful, but the validity of this procedure depends palpably on how well that statement agrees with clear and common cases, which must therefore be the ultimate appeal.

15. THE CODIFICATION OF RULES

[Generalizations regarding when an act is in conformity with and/or in violation of a rule are called *codifications of rules*. In the case of statutory rules, the statute itself may often though not always be
275

directly converted into a codification of the rule. This affords fresh occasion for considering why some regard all rules as statutory. Certain limitations on the generality of a codification are observed, and a number of typical kinds of occasion for seeking such generalizations are noted.]

Generalizations that make explicit what it is for behaviour to be in conformity with and/or to be in violation of rules, I call *codifications of rules*. Such formulations presume that there is a rule to be formulated. If this condition fails, the formulation in question devolves into a simple generalization about behaviour. To codify a rule is to engage in the theory of the practice—it is to say what the practice is or to describe how it is engaged in. In the case of statutory practices, it is frequently, but not invariably, the case that the originating statute can be converted into a rough codification of the rule. It is not possible in cases like promises, where the statute (the promise) does not say that such and such is to be done. But where that is stipulated by the statute, and where there is a general expectation that the statute will be operative,[1] then, by recasting the statute as a statement and by attaching codicils regarding occasions of application and exceptions, one may secure the desired codification.

Armed with the observation that the codification of rules is a part of the theory of the practice, we may return to consider why some have thought that all rules are statutory.

One consideration in favour of this belief is that rules, in the literal sense, are statutes. But that does not count for too much, for all will agree that the rule is realized in practice, depending as much upon occasions for engaging in the practice as upon the forms followed. One does not add up bridge scores by following the rules of deduction set forth in Church's book on Logic; but the rules do not tell you that. Even the most formally formulated rules do not apply themselves. There remains an irreducible distinction between practice and statute, and the practice cannot be absorbed into the statute, or even completely anticipated in so many words.

Another factor which may induce us to regard all rules as statutory is the idea that reasons must be premises (see Part II, no. 9, pp. 97f.). To conform to a rule is to act for a certain kind of reason. Now if one supposes that reasons must be formulated as premises, then it would follow that before one could act with the reason that such and such a rule obtained, he would have to be able to say what the rule is. The intimated conclusion is, no rule without a formulation; therefore, all rules must be statutory in the defined sense, since they would not

---

[1] Not always the case—as 'No-Smoking' signs in University of California classrooms well show.

276

exist without a statement telling what conformity demands. But I hope long since to have disabused readers of the prejudice that reasons must be premises.

The chief source of error here, unless I miss my guess, is confusion of theory and practice. Statutory practices must wait upon the formulation of a statute, whether or not the statute can be converted into a codification of a rule. But non-statutory practices may well exist in advance of any formulation—statute, code, or what have you. By insisting that a codification must, as a kind of statute, institute the practice, one falls into a mistake which I dub the Socratic Assumption, that of holding that we must know what we are doing before we can know how to do it. But the usual order is just the reverse. To codify a rule, even a statutory rule, is, precisely, to become explicit about a pre-existing practice. It is to say how one must conduct himself in order to conform. To have a rule (though not a codified rule) it is quite sufficient to have a practice, behaviour susceptible to objective distinctions of correct and incorrect. Public criteria indeed are wanted, but they do not need to be expressly formulated. An agent's behaviour is subject to rule if he only *know how to* conform, even if he cannot begin to say what it is he conforms to. (This is apparently so even for phases of chess-like games such as the Japanese Go, the playing of which *is* a statutory practice. I have been told that the masters of this game have never succeeded in saying precisely what brings a game to a close; nevertheless, there is never any disagreement about when a game is over.) The agent may not even be able to say the equivalent of 'correct' or 'incorrect'. But for us, theoretical onlookers, to speak of a rule it is necessary and sufficient to be able to know that such distinctions can be made, and we begin to know *what* rule if we can explain why this item of behaviour is correct, that one incorrect. With that we begin to become explicit about the rule; but do let us be clear that the *modus operandi* is not inevitably an appeal to prepublished statutes.

It may be contested that we cannot decide correctness in the absence of a formulation, which is the statute. Against this, observe first, it is again the observer's decision that we have in mind here. But, second, appeal to statute is itself never enough for deciding, as we have already seen. Third, there is also an appeal in the case of non-statutory practices, *viz.*, to that to which one would appeal for confirmation of one's codification of the rule—clear cases of conformity and infringement and established precedent. The appeal, in short, is to the practice itself.

Allowedly, the codification of a non-statutory rule may yield a code which approximates to a statute as an object of appeal; but such guide lines are drawn in after the fact, and the content of the code is always subject to alteration in consideration of what we may later discover about the practice.

Our previous conclusion remains intact, *viz.*, that rules may be in force without in any way having been made explicit, in the utter absence of any kind of formulation. To be sure, in order to conform to a rule the agent must *know how to* distinguish correct from incorrect, and he must be (practically) aware of certain features in the situation which make it appropriate to behave as he does and by reference to which he regulates his behaviour. He need not to this end be able to state what he finds or be equipped with a formulated code which he follows. One may act in conformity with rules, and even recognize conformative behaviour done by others, without being able to put the rules into words. However, any rule is codifiable, and indeed in principle it must be possible to become quite as explicit as circumstances demand. But seldom shall we be able to gain a formulation covering all past cases and anticipating all subsequent ones, and that much is never called for. That this should be so is not generally due to want of diligence or foresight on the observer's part, but is commonly an essential fact about the kind of practice in question.

To codify a rule, then, is to become explicit about its practice, perhaps in order to arrive at some further generalizations of an anthropological, sociological, or linguistic kind regarding those for whom the rule matters. Or, again, one may desire to make a code or canon available for clarifying or enhancing the regularizing effect of the rule on community behaviour, or as an aid to strengthen one's own resolve, or as a guide to administrators.

Now, in order to become explicit, we shall certainly have to observe what behaviour counts as correct and incorrect. If we get the facts right, then we codify the rule that was operating; if we get the facts wrong, we may indeed publish *a* rule (though we need not) but certainly it will not be the one about which we thought to be explicit.

The collation of the relevant facts may or may not involve generalizing about behaviour. (On the negative side, consider the lexicographer who simply turns up specimens.) But the result is in the nature of a generalization about the practice. Ideally, such formulations should be completely explicit regarding the composition of the community, and the practice engendered, and all known qualifications and exceptions should be mentioned. But the ideal is never attained, and often it is even logically impossible to summarize a whole practice in the formulated code.

16. SUMMARY AND APPLICATIONS

In summary, then, we can say that community rules are either statutory or non-statutory, restrictions or enabling rules, constitutive or non-constitutive for practices, and they may or may not be rules for succeeding. It is not always an automatic matter to place a given rule in this scheme, partly because kinds of rule are related in various ways. Thus systems of enabling rules may engender practices subject to various kinds of restriction; again, as we remarked concerning rules of good manners, restrictions may convert into enabling rules; *e.g.*, restrictions by conformity to which one acts in polite ways may convert into rules by conformity to which one may be a polite person. However, this scheme will be a serviceable guide to the further analysis of conformative behaviour. In this last section, I should like to sketch indications of how I envisage that such applications might be made.

There are many and various areas of life and kinds of practice in which rules operate. In the sense of 'rule' here adopted, there are rules of law and morality and manners, rules of Language, tongues, translation and orthography, rules for games and rules for calculation, rules for telling time and for reading musical scores, rules of the road and rules of the sea. It is doubtful whether any of these areas of life or practice admit of only one kind of rule. Thus certain moral rules seem to be statutory, and others not; certain rules of English are constitutive, others not; some rules of law are clearly restrictions, while others (chiefly what Hart calls 'secondary legal rules') appear to be sometimes enabling rules. Still we may expect that certain practices will *typically* call for one kind of a rule rather than another. It is not to be expected that such a typification will ever be 'categorical', for radically distinct kinds of rule may achieve the same kind of characterization within our scheme. Nevertheless, I submit that it would tell us a great deal about these practices if we could say what kinds of rule typically underlie them. That is the strategy behind the sketch analyses which now follow.

Rules for morality are typically non-statutory, non-constitutive restrictions, which are not rules for succeeding.

Primary rules of law are typically statutory, non-constitutive restrictions, which are not rules for succeeding.[1]

---

[1] 'Primary rule of law' is Hart's phrase. They are legally enforced restrictions, usually backed by social pressure, which are thought to redound to the benefit of society at large. They may, in large measure, be regarded as supplements to or replacements of rules of customary morality, suitably codified and enforced. The operation of such laws serves to protect morality both by providing enforcement against wilful infractions and by filling in during periods of social transition or

Rules of Language are typically non-statutory, non-constitutive, enabling rules for succeeding.

Rules of tongues are typically non-statutory, constitutive, enabling rules for succeeding, as also are rules for translating from one tongue to another.

Rules of orthography are typically statutory, constitutive, enabling rules for succeeding, as also are rules for calculating and rules for reading musical scores.

Rules of games are typically statutory, constitutive, enabling rules, which are not rules for succeeding.

In the sequel to this volume, I shall seek to draw out in greater detail what is implied by the above sketch definition of a rule of Language.

---

fusion when previously accepted rules are falling into disuse or when there is too little agreement on fundamentals to assure widespread compliance. Unlike counterpart rules of morality, primary rules of law should be expressly promulgated, are regularly provisional contrivances alterable by due process, and carry specific sanctions. In my view, Locke's discussion of Civil Society and its relations to the State of Nature is still worth reading on the nature of Civil Law and its relation to morality. Primary rules of Law are contrasted by Hart with secondary rules of law, which latter are designed chiefly to regulate formal legal proceedings. It is not clear to me whether secondary rules of law are always, sometimes, or never enabling rules. Such rules may seem necessary in order to conduct legal proceedings. But this view may give undeserved weight to the highly codified legal procedures of our society. Is it not possible in small societies that disputing parties should naturally and without benefit of enabling rules submit their differences to a common authority for adjudication, much as quarrelling children may submit themselves to the judgment of their parents? I suspect that some secondary rules of law are restrictions and others (*e.g.*, rules for appealing to the Supreme Court) are enabling rules. But which are most typical I would not hazard to say.

Part Four

CONVENTIONAL BEHAVIOUR

---

1. THE CONVENTIONAL AS WHAT NECESSARILY INVOLVES WHAT MIGHT HAVE BEEN DIFFERENT

[It is natural and even common to describe certain kinds of behaviour, including the use of Language and religious and ceremonial observances, as *conventional*, where 'conventional' does not mean artificial, arbitrary, original, usual, what has been agreed to, unnatural. An interesting fact about the most typical examples of conventional behaviour is that the conventions might have been different; *e.g.*, I might have written what I say here in German or French, different nations have different ways of saluting. In short, the conventions might have been different and the behaviour remained the same. Most forms of conventional behaviour are such that some agents might expressly accept alternative conventions. It thus typically appears to be an essential feature of conventional behaviour that there should be in it something which is inessential.]

It is natural and not uncommon to speak of Language as conventional; and we may speak of this or that general or special (linguistic) convention. It would be nearly as natural to speak of the use of money, marriage, worship, and saluting as conventional, and again there would seem to be room for discussing general or specific conventions for purchasing goods and services, formalizing nuptials, conducting worship, or indicating recognition and order of authority. These latter types of action do not, at least superficially, appear to be uses of Language, but I believe that the force of 'conventional' is exactly the same as when applied to Language. [1]

---

[1] The common characterization of the use of Language and ritual observances as conventional is entirely natural, so much so as to be almost automatic. See, *e.g.*, J. L. Austin, *How to do Things with Words*, pp. 19f., 120f., 127. Also Saussure

281

While the use of 'conventional' is easily understood, it is, I fear, almost as easily misunderstood. Attempts to *explain* this employment of 'conventional' are apt very quickly to come to an impasse.

A source of trouble is that we are also quite naturally able to speak about Law and Morality as conventional, and we call styles of music, architecture, behaviour, thought, conventional; also, we may be over-impressed with the force of the verb 'convened', and by the institution of business, professional, and political conventions. *Conventional* might seem to mean that which is arbitrary, artificial, unnatural, contrived, agreed to, regular, uninspired, commonplace, usual, standard, familiar, original, fashionable, ordinary, received, insincere, and, I am sure, much else besides. (And these may even *seem* to conflict. A conventional or standard gear-shift has become a bit dated, hence not fashionable, though hardly unfashionable either.) All this is extraneous to using Language, and using money, curtseying, presenting arms, saluting, raising the host, and kissing the Pope's toe, examples of behaviour which seem eminently conventional in some way or other. The danger is that the employment of 'conventional' may bring us to think incorrectly about Language, worship, *etc.*

However different the force of 'conventional' may be as we change from one context to another, it is *not* that the word has a number of different, distinct senses. It is, rather, part of the sense of the term as employed in English that it should change its force in this way, that it should be used now to make contrast with the natural, now with the inevitable, now with the unusual. An essential part of the meaning of 'conventional' is that it have this contrasting thrust. 'Conventional' in this way resembles 'real', 'true', 'ordinary', 'plain', 'normal', 'usual', all of which, following the terminology of Hall, we might call 'excluders'.[2] Almost all adjectives, to be sure, signalize features by virtue of the presence of which objects may be contrasted with other objects. Excluders are not employed to assign specific features, but directly to signalize a *kind* of *open* contrast, which is cinched up by the circumstances of discourse, but which may even then remain open. Thus 'normal' may be used to indicate a contrast with *infrequent*, *aberrant*, that which *deviates* from a statistically normal distribution,

[2] 'Excluders', R. Hall, *Analysis*, 1959, pp. 1–7. Also, J. L. Austin, *Sense and Sensibilia*, Chap. VII.

(*Cours de Linguistique Général*, pp. 33, 97–103), directly if somewhat confusedly, assimilates Language, religious rites, political forms, and ritual in general as conventional. (The confusion, a common one, results from a failure to consider carefully whether it is the use of Language itself or particular conventions for using Language which are properly speaking called conventional. I shall hold that it is only the former.)

etc.; and once that is settled, there may still remain no set measure for infrequency, aberrancy, *etc.* It is much the same with 'conventional', which, in this circumstance or that, may mark a contrast with the natural, the artificial, *etc.*, where usually there would be no antecedently set measure for naturalness, artificiality, *etc.* It will not have escaped the reader that we seem naturally to explain an excluding use by specifying a family of overlapping, contrary excluding uses; 'natural' is quite as much an excluder as is 'conventional'. [3]

These remarks go some way towards explaining why philosophers' accounts of this or that which trade on the use of 'natural', 'normal', 'ordinary', 'conventional' so infrequently give satisfaction; why (*e.g.*) 'conventional' seems so much of a weasel word. This kind of terminology simply does not by itself signify those definitive 'features' of things which we may be seeking. It invites embarrassing demands for 'What do *you* mean by "natural"?'; and it easily suggests obvious counter-examples. But this kind of terminology is not, for all that, any the less inevitable. The appositeness of an excluder within a certain domain points up the relevance of certain questions. It is part of our conception of 'natural kinds' (*e.g.*, men, trees, mountains) that examples may in many respects be normal and abnormal. It remains that such appeals are unavailing unless the theorist is prepared to specify the features by virtue of which instances of the case in hand are to be regarded as normal or abnormal, conventional, real, regular, natural. [4]

Now we are looking for a definition if you wish, the specification of the features by virtue of which the use of Language is conventional.

[3] Linguists have observed that a language will impose certain constraints upon the order and position of the adjectives which concurrently modify a noun. Thus we may say 'A real, good, solid red table' or 'un vrai bon vin rouge' where no other order of the included adjectives is admitted. Ziff (*Semantic Analysis*, no. 208) speaks of 'real' as being of higher *rank* than 'solid', *etc.* The rank of an adjective, syntactically signalized by its position of occurrence in a string of adjectives, tends to be a measure of its freedom of occurrence in connection with different subject matters, of the 'topic inspecificity' of its meaning. (Other factors must also matter. The meaning of 'old' is less topic-specific than is the meaning of 'intelligent', for only animals may be or fail to be intelligent, whereas animals and other things as well may be or fail to be old. Yet 'intelligent old man' seems more admissible than 'old intelligent man' yielding the conclusion that 'intelligent' is of higher rank than 'old'.) From what has been said, it is to be expected that excluders should have relatively high rank, and that it be part of their meaning that they should effect variable distinctions, highly dependent on context, *e.g.*, 'a conventional, square, mahogany, bedside table'.
[4] To take a recent instance, I am dissatisfied with the Hart-Honoré account of causation in terms of abnormal features of things (*Causation in the Law*, Chap. II, Part III, esp. pp. 31–38) because the authors' efforts to explicate the abnormal, mostly in terms of 'ordinary' and 'reasonable', while useful, are not useful enough as an index to abnormalizing features.

Therefore to say that (*e.g.*) Language is conventional is not to answer a question but to raise one. In what manner conventional? Surely there is something importantly right in our quickness to say that Language is conventional; and just for that reason it behoves us to try to supply the required specification.[5] We want to say what is common to and characteristic of using Language, performing cere-monies, showing respect, *etc.* We must do for 'conventional' rather what Gauss' curve did for 'normal', and more so; the idea of normal distribution may be harnessed to populations of almost all kinds, where our aim is to define *one* kind of *behaviour*.

But, it might be protested, surely what we are seeking to understand must be 'conventional' in its ordinary sense, the sense which we so naturally apply to Language. Therefore some kind of contrast is indicated. Which kind then? Take Language as the control: pretty clearly the existence of Language does not wait upon express agree-ment or convention; nothing could be much less arbitrary and arti-ficial or much more natural in the life of man than the use of Lan-guage. Now 'conventional' or, better still, 'merely conventional' sometimes seems to mark a contrast with the 'essential'; the conventional is what 'need not have been', what 'might have been otherwise'. But surely it is not that we mean to say that we might not have had Language, worshipped gods, or saluted our fellows. It is rather that it is essential to our idea of (*e.g.*) Language that there should always be something inessential about it, something that does not matter, something that is 'merely conventional'. Now, what is it about what I said that does not matter for what I said? What is it that must be there but which somehow seems inessential? What is it that might have been different? Well, what I said, I said in English; but I might have spoken or written in French. I might have said what I said otherwise than I did; but it is essential that I should have said it somehow. Similarly, almost every nation has its own salute and its own currency. Baptism, even within the Catholic Church, may be administered with more or less ceremony, by nurses as well as by priests.

Roughly put, the distinction is between *what* and *how* the deed is done, where the *how* is inessential and might have been different,

---

[5] Though some have denied the premise, notably Ziff (*op. cit.*, pp. 25f.). Ziff, for all his good counsel against the misconstruction of usage and his understanding of high-ranking adjectives, concludes that, since the use of Language is natural and since it does not depend upon express agreements, it is not conventional. That is a non-sequitur. I allow that Language is not non-natural. We are not slaves to onomatopoeia. We are seeking a different contrast to conventional. Interestingly, Ziff sees part of what is wanted when he observes that the non-conventional regularities of a natural language could be replaced by conventional ones.

though that there should be such an inessential *how* is required by the *what*.

That is so for many kinds of behaviour, *e.g.*, for all kinds of conformative behaviour underlain by non-constitutive enabling rules. An additional feature of most forms of conventional behaviour is that *some* agent could *expressly adopt* conventions alternative to those which may actually be in force. It is this possibility of *adopting* alternatives which comes closest to capturing the essentially inessential relation of particular conventions to the behaviour they underlie. Our formulation does not imply either that conventions come into force by express adoption (though that sometimes happens) or that anyone capable of engaging in a conventional practice is either able or free to adopt his own conventions; it implies only that alternative conventions could be adopted by someone, by an agent who had attained a certain level of behavioural sophistication and was left free or was authorized to legislate on usage.

The stipulated condition is that conventional behaviour is conformative behaviour underlain by rules alternatives to which could be expressly adopted by some agent. The conventional is a kind of doing done by following conventions, which might have been different. But this will not do as a definition of conventional behaviour, and for two reasons.

First, it is not necessary. There appear to be conventional acts which can be done in only one way, *e.g.*, curtseying, giving a 21-gun salute, and writing one's name. The stipulated possibility of adopting alternative conventions holds only under the condition that such cases have been excluded. Later we shall establish that the possibility of adopting alternative conventions is indeed necessary and sufficient for all *other* kinds of conventional behaviour, but to state that result presupposes a more general definition of conventional behaviour.

Second, the stipulated condition states that alternative conventions or rules could be 'expressly adopted'. But only animals having a quite advanced mastery of Language could propose and adopt alternative conventions, and, of course, the use of Language is itself a form of conventional behaviour; 'expressly adopt a rule' therefore includes in itself the whole complexity of conventional behaviour and cannot be appealed to for purposes of defining conventional behaviour.

The possibility of adopting alternative conventions is, as things presently stand, only a lead to a more correct characterization of conventional behaviour; and what there is of truth in the thesis that conventional behaviour is conformative behaviour for which someone could expressly adopt alternative rules remains to be discovered and explained.

285

2. THE CONVENTIONAL AS WHAT REQUIRES
CONFORMITY TO CONVENTION

[That in conventional behaviour which might have been different is the convention. A convention, what one follows when doing a conventional act, is in the nature of a rule. The indicated conclusion is that conventional behaviour is a kind of conformative behaviour, the underlying rules being typically non-constitutive, enabling rules. This may be qualified to allow for conventional acts which can be done in only one way, in which instances the rule is constitutive of the conventional practice. Not all conformative behaviour, even when underlain by non-constitutive, enabling rules, is conventional.]

Supposing it true that conventional behaviour might have been different, what is it about this behaviour that might have been different? Surely not the existence of Language, worship, and rank, for these are substantially irreplaceable phenomena. What might have been different is the *way* in which acts of these kinds are done. One may speak or worship according to one set of conventions or another. So, compressing somewhat, we can say that what might have been different are the conventions themselves.

Now, your being a member of this community, church, army, *etc.*, entitles others to expect that you will speak, worship, salute in this way rather than another. It would seem then that conventions are rules, as we explained them in Part III. It would follow that conventional behaviour is a species of conformative behaviour. Furthermore, to the extent that it is true that the conventions might have been different, the rules in question are 'non-constitutive'.[1]

We observed that normally it would seem to be *essential* to a conventional act that there be something about it that might have been

---

[1] That conventional behaviour, especially the use of Language, is a species of conformative behaviour is certainly the 'received opinion', well represented by Wittgenstein's *Investigations*. But here again Ziff would be the iconoclast. In an appendix to Chapter 1 of *Semantic Analysis*, he implicitly defends his faith in 'regularities' by disparaging the appeal to rules as being as irrelevant to the understanding of Language as '. . . an appeal to the laws of Massachusetts while discussing the laws of motion' (*op. cit.*, p. 35). He supposes that rules would have to be laid down in the teaching of Language, but, he says, languages are mostly learned not taught. He suggests that rules must constrain (p. 36) or that they enter into the formation of plans and policies (pp. 36ff.). But, of course, putative rules of Language do not do that. And no one ever thought they did. We may allow that Ziff is right that rules of Language in the literal sense of 'rule' are rare. Actually his own conception of rule seems to me to be only a distant relative of the literal sense of 'rule'. Apart from that, my claim is only that conventional behaviour, including the use of Language, is a species of *conformative* behaviour, an analysis of which I have supplied, partly to lend substance to the intuitive, unanalysed, philosophical appeal to rules. Rules in the literal sense concern me only as a special case (see p. 236).

different. What there is of truth in this we can recast in a more accurate way. Conventional acts are ones which cannot be attempted except by conforming to some one or other convention. If an act is of that kind, the purpose itself may be called conventional. But if one cannot attempt the act except by following a rule, the rules in question must be what we called 'enabling-rules'. We conclude that conventional behaviour is enabling-rule conformative behaviour. In the usual case the rules will also be non-constitutive. The qualificatory 'usual' makes allowance for kinds of action which, while conventional, seem on the surface to require conformity to quite specific rules, *e.g.*, giving a 21-gun salute or writing one's name. Here the rules may be 'constitutive'. Examples of such rules or conventions are: 'I' may be employed as a first-person singular pronoun; 'the' may be employed as a definite article; a person may validate a document by writing down his name in his usual way. Clearly, in a single 'conventional act' the agent may conform to a number of different rules.

Contrary to suggestions I have felt in certain writings, not all conformative behaviour is conventional in our sense. The rules capsulated in recipes and road maps do not underlie a species of conventional behaviour. There is nothing about the very ideas of cooking and travel which is conventional. Conventional behaviour is underlain by enabling rules. But even that is not enough. Rules for getting TV or radio programmes into a room are usually non-constitutive enabling rules; but making programmes present in this way is not a kind of conventional behaviour. We must supply a narrower specific difference.

3. CONVENTIONAL BEHAVIOUR IS SELF-IDENTIFYING [1]

[What is at once most essential to and profoundly perplexing about (*e.g.*) the use of Language is that (with qualifications) one can say something only by showing what he means to say. It is the same with other kinds of conventional behaviour. In saluting one must show that he means to salute. But this must be carefully qualified, because, first, the agent may succeed in saying what he means to say even if no one understands, and second, it may not actually be part of his purpose that anyone should understand. Taking note of these considerations, a conventional purpose is explained as one which cannot be attained except by the agent's making such movements as would make the purpose identifiable in the practical sense. Conventional action is

---

[1] In this section, I modify an idea adapted from H. P. Grice's paper 'Meaning', *Phil. Rev.*, July, 1957, esp. pp. 385f.; a wisp of something similar is also in Austin, *op. cit.*, pp. 121, 127, n. 1.

provisionally explicated as conformative action which can succeed only if the agent makes such movements as will make his purpose identifiable. His *reason* for making the movements he does is that the occurrence of those movements would make his purpose identifiable. Two important consequences of this explanation are these. First, one could not identify a conventional act if he did not know how to do that kind of act, identified in agent-neutral terms. Second, conventional behaviour implies possible self-consciousness, at least practical knowledge by the agent of the conventional purpose with which he acts.]

Supposing it established that conventional behaviour is a species of conformative behaviour underlain by enabling rules which are usually non-constitutive; let us take a fresh look at what must be typical examples of conventional behaviour to see whether we can descry a specific difference. It will be well to remember that kinds of action may be defined, purposes may be identified, by specifying conditions of success. Otherwise: we may begin to explain a type of action by specifying characteristic reasons or mistaken reasons for which it is done.

The use of Language surely must count as entirely typical of conventional behaviour in the sense we wish to explain. What is at once most essential to and perplexing about Language is that it speaks for itself. In seeing me do whatever it is I may be doing, *e.g.*, shooting at the top of the target, you may not know what I am doing. But if you hear me say something you will there and then come to know what it is I mean to say. My choice of words is calculated to tell you what I mean to do with those words. They speak for themselves. Similarly the captain will recognize from the corporal's salute that the corporal means to salute him; similarly, the queen will see in the act of curtseying the intent to curtsey.

On several counts this must be hedged in. First of all, in asking a question, I do not also *state* that I mean to ask a question; nor when I make a statement do I state that I mean to make that statement. In such acts, it is not part of the purpose that purpose should be made identifiable. Rather, my words or my movements are calculated to indicate and, in a certain sense, *must* indicate my purpose, if I am to act to attain that purpose. My act is not one of saying what I intend to do; but rather my act, if it be conventional, must *show* what I mean to do (see Part II, no. 22). This, I think, is part of what lies under Wittgenstein's remark that the assertion *shows* its sense, and *says that* things are so (*Tractatus*, 4.022). That one's purpose should thus be made manifest appears as very like a condition of success for a conventional act. Now, no matter the kind of act, it must be that the

288

purpose should be identifiable in the agent's movements. But only in the case of conventional acts does this become like a condition of success. But on this point great care must be taken. One may success-fully do a conventional act, and his audience not 'understand'; one might even mean them to be misled; indeed, one might speak in the absence of any audience at all. It is not one's purpose in doing a conventional act that he should be understood, or misunderstood either. That one's purpose *should* be identified is not a condition of success; only that it be made identifiable. Putting it rather more generally, an agent does a conventional act only if he can attain his purpose only by adopting means which would enable others to know that he was acting to attain that purpose. That suggests that a conventional purpose is one that can be attained only by the agent's making, in the circumstances in question, such movements as would enable another to identify that purpose. Or, reversing it, if we know that the agent is not acting in that way, then we know that he does not have a conventional purpose. The agent's purpose is of such a kind that it cannot be attained unless he makes it identifiable in his movements. Making purpose identifiable may be provisionally and conditionally treated as a condition of success for conventional action. Alternatively put, an agent does a conventional act only if among his *reasons* or *mistaken reasons* are that his making of such and such movements (his uttering of such and such words, say) would show that he means to do (means to say) such and such.

With all this in mind, let us now lay it down that a purpose is conventional if and only if it is one, action to attain which requires that the agent be conforming to or violating rules, and it can be attained only by the agent's making such movements that another, suitably prepared, could, disregarding further purposes to which the act might be collateral, identify the act, practically recognize the purpose, from the very fact that those movements were made, circumstances being in other relevant respects determined. Behaviour identified by a specification of purpose of this kind is conventional behaviour. This proposal is provisional and will be modified in no. 5 below.

About this explication of the conventional, observe, first, con-ventional behaviour is a kind of conformative, hence a kind of pro-ficient, action. This matters, for it sets conventional behaviour off from non-purposive behaviour like twitching and also from other self-identifying kinds of action in which the purpose is to make certain kinds of simple movement and hence to be identified from those movements, *e.g.*, *kicking*.

Second, notice that acts of deceit and deception, *e.g.*, lies, have kinds of 'further purpose' to the attainment of which conventional behaviour might be collateral, and hence are to be disregarded, *i.e.*, are irrelevant to the definition of conventional behaviour.

Third, the reference to circumstances is required because the occasion and the state of the world and of the agent might so vary as to allow different conventional purposes to be attained by way of the same movements ('Yes'). As it turns out, these conditions, which are among the conditions of success for the act, and so definitive of the purpose, are what may call for one movement rather than another; *e.g.*, his presence calls for 'him' while his absence may recommend his name.

Fourth, a conventional act may fail even though the purpose is made identifiable in the movements. That, if it be a condition of success at all, is only one condition of success. There will certainly be others, the failure of which would nullify the success of the act, *e.g.*, that there be an object answering to a name. Self-identification is not self-validation.

Finally, my proposed explication is not yet a definition of conventional action. As a definition it would be circular. This will be explained, and a definition of conventional behaviour supplied in no. 5 below. The crux is that being self-identifying must be, not a condition of success, but a condition of doing for conventional behaviour.

The movements by which one makes his purpose identifiable in a conventional act we may call *conventional movements*. The rules to which one conforms in doing the act we may call conventions. Though it does not yet follow from our account, let us take it that one makes his purpose identifiable by following the rules, by conforming to the conventions. An observer is not properly qualified, be it noted, unless he has or directly comes to have at least practical knowledge of these conventions.

One cannot do a conventional act whether or not successfully except by conforming to conventions. These are enabling rules. But, in general, the conventions could be different; hence the conventions will, as we have seen, usually be non-constitutive.

It is this last, I suppose, which inspires some to hold that determination of vocabulary in the use of Language is 'arbitrary'. It might have been different. But there is also something in the thought expressed by Wittgenstein in the *Philosophical Investigations* (Part I, no. 510) and made explicit by Hampshire (*op. cit.*, pp. 136f.), that one cannot simply make his words mean something other than what he knows them to mean. In view of the explictly technical adapting of familiar terminology, which occurs so often in algebra ('ring', 'group', 'ideal'), the thought is plainly somewhat exaggerated. But it intimates the truth that in using words one is employing devices which, at least practically, he knows will make his purpose identifiable. He cannot use them except by conforming to a convention, to a usage. One of the agent's reasons or mistaken reasons is that the utterance of *these* words would make his purpose identifiable. Conformative behaviour, we argued in no. 7 of the last chapter, is primarily 'public'. This is even more obviously so in the case of the conventional kind of conformative behaviour. In learning to do conventional acts, and in coming to the place where one can have such purposes, one must also learn how to disclose those purposes. It is partly for this reason that the possibility of the agent's being 'understood', in some sense of 'understood', coincides with successful conventional action. For another understands only if he is aware of how the agent discloses his purpose in attaining it. From this it does *not* follow that the agent cannot conform to private convention, or that he need be understood by anyone; all that follows is that if anyone came to know that these were the operating conventions, he would also then and there come to know what the agent's purpose was when he acted in conformity with those conventions, and the agent knows that.

Our explanation of *conventional* has been framed in terms of the identification of the agent's purpose by a possible observer. This misleadingly suggests what need not be the case, that a conventional act cannot succeed in the absence of observers or despite the misunderstanding of whatever observers there may be. Our final definition of conventional action will avoid that suggestion. But the present proposal has the compensating advantage of suggesting an explanation of what is surely one of the most important facts about conventional behaviour. I may know that French is being spoken even if I cannot speak a word of French. The sounds are enough. I may recognize that one is batting in a game of cricket, though I may have no idea of how to bat in cricket. Similarly, as a child, I could tell when my parents were playing bridge, though I knew not how to play. But it is quite different with Language. I cannot identify what is said (*e.g.*, in French or in English) unless I know how to say it myself, perhaps in French or in English or in some other tongue. More generally and carefully stated, it is a necessary condition of an act's being conventional, that an observer is prepared to make a correct and direct identification only if (but not *if*) he know how to do that kind of act, insofar as he could not know that this kind of act was being successfully done if he could not also act to attain that purpose, were it described in terms neutral as between different agents.[2] The qualification that the observer's identification be 'correct and direct' is attached to eliminate cases where the observer is told or guesses that the agent is doing a kind of conventional act which the observer has heard

[2] The limitation to recognizing *success* will be expunged in no. 5 below, where it will be seen that conventions are rules for succeeding.

about but cannot himself identify from the performance, *e.g.*, identify what is being done from the movements. His proficiency need go only as far as his capacity to identify, *e.g.* to identify a question as such he need only be able to ask questions, whereas to identify the question whether Puerto Rico is a state, he must know how to ask that question. It is consistent with this thesis that the observer could do this kind of act only by way of other movements (in gesture or in another tongue); or that he comes to know how only when he finally realizes what is presently being done (*e.g.*, as when he learns a new use of Language); but the condition remains. The qualification that the purpose be identified in agent-neutral terms is actually redundant (because of the 'know how to'), but is added explicitly to exclude cases where, in point of logic, only people of a certain kind, indeed perhaps only a single person, may attain the purpose in question; *e.g.*, one may give only *his* promise, cast *his* vote, and only women can succeed in curtseying.

That this is a necessary condition follows from the stipulated condition. Suppose one identifies the act and sees it is successfully done. Then he must have at least practical knowledge of the conditions of success, and know that all of them are satisfied. Among these conditions is that the act should be made identifiable in the movements; so the observer must have at least practical knowledge that the condition is satisfied by the movements that he observes. Since he also knows (in at least the practical sense) what conditions of the agent are conditions of success, he knows what the agent must do to succeed in the act. It follows that he knows (in at least the practical sense) that were he that kind of agent, in these circumstances, he could do that kind of act by way of making just those movements he observes the agent to make. That is sufficient to say that he knows how to. (This explanation seems to me to be, by the way, an almost inevitable description of how one comes to learn Language by way of coming to understand it.) Conventional behaviour differs from other kinds of behaviour underlain by enabling rules (*e.g.*, talking French, batting in cricket, and bidding in bridge) just by the fact that the movements are enough. I know that he succeeds in batting a cricket ball from my knowledge that this is cricket, and from the applause that I hear. The applause is not a condition of success, but that is what tells me that the act succeeded.[3]

An interesting further conclusion bearing particularly on Language

---

[3] It is interesting that ability to identify non-conventional but conformative behaviour underlain by enabling rules does seem to presume that the observer have acquired capacity for conventional behaviour. So much verbal stage-setting seems to be required. I only note this, without trying to give a demonstration.

acts and Language dependent states and acts, is that there are no 'ineffable thoughts'. To think, I submit, is to 'mean something', which is to have a kind of conventional purpose, without necessarily acting upon it. But, by the conclusion we have just established, one could not know what thought, if he did not know how to make it identifiable, *i.e.*, express it. More generally, the conclusion supports the Platonic (as against Aristotelian) idea that unexpressed thought calls for the inhibition of expression, is 'internal talking'.

To the conclusion that an observer of the conventional must know how to do what he identifies, I shall now argue that we may add the further consequence that the agent must know what he is doing, in the sense that he must be capable of (at least practical) *self-consciousness of purpose*. Stronger still he must be capable of knowing what he is doing if what he is doing is a conventional act. We can, I submit, truly say of a conventional agent that he must be capable of becoming aware of himself as an agent, and that the conventional agent must have at least practical knowledge of his own purpose. Not only must he be conscious of those facts which are his reasons, but he must also be conscious of himself as an agent doing a particular kind of act. This, if we can be satisfied that it is true, is of first-order interest. It gives us a sufficient though not a necessary condition for self-consciousness. If my earlier conjecture (Part III, no. 11, pp. 265f.) is true—that capacity to engage in practices underlain by enabling rules is sufficient for self-consciousness—then the thesis that one who does a conventional act is capable of self-consciousness is trivially true. But I am not entirely confident of the correctness of the argument put forward in support of that conjecture. At all events, the conclusion of the present thesis, that if an agent is doing a conventional act, then he must be capable of knowing that he is doing that kind of act, is somewhat stronger insofar as it requires possible self-consciousness of one's actual purpose and not merely possible self-consciousness of something. So let us consider it on its own merits. Does it seem to be true?

Well, one might see a banana and eat it without knowing that he is eating a banana. One may recognize bananas and have learned to eat them before he has learned to recognize that others are eating bananas. But if one has not learned to identify ingestive acts in others, he cannot have even practical knowledge of this kind of deed, whether done by himself or by others. Similarly, one can speak French without knowing that he is speaking French. This is perhaps a poor example, because the agent's purpose would then surely not be one of speaking French. (See discussion of this kind of case on pp. 265f.) But surely one could not *succeed* in saying or even in thinking something without knowing what he 'means'. We now can see vaguely why that is so. In conventional behaviour the purpose is, so to speak, displayed or enacted in the movements. By doing the act, the agent makes the purpose identifiable, to himself as well as to others. But that is too vague. It would pay to be more systematic, so let us try. We identify purpose generally by reference to the agent's knowledge of the conditions of success which explains his movements. We have stipulated that a condition of success in conventional behaviour is that the agent should make his purpose identifiable. He does that by conforming to certain rules. A condition for doing such an act is that he know or believe that there are such rules. His knowledge or belief that there are such rules explains his doing the act in the way he does. But clearly he could not believe that these are the rules by conformity to which he would make his purpose identifiable, unless he knew what his purpose was. Our stipulation therefore requires that the conventional agent must have at least practical knowledge of his purpose. Following the conventions enables him to do the deed, only if he knows that this is the kind of deed he wishes to do. So the conclusion is that to say truly of an agent that he was doing a conventional act implies that he has at least practical knowledge of what he is doing. The consequent of this conclusion is stronger than that of our conjecture that capacity to engage in a practice underlain by enabling rules is sufficient for self-consciousness; it was there not required that the agent should be able to know that he was doing the kind of act underlain by the rules (see the example of speaking French above); but if one does a conventional act, he must be capable of at least practical knowledge that he is doing an act of that kind.

It may now be thought that I have proved too much and that the argument must be unsound. It may be held that this congenial conclusion which accords so well with our first intuitions about Language is in fact not true. If it were true, it would imply that a speaker must always be capable of understanding what he says. Two kinds of counter-example may be offered. First, we have the case of the mechanically stupid wife whose car breaks down on the road. It is hauled off to the garage, where the mechanic tells her that the car has thrown a piston rod. We are to suppose that the wife has no more idea than a chimpanzee what a piston rod is. But she nonetheless duly reports to her husband that the car threw a piston rod, this said on the unquestionable authority of the garage-man. The second kind of example is that of the non-professional report that a mutual friend has silicosis. The party making the report is supposed to be ignorant of the true nature of silicosis; in a sense, he does not know what he says, and yet he says it.

The second ostensible counter-example is the easiest, so let us consider it first. Observe that the imagined speaker could equally well have said, 'He has what the doctor *calls* silicosis', whereas a specialist in lung diseases surely could not have said, 'He has what the doctor calls silicosis', in just the way that neither the friend nor the doctor could say, 'The book is sitting on what furniture makers call a table'. The point is that the friend reports something different from what the doctor would report. It is true, then, that the friend does not say what he does not understand; he says something else. The difference is reflected by the fact that, while the doctor would verify the presence of silicosis by taking X-rays, testing lung cultures, *etc.*, the friend would verify what he says by consulting a doctor. Of course, if he did not have silicosis, the friend would have been wrong in saying that he did, but not wrong in the way in which the doctor would have been. Any of us would be wrong to say that Cortez conquered Mexico should it turn out one hundred years hence that the job was done by Cortez' assassin. We would trace our error to the error of one chronicler, but our error would be of different order from his. But what chroniclers have said is all we have to go on. So, too, all the friend has to go on is the doctor's report. The friend's misconstruction of the doctor's report would falsify what he says. The correctness of the doctor's report is presumed; it is a 'presupposition' not a truth-condition of the friend's report. (This kind of case could be dissected in greater detail. It is clear, for one thing, that pathological syndromes that go by fancy medical names are usually [not always] to be distinguished from the common cold, measles, and mumps. One would not say, 'He's got what doctors call a common cold'. Refinements of diagnosis, marked by a ponderosity of jargon, which take us beyond the gross symptomatology of things, alter the subjects.)

Let us now return to the first, more difficult kind of ostensible counter-example, illustrated by the uxorial explanation of the car's breakdown. It is assumed that the wife is not merely parroting words. She is conveying information to her husband, and, what's more, she knows that she is. Nor in this case, unlike the other one, is it plausible to suggest that what she conveys is that the mechanic told her that the car had thrown a rod. She wants to tell her husband what is wrong with the car, and not what the mechanic told her. But, since she does not know what she says, she seems to be saying what she does not understand. My answer is this: She conveys the information and she knows she does, and she does this and knows she does this by giving the appearance of saying something in particular; but what she conveys is not what she says. It is a principle of our theory that any kind of act could be done on its own, without being collateral to any further purpose. Suppose, then, that the woman were in fact saying what we suppose her to be saying (that the car threw a rod), but only to herself and without meaning to convey information to anyone else. Her act would then indeed be a kind of parroting, a mouthing of empty words. But she was not parroting to her husband. The conclusion is that, while her act surely was one of conveying information, no one of the acts done collaterally thereto was a conventional act of saying that the car had thrown a rod. She could just as well have simply shown her husband the car, and pointed out the place that the mechanic had pointed out to her. That indeed is a conventional act, but not one of saying that the car threw a rod. Now our stipulation required that we consider conventional action in abstraction from further purposes which it might collaterally subserve. But if in the present case we excise the further purpose of conveying information, the collateral act with which we are left is not the conventional act of saying that the car threw a rod, though it may still be a conventional act. It is worth remarking that performances of the kind we imagined could certainly not be done by anyone who was not already a past master at conveying information in conventional ways. The wife certainly gives the appearance of saying something. But what she says, if she says anything at all, is not that the car threw a rod.

I assume that our thesis, that conventional behaviour implies capacity for knowing what one is doing, is redeemed.

This conclusion suggests that we could *define* a conventional act as one which could not be attempted except by an animal who could be aware of what he was doing. That would not work. There are kinds of acts, not themselves conventional by our stipulation, that presume the use of Language, and even full self-consciousness on the part of the agent, *e.g.*, things done while browsing in a library or looking up a book in a card file. Such performances require that the agent know what he's doing, but not that he make this identifiable in his movements. I would hope, furthermore, that all would agree that these are not examples of what we would want to mean by conventional action.

Corollary to the general point about self-consciousness which has just been established is the further fact that, if the conventional act in question is a Language act, then the agent can progress from practical awareness of his purpose to theoretical knowledge of it by simple reflection, if he can reflect, by simply considering his own movements. To have a conventional purpose, the agent, we saw, must know how to act to attain it; but the expressions by repeating which he would do this, and so make his purpose identifiable, the words by which he would say what he means to say, are also the very ones from which he himself would theoretically identify the deed. He would report what he means to say by saying what words he would utter.

For this to count as a theoretical identification of his (conventional) act, the speaker would also need to be able to refer to himself and to his purpose. Only then could he have theoretical knowledge by simple reflection that his purpose was to say p. In short, that he should be able to have 'reflective (non-observational) knowledge' is not assured just by his having the use of Language, but also demands that he should have acquired the capacity of referring to himself as an agent. In summary, our stipulation, if it be justified, makes it appear that practical knowledge of one's own purpose is assured by a capacity for conventional behaviour, while theoretical knowledge of one's own purpose waits upon the ability to refer to oneself.

Some may still wonder how an observer's (practical) identification of conventional behaviour differs from the identification of any other kind of action. Do we not always identify an agent's acts from his movements, if circumstances are in all relevant respects determined? Yes, but the force of this formula is quite different in the case of conventional acts. What is peculiar in conventional action is that the agent must act so that (but not 'with the purpose that') his purpose may be identified. His choice of word or gesture is calculated to indicate what he wants to do (say). To recognize this and identify the act, the observer must, as it were, be able to put himself in the agent's shoes. The difference can be seen from the two sides. First, as we have already noted, for an observer to identify the act it is implied that he should know how to do it on his own. It is different, for example, with playing a piece of music; I might identify that he was playing a certain piece of music on the flute, though I know not how to play the piece on the flute or on any other instrument. Second, it is implied that what is observed is an agent who is aware of himself as an agent and can know what he is doing. These two factors contribute to the self-identifying or conventional syndrome.

4. THE CONVENTIONAL AND ALTERNATIVE CONVENTIONS

[It is shown that our stipulation regarding conventional behaviour is a necessary but not a sufficient condition for conformative behaviour underlain by enabling rules being such as to call for conformity to rules for which alternatives might have been expressly adopted. It is considered whether we may possibly always regard kinds of conventional behaviour which do not admit of alternative conventions (*e.g.*, curtseying, raising the host) as being hybridized from a conventional Original Purpose whose attainment does allow for alternative conventions (showing respect to one of higher rank; symbolizing the presence of deities). The conclusion is that this would distort our common ways of thinking about familiar types of conventional behaviour.]

It was originally suggested that typically conventional behaviour essentially involves something which might have been different, where that turns out to be precisely the operating rules or conventions. We observed that alternative conventions can usually be expressly adopted by someone. Certain exceptions to this were noted, *e.g.*, acts of curtseying, giving 21-gun salutes, and making certain kinds of invocation. Here, within limits, there is only one way in which the act can be done—by bending the knee, firing the cannon, or singing the service. Nonetheless, there seems to be something important and natural in this idea of possible alternative conventions, and it would be well to see how it lines up with our stipulation regarding the self-identifying character of the conventional given in the last section.

The idea is, then, that the conventional is that for which there might have been alternative conventions, each in itself suitable for attaining the conventional purpose. It is with the idea of a conventional purpose that our explanations of the last section began. Let us see if and how the two accounts come together.

Now to say that there might have been alternative conventions must in this case be taken to imply that someone might have explicitly adopted alternative conventions. It is not that one *does* so adopt a set of rules; only that someone *could* have. So a convention is something for which alternatives could (but need not) be explicitly adopted in its stead. That for which two different conventions may be adopted is what we would identify through the conventions in different conventional acts. That which we identify through the convention is set by reference to the presence of certain fixed features in the circumstances in which the act would be done; these fixed features constitute all that is relevant in the circumstances for identifying what kind of act is done. Thus we should determine that another was eating through the most alien of table manners or conventions in consideration of the presence of comestibles, masticatory movements, and so on. Knowing the force of the conventions, we can, from the movements, identify the act as of a kind. We have held that an act is completely determined by a specification of the agent, together with the elements of movement, circumstance, and purpose. Suppose, then, that the agent is given and the occasion fixed in all relevant respects as is demanded by our stipulation regarding the conventional, we then identify the movements and, in so doing, determine the other elements of the act. These can be only the elements of purpose. That means that we identify the purpose in the movements. But that is just

what my stipulation regarding conventional behaviour demands—
that the purpose be made identifiable in the movements. It therefore
seems to me that, for an act to be conventional in the sense of there
being alternative rules, it is necessary but not sufficient that it be conventional according to the stipulation. Pretty clearly this argument
exploits special features of those rules which we have called 'conventions'. Otherwise it would lead to the obviously false conclusion
that any practice underlain by non-constitutive enabling rules is
conventional according to our stipulation, *e.g.*, the practice of tuning
in a certain TV programme. The special features exploited were,
first, that conventions *can* be expressly adopted, and second, that we
identify what is done through these conventions.

We have already seen that our stipulation does not imply the possibility of alternative conventions. There are kinds of acts that can
succeed only if the purpose is made identifiable in the movements,
which cannot be done in alternative ways. When a girl is taught to
curtsey, she is also taught that this is the proper *way* to curtsey. She
cannot be taught the one without the other. Similarly, giving a 21-gun
salute requires the firing off of guns. I assume that an incantation,
say in voodoo, *requires* that the agent should make certain sounds
and gestures in a certain way. Some leeway remains, of course, in the
exact movements made and sounds issued; but there is a kind of
pattern or outline which must be conformed to. Now, since it is the
very movements which one is attempting to make in doing such acts,
it seems to me that they are all of that kind which we called endotychistic (Part II, no. 19). But if the movements are not essential in the
sense that to make the movement is part of the purpose, then one
might have attained the purpose by way of alternative movements.
So one might have adopted alternative movements to make the
purpose identifiable. The conclusion is that if an act is not endotychistic, then it is conventional according to our stipulation if and
only if it is enabling, conformative behaviour for which some agent
might adopt alternative conventions. The results of nos. 1 and 3 are
mutually supporting.

Suppose now that we have the more common (non-endotychistic)
kind of case, a conventional purpose which might be attained in
alternative ways, *e.g.*, by following the conventions of German,
French, or English. It might be one's purpose to do such an act in a
particular kind of way; *e.g.*, one may, when travelling in France, not
merely order his meal in French, but make the attempt to give the
order in French. That he should do it in French is part of his purpose
as may well be understood by the solicitous waiter who, commanding
a good knowledge of English, lends aid to his struggling client. Such
would be a kind of hybrid act, as we introduced that idea in Part II,

no. 15, with a conventional Original Purpose and a non-conventional Original Way. Let us call such acts *hybridized conventionals.* There is another kind of case. One may act to attain a non-conventional purpose in a conventional way; *e.g.*, one may eat in a conventional way, or serve the food according to Emily Post. What is conventional here will usually be the *way*; but it might become part of one's purpose that his movements should show that he means to eat or to serve in this way. That would be a kind of hybrid act, for which the Original Way is conventional but the Original Purpose most likely not. The hybrid purpose in question could not be attained unless the agent made the fact that he meant to attain the Original Purpose in the Original Way, identifiable in his movements. This kind of act we call a *conventional hybrid.* Usually, of course, there will be alternative ways of being polite, proper, mannerly, *etc.*

Once we have made explicit these ideas of hybridized conventional and conventional hybrid, some may be led to suppose that those types of conventional acts which can be done in only one way are in fact hybridized conventionals. It could be argued that curtseying, for instance, is a kind of act for which the Original Purpose is showing respect to superior rank, which surely can be done in many ways. I think that would distort the facts. Allowing that one could have first learned to show respect to superior rank, and then have come to learn to do it *by* curtseying, that is not the normal way. Normally, it is curtseying, not showing respect to superior rank, that would be the more natural unit of action. It is rather as when one *first* learns to talk in a certain tongue.

Now highly sophisticated creatures may wish to refashion their practices out of highly abstracted types of behaviour. They may systematically replace all forms of endotychistic conventional behaviour, and the accounts of no. 1 and no. 3 would have equivalent application to their behaviour. But that is fanciful. Besides, no one could become so detached from particular conventions without first having acquired the capacity to do (endotychistic) conventional acts which do not admit of alternative conventions. Such types of action are irreplaceable by hybridized conventionals.

5. FINAL DEFINITION OF CONVENTIONAL BEHAVIOUR

[Our stipulation regarding conventional behaviour as conformative action which can succeed only if the agent makes his purpose identifiable in his movements carries the misleading suggestion that there must be an interlocutor, and it is ambiguous at the essential 'only if', leaving unexplained the connection between the two conditions of being conformative and being self-identifying. Also, the stipulation, if taken as a definition, would be circular: For what it requires is that one of the conditions of success for conventional behaviour is that the purpose be made identifiable, that all the conditions of success be indicated. This argument suggests a more suitable definition, making the self-identifying condition, not a condition of success, but a condition of doing a conventional act. More exactly, conventional behaviour is defined as conformative behaviour where conformity to rule enables the agent to indicate all possible circumstances in which the act might fail; that any of these circumstances does not obtain would then count as a condition of success, for the type of conventional action in question.]

Our stipulation regarding conventional behaviour according to which it would be a species of conformative behaviour which can succeed only if the agent makes his purpose identifiable in his movements strikes, I believe, close to the heart of the matter. Yet it is set forth in terms which are at once somewhat obscure and likely to provoke suspicion. For this reason I have not put it forward as a definition, but only as a stipulation. The difficulties are these: First, it irrelevantly suggests the presence of interlocutors, however hypothetical; it would be well to remove that suggestion. Second, it separates the self-identifying character of the conventional from its character as a species of the conformative. Now, while it is true that behaviour may be self-identifying without being conformative (*e.g.*, kicking), conventional behaviour is self-identifying only *by* being conformative. The rules in question are enabling rules. Our definition ought not to efface that fact. Also, third, the 'only if' in the explanation embodies an important ambiguity. It is an essential feature of our first intuitions about Language and other kinds of conventional behaviour that if only one says it, he will succeed, provided no essential condition fails. (*I.e.*, the rules in question are rules for succeeding.) But now some such conditions might fail and, even if not, the hypothetical interlocutor may not be able to identify what was done. For this reason the 'if only' gave way to an 'only if'. Now interlocutors do not matter, and the continued presence of 'only if' leaves it open that the act might fail even if all conditions of success are satisfied, which is counter-intuitive. Finally, and most importantly, our stipulation, if taken as a definition, would appear to be viciously circular. We stipulated that a condition of success for a conventional act is that the purpose be made identifiable in the movements. A principle of our theory is that we theoretically identify a purpose by specifying conditions of success. It follows that an observer would identify a purpose only if he were to become at least practically aware of the conditions of success. So, I conclude, our stipulation would have it that a condition of success for a conventional act would be that the agent should indicate all the conditions of success, including that condition of success itself.[1]

Our stipulation required that an agent does a conventional act only if he indicates what he is doing. He therefore would not even do such an act unless he satisfied the stipulated condition of success. But, clearly, the attempt must be held distinct from the success of the act, a principle which would be jeopardized were we to insist upon taking the stipulated condition as a condition of success.[2]

This codicil to the argument for circularity suggests the following escape, which would at once capture whatever truth there is in the stipulation while avoiding the difficulties it engenders. The mentioned condition that the agent should make his purpose identifiable is not a condition of success for conventional behaviour, but rather a condition of doing for conventional behaviour. A condition of doing a conventional act is that the agent should indicate all the conditions of success for that act. We might furthermore hope to recast the condition as a condition on the nature of the rules which underlie conventional behaviour, disregarding the possible presence or absence of interlocutors. That would establish the wanted connection between the conformative and self-identifying character of conventional behaviour, requiring, by the way, that conventions should be enabling rules.

The desiderated definition is already almost at hand. We have recast the stipulated condition to read: A condition of doing a conventional act is that the agent should make his purpose identifiable in his movements. That, in turn, must mean that a condition of doing a conventional act is that the agent's movements should indicate all the conditions of success for the act. To be sure, the agent's movements do not 'say' that such and such are conditions of success; rather, they indicate those conditions in that 'one who understands' would there and then know in the practical sense that those conditions must be satisfied if the deed is to succeed. But now we must furthermore require that one would indicate the conditions of success by conforming to rules, and only in that way. For that purpose it is sufficient to say that conventional behaviour is conformative behaviour underlain by enabling rules of the required kind. Now we

---

[1] Many have felt that Grice's original formulation of the condition (see p. 287, n. 1) is circular. The above argument supports that feeling.

[2] Actually, misuse of the stipulation as a definition once led me into the absurd view that one could not speak meaningfully without succeeding in saying what he meant to say, a conclusion I adhered to with great obstinacy to the horror of my then near collaborator, W. P. Alston.

noted that our first feelings about conventional behaviour were that such action would succeed *if only* the agent conformed to the rules, provided that all the conditions of success were satisfied. Conformity to rule should leave no room for failure provided that all the indicated conditions are met. The way to accommodate this is to say that if the act fails, the reason could be anticipated and the contrary of the statement that that circumstance obtain could be cast as a condition of success. Putting this all together, I would finally define conventional behaviour as *conformative behaviour where conformity to rules enables the agent to indicate all possible circumstances in which the act might fail.* A condition of doing such an act is that the agent should conform to such rules. (The rules to which he conforms need not be those of accepted usage. They may in varying degree be private to himself.)

The definition makes it quite explicit that conventional behaviour is a type of conformative behaviour, and that the underlying rules are enabling rules. It clearly allows for alternative rules, though it does not require them. It captures the essential self-identifying character of conventional behaviour. 'All possible circumstances in which the act might fail' at least includes the contradictories of all conditions of success, the indication of which makes the act identifiable; but, since these possible circumstances of failure are indicated, that they should not obtain are conditions of success. Herewith it immediately follows that conventions are rules for succeeding, that one will succeed in such an act provided he conforms to rules and that all the indicated conditions of success are satisfied. Actually, the negative formulation of our definition in terms of circumstances of failure is preferable, for reasons discussed in no. 18 of Part II. One can indicate all circumstances of failure without being able to give in advance a list of these, in that the rule may accommodate the theoretical drawing of distinctions in and the division of prespecified conditions (*e.g.*, giving a gift requires not only that one deliver an object, but also that it *belong to* the donor). This will later become of importance when we inquire into the typical character of rules of Language or conventions. Finally, in connection with the last point, the condition that one should make his purpose identifiable is no longer cast as a condition of success, but rather as a condition of doing, a condition of success-or-failure. It becomes, if you wish, a truth-condition for the observer's statement that the agent is doing a conventional act. That, we have seen, obviates the circularity in our original stipulation regarding conventional behaviour.

It remains to consider whether the two major conclusions concerning the nature of conventional behaviour drawn from the stipulation continue in force. The conclusions were (1) one could not identify a successful conventional act unless he knew how to do it himself;

and (2) conventional action implies self-consciousness of purpose on the part of the agent. The crux of the previous argument for the first conclusion was that, since the observer perceived that the conventional act succeeds, he must also observe that all the indicated conditions, including the stipulated condition regarding self-identification, are satisfied. He then must see that he could also indicate those same conditions by making those same movements in the same circumstances. All of that carries over. Only now we can strengthen the conclusion, releasing the condition that the observed act should have succeeded. To identify the act as a conventional act, the observer need only perceive (in the practical sense) that such and such are the conditions of success and that they are indicated as such by the agent's movements. If he perceives that, then, whether or not the act succeeds, he identifies the act. He therewith also sees that he could indicate the same conditions by making the same movements in the circumstances of the agent. That is sufficient to say that he knows how to do the kind of act in question.

The crux of the previous argument for the second conclusion, that self-consciousness is a necessary condition for conventional behaviour, was that the agent's conformity to the rules by which he indicates conditions of success required that he be aware of what conditions of success he would thereby indicate, and hence in the practical sense be aware of what he was meaning to do. That argument carries over intact.

6. CONVENTIONS ARE RULES FOR SUCCEEDING

[Proceeding directly from the definition of conventional behaviour, we gain the conclusion that conventions are rules for succeeding. This exposes another important factor in the conventional or self-identifying syndrome. A convention is a rule according to which the agent may indicate a set of conditions of success by making a certain movement. This occasions the introduction of some terminology for talking about conventions, which anticipates the application of our definition of conventional behaviour for the analysis of the use of Language.]

It was earlier remarked that one of our first intuitions about conventional behaviour, in particular the use of Language, is that the agent will succeed 'if only' he does the act (e.g., 'utters the words'), provided that all necessary conditions of success obtain. One gets the deed done simply by doing it. The success of the act depends upon nothing extraneous to the act itself, nor will it fail on account of unfortuitous circumstances. All possible causes of failure are, so to speak, anticipated in the act itself. All of that is secured by mere conformity to the conventions whereby the agent makes his purpose identifiable by indicating all possible circumstances of failure. This feature of conventional behaviour is succinctly captured in the formula that *conventions are rules for succeeding*. Our definition of conventional action was framed to yield that conclusion. Let us now look at the details.

Rules of succeeding were defined as rules conformity to which would assure success in action, provided that all conditions of success for the act were satisfied (see Part III, no. 13). Examples of such rules are rules for calculating and (perhaps) the rules embodied in our use of road maps. Following a rule for succeeding does not, to be sure, guarantee that all conditions of success are satisfied, and failure is surely a possibility. If the numerals with which one would calculate vanish immediately upon being written down, one could not succeed in the calculating; if conflagration destroys the town, the map will not help you get there. On the other hand, if no such conditions fail, then one is bound to succeed simply by following the rules. My claim is that conventions are such rules.

Our final definition of a conventional act was a conformative act where conformity to rules enables the agent to indicate all possible circumstances in which the act might fail. Suppose now that one conforms to the rules, thus indicating all possible circumstances of failure. These are circumstances of failure; so, given any such one, as may be abstracted from the general indication and specified, we may take it as a condition of success that such a circumstance not obtain; but we should now be picking out conditions from all possible circumstances of failure; so, if all conditions of success are met (however unformulatable they might be *in toto*), then the act succeeds. The rules thus qualify as rules for succeeding. Now the rules by following which one indicates all possible circumstances of failure are rules by following which one makes his purpose identifiable. Such rules fall under our definition of conventions. So conventions are rules for succeeding; and conventional acts are ones which are done and done only by conforming to rules for succeeding.

It does not follow that conventional acts always succeed. Possible circumstances of failure can obtain. I do an act of promising perhaps by saying 'I promise', which indicates among other things that a condition for success is the existence of a promisee. Should there be none, I shall not make a promise. Nor will one succeed in her act of curtseying if she does not wish to give another reason to suppose that she thinks him or her to be of higher rank. That is a condition for succeeding in a curtsey (though not a condition of success, *e.g.*, for practising curtseying).

What does follow is that failure in conventional action must be accountable for by some assignable reason which was prefigured in the act. A miracle could not interfere. The cause of failure could be determined by measuring the facts against what is indicated or shown in the act.

This result complements the conventional or 'self-identifying' syndrome. We earlier concluded that a conventional act is one which could not be identified except by one who knew how to do it, and that conventional behaviour implies self-consciousness. We now add that a conventional act is one which the agent gets done simply by doing it, insofar as the act itself prefigures all possible circumstances of failure.

Here is one place where the conventional (in the defined sense) does indeed contrast with the 'natural'. Animal behaviour may be looked upon as a grandiose attempt to use, duplicate, and supplement 'nature'. The products and effects of action—tables and chairs, or the music of the flute—may be taken as deliberate improvements upon the slabs and stones and harmonious breezes supplied by nature unworked and unsolicited. But the workings of nature are incalculable, and natural materials are obstinate. Conventional behaviour is an attempt to obviate a dependence upon the unpredictabilities of stubborn matter. It does that either by enabling us to produce completely independent, non-material objects ('conventional upshots', as I call them) or by conventionalizing the effects of action, now conceived in abstraction from any interfering impingements, obstructions, *etc.*

The conclusion that conventional acts prefigure all possible circumstances of failure must be employed cautiously and modestly. It is not implied that anyone should ever be able to give an advance listing of 'all possible circumstances of failure' for any conventional act, or even that there is any such collection to be listed. What follows is that we can always determine from our identification of a conventional act whether 'these circumstances' could cause the act to fail, whatever 'these circumstances' may be. We may always trace the failure of the act to a condition indicated in the act. It is rather as with real numbers: No advance listing of transcendental real numbers can be given, for they are non-denumerable. Yet we can decide for any real number whether or not it is transcendental, however difficult that job may be in detail. We have observed that the identification of purpose is always incomplete. Our result is that any uncertainty over the success of a conventional act is to be traced to an incomplete identification of the purpose.

A word, now, about conventions. Obviously I have *linguistic* conventions mostly in mind. What I shall say now anticipates the application of our definition of conventional behaviour to the analysis of the use of Language. But there are other kinds of conventions too—the conventions embodied in gestures, signals, *etc.* Now generally a convention would be defined by saying what conditions of success would be indicated by making a particular kind of movement. An agent who knows the convention is enabled to indicate the conditions by making that kind of movement. Taking the use of Language as model, I shall say that a description of the kind of movement defines an *expression*, and a list of the conditions of success defines a *use* (of words), and that the convention is specified by saying that the expression *has* the use of words. Finally, if an agent, in the course of doing a conventional act, *A*, makes a movement which is an instance of an expression, therewith indicating the conditions of success the listing of which would define a use, *U*, I shall say that he *realizes* (the use) *U* in *A*.[1]

A number of observations are in order:

(1) A given expression may in fact have a number of different uses, or a use be had by a number of different expressions. In both kinds of case, different conventions result. It proves convenient, then, to say that an expression has such and such use *in* a convention, or that a use is had by an expression *in* a convention.

(2) Generally, in doing a conventional act, the agent conforms to a number of conventions and thus realizes a *number* of uses. In the case of spoken Language, a lower bound on that number would be determined by a count of the occurring 'morphemes'.

(3) Generally, the same kind of conventional act may be done and the same uses realized by conforming to alternative sets of conventions. The act is derivatively identified by a list of the sets of conditions of success (uses) which are separately but concurrently indicated by the occurring expressions.

(4) A language may be regarded as a set of conventions for the use of Language. I make this explicit by saying that a convention *pertains* to the language. Usually conventions which pertain to languages go in families, in that an expression will generally have a variety of

---

[1] Some may protest at my employment of 'use', both in the phrase 'use of words' and later in the phrase 'use of Language' (see, *e.g.*, J. N. Findlay, 'Use, Usage and Meaning', *Proc. Arist. Soc. Supp.*, 1961, pp. 231–242). I sympathize with the complaint, for these are certainly not ordinary uses of 'use', but I will not withdraw. There is no other term I know of that does the job as well. 'Use' has already come to be employed by philosophers in usages close to mine, and for the excellent reason that vernacular usage strongly suggests this technical use; 'use' has the advantage of insisting on a connection between 'meaning' and behaviour. But let it be well understood that these are technical employments of 'use' that need and are given explanations.

different, related uses. For example, 'lion' is in English used to *predicate* the characteristic of being a lion, to *refer* to the animal-type lion, to *determine* the class of lions, *etc.*

When the families of uses are thus systematically related, we define a *meaning* of the expression in the language by saying that that expression has that family of uses. The automatic assignment of several related uses to a given expression is largely achieved by the morphology-cum-syntactical-transformations available in the language. Because expressions pertaining to a language may have different uses which are not thus systematically related, an expression may have several meanings in a language.

(5) What has been said foreshadows the development of a general theory of Language and conventional behaviour. Such a theory would afford means for isolating particular expressions and particular sets of conditions of success, and provide appropriate terminology for classifying and otherwise characterizing expressions and uses. Traditional grammar is such a theory, however imperfect. We may, within it, for example, state that according to a convention pertaining to English, 'I' is a first-person singular pronoun, or that, according to a convention pertaining to German, a dative ending may be used to indicate indirect object. Doubtless all this is confused. Modern structural linguistics seeks chiefly to work out a better theory, concentrating particularly on the isolation and characterization of expressions. In a sequel to this volume I shall attempt a similar improvement, but one which concentrates particularly upon isolating and characterizing sets of conditions of success—uses of words.

7. ENDOTYCHISTIC, EFFECTIVE, AND PRODUCTIVE
CONVENTIONAL ACTION, WITH SPECIAL ATTENTION TO
CONVENTIONAL EFFECTS AND ACHIEVEMENTS

[Conventional acts may be either endotychistic, effective, or productive, in the senses of no. 19 of Part II, and there are conventional acts of all these kinds. Attempts are made to counter charges against the legitimacy of conventional effects and conventional achievements.]

In Part II, no. 19, it was conjectured that all acts are either productive, effective, or endotychistic. This classification of action is given in terms of the 'measure of success'. An act is productive if and only if it is successful only if it contributes to bringing a product into existence. An act is effective if and only if it is successful only if it brings about some specified effect upon some independently existing object. An act is endotychistic if and only if it is successful only if certain specified movements are made by the agent, in which event the act is called an *achievement*. These classifications are not exclusive.

This tripartite classification of action carries over to conventional behaviour. It remains only to observe that there are conventional acts of all three types. If one successfully makes a conjecture, makes a promise, or asks a question, he produces a product—the conjecture, promise, or question—whose existence depends upon action, and which might be reproduced in different acts. But making conjectures and promises and asking questions are obviously types of conventional behaviour, hence of conventional, productive behaviour.

If one successfully deeds a plot of land to another, he does a conventional act which affects the property in respect of legal ownership. The property is not brought into existence by the deed, but surely it is changed. It is the same with naming heirs and nominating people for office. These are all types of conventional effective behaviour.

Curtseying, saluting, and calculating are types of conventional action. But they are also types of action which succeed only if certain movements are made. Hence they are endotychistic.

These examples are not proven. I have not actually demonstrated that the types of action in question are conventional and productive or effective or endotychistic, as the case may be. But they clearly are examples of what they are meant to be examples of.

Conventional acts may be of several types. Thus 'signing a document' identifies a type of conventional behaviour which is both effective and endotychistic. More disconcertingly, there may be hard questions whether a conventional act is of one kind or another. Thus whether 'giving a benediction' identifies a productive, effective, or endotychistic type of conventional action may be theologically controversial.

The measure of success for a conventional act is a conventional product, effect, or achievement. All these are seriously problematical. Conventional products will seem especially suspicious to many, and I shall consider their 'status' in detail in the next section. But some may have qualms even about conventional effects and achievements, qualms which I should like to quiet.

The legitimacy of conventional effects may seem uncertain to some because they can discern no effects. They have trouble allowing the mere possibility of any interaction between physical nature and conventional arrangement. They think of interaction in exclusively physical terms. How can a non-conventional thing like a plot of land be materially affected by mere convention, undergo a purely conventional change? Yet surely they would admit that their land could become the property of another. It may ease the acceptance of this fact by recalling the following:

309

(1) The conventional act which has the effect upon (say) the land does not of course bring the land into existence. That there should be a plot of land to be found between such and such boundaries is a condition of success for the act.

(2) Of course, nothing physical happens to the land immediately on account of the sale. Luckily, too, for otherwise I could not be sure of what I bought. But for all that something happens to the land when you sell it to me—your view of it and mine will certainly change.

(3) Finally, the change in question does not generally depend upon any particular type of physical change, effectable, say, with a plough; and it can be effected by use of alternative conventional instruments.

We earlier observed that effects, unlike products, do not depend for their existence upon animal action, and we anticipated that this would also hold of conventional effects (Part II, no. 19, pp. 160f.). The mere passage of time may create property rights in stolen goods, as the richness of both Le Musée de Louvre and the British Museum well demonstrates; similarly, civil authority founded on conquest and so-called 'common-law marriage' involve the bringing about of conventional effects, as it were, by inaction. But conventional effects do have a closer dependence upon conventional behaviour than 'natural' effects do upon ordinary behaviour. One could not identify a conventional effect unless he knew how to do some kind of conventional act by which such an effect would be produced. Common-law marriage is regarded as something other than mere natural union because there exists a controlling contrast with ceremoniously constituted marriage, and no one could grasp the sense of 'common-law marriage' unless he knew that people could be 'properly' married through the conventional agency of some constituted authority. Possessions merely taken may become property only because we have available forms of conventional behaviour by which property rights are created and confirmed, and these even work to protect one's claim of rights in property originally stolen. These observations have evident application to classical questions over the nature of citizenship and its dependence upon 'consent'.

Doubts about effective conventional action are mostly a matter of 'feeling', reflecting a disdain for the merely conventional arrangements of life. But the objection to conventional achievements is of a different order—it is based on an argument. The difficulty is this: A conventional achievement *is* a successful, conventional, endotychistic act. That it be both endotychistic and successful implies that it is constituted in part of particular movements. That it be conventional implies that some of the movements which constitute it must also indicate what movements must constitute it if it is to be successful. The movements actually made must indicate that they are the movements that are to be made. But that would seem an impossibility. For suppose the act had failed, as any type of act might; then the movements were not made. But if they were not made, neither did they indicate that they were the movements that were to be made. It appears then that one cannot do such an act without succeeding. But such acts fail—one may fall on her face in curtseying, or salute a robot. The argument went wrong in two places: (1) It assimilated the conditions of success and all such conditions to movements, constituting the act. But statements of the conditions of success do not refer exclusively to movements, if at all. (2) It regarded each constituting movement as itself self-indicating. About the latter, it is certainly possible that an agent should make certain movements which would indicate that he would have to make certain other movements to succeed in his act. About the first-mentioned mistake, all types of endotychistic action have certain conditions of success which do not concern the agent's movements. Take the non-conventional case of high-jumping. A condition of success is that there be a bar over which the agent is to move. In conventional endotychistic action these conditions are indicated in the movements, but surely these conditions are not for that reason to be regarded as part of the movements. A condition of success indicated in an act of curtseying is that a person of higher rank than the agent should be present; but the presence of such a person is not a movement.

An achievement, in brief, is not simply movements made, but movements made in certain circumstances. So I can and must fail at such an act if the circumstances are not as I indicate them to be.

8. CONVENTIONAL UPSHOTS

[It is argued that products produced by successful productive conventional acts are always non-material products, or upshots. A salient differentiating feature of conventional upshots is that they are produced by as well as identified in their productions. A promise is at once produced by and identified in a successful act of promising, whereas an edition of a newspaper—also an upshot—is not produced by its copies—a kind of production—but perforce before the type is set. A second differentiating feature of conventional upshots is that no one could identify such an upshot without knowing how to produce it. While not all upshots are conventional, it appears that the existence of a non-conventional upshot always depends upon the existence of a conventional upshot. Anticipating results of Part V, it is conjectured that all conventional upshots are Language upshots. Conventional upshots have their own kinds of characteristic, and are presumably

311

analysable into elements. Warnings are posted against confusing the elements of an upshot with the objects to which the agent may refer in producing the upshot.]

It was observed in the last section that some types of conventional action are productive, leading if successful to the production of products. Examples were promising, conjecturing, questioning. Promises, conjectures, questions are conventional products. It remains to consider what kinds of products these are and to consider such special features as they may possess.

Products, recall, are of two kinds: material products and nonmaterial products which I also style upshots. Material products are individuated with respect to space and time. They cannot be reproduced, if they can be reproduced at all, until they have been destroyed or dismantled. Examples of material products are artifacts, and performances of plays or of musical compositions, *etc*. Upshots are products which can be reproduced without having to be first destroyed or dismantled. Upshots, so characterized, are not really a proper species of product; they are the remainder left upon the removal of material products. We have not yet specified nor shall we be able to specify suitable differentiating criteria of individuation, identity, *etc*., for upshots generally, as we have done, in an open way, for material products. We have said only that upshots are not material products. Doubtless upshots may be of many kinds: Corporations, teams, constitutions, newspapers, editions of newspapers, openings in chess, and musical compositions are all upshots. So too are conjectures, promises, and questions (in one understanding of 'conjecture', *etc*.). The proof of this is that one can make or ask the same conjecture, promise, or question in two separate acts of conjecturing, promising, or questioning, without destroying the object before doing the second act.

It is obvious that conventional products will all have to be upshots. But it is worth considering why that is so. It follows from our earlier conclusion that conventions are rules for succeeding. Material upshots are either themselves material bodies or their production essentially involves animate workings upon matter; but matter is capable of being unreasonably refractory, refusing to assume the shapes we would impose upon it. It might crumble or be destroyed from without, just before we finish the job, and that despite the fact that no condition of success fail. Now a conventional product is produced by conforming to rules for succeeding, provided only that all the indicated conditions of success are satisfied. If no condition of success fails, then, if only one follow the rules, he will succeed; in this case, he will produce the product. Using our definition of conventional behaviour, one will produce the product by conforming to the rules, if he makes his purpose identifiable, provided none of the conditions of success thus indicated should fail. But nothing in the realm of external matter can effect that. I conclude that all conventional products are upshots.[1]

We have now accounted for the characteristic and to some the suspicious self-subsistent nature of conventional upshots. If the product is bound to be produced provided all the indicated conditions of success obtain, the existence of the object is guaranteed by the act and identified in it. Conventional products are brought into existence merely by successful action within a body of practice; unlike artifacts, conventional upshots are not replacements for or improvements upon articles which nature supplies, free and unsolicited. They duplicate nothing in the preconventional order of things, and depend only upon what the producing act prescribes.

The self-subsistent character of upshots is what is most apt to stir distrust and provoke nominalistic compunction. I have already tried to forestall this reaction (Part II, no. 19). Let it be clear, however, that, far from assimilating promises and questions to tables and chairs, I should rather be taken to be marking the differences. However, it remains that we do allow for questions whether the agent made the *same* promise or another one, asked the same or another question, and we have ways of establishing answers. Also, I have defined products and classified them in advance, and it is a result of our investigation that promises, say, are a type of non-material product. One may still protest that to posit a promise additional to the act of promising is to make a spurious duplication. The promise is only a verbal figment, an 'internal accusative' to the act of promising; that assessment, one might claim, is but confirmed by the observation that the suppositious promise is identified in and produced by the act of promising. I respond, first, that the act of promising may fail and no promise be made, and second, the same promise may be identified in different successful acts of promising. It follows that the promise would be wrongly equated with the act of promising, however much the product may depend upon and be classifiable as an "internal accusative" for the conventional practice of promising. One may,

---

[1] Clearly this argument assumes that we cannot make it a condition of success for producing, *e.g.*, artifacts that the materials employed will not fail us. That surely cannot be a genuine condition. Of course, we might discover what went wrong, *e.g.*, that this particular kind of substance would not bear the treatment given it; that we should not employ such material could then become a condition of success. But we could not anticipate once and for all any and everything that might go wrong with our materials. That is, I think, an important fact about our idea of matter.

furthermore, say things about the act of promising which cannot be meaningfully said about the promise, and conversely: thus, the act of promising was quick or slow, in English or German, but not the promise; the promise was kept or broken, first made on such and such occasion, but not the act of promising. Finally, one may refer to a promise without referring to a particular act of promising, although to speak of a promise implies that some or several acts of promising occurred. In concession to the nominalist it must be allowed that the defender of conventional upshots must recognize the demand to say how the existence and identity of a particular kind of upshot is established, especially as we cannot provide any positive such account of upshots in general. I have already begun to do that, and wish now to get on with the task.

We have been blandly speaking about identifying upshots in the producing act. That is their single most important feature. It may mollify the nominalist to recall that upshots are characteristically brought before attention in a concrete spatio-temporal form. Newspapers have *copies*; symphonies are *performed*; promises are *made;* and questions are *asked*. In our earlier discussion of upshots such perceivable manifestations of upshots were called productions. It is essential to any one sort of upshot that it should have particular, characteristic forms of production. It *must* be that an upshot *may* have a production. Particular productions of an upshot *are* material products. (Recall that the production is not related to the upshot as instance to universal. The upshot is also a particular, not a universal. On the other hand, 'production of upshot-U' is a schematic name for an associated universal, of which the productions are instances.)

I hold that some modes of production are *essential* to the upshot. The force of this 'essential' depends upon the general consideration that any kind of object is primarily to be identified in a characteristic medium, *e.g.*, bodies in regions of space at given times, colours in material surfaces, numbers in numerical expressions. Other ways of identifying the object depend upon the possibility of the primary kind of identification. We are able to give the primary type of theoretical identification by reference to the 'instantiating medium', because all depends upon our capacity to make practical identifications of this type of object in the instantiating medium. Now upshots, I hold, are primarily to be identified in their productions. Newspapers are identified in their copies, laws in documents, pieces of music in performance. If they could not thus be (practically) identified, they could not be identified in any other way. Thus, while I may know from the looks in the listeners' faces that what is now playing is Rasoumovsky no. 2, that would not be possible were no one able to identify the music by listening to it.

314

Now conventional upshots also have their productions. It appears that these productions are no other than the very acts of promising, conjecturing, questioning by which the upshots are produced. The conclusion would be that *conventional upshots are produced in their productions*. That in fact is true, as we may quickly convince ourselves by a simple argument.

In performing a conventional act one must make his purpose identifiable. The purpose of a productive conventional act is to produce the upshot. Therefore, if the act succeeds, the agent thereby shows that it is his purpose to produce a particular upshot. Hence, if the act succeeds, the upshot is made identifiable in the act which produces it. But the upshot is identified in productions. Hence the production is the act of producing. This is the single most important fact about conventional upshots.[2]

To this result about the identification of conventional upshots, we may now add the further conclusions that one could not practically identify a conventional upshot unless he knew how to produce it. That follows as corollary from our earlier conclusion that one could not identify a conventional act without knowing how to do it. For one to identify an upshot implies he could identify it in a production, hence identify the production; but the production of a conventional upshot is the producing act. Therefore to identify the upshot requires that one be able to identify a producing conventional act which in turn requires that he know how to do such an act.

All conventional products are upshots; but not all upshots are conventional. That is clear from our examples of newspapers, pieces of music, *etc.* But, using the two results just arrived at, we are now able to give something like a proof. Beethoven's 9th Symphony is an upshot. I am generally able to identify it in its productions (performances), yet I am completely incapable of performing it for myself, and even less would I be able to produce it (write it) on my own. (If a symphony seems too large a thing to be produced by an act, a simple tune would be enough to illustrate the argument.)

But there are relations between conventional and non-conventional upshots. I conjecture that non-conventional upshots depend upon conventional upshots in that an agent could not produce any upshot unless he had attained the level of productive, conventional behaviour, nor could we *prove* the identity of (as against practically identify) any upshot without appeal to a conventional upshot. Without a

---

[2] This fact more than any other may lure us into contra-Platonistic conclusions, of the kind set out, say, in Wittgenstein's *Tractatus*. Wittgenstein, if I understand him, wants to say (as against Frege and Moore) that there are no conventional upshots, only acts of asserting; no 'propositions', only acts of 'presenting' (*darstellen*) sets of truth-conditions as pictures of the world.

positive characterization of upshots in general, I cannot supply a proof. But the conjecture seems entirely plausible. The substance of the conjecture is in two parts. First, the producing of an upshot, whether or not conventional, always depends upon the collateral producing of a conventional upshot. In the sequel to this volume, I shall argue that writing music involves Language acts, hence conventional behaviour. Now Beethoven wrote the 9th Symphony by writing that piece of music which became the 9th Symphony. Similarly for those contracts, recipes, plans, formats, *etc.*, which are produced in producing corporations, kinds of dish, chess-openings, newspapers. Let us call these *diagrams*. My submission is that one produces an upshot only by producing a (conventional) diagram. This thesis is supported by the second part of the conjecture, which is that one may prove identity of an upshot only by comparison with a diagram, which is a type of conventional upshot. Hence, since having an object requires a method for proving identity, the existence of an upshot always depends upon the existence of a conventional upshot. One must have a diagram before identity questions over a (non-conventional) upshot can arise. Now here I speak about *proof* of identity, not practical identification. Obviously I could practically identify a piece of music in a production of it, even if I did not myself know how to write down music, that being evidence that the piece of music is not a conventional upshot. Comparison to a conventional upshot, the diagram (itself identified in a production, *e.g.*, a score), is a method of proof of a statement of identity. What I have now claimed is conjecture. I can only say that it *seems* true. It simply records the *observation* that there seems to be no other way of establishing identity available. Counter-examples, or proofs pro or contra the truth of the thesis, would be welcome. But the conjecture may gain credibility from the following consideration. An upshot or non-material product has no material existence apart from producing animals, as material products do once they have been completed. Now if the 'instantiating media' (the 'performances') do not provide some assurance for existence and identity, such as we find in conventional behaviour, then these questions over existence and identity must be referred to something else. It seems unlikely that we can make (non-material) upshots depend in this way upon material objects. Our only recourse would then be to some kind of self-assuring, self-identifying standard, and the only likely candidates are conventional upshots, which we know are identified in their producing acts, that always yield the upshot provided all conditions of success are satisfied. All examples of types of upshot (for which, of course, criteria can be delivered and proof or disproof of the conjecture be provided) seem to be of this kind: they either are themselves con-

316

ventional or depend upon conventional upshots, namely diagrams.

All our examples of conventional upshots—promises, questions, conjectures—belong patently to the realms of Language. I think that is no accident, and I conjecture that it must be so. I can offer no 'proof', only considerations in support of the thesis, which is that all conventional upshots could be produced by Language acts. In Part V, Language acts will be defined as conventional acts whose purpose is attainable by making inscriptional movements. Now what is special about conventional upshots, as against conventional effects and achievements, is that they are conceived of apart from any particular movements that may make them identifiable in the act. One might either speak or write, or signal, or tap out a question. That strongly supports the conjecture that all conventional upshots are upshots of the use of Language. If it is not a part of a productive conventional purpose that certain movements should be made, there is no obvious reason to think that the products in question might not be produced by any kind of movements, hence by inscriptional movements. But a conventional act which can be done by way of inscriptional movements is a Language act. But if an upshot can be produced by a Language act, it is a Language upshot. The conclusion would be that all conventional upshots are products of the use of Language.

A conventional upshot is an object in its own right which may be referred to and spoken about in characteristic ways. Thus we can speak about the *form* of a conjecture or a statement—ask and answer whether it be singular or universal or whether it be a statement of existence or identity or whether it be of the subject predicate form; or we may ask whether a promise was *kept* or broken; or whether a conjecture is *true* or *false*. Still again, conventional upshots may be more or less vague.[3]

It is reasonable to expect that we should be able to analyse conventional upshots into elements. The assumption that we can is implicit in much of our talk about creatures of Language. Thus we speak about the subject and the predicate of a statement, or we may distinguish the two references which contribute to a statement of

[3] For discussion of an interesting case, see J. L. Nelson, 'Are Inductive Generalizations Quantifiable', *Analysis*, 1962, pp. 59–65. Nelson considers the statement 'Ants attack spiders', which he argues has a different force from 'All ants attack spiders' and 'Some ants attack spiders'. Though he marks the contrasts in terms of 'ambiguity', that is the wrong word. What he is really drawing attention to is relative vagueness of upshots. The upshot *Ants attack spiders* is more vague than the upshot *All ants attack spiders*. It is, I hope, clear that the utterance of the statement is vague only because the upshot (the statement) is. In saying that ants attack spiders one says exactly what he wants to say, and could not say it any better.

identity. In the study of Language which follows this volume, we shall pursue the investigation of the elements of conventional upshots in considerable detail.

To speak about a conventional upshot requires that we refer to it. That will normally imply a *theoretical identification* of the upshot. This kind of identification must be strongly contrasted with the practical identification of the upshot in a producing act. For one thing, a conventional upshot is not theoretically identified in the producing act, though, from the fact that someone makes a theoretical identification of the upshot, it follows that he could practically identify it in a producing act and that he know how to produce it. The difference may be obscured by the fact that we normally refer to conventional upshots by, as it were, simulating the acts which would produce them. We say, for example, 'The statement that Bess is a bore', where we would naturally make that statement by saying 'Bess is a bore'. But this is not invariably required. One might refer to that same statement as the subject-predicate statement consisting of a diminutive personal name reference after 'Elizabeth' to a person presumed known to the speaker plus a characterization tested for in such and such a way. One of the things we would hope to accomplish in our theory of Language is the development of categories for giving such theoretical identifications of Language acts and their upshots.

It may be worth observing at this point that when we do make theoretical references to conventional upshots or their elements we are not necessarily referring to anything else. This becomes especially important when we are concerned with the analysis of productive Language acts in which we make reference to other things. In particular, care must be taken not to suppose that the element which we refer to and hence identify in performing the conventional act—the referent, if you wish—is identical with the corresponding element of the upshot—which we might describe as a reference to the object. This distinction is connected with the much advertised distinction between the 'extension' and the 'intension' of an expression. The distinction, though familiar, is overlooked even by philosophers and logicians who ought to know better.[4]

---

[4] Thus Strawson (*Individuals*, pp. 15ff.) seems to hold that when an audience hears a speaker refer to, hence identify, a referent, they also directly identify that referent; in fact, what they identify in the first instance is the speaker's reference to the object, and then perhaps the identification is only practical. To appreciate the necessity for this intermediary identification of the reference, observe that Strawson's characterization of identification would equally well apply to selecting or picking out or laying hands upon the object physically. The initiating agent selects an object; his respondent then selects an object; and there is a question whether they have selected the same object. But verbal identification is patently something different from selection. It necessarily proceeds by way of a conventional

9. THE CONVENTIONAL SYNDROME

In the course of this part we have observed a number of characteristic features of conventional behaviour which when assembled together into constellation reveal in a striking way the self-identifying nature of the conventional. First, one could identify a conventional act only if he knew how to do that kind of act, were it specified in agent-neutral terms. Second, an agent could do a conventional act only if he 'knew what he was doing', in the sense of being able to identify that act in the behaviour of others, and be capable of self-consciousness. It is but a small step from there to the use of Language, the possession of which in sufficient degree affords the possibility of (theoretical) knowledge by reflection of one's own purposes. Third, conventional behaviour is a type of conformative behaviour underlain by enabling rules which are rules for succeeding. Finally, for the special case of productive conventional acts, we have seen that conventional upshots are produced in their productions, there being no need for any external standard against which identity would be determined, and, furthermore, one could not identify such an upshot unless he knew how to produce it on his own. None of these conditions taken singly appears to be a sufficient condition for conventional behaviour. There are many kinds of non-conventional conformative behaviour underlain by enabling rules, capability for which would seem to imply self-consciousness, e.g., batting a baseball. There also seem to be kinds of non-conventional behaviour which one could not identify without knowing how to do in some small degree, e.g., plugging in an electrical cord. There may be rules for succeeding which do not underlie conventional behaviour, e.g., the rules embodied in maps. There are finally non-conventional upshots which are produced in

---

intermediary; when it is verbally identified, the object is, if you wish, selected, *via* a reference. The listener must suppose he has identified the speaker's reference before he can himself proceed to identify the object.

The same mistake is embedded in the Carnap method of designatory rules (*Introduction to Semantics*, no. 12). Carnap sometimes supposes that you can fix the sense of a referring expression by saying what its referent is. But here, surely, Frege was right. You can give the sense, not by giving the referent, but only by giving the sense, or what Carnap himself in other places called an *individual concept*.

Clarity regarding these matters demands, as it turns out, that we distinguish not only the (possibly non-conventional) referent and the reference, which is an element of the conventional upshot, but also (what I call) the *referring use*, which is an element of the conventional act by which the upshot may be produced. The use may be 'realized' even if the act is unsuccessful and no reference be 'contributed' to the upshot. Also the same reference may be contributed by way of realizing different uses.

their productions, notably (linguistic) sentences. This last example makes it appear doubtful that even the concurrent presence of these features is sufficient for conventional behaviour. But they are a mark of the conventional. They are, in medical language, a syndrome of the conventional.

Part Five

THE USE OF LANGUAGE

---

1. LANGUAGE ACTS

[The use of Language is defined as conventional behaviour which may be done by way of collateral acts of inscribing, *e.g.*, by writing. The chief novelty of this procedure is to bring the idea of saying something into connection with the possibility of failure. The restriction of Language to what is possibly inscriptional is apparently somewhat *ad hoc*, though it seems to impose the needed delimitation. This definition is not to be so construed as to make written forms of expression in any way primary, and does not conflict with the linguist's working conception of Language as speech. This definition of the use of Language is not in terms of what is or might be understood; it is abstracted from the use of Language for purposes of communicating, recording, or from any other such further purpose; it is directed to the behaviour of a single agent, hence does not much consider the kind of reciprocity characteristic of contracts. While the use of Language is usually collateral to the attainment of some further purpose, examples of Language acts as such can be found. Language acts may be productive, effective, or endotychistic; endotychistic uses of Language are alternatively called calculative. Finally, Language acts are contrasted with hybridized conventional action and conventionalized hybrid action, and with Language-dependent states, especially states of mind.]

We now enter onto the last lap of our investigation, the use of Language, which we wish to define as a species of animal behaviour. If asked to say in a rough preliminary way what I take the use of Language to be, I should come forward with something of the following sort. The use of Language is a type of behaviour that requires the employment of conventionally determined upon, repeatable devices, these to be called expressions, that employment to be in conformity with rules that can be taught and learned, where the devices in question may be of many sorts, including written and spoken words, symbols, gestures, winks and nods, lighted lanterns, and indeed almost anything that can be made or moved on repeated occasions by animals. The use of Language, or, more briefly 'Language' (read: 'capital language'), is to be contrasted with (1) *languages*, here taken to comprise the various tongues of mankind, natural or contrived, and every manner of notational system, (2) subject-matters and theories, which I call *departments of Language*, and (3) *manners* of using Language, *e.g.*, written, spoken, or gestural forms, the characteristic styles of science, mathematics, literature, and daily life, *etc.*, all of which I shall call *styles of linguistic modality*. In a sequel to this volume, we shall look at these other ideas and relate them to the central idea of the use of Language.

We are now in position to make the provisional explanation of Language more concrete.

Our programme has been to provide in order definitions of behaviour, action, proficient behaviour, conformative behaviour, and conventional behaviour, each being a species of what precedes it in the list, the line of definitions representing a growing behavioural sophistication in agents as viewed by observers. We may now back up the appeal to 'conventionally determined upon', and shall proceed to define the use of Language as a species of conventional behaviour. A *differentia* is wanted, for there appear to be kinds of conventional behaviour which are not Language. Standing sentry, by no apparent means a Language act, may require the display of costume and emblem, where these are certainly conventional devices which may be put on time and time again. Likewise with curtseying, purchasing, and saluting. Consider also raising the host: the priest does the act by making conventional movements in conformity with the rules, and he may succeed or fail; but such a sacramental performance does not look like a use of Language.

I shall take it as given that the following are clear cases of kinds of Language action, or, as I shall dub them, uses of Language.[1] Asserting propositions, *e.g.*, that $e = 4\cdot770 \times 10^{-10}$ e.s.u., that π is a transcendental number, or that Akbar was a Mogul emperor, questioning (which may be of many kinds), conjecturing, making assumptions (as in 'Let us assume'), postulating; expressing intention, hope, desire; reporting pains, memories, dreams; promising, ordering, welcoming, thanking, praying; cursing, cheering; writing one's name, naming, and counting. (Some may regard the latter three items as question-

---

[1] These are examples of Austin's *illocutionary forces*. See *How to do Things with Words*, esp. Lectures VIII–XII.

able.) Examples of kinds of conventional behaviour which do not at least on the surface appear to be uses of Language are curtseying, purchasing, saluting, raising the host, and presenting arms. These are small samples. But they already suggest a *differentia*. All the types of apparently non-Language conventional behaviour are ones in which the performance is, as it were, imprisoned in a single medium. Curtseying, saluting, *etc.*, are themselves quite special kinds of movement. In our terminology, such types of action are endotychistic. The underlying conventions are constitutive of the practice. That is also true for certain of our examples of uses of Language, *e.g.*, writing one's name, which is something that requires writing. The suggestion, one which accords well with the logician's commonest first view of Language as a system of signs, is this: *A Language act is a conventional act, the purpose of which could in principle, on some occasion, by someone, be attainable by way of a collateral act of inscribing, that is, by way of the use of inscribed or graphic expressions.* As a general rule, if no restriction follows from the characterization of a type of conventional action regarding how the purpose in question might be attained, we may assume the possibility of collateral, inscriptional action, and hence that the act is a Language act.

I shall presently attempt to justify the choice of *differentia*. But for the moment it may be well to observe that our definition certainly does not conflict with the linguist's first view of Language as *speech*, as something lingual. I would gladly agree that Language acts are most characteristically and commonly done *viva voce*. All that I wish to claim is that acts of the same kind, if the kind is a use of Language, might also be done inscriptionally; I am saying that Language is something which some speakers could learn to write, even if no one ever does.[2]

Let us now consider the proposed definition step by step. We shall suppose that an observer is telling us about someone who is using Language, and shall consider whether or not what the observed agent does would meet our definition. When one speaks, writes, gestures, *etc.*, something happens on a particular occasion, at a particular time,

[2] Some conjectured equivalences: what linguists commonly call an *utterance* is a spoken Language act. Similarly, what Austin (*op. cit.*, *e.g.*, pp. 95–97) calls a *rhetic* act is a spoken Language act, a 'speech act'. I think that Austin's rhetic acts are all of them what he calls *locutionary acts* (*e.g.*, pp. 94f.). Whether all his locutionary acts are also rhetic acts is not entirely clear. I believe they are not, in which case I conjecture that Austin's 'locutionary act' corresponds with my 'Language act'. Austin's 'illocutionary forces', as noted earlier, correspond to my 'uses of Language'. For Austin, every locutionary act is an illocutionary act and conversely. This would correspond to a thesis, which I maintain, that every Language act is of some one or more kinds—is an instance of some one or more uses of Language—and that every use of Language is a type of Language act.

within the body of some one particular animal; *i.e.*, a sequence of animal movements occurs. We familiarly suppose that a talking, writing, gesturing, *etc.*, creature may be held accountable in various ways for what issues from his movements; hence, this is behaviour. What he does, moreover, is something which a true report would imply that he was meaning to do, *i.e.*, *say*. The verbal test for action gives a positive result. What is at once most novel and suspicious about our definition is the way it brings Language under the possibility of success and failure. One may feel that if someone speaks and says his words, there is no room for failure. But, nevertheless, we can turn up ways in which failure is possible, and in doing that achieve what I think is a rather penetrating view into the workings of Language. Consider the case of promising: It is essential to an act of promising that the promise should be given to some one or other intelligent creature in particular. This can be taken as a condition of success for promising. I cannot make a promise to a robot; so, should I do an act of promising, addressing myself to a robot which I take to be a man, I shall fail to make the promise, though I am, nonetheless, meaning to make a promise.[3]

It remains to see that other hasps to which the concept of action, and conventional action in particular, are fastened are available for securing the use of Language. The completion of a Language act will always involve some type of collateral action, *e.g.*, writing down a sentence. But, as our theory demands, acts of these characteristically collateral kinds may be done on their own, as when one simply mouths (meaningful) words. Language acts may themselves be done collaterally to something else, and usually are, as when one person says something in order that another may know. But again, Language acts may be done simply on their own, without collateral connections, as when I comment privately but vocally on the state of my garden, or even when I make a promise, committing myself thereby, of course, but not as a means of doing something else, such as imparting confidence to my respondent. (I may succeed in the act of promising even though my respondent doubts that I shall do as I promise.)

I claim, in short, that the use of Language fits very well indeed within our analysis of action. It is, furthermore, clear that the use of

---

[3] Such conditions of failure correspond to Austin's A-2 infelicity conditions, *op. cit.*, pp. 34f. I have heard people expressly deny that one may utter meaningful words meaning to say something and fail. But since the question is seldom explicitly raised, the denial is more often implicit. Thus E. J. Lemmon ('On Sentences Verifiable by their Use', *Analysis*, 1962, pp. 86–89) argues that utterances of the form, 'I promise that P' ('I promise to do A'?), are verifiable by their use and that we may succeed in promising 'merely by using such sentences' (p. 89). An intriguing idea, but it will not stand without qualification, for the utterance cannot by itself assure the satisfaction of all the indicated conditions of success.

Language is something that can be acquired, that one can learn to do. It is something at which one cannot fail, unless he *knows how*, e.g., I cannot fail to make a promise unless I know how to make promises. Moreover, I cannot promise unless I be capable of finding words to accomplish the task. So the use of Language apparently is a kind of proficient behaviour. Now a person may know how to use Language according to one set of conventions or another, in English or French or in semaphore signalling. He would then need to have learned the rules of English, French, or semaphore. So the use of Language appears to be a species of conformative behaviour. Finally, the use of Language is conventional. What one learns to do in following a convention is to make his purpose identifiable in his movements, in the expressions, he employs. Nowhere is the self-identifying nature of conventional behaviour more easily illustrated than with Language. Somehow or other one succeeds in saying what he means to say, only by saying what he means. It may seem impossible to separate what he is doing from what he shows himself to be doing, just because success depends upon his showing what he is doing in doing it. That is of the essence of conventional behaviour, which I hope has now been sufficiently investigated to secure a collateral demystification of Language.

We may usefully contrast the use of Language with what it might replace in the preconventional life of man, for thereby we may anticipate and counter an objection which might otherwise be lodged against our choice of a specific difference for the definition of Language. One might have protested that there is a use of Language which surely must be spoken out, cannot be done in script or print, *viz.*, an expression of pain. But it seems to me that what lies under this protest does not damage but rather vindicates our choice of *differentia*. So let us compare saying 'It hurts' with an unrestrained 'ouch' and also with a completely untutored scream of pain. In saying 'It hurts' one would indeed be doing a Language act. A person would not succeed in such an act were he not to make the fact that he was reporting pain identifiable from his words. But one might also do that by writing it on a piece of paper (say, before the doctor's eyes). Reports of this kind can be given in script. Now a report of pain is surely not a *mere* expression of pain. An example of this last might be the untutored scream of the infant or the puppy-dog. Such would not necessarily even qualify as behaviour. The scream is, if you wish, a 'natural sign' of pain. No creature in this world ever completely surmounts the threat of suffering in that way. Not even the staunchest could always put down every sign of every kind of hurt. It is nonetheless true that at a certain stage of development some animals learn to suppress expressions of pain sometimes, which

325

expressions, if they occur, thus come to qualify as a kind of behaviour. Interestingly, we might come to express pain by uttering a sound like 'ouch' which we have been conditioned to let out when in pain and which, indeed, might on *other occasions* be uttered as a word, as an element of a conventional pain report. But in such behaviour 'ouch' clearly is not always pronounced as a word, but may also erupt as a 'natural sign' of the pain, a surrogate wince, entirely a part of the agent's suffering. The 'ouch' is rather like what the sea, by some quirk, might seem to write along the shore, or what the wind might cast across the sky in clouds. The immediate conclusion is that the expression of pain is not always a kind of use of Language, and it is therefore no objection to this account that we cannot always write down our screams.

Consider now when one would utter the sound 'ouch'. There would seem to be at least four cases. First, the sound 'ouch' is driven from one by the blow; he could not possibly have been expected to keep it in, and the vocal pain reaction does not even qualify as behaviour; it is something that happens to the animal, like palpitations or blanching. Second, one says 'ouch' but might by sufficient exercise of self-control have stifled it; in this case sounding 'ouch' is an item of behaviour. Third, one says 'ouch' with the intention of drawing the attention of another to his pain; the child loudly complains in his mother's presence; in this case he acts, though he is not necessarily doing a Language act. Fourth, one says 'ouch' wishing to draw the attention of another, say his mother, to his pain by way of making her understand that he wishes her to see that he is in pain; that is a conventional and a Language act. It is essential to this latter kind of act that the child should show in his act that he wishes his mother to know that he is expressing pain. There are any number of ways in which he could have done this: by turning his face, or accentuating a wince, or sending a note. But the result is Language and not a mere expression of pain.[4]

The burden of this discussion has been to show that vocal expressions of pain are not counter-examples to my thesis that a Language purpose could in principle be attained by way of inscriptional collateral acts. There is another type of counter-example which I acknowledge. Certain rituals may require the recitation of prayer by a priest. We are certainly inclined to allow that such praying is a form of Language, in contrast, say, with the conventional acts of opening the Ark of the Covenant or making the sign of the cross. But

---

[4] Expressing pain as a use of Language will be examined in the sequel. The above example was rough at best, and properly not a Language act at all, but rather an act to which the use of Language is collateral, that of letting mother know.

if ritual demands that these prayers be *recited*, they could not be done inscriptionally and hence would not qualify as Language by my definition. Allowing this, I would explain it by appealing to my choice of a *differentia*, which would thereby achieve additional support as an analysis of other, more straightforward kinds of case. Using my criterion for Language, I would submit that we are inclined to call the ritual recitation of a prayer Language and the opening of the Ark not, only and precisely because the prayer is sung or spoken in a language which could be written down, while nothing comparable could be said about the opening of the Ark. But then it also seems that the prayer itself could be written down as a private supplication to God. Perhaps the uttering of a prayer in full service is indeed a different kind of Language act from the mute penitant's pious letter to God—that is a question that is hard to resolve—but even if it is, leaving the counter-example intact, still the ritual recitation of a prayer is regarded as Language only by cause of its immediate associations with praying generically taken, which, we noticed, may be done inscriptionally.

I must now say something in justification of the *differentia* of the use of Language, that the purposes in question should be attainable by way of inscriptional movements. I have already stated that this does not conflict with the linguist's preferred view of Language as speech. Nor does it embarrass the priority of gesture. What is wanted is something which sets Language off from other kinds of conventional behaviour; and, with an eye on our examples, I suggested that Language is something possibly done by graphic or inscriptional means. Some, perhaps conceding that this works well enough in fact, may still find it inadmissibly *ad hoc* and artificial. I do not think that it is, but neither do I think that the distinction is very important. As it turns out, most types of conventional behaviour may, at a certain level of abstraction, be replaced by the use of Language. The crippled girl may put words in place of a curtsey, may signalize her respect in that way; or some other kind of God-displaying demonstration might take the place of elevating the Host. Paying respect and invoking and displaying the presence of God are abstracted from and become possible replacements for curtseying and raising the Host. But even if such 'abstraction' is always possible (which is at least questionable) we ought not to legislate the less abstract out of existence. Something like a formal criterion distinguishing Language from other kinds of conventional behaviour is therefore desirable. I think the suggested criterion works, possibly with doubtful inclusions and rough edges. Apart from the possible counter-example of ritualistic prayer, uncertainty arises especially for those types of conventional behaviour which can be done only

327

inscriptionally. I harbour doubt whether all these do qualify as uses of Language. Examples are calculating, in the literal sense, as when we add or multiply or differentiate functions. My immediate (hence, in this kind of case, most reliable) inclination is to say that these do count as Language; but I suspect that some would move in the contrary direction. Now I think that something really justifies my appeal to inscriptions; it is not merely *ad hoc*. While the original and usual medium for the use of Language is probably speech-cum-gesture, and certainly not script or print, it does seem that, for the purpose of theoretical investigation, conventional upshots are best presented as produced in script. The reason is quite simple: The traces of the product left in script on stone or paper are less ephemeral than, and can be reproduced in ways which are relatively independent of, such personal factors as the pitch of the voice, and all else which makes phonemic analysis a difficult technique. The demand that the purpose of a Language act could be attained by way of inscriptional movements is companion to our conception of Language as something conventional that is produced in its productions. For purposes of illustration and study we want something that at once replicates the producing act and that may be put together independently of and preserved beyond the life of the producing act. Until recently mankind had devised nothing superior to the use of writing for that purpose. Writing has thereby become a kind of controlling vehicle for the use of Language. It might have been different if our ancestors had had the use of tape recorders or sound-preserving boxes instead of styluses and chisels.

This is not 'proof', only explanation. Indeed there is some risk here of obscuring an important distinction, that between transcribing something and writing something. The observation if true might be taken to show that graphic means have evolved historically to facilitate the *transcription* of Language, and some linguists have held that view. But now we may transcribe types of phenomena which are not themselves instances of Language acts, *e.g.*, bird songs. Transcribing a Language act, as done, say, by a field linguist, is no more an act of the kind transcribed than transcribing the hoot of an owl is the hoot of an owl. Now I am not making the trivial claim that Language can be transcribed; I hold, rather, that any kind of Language act may be done by way of a collateral act of inscribing; a collateral act of inscribing may therefore be at least part of a Language act of any kind. Transcribing, I would argue, is itself a special type of use of Language, instances of which not merely may but must be done by way of collateral acts of inscribing. Now transcriptions of phenomena are characteristically made for purposes of record and theoretical perusal. These same purposes, I have held, explain why inscriptional

328

forms have evolved to subserve the use of Language. The conclusion is that not all inscriptional Language acts are acts of transcribing, though all acts of transcribing are inscriptional Language acts. What is the difference? The key word in my statement was 'replicate'. An inscriptional act 'replicates' a possible Language act, whereas an act of transcribing certainly does not necessarily replicate what is transcribed. Where there are known ways of writing, established orthographies, *etc.*, as today there are for most natural languages, the possibility of inscriptional replication is assured by the existence of variant written expressions. Elsewhere, *e.g.*, for hitherto unwritten languages and for gesture, I claim only that the same Language purposes which may be sought by use of such expressions could be attained by *equivalent* inscriptional means. When a conventional purpose cannot be thus attained, *e.g.*, the opening of the Ark of the Covenant, that purpose does not determine a use of Language.

An inscription, literally conceived, is not an inscriptional act, but the residue or record of such an act. I have observed that it may be important that we should have such records. I shall, however, also tendentiously employ 'inscription' to mean both a kind of inscriptional movement and the product of a productive, inscriptional act.

It will be well now to stop and consider how our view of the use of Language differs from that of the linguists. By and large, those modern linguists who derive from Bloomfield (*Language*) and Z. Harris (*Structural Linguistics*) are conscientiously sceptical about any appeal to 'meanings'. They generally (though not consistently) suppose that the occurrence of ultimate units, so-called phonemes, may make a difference in the meanings of utterances, and that other units, so-called morphemes, mark specific differences in the meaning of utterances. But we are admonished not to talk about meaning *per se*. These facts, about difference in meaning, are to be determined by noting the differing reactions of native speakers to utterances that contain recurring and alternately occurring phonological patterns. In contrast, I feel no compunction about 'meanings', and shall indeed work out a scheme for defining meanings in terms of the indications of conditions of success that must be part of any conventional act.

The linguist declares himself to be engaged in a part of the study of interpersonal behaviour. The field of study, more narrowly defined, is that of characteristic responses that people make to sounds made by other people in specifiable social situations. We need not for present purposes niggle over what strikes me as an unjustified restriction of the field to (1) human animals, (2) speech, and (3) social intercommunion, for perhaps these are the predominating and hence controlling kinds of case. What is more objectionable is that the linguist appears to hold that there really is no such thing as linguistic

329

behaviour. So far as I can see, he would have to allow that sneezes and belches are meaningful utterances, duly consisting of morphemic and phonemic elements. Part of what inspires my efforts is the desire to be able to explore the gulf between saying something and such obviously non-linguistic happenings as sneezes. The linguist appears to hold that we can pass from the analysis of acts of uttering sounds to the analysis of acts of communicating with fellow creatures, to the almost total neglect of acts of saying something—the use of Language—which lie sandwiched between. They regard the study of meaning, when they even consider it, to be part of the investigation of interpersonal behaviour. From grammar to communication, and Language be damned. My efforts are to explain what it is to say and to mean something, where this is but one important type of performance which is regularly collateral to the ends of conveying information and social intercommunion in general.

The linguist understandably puts great emphasis on the 'social situation'. In order to isolate the relevant elements of utterances it must be assumed that relevant features of the 'social, cultural, and interpersonal situation' remain constant. It is they which give meaning to the utterance. Often, it seems, the linguist feels he need do nothing more about meaning than make some blanket allusion to the 'social situation' (see, *e.g.*, Harris, *op. cit.*, pp. 12–41, pp. 172f., and appendix, pp. 186–95). In a more systematic frame of mind, he may go on to suggest that perhaps, if we cared to, we could isolate elements of meaning by considering the responses provoked by the substitution of complete utterances into varying social situations. This appears to effect an extension upon the linguist's method of agreement and differences by, as it were, enlarging the scope of the utterance to include the social situation itself. Just as in morphological analysis one part of the utterance is regarded as a context for the other part, so the whole utterance is now regarded as part of the context for elements of the social situation. Now this way of bringing in elements of the social situation as elements of meaning initially looks quite promising, suggesting something like what I call conditions of success. But what is missing, again, is any awareness that the relevant elements of the situation must be indicated in the utterance.

I suspect that the linguists may sometime soon have a great deal to tell us about the phenomena of Language. But that will not happen until they leave off avoiding the subject, which is not so much the making of sounds for purpose of social intercourse, but acts of saying something. I would be gratified if my own second-order investigation of how we think about behaviour in general and the use of Language in particular would be of any value in drawing their trained attention to the interesting range of facts which they have hitherto mostly passed by with little more than a disparaging glance. At any rate, I shall, in a sequel to this volume, have occasion to draw further comparisons between this theory and structural linguistics.[5]

My definition of the use of Language may not be exactly what the reader might first have expected. I have quite deliberately steered away from defining Language in terms of what might be *understood*, or in terms of *communication*. 'Understood' suggests the presence of an audience to which the act is being addressed. But that is not required for using Language. Admittedly, interlocutors are sometimes necessary for the success of Language acts, *e.g.*, promises; also, the speaker's attainment of the further purposes to which his use of Language is collateral normally depends upon his getting his interlocutors to understand what he says. But the achievement of understanding does not affect the identity of what the speaker says. Even with interlocutors present, one does not normally speak to get the others to understand; one may speak in the hope either that the others will or will not understand, or without considering the question at all. 'Understand' is, at all events, an intolerably vague word, which seems to grow vaguer with every new book on aesthetics and psychology. It covers a gamut comprehending everything from the merest identification of what goes on to the most impressionistic penetrations. Even if we take 'understand' in some usefully confined sense, where we always understand *what* and not *why*, and where understanding is in consideration of convention, we must not forget that the use of Language is not the only kind of behaviour which qualifies, and hence that being understandable does not afford a sufficient delimitation of Language acts. It would seem more promising for us to try to explain 'understand Language' by way of explaining what it is we understand, rather than *vice versa*. Another *possible* objection to the use of 'understand' is that it is not clear whether it is only *successful* Language acts which can be understood. Now I think that our account does reveal what it is about 'understand' that makes such a strong appeal. Our first stipulation regarding the conventional was in terms of making purpose identifiable in one's movements. We laid down as a necessary condition for the success of a Language act that a suitably prepared audience should be able to identify, in the practical sense, what was said. Language intent or purpose must be open to public inspection. Now 'understand' seems, in a usefully narrow and familiar sense of the word, to mean something like identify what is said from the words. The possibility of being understood in that sense of 'understand' is indeed

[5] Some linguists do not fall under my ban. I daresay that most traditional descriptive linguists do not; nor do those structural linguists who avow an interest in what they variously call 'semantics', 'sememics', 'semasiology', *etc.*

a necessary condition for having succeeded in the use of Language. 'Communication' is also a word of uncertain meaning. It has become common to speak about communication between birds or even between robots. So employed it appears to mean something like interresponses between objects that are at least analogically animate. But let us confine it to instances where one animal takes measures to let other animals know how things are. Communicating in this sense clearly does not necessarily involve the use of Language. If words fail him the bartender may let the drunk know how things are by simply tossing him out of the bar. He brings about the desired effect without recourse to Language, although Language might normally have been employed for the task. If, however, we return to a more familiar sense of 'communicate' which might be glossed as requiring use of Language, we would be bringing in too much. A person may use Language without meaning to communicate, as when he writes down his observations without intending to pass them on to others, or even without meaning to consult his notes on some later occasion. Also, it seems to me that one might very well succeed in (*e.g.*) making a report, and yet fail utterly to communicate. Hence Language is separated from communication as something which is at most characteristically collateral to acts of communicating. And even if we tighten the idea of communication to mean having an effect by way of using Language, that makes only more obvious that 'communicate' will not do for defining the use of Language.

Relatedly, it is worth noting that the use of Language usually involves only a single agent, whether animal or corporate. Reciprocal action between agents is behaviour of a different order. Thus promising (which is a use of Language) may be set off from a number of different kinds of things which lawyers sometimes classify together as promises, including contracts, agreements, and dispositions of various kinds. A contract differs from a promise in that it involves two agents at a minimum. I am prepared to allow that in making a contract each party, by the way, makes a promise; but I think that in this case the act done by each party is a hybrid which has as its Original Purpose the binding of the other party to do as promised. The case is in its relation to the use of Language closely analogous to that of communication. A principle of our theory is that any kind of act might be *The* Act done: that there is no kind of act which *must* be collateral to something else, or which can exist only as an abstraction. We have been using this principle in order to argue that it would be unavailing to try to define the use of Language in terms of communication. It is essential that agents may do Language acts *simpliciter*, however it may be that Language is introduced within more encompassing spheres of behaviour.

I have already indicated examples of Language acts *simpliciter*. These are most easily found if we consider people who, momentarily free of the pressures of the world, have nothing else to do but talk. Thus an unaccompanied spectator at a football game may pass the time by counting up the officials on the field, or by calculating an estimate of the number of spectators on the other side; or he may cheer when the home team scores, just cheer without any further purpose. Again, a carefree ambler with a naturalistic bent may find himself vocally identifying the kind of trees he passes by. These are examples of Language acts *simpliciter*.

Evidently Language acts *simpliciter* are relatively rare. We usually use Language collaterally to the attainment of further purposes. It is that which accounts for the appeal of 'communicate' for defining Language. In some quite broad sense of 'communicate', Language acts are usually done collaterally to or hybridized into acts of communication. One could plausibly argue that the importance of Language in our lives might be traced to its use for purposes of communication; that communication is the ultimate rationale of Language (whatever might be the ultimate rationale of communication). That is probably true; we first learn to produce Language for purposes of *presenting* what we produce *to others*. Though, as I have argued, we may later learn to inhibit the presentation, much as we might make and discard a work of art.

The fact that one might do a Language act collaterally to nothing else gives licence for treating Language as an autonomous form of behaviour. There is no other workable alternative. Should we attempt to chart the ways in which the use of Language contributes to the affairs of life, we should never end. There is very little to which the use of Language might not be collateral. The use of Language, even taken autonomously, restrictedly reveals what these further connections regularly are, particularly in the commitments engendered by the use of Language, *e.g.*, the commitment to keep a promise, or one's commitment to the truth of a statement he makes.

Certainly, a person may successfully make a promise without intending to do as promised or without intending to do anything else either, such as assuring the other party or binding him in his turn; relatedly, one may make a promise he fails to keep. But these characteristic intentions and commitments (Austin's Γ conditions, see *op. cit.*, Lecture IV) may nevertheless be brought into connection with conditions of success, mention of which would contribute to the definition of a use of Language. An agent cannot at one and the same time succeed in making a promise and *express* his intention not to do as he promises. The condition in question, that the agent should not express an intention not to do as he appears to say he will, figures even more strongly, as a condition for doing an act of promising. For, if one is making a promise he must be taken to know, hence believe, that he is committing himself to do a certain act; that belief would be nullified by an expression of intention to the contrary.

Our method, then, will always be to define a use of Language in abstraction from the further purposes it may subserve and the meeting of commitments it engenders, except so far as those purposes and commitments must be mentioned and indirectly brought into the definition. There are dangers in this method. For one thing, it must always be clear that we are dealing with the agents who are capable of simply talking without further purpose, of that kind of detachment from the pressures of life. This analysis may encourage us mistakenly to cast as conventional hybrids, types of action which are probably better described as units from which Language acts are abstracted. We shall, for example, explain acts of instructing and persuading as hybrids in which the Original Way is a type of Language action. The result is a distortion, and therefore objectionable. The supposed agent would most likely first have learned to convey what he wishes to say to others, before becoming able simply to say it with indifference to any further purpose. However, if we do assume animals of sufficient sophistication to do Language acts *simpliciter*, then, in their lives, those hybrids into which we shall analyse acts of communicating, persuading, *etc.*, may be thought of as replacing the more primitive attempts to get through to other people.

Uses of Language are either endotychistic, productive, or effective; the respective measures of success are conventional achievements, products (upshots), and effects. Examples of endotychistic uses of Language are writing one's name and calculating, in the formal literal sense. As a more perspicuous name for such types of behaviour I propose 'calculative uses of Language'. Conjecturing and promising are productive uses of Language, and the corresponding upshots are conjectures and promises. Giving gifts and introducing people are effective uses of Language; transfers of property and introductions are corresponding conventional effects. A given use of Language, *e.g.*, signing a document, may be all three, endotychistic, effective and productive. We shall in no. 4 consider these three types of Language use and their relations in greater detail.

Before quitting this introductory section it would be well to notice that there are a variety of kinds of action, state, disposition, and occurrence which, while depending upon the fact that the supposed agent have acquired various Language uses, do not themselves qualify as uses of Language. Examples are conventional hybrids, such as acts of communicating, and such other types of act as looking up a book in a card catalogue, and episodes of reciprocal conventional behaviour like the drawing of contracts. When we ascribe such acts, states, dispositions to an agent, we imply that the animal be able to say what his act, disposition, or state, *etc.*, is, though these acts, *etc.* need not actually qualify as Language acts. Included here is everything which dwells within the halls of deliberative, contemplative, and reflective *thought*: wishes, hopes, and regrets. These may reveal themselves in dispositions to use Language or as 'mental acts' of inhibiting the use of Language, or states thereupon consequent.

In the balance of this part we shall be largely occupied in isolating Language acts from acts collaterally done thereto and from acts to which Language acts themselves may be collateral or into which they may be hybridized.

2. LEXICAL ACTION

[Language acts are always done by way of collateral acts that consist of sequences of meaningful movements. The immediate purposes of such collateral acts might be attained although the ultimate Language purpose is not attained; also, the immediate purpose of the collateral act could be the (ultimate) purpose of an act. Acts having such a purpose are called *lexical acts*. While lexical action is defined with reference to the use of Language, it is not itself a species of the use of Language. The relation between the use of Language and lexical action consists in the facts that (1) a condition for doing a Language act is that the agent should do a lexical act, and (2) a condition of success for a lexical act is that all the constitutive movements should have uses (meanings) in conventions pertaining to a single language. This last is made explicit by stipulating criteria for lexical action according to which we prove the existence of lexical action by applying tests to Language acts, where typal identity is established by giving an ordered enumeration of the types of movements (having uses in conventions) which are made. Lexical action is a type of conformative but non-conventional behaviour that may be either productive, endotychistic, or both.]

Language acts are conventional. Such action requires that the agent should make a sequence of movements indicating conditions of success; the purpose of the act would be identified by listing these conditions. In the case of conventional action, the agent must have learned to make the behaviour-constituting movements. It follows that the making of a sequence of movements constituting a Language act itself qualifies as a type of action.

The type of action in question has been introduced in association with the use of Language. That is no surprise. We are taught to do such acts in tight connection with the acquisition of conventional proficiencies. The purposes of such acts continue to be most commonly sought collaterally to the use of Language. We may describe the movements as 'meaningful movements', because they have meaning or use in conventions, *i.e.*, conventions allow that conditions of success could be indicated by the making of such movements. But for all that, the type of action in question—that of making a sequence of meaningful movements—must be separated from the use of Language with which it has these tight collateral affiliations. The reasons are clear. (1) The same Language purpose might have been sought and attained by way of different lines of collateral action: I can say that I am going to buy a particular book by uttering these words, 'I am going to buy the book' or by saying, 'Voy a comprar el libro' or by simply saying 'yes' to the question whether I intend to buy the book. (2) Acts of making the same meaningful movements may be done collaterally to the attainment of different Language purposes, *e.g.*, 'yes'. (3) One may succeed in making meaningful movements without succeeding in saying anything at all, as when I answer 'yes' to the question how many people are coming for dinner. Finally (4) one may succeed in making meaningful movements without meaning to say anything at all, either (a) collaterally to the attainment of some other kind of purpose (*e.g.*, 'The rains in Spain fall mainly on the plain') or (b) collaterally to no other purpose at all, as in vacant mumblings and doodling. This type of action—making meaningful movements—though clearly related to the use of Language, as is intimated by the word 'meaningful', has characteristically different conditions of success. The relation between the two kinds of action is that a condition for *doing* a Language act is that the agent should collaterally do an act of making meaningful movements. For want of a better name, I shall call this type of action *lexical action*— an act of making meaningful movements, whether or not done collaterally to a Language act, I call a lexical act.[1]

The idea of lexical action has been introduced in relation to the use of Language. All the more reason why we should be on guard to observe the distinction between lexical action and Language. Though a Language act will always involve a collateral lexical act, a lexical act is not a Language act. That is what I have been so far chiefly concerned to argue. But I am confident that there are those who will continue to resist the distinction. Indeed, it is natural if wrong to

[1] Spoken lexical acts are what Austin calls *phatic acts* (*op. cit.*, pp. 92, 95f.). I prefer 'lexical' because I want something that will free me from confinement to phonetic expression. 'Lexical' suggests *word*, where words may be both spoken and written. 'Lexical', unfortunately, is still not right, for I want to allow for gesture, signalling, *etc.*, as well as for the utterance of inscription of words.

think about Language acts as though they are and could be nothing more than acts of repeating sequences of expressions (making meaningful movements). One does a Language act only by doing a lexical act. The question then is: what must be added to the lexical act to achieve a full-blown Language act? Clearly nothing more of the same kind, *i.e.*, nothing more in the way of meaningful movements, for surely the uttered or written words suffice.

The answer has been supplied in our observations that lexical action is usually only collateral to Language action and need not be even that. We may sum this up in the terminology of no. 14 of Part II. A necessary condition for doing a Language act is that the agent should do a collateral act having an immediate lexical purpose and an ultimate Language purpose, where the immediate purpose of the collateral act could be the purpose of an act, in which case The Act would be a Language act. The conditions of success by which lexical action is defined are different from those by which a use of Language would be defined. Nowhere is the utility of our general theory of action better seen than in its easy resolution of this difficulty. One may do a lexical act, addressing a sequence of meaningful words, 'I promise to . . .', to a manikin which he takes to be a man; he succeeds in the lexical act, though he fails in the act of promising. Again, a speaker may wish to raise a question about the ownership of an object which in fact does not exist; he gets the words out all right, and they also carry a meaning, and he succeeds to that extent—in his lexical act; but The Act is one of questioning, and here the speaker does not succeed in asking a question, in raising an issue of true or false. The existence of a suitable addressee or of a referent is not a condition of success for the types of lexical action in question, though just such lexical acts are usually done with an eye to indicating that such conditions are conditions of success for Language acts.

This way of separating the two spheres of action also brings out why they are so closely affiliated. In the terminology of our account: (1) A condition for *doing* a Language act is that the agent should do a lexical act; (2) a condition of *success* for lexical action is that there exist conventions in which every one of the movements constituting a lexical act has a use, *i.e.*, there are conventions in conformity to which such a movement, if made in course of doing a Language act, would indicate a package of conditions of success. That the constituting movements should thus have uses is also a condition for doing a Language act.

A lexical act may be summarily explained as an act of making a sequence of movements all of which are of a kind having uses in conventions pertaining to a single language, where the conditions of success defining the use could be conventionally indicated to yield a

Language act. The definition raises many questions for which we must, at the present juncture, simply assume that there are answers available. The first of these concerns how we might set about determining that the conventions in question all pertain to a *single* language. Examples of languages are tongues, dialects, ideolects, systems of notation, signalling, or what have you. The specification of the language is, in a broad sense, a task for the working linguist, or for the contriver of the notation, *etc.* There will often be a good measure of indeterminateness here, *e.g.*, over what French words may be viably transplanted into English and over the hybridizing of gestures and vocable items, as well as over the breadth of the language community.

Another more interesting question concerns how we would establish that different packages of conditions may be concurrently indicated in a single Language act. This is a large part of the notoriously difficult problem of fixing the distinction between sense and nonsense. Assuming familiar conventions pertaining to English for the words 'the', 'chair', 'is', and 'equal', there would appear to be no sense in saying 'The chair is equal'. The reason for that is that the conditions indicated by 'equal' must, to achieve a full Language act, be complemented by two independent sets of conditions which would be indicated by employment of so-called referring expressions, *i.e.*, two sets of conditions regarding the existence and the identity of objects. (See my *Modes of Referring*, Chap. I, nos. 2, 5.) That would come out once we had actually defined the use of 'equal' in terms of conditions of success. The assurance of systematic solutions to such problems clearly waits upon the provision of a well-wrought theory of Language, including what I would call a theory of conceptual valence. First steps towards such a theory will be taken in the sequel to this volume. Meantime, we can only assume that the problems have solutions.

Clearly, the use of Language dominates the notion of lexical action. The operating criteria are brought down from the criteria for Language. It will pay to make that more explicit. We have previously had occasion to anticipate the articulation of a general theory of subject matters and kinds of object according to which we specify a subject matter and define a kind of object by specifying various tests or criteria, including tests for existence and identity. (See esp. the definition of *purpose* in no. 10 of Part II.) It is always assumed that the objects are practically identified in a controlling kind of circumstance, medium, *etc.*, and that we establish existence, identity, *etc.*, by applying tests to those circumstances, *etc.* Thus, material bodies are located in regions of space at points of time; colours are located in the surfaces of bodies, natural numbers in numerical expressions;

338

purposes in items of behaviour. To be sure, the objects might not be found in or referred to as in such circumstances; *e.g.*, a number may be referred to descriptively ('the first odd perfect number'); or a colour be discerned in a beam of light; or a purpose manifested in the wishes, not the behaviour, of an animal. But proof of existence must finally involve operations upon the 'instantiating medium' or within the 'locating circumstances'. Though this form of explanation of subject-matters and objects is still far from adequately defined, it should be well enough understood to be used for present purposes.

A lexical act, I say, is located in a Language act. That sweeps in the one speck of truth in the formalist view that a Language act *is* a lexical act. The clarity of the thesis may be muddied by the fact that a Language act is in its turn located in an act (of making movements). Transparency is restored by observing that whether or not these movements are 'meaningful' and hence constituents of a lexical act is determined with reference to a Language act. The importance of this is that lexical acts are located in their collateral connections. It is by now evident, however, that a lexical act need not always be found in such a connection; it may be found on its own, just as a colour may be seen in a beam of light or a purpose be discerned in the expressed wishes and not in the behaviour of an animal. What remains essentially true is that a lexical act could be done collaterally to a Language act, just as a colour could be the colour of some body or a purpose acted with. What has just been said better captures the dependence of lexical action upon Language, which has hitherto been described somewhat openly and figuratively.

We establish the *existence* of a lexical act by parsing the Language act in which it is located into a sequence of movements each of which is then shown to have a use in some convention, all of which conventions pertain to the same language.

We individuate a lexical act as an act, *i.e.*, as a sequence of movements. Criteria of identity follow in train (see no. 21 of Part II).

We establish the *kind* of lexical action with reference to the kinds of movement into which the instantiating Language act is parsed, and relatively to the language: We give an ordered enumeration of the (meaningful) movements that constitute the act. Clearly, lexical acts of the same kind may be done collaterally to different kinds of Language act, and a lexical act may even be 'ambivalent'. Combining this stipulation regarding the typal identification of lexical action with our general theory of purpose and the typal identification of action (nos. 4, 10 of Part II), we get the (desirable) consequence that the conditions of success which determine a type of lexical action have chiefly to do with the existence of kinds of (meaningful) movement having uses in conventions pertaining to the same language.

339

Lexical acts will have other features: *e.g.*, they will be brief or long, English or Chinese, ambivalent, phonetically balanced, *etc.*, *etc.* The most interesting of these features (*e.g.*, ambivalence) would be defined by test-specifications that would have to mention the use of Language.

If what I have proposed has any merit, it would be futile to seek a totally non-conventional determination of utterances (lexical acts), or the elements of utterances, by pure statistical canvassing, say. (See K. Buehler, 'Phonetik u. Phonologie', *Travaux du Cercle Linguistique de Prague*, 1931, pp. 22–53; cited by Quine in 'The Problem of Meaning in Linguistics'.) I shall return to this point at the end of the next section.

I have now schematically stated criteria for lexical action. It remains to consider what kind of action lexical action is: conformative or non-conformative; conventional or non-conventional; endotychistic, effective, or productive.

Lexical action clearly is conformative. One cannot do such an act except by conforming to rules which are also conventions of the language in question. This does not mean that the agent is actually thereby meaning to say something. He may merely be repeating or taking down words upon the request or in mimicry of another. But his efforts might still be corrected and he would have to understand that. He conforms to (or infringes) expectations which, as he regards them, are 'warranted' or 'legitimate'.

The rules in question are rules of a language and therefore also rules for the use of Language. But the agent may not be conforming to them as rules of Language; he may, that is, not be meaning to *say* anything when he enunciates his words. But he must, if he is to succeed, at any rate conform to some of the rules of the language in question, especially derivative rules of syntax where these rules may be very fluid indeed. I am inclined to say that we could define the language by specifying the conventions, allowing that there will usually remain considerable flexibility and large tolerances. Since a lexical act is typified relative to a language, it appears that rules underlying lexical action are constitutive, this being subject to certain flexibility qualifications.

Occasionally, for so-called formal languages, such rules are actually laid down in advance, and by implication stipulate criteria of correctness. For such languages, the rules are *statutory*. For the more important case of 'natural languages', chiefly the tongues of the world, the rules are surely not usually statutory. They are codified only after the fact, as useful guides for or summaries of existing non-statutory practices.

The rules are clearly enabling rules. Lexical action is relative to a language. There is no language without conventions, and it is precisely the conventions that enable one to engage in that practice and, derivatively, to do lexical acts.

Finally, the rules are rules for succeeding. By merely conforming to the rules of a language, principally the derivative rules of syntax, the agent will succeed in his act of putting together a meaningful string of movements of meaningful types, provided that all the conditions of success are satisfied, chief among which are that he actually make the movements in question and that these movements all have uses in conventions pertaining to that language. It is, by the way, clear that this last condition may not be met. Thinking that a sequence of nonsense sounds I have heard are meaningful in the other speaker's language, I may repeat them and thereby attempt a lexical act; but I shall fail. Again, I may try to pronounce a Polish sentence and interpolate sounds that are not instances of Polish words; again I fail.

We have now arrived at the conclusion that lexical action is a species of conformative behaviour where the underlying rules are typically constitutive, non-statutory enabling rules for succeeding. The more interesting question is whether lexical action is conventional behaviour. The answer is that it is not. It is true that in doing a lexical act the agent means to conform to rules which are conventions. But it is not a condition for doing such an act that he should thereby indicate the conditions of success for his act. So long as the agent believes that these are the conventions of some single language, he need not know or even have an opinion of what the conventions are. He would, that is, have no idea what conditions of success could be indicated by conforming to those conventions. Obvious examples are lexical acts that the agent does in the course of mimicking another or as exercises in pronunciation. In short, while one does a Language act by doing a lexical act, thereby indicating conditions of success, one does not do a lexical act by doing a lexical act, and conditions of success need not be indicated. Lexical action is not conventional behaviour. A clinching argument if it is needed is this: a child may recognize a foreign language and even identify what words are being spoken in that language, thus identifying the type of lexical action in question, without himself knowing how to do such acts. But one who can identify a conventional act must also know how to do such acts (see nos. 3 and 5 of Part IV).

I turn now to the question whether lexical action is endotychistic, effective, or productive. The answer is not obvious, for it might be thought that lexical action is any or all of these. The agent will succeed at such acts if only he make movements having uses in conventions pertaining to a language in conformity with the syntactical rules of that language. It would appear then that all such acts are endotychistic. But also it might be thought that he would succeed only if he set the air resonating or got the paper, slate, or stone suitably inscribed, which suggests that such action is effective. The answer to both of these suggestions is the same. The types of movement in question have uses in conventions for Language. But we stipulate that a Language act could be done inscriptionally. The expressions employed, therefore, may, according to the operating conventions either be inscriptional or have inscriptional variants. To the extent that the latter is the case, the movements may also have any number of other variants, e.g., phonological or gestural ones; it is doubtful that they could be defined kinematically or by reference to characteristic effects. The types of movement are ideally to be regarded as equivalence classes constituted in part by possible orthographic conventions. Words, as we normally conceive them, are the chief example of expressions which have variant forms. The conclusion is that not all lexical acts are either endotychistic or effective. If our schemata (of no. 19, Part II) are to stand, then at least some types of lexical action—those which consist of stringing words together—must be productive. That, I believe, agrees with our usual way of thinking about such acts. So let us consider what the products of such action might be.

Allow first that it may be essential that such a lexical act be performed in one variant or another—sound or gesture or writing—collaterally to the attainment of some further (non-conventional) purpose such as mimicry or speech improvement. Nevertheless, we are also accustomed to speak of agent's uttering or writing down the same *sentence* over and over again. If the agent fails in producing the sentence in such cases, he fails in his lexical act, whether or not he also meant to say anything thereby. Now sentences, in the everyday sense of the word, are indeed *products* of human action, ones which competent agents can reproduce, almost at will; hence, they qualify as upshots. Because such objects are very familiar and because the production of such objects may be the measure of success for lexical action, I find nothing intrinsically unsatisfactory in the thought that lexical action may be productive. We may also allow that lexical acts may be endotychistic. But there is nothing to keep the same act from being both endotychistic and productive. I hazard the opinion that even many lexical acts consisting of expressions which are exclusively gestural or notational may be regarded as productive. What we need are tests for establishing the existence and identity of products similar to sentences. These, I think, can usually be supplied by invoking some standard way of transcribing the non-inscriptional phenomena. These are trivially available for acts which are actually done inscriptionally, by use of some system of notation. We also have stipulated that a Language purpose may be attained by inscriptional means; we are therefore assured inscriptional *equivalents* for non-inscriptional lexical acts. This promises some measure of success in our efforts to establish systematic methods of transcription and hence the possibility of regarding a broad range of lexical action as productive. I do not claim that all lexical action is productive. However, I do propose to generalize the problematic everyday notion of sentence, as follows: A sentence is a product of a successful productive lexical act. Application of the criteria of identity for such objects requires the rendering, directly or by transcription, of the movements of the successful act into a written form. Lexical acts that may be reasonably submitted to this kind of analysis are productive; such acts, if successful, produce sentences.

3. SENTENCES

[Generalizing upon the everyday notion, we define a sentence as the product of successful, productive lexical action. Such products are non-conventional upshots that are produced in their productions. Sentences in this conception are 'types' and not 'tokens'. They are sequences of types of movement. Sentences are not to be equated with the sounded or written traces which the act may leave reverberating in the air or inscribed on a page. However, the test for theoretical identity calls for inspection of the inscription which results from the transcription of the lexical act onto a piece of paper, say. It is only because there is some such test available that we are able to abstract the sentence as an object from a successful lexical act. The transcribing of sentences would appear to be a kind of endotychistic conventional behaviour, and is to be distinguished from non-conventional lexical action of producing sentences, say by writing. Sentences have various characteristics, the most interesting of which depend upon the fact that they are products of lexical action itself defined with reference to the use of Language. Any sequence of kinds of transcribable movements that could be made collaterally to the performance of a successful Language act produces a sentence. A result of this is that elliptical, ungrammatical, and 'bad' sentences generally are still sentences. A sentence may be analysed into a sequence of types of movements. Each such type of movement is a (meaningful) expression. Expressions may be classified in various ways. Provisional suggestions are made regarding the definition of non-sentential sequences or expressions, especially so-called phrases and clauses. Any attempt to elucidate these notions of sentence, expression, *etc.*, without reference to the use of Language would be unavailing.]

343

At the end of the last section, it was argued that lexical action is oftentimes productive. I proposed that we call the product of a successful lexical act a *sentence*. I believe that this touches close to the heart of our ordinary, everyday notion of a sentence. Though the notion of a sentence is notoriously problematical and I cannot claim to have resolved all the issues, it seems to me fairly clear that sentences in our ordinary conception are regarded as products of lexical action.

This definition potentially effects an extension upon the ordinary notion of a sentence. Sentences literally taken pertain only to tongues, and have both written and spoken variants. Now it may turn out that only such modes of lexical action are in fact productive. But that is not obvious. Should other modes of lexical action, *e.g.*, signalling, also prove to be productive, there will be sentences to correspond. While sentences literally taken are strings of words, I allow for the possibility of a sentence consisting of a string of symbols or gestures. The test of identity, as we formulated it in no. 2, will always involve the inspection of a written transcription. Also, ordinarily 'sentence' carries an assessment component which is absent from my definition. We are inclined to say that grammatically malformed or foreshortened strings of words are not sentences, though they might be let in by my definition. I make no apologies for these technical arrangements. It is not to be expected that such a problematical, ordinary notion as that of sentence should fit snugly into our theory. I believe, furthermore, that my notion of a sentence is a natural extension upon the everyday idea, one which has been prefigured in the writings of the other theorists.[1] I shall therefore use my notion of sentence without further compunction.

---

[1] Formal logicians are fond of calling their formulas sentences. That is not 'ordinary usage', though it probably conforms to my definition of a *sentence*. I do not deny that there are dangers in this manipulation of terminology. Indeed, I suspect that certain characteristic misconstructions made by the formal logician regarding the relation of his systems of formulas to other uses of Language are abetted by his employment of 'sentence'. Thus '$(x).\phi x \supset \psi x$', for example, is simply a formula belonging to a system of formulas, and employed in conformity with formal rules. The use of Language in question is of a kind I have called *calculative*. Now, this formal system may be employed for purposes of theorizing about other uses of Language, especially, for stating relations of entailment between Language upshots and for characterizing those upshots as necessary or contingent, or as having certain forms. In such applications the formula '$(x).\phi x \supset \psi x$' functions not as a sentence but rather more like a word employed to characterize propositions and other conventional upshots. Thus, for purposes of a certain analysis, we might wish to assert that the proposition that all cats like cheese is of the form $(x).\phi x \supset \psi x$. But the logician is apt to describe his analytic exercises in a different way. He thinks of the formula, called a sentence in the formal calculus, as rather like a skeleton of sentences that would ('should'?) be

Sentences, then, are products. It is evident that they are non-material products or upshots. One may articulate and hence produce the same sentence many times over, and others do the same. They are not conventional upshots of course, because lexical action is not conventional action. One may practically identify a sentence without knowing how to produce it oneself. However, sentences, like conventional upshots, are produced in their productions. They are produced and most fundamentally, practically identified in the same 'medium', *viz.*, a lexical act. The reason for this is as follows. Sentences are characteristically produced collaterally to the attainment of some Language purpose. The definition of a sentence on that account requires an upward reference to forms of Language. The productions in which sentences are practically identified must preserve that connection to Language action; now a sentence-producing act is just a lexical act, of a kind normally collateral to Language action. The connection between the production and the use of Language is secured by taking the producing lexical act as the instantiating production.[2]

---

[2] Some would seem actually to equate the sentence with a type of lexical or Language act. I have argued that that was Wittgenstein's opinion in the *Tractatus* (in my review of E. Stenius' book *Wittgenstein's 'Tractatus'*, *Mind*, 1963, esp. pp. 281f.). It is also implicit in Ryle's controversial advocacy of the view that there is a sharp distinction between words and sentences, a thesis which is strongly supported by my analysis of sentences as products. Ryle holds that words are *used*, while sentences are not; and he maintains that words belong to *languages* whereas sentences belong to *speech* (see 'Ordinary Language', *Phil. Rev.*, pp. 167–86; 'Use, Usage and Meaning', *Proc. Arist. Soc. Supp.*, 1961, pp. 223–30). The obvious objection is that some sentences are single words. But I think that Ryle could plausibly respond that there remains a difference. Words and stock phrases are listed in dictionaries; but to regard a word or a stock phrase as a sentence is to lift it out of the dictionary and to imagine it put to work in actual speech. Ryle, wrongly in my view, suggests that a sentence is a speech act— sentences certainly may be considered in abstraction from the acts which produce them. But the suggested equation comes close to getting at something true. A sentence, even if it consists of a single word, is, unlike a word, a *product* of speech or other modes of using Language; words are the raw materials which are employed to produce such products. Something, at all events, must be added to the utterance of a word in order to produce a sentence, if not other words then at least the circumstances of action. We have now discovered a still closer connection between sentences and Language acts with the observations that sentences are not only produced by but also identified in lexical acts, hence usually in Language acts. These observations almost validate Ryle's dictum that words have uses whereas sentences do not. We are able to employ a word to produce a sentence as well as

---

employed to express propositions having a form that the formula, in the application of the formal calculus, is used to ascribe. '$(x). \phi x \supset \psi x$' is regarded as a kind of stripped-down rendering of 'All cats like cheese', of which '$(x). cat\ x \supset$ likes cheese x' is held to be a useful and exact reformulation.

What has been said concerning sentences calls for some remarks and will possibly provoke an objection which I must try to answer. First, sentences are what, following Pierce, are called 'types' and not 'tokens'. A token of a sentence would be either the particular movements made in a particular lexical act or the actual sounds, scribblings of graphite or ink produced by the act, or such other material traces or marks as it might leave. But a sentence has been defined as a sequence of types of movement, and the same sentence may be produced over and over again as the upshot of different lexical acts. (Note, however, that the sentence is not a 'universal', *e.g.*, not the universal that might be referred to as 'production of the sentence', but an upshot. See no. 19 of Part II.) While it is required that the type have a sense, the determination of *what* sense it has is not required for establishing the identity of the sentence. Indeed, a sentence may be ambivalent, that being one possible characteristic of sentences.

The second remark is that the determination of the identity of a sentence is relative to lexical action and hence relative to a language. Allowing of the possibility of one-word sentences, the English sentence 'Rot!' is different from the German sentence 'Rot!', and the Spanish sentence '¡Red!' is different from the English sentence 'Red!'.

The objection I anticipate is this: It is incorrect to hold that a sentence is produced in its productions because a sentence is identified, not in lexical acts that produce it, but rather in the sounds or in the squiggles of graphite or ink that such acts leave traced in the air or on paper. The sentence would then be a type of mark or a type of sound. Let me first concede that surely we may identify the sentence from tracings of sound or script. But such tracings are not always available; for example, they are not available in gesture. That might licence a generalizing retreat to the common factor of movement. But I want to base myself on firmer ground than that. It is, I believe, essential to our conception of a sentence that an observer should be able to identify the sentence *in* the producing lexical act, albeit perhaps *from* the sounds he hears or the squiggles he sees. If sentences could not be practically identified in lexical action, they could not be identified in any other medium either, say on the printed page. 'But why, then, do we refer to this sentence in *this* way?'

To understand why, we must observe the distinction between the practical identification of the sentence in a lexical act (perhaps from

---

to do a Language act only because the word has a use; but then sentences, being products of successful action, are not similarly employed and have no need for uses. My view, in brief, is this: while a sentence is not to be equated with an act of saying, as Ryle suggests (*loc. cit.*, p. 229), it is dependent upon acts of saying in that it is a product of such acts, and identified in them.

the tracings) and the test by which we *theoretically* establish identity. Our definition of a sentence requires that it might be transcribed, which transcription will produce a mark on paper. We then establish, first, that a sentence has been produced and, second, which sentence has been produced by making certain observations on the mark. For example, we look up the supposed words in a dictionary, which words are themselves duly counted and identified. Indeed, it is only because there is some such test available that we are able to extract a product from the movements constituting a lexical act. But some capacity for making practical identifications of sentences in lexical acts is a precondition for giving theoretical demonstrations of identity by operations upon the written word or other transcription. The situation for sentences is closely comparable to the case of music. There we practically identify the piece most fundamentally in the performance and demonstrate identity by use of a score. (The difference is that the piece of music is brought into existence by writing the score, whereas the sentence is not brought into existence by the transcription.) How then are we to regard the mark on paper? We conjectured in no. 8 of Part IV that we establish the identity of non-conventional upshots by making a comparison with a conventional upshot. That suggests that the transcription of a sentence is a production of a conventional upshot. That suggestion is borne out by the observation that transcribing a sentence, which may be an exercise in orthography, would seem to qualify as a kind of conventional behaviour, that is both endotychistic and productive. In doing such an act, the agent must indicate that what he means to do is to write down a certain putative sentence. If I am correct, then, the conventional action of transcribing sentences must be distinguished from producing sentences, say by writing. However that may be, the thesis that sentences are practically identified most fundamentally in producing lexical acts is sustained. This does not deny that sentences may also, in a subsidiary way, be identified in transcriptions.

Using our method of criteria, a sentence may be summarily explained in the following way: Sentences are located in lexical acts. A single successful lexical act individuates a single sentence. We establish the existence of a sentence in the act (and therewith also the success of the act) by making a transcription which we then lexicographically scrutinize with the aid of some dictionary, glossary, or code to determine that each of the transcribed types of movement has a use in a convention pertaining to a single language, also consulting rules of syntax. We establish the identity of the sentence by enumerating the transcribed kinds of movement in order.

We may immediately define a variety of types of sentence characteristic in terms of related procedures. An enumeration of the transcribed movements will derivatively give a measure of the *length* of the sentence. The particular dictionary to which we appeal determines to what language the sentence belongs, and so whether it be French or Chinese, Esperanto or PM-ese. By submitting the sentence to syntactical transformations or, better, by observing what uses the dictionary assigns to the occurring expressions, we may determine whether the sentence is or is not *ambivalent*. Sentences may have many other characteristics as well, which are not easily summarized in a formula. They may be clear or obscure, vernacular or technical, elegant or ponderous, grammatical or ungrammatical, good or bad. The most interesting of these features would be determined by tests derivative from a lexicographical analysis of a transcription. All such properties are relative to a language and so, implicitly, to the use of Language.[3]

The fact that we may speak of grammatical and ungrammatical or, more generally, of good and bad sentences, shows that our notion of 'sentence' is not normatively prejudiced. A sentence, no matter how bad—and the criteria for better and worse are obviously various—is still a sentence, though it may not 'be English'. If the conventions of a language are such that one could do a Language act by producing a questionable sentence, then it is a sentence, no matter how 'bad'.

A sentence is a sequence of types of (meaningful) movement, perhaps only one ('yes'), the instancing of which movements would be sufficient to constitute a Language act according to the conventions of the language. The sentence, unlike the act of producing the sentence, is a sequence of types of movement and not a sequence of movements of the types. The sentence may be analysed into those types of movement. Each such type of movement is what we have called an 'expression'. The analysis of a sentence will lead to 'ultimate constituents' or simple expressions. Borrowing from the linguists, we may denominate as *morphology* the study which seeks to determine and classify the simple expressions of languages. Morphological investigations are relative to the interests and purposes of the theoretician. Field linguists, who are chiefly interested in unravelling the intricacies of natural, spoken languages, regularly attempt to isolate the simple expressions of a language—so-called morphemes—in terms of phonological elements characteristic of the speech of the community, so-called phonemes—which elements are not necessarily themselves expressions having uses, though their occurrence serves to differentiate such expressions.[4] Such phonological distinctions are

---

[3] I am tempted to call them 'semantical properties', but that would be to perpetrate another outrage with and upon an overworked word.

[4] As it turns out, the linguists' idea of morpheme does not correspond exactly with my notion of a simple, vocable expression. Any expression, none of whose

of course roughly represented by the letters of an alphabet. Philosophers and formal logicians who often work with systems of notation of their own invention, where each simple symbol is introduced as such, have no occasion to operate upon any lower level of analysis. Despite these differences, our discussion implies certain general principles of morphological analysis. The first of these is that the analysis is always relative to a particular language or family of languages. For example, 'Zer' (as in 'Zerlegen') is an expression of German but not of English; '⊣' appears to be a different expression in the formal notations of Frege and Church. The second principle is that the determination of simple expressions is relative to the use of Language. A simple expression is a type of movement, which if made in conformity with a convention pertaining to a language in the course of doing a Language act, would indicate a package of conditions of success, where there is no convention pertaining to the same language according to which complementary physical parts of such a movement could be made to indicate conditions of success. The indicated conditions of success define a 'use'. It follows that the uses available to the speakers of one language might not be available to the speakers of another, though we may expect that the same complete sets of conditions of success may, in various ways, be indicated by conformity to the conventions of different languages. There are perhaps circuitous ways in which English speakers can say what Germans would more simply say with the (colour-verb) expression 'blaut'. Finally, while the determination of simple expressions is relative to the use of Language, the identity of the expression does not depend upon the particular use or uses (meanings) the expression has in conventions pertaining to the language.[5]

---

[5] These principles would seem to be acceptable to most linguists. They always rightly insist that their investigations are relative to the language or to a speech community. According to standard descriptions of correct linguistic procedure, that of Harris, say, the linguist fixes the morphology of a language by attempting to generate both utterances and non-utterances out of utterances by appending, deleting, interchanging, and replacing putative morphemes. But the determination of utterances and non-utterances is made relatively to the responses of hearers, where those responses must be seen as responses to the use of Language: utter-

---

physical parts are expressions, would be a simple expression for me, *e.g.*, 'me'. But, in line with principles of linguistic analysis, 'me' would consist of at least two morphemes, *viz.*, [I] + obj. Also 'en' and 's' (as in 'oxen' and 'dogs') would be two distinct simple expressions having the same use for me, but they would be allomorphic variants of a single English morpheme for the linguist. Some of these complications would be obviated by the addition of lexemic stratum, such as is actually employed in some duplicated materials I have seen by S. M. Lamb; Lamb, rightly in my opinion, also adds a sememic stratum to the apparatus of structural linguistics. 'Me' is indeed sememically complex, though lexically simple.

Simple expressions may be classified in various ways. They may be written or spoken or gestural, words, symbols, signs, and signals, identified from sound, script, or smoke. Linguists, who are much concerned with such questions, have worked out a terminology for the classification of morphemes, which, while not always self-applying or completely adequate, has proved useful. Thus a morpheme may be bound or unbound, according to whether it must occur in combination with other morphemes of definite types. Using these distinctions, we might define a simple word as an expression (not necessarily a simple expression) having both phonological and inscriptional variants, where no one of the parts of the word is an unbound morpheme. ('Milkman' is not a simple word.)

A sentence is the product of a successful 'complete' lexical act. 'Complete' means that the movements in question could without further addition constitute a Language act. In our theory of the language in question, we would like to be able to capture the phenomenon of a complete lexical act by finding the principles according to which a sentence may be put together out of simple expressions. That would be part of the syntax of the language. Sentences are not the only ordered sequences of simple expressions which we may wish to isolate. We may call such non-sentential sequences of expressions 'incomplete sentences'. They are strings of expressions which may be supplemented into sentences. Examples are 'is a' and 'the eager one'. There are various types of incomplete sentences, which may be completed in various ways. Some of these are called 'words', others 'phrases', others 'clauses', and some have no distinguishing title at all. Proceeding in the other direction, we may begin with (complete) sentences and try to break them down into 'immediate constituents', these being expressions or sequences of expressions which have use in the language. The attempt to state principles for distinguishing incomplete sentences which do and do not have use, and for classifying those that do, is another large part of the so-called syntax of the language. This study is bound to be an extremely untidy affair, for the same sequence of expressions which would be the product of a complete lexical act might *also* be analysed as a type of incomplete sentence; for example single words. Heeding this difficulty, I would still make a rough and provisional attempt to define the notions of phrase and clause. These explanations permit the same expression to be both sentence, phrase, and clause.

A phrase is a sequence of expressions which has a use, *according to*

ances must have 'sense'. Meaning must be present, even though, as most linguists insist, we do not need to know what meanings a proven morpheme has. Meaning may be submitted to structural analysis, and Lamb's structurally defined notion of *sememe* approximates to my *use*.

the conventions of the language. But now how are we to understand 'according to'? Clearly, the phrase is not *assigned* a use in any particular convention. Rather, it has a use as a result of the component simple expressions having uses in different conventions. We can only make appeal to rules of syntax which presumably follow from the conventions. But how are we to draw the conclusions and find the principles? Modern so-called transformational grammar helps a good deal, but not enough.[6] The guiding principle is this. There is some category into which the phrase may be classified; *e.g.*, it may be a substantival or a verbal or a prepositional phrase. Phrases, then, are to be classified according to *use*. Now uses are defined by listing the conditions of success that would be indicated in a Language act by the employment of expressions having those uses, and uses are to be classified according to certain of those conditions. Among the conditions of success defining a substantival use, for example, are ones concerning the existence and identity of objects. Applying these thoughts, a phrase would seem to be a sequence of expressions having uses in conventions pertaining to the language, where, among the conditions of success that would be concurrently indicated by the occurrence of those expressions in a Language act, there are conditions characteristic of some specified kind of use. About this definition, notice (1) it allows that a phrase may be both a sentence and an incomplete sentence; the decision is expectedly relative to a particular utterance and the determination of whether the occurrence of the phrase would indicate a 'totality' of conditions. (2) The definition, again expectedly, makes systematic upward appeal to the use of Language. (3) The determination and classification of phrases depends upon the availability of a theory, howsoever rudimentary, for the analysis of the use of Language and the classification of uses. (4) Phrases will usually have uses of a kind which simple expressions also have in conventions pertaining to the language; *e.g.*, a substantival phrase is classified with simple nouns and pronouns; but that is not inevitable.[7]

[6] This analysis, perhaps usefully, would classify as phrases sequences of expressions which, in learning schoolboy grammar, we would not naturally think of as such, *e.g.*, 'He knows . . . very well' as in 'He knows John very well'.

[7] See Harris, *op. cit.*, p. 264, n. 10 and appendix to 16.22. The decision in any given case is flexible. First, it is not settled once and for all how narrowly uses are to be defined. We may want to say that 'The lion' both does and does not have the same kind of uses as 'John' or as 'me'. Again, if our analysis into immediate constituents would parse 'Felix is a cat' into 'Felix' and 'is a cat' (as it may do), then 'is a cat' may be thought of as a phrase having a use of a kind (a predicating use) which presumably no simple expression has, though a single verb form with inflections may. But it would be different if we analysed 'Felix is a cat' into 'Felix', 'is' and 'a cat'.

351

Clauses are of many kinds, including so-called co-ordinate, sub-ordinate, and relative clauses. They seem to have this common feature: *Either* (1) the clause or a part of the clause is itself a (com-plete) sentence *or* (2) the clause could be converted into a sentence or a clause (sense) by replacing certain constituent expressions by other expressions of definite types. A co-ordinate clause is one the whole or part of which is a sentence, but where the clause itself is regarded as an expression that would be produced by the completion of one collateral stage of a Language act. Relative clauses are ones that would be converted into sentences by replacement of one expression— the relative pronoun—by another expression. Perhaps the most interesting kinds of clauses are subordinate clauses. They are of many sorts, but I think that they have common features. Such a clause may contain parts that would have to be dropped or replaced to yield a sentence; *e.g.*, conjunctions would have to be dropped and sub-junctive or conditional forms replaced by indicatives. But now these deleted or altered expressions generally secure a systematic kind of alteration of the sense of the other occurring words. In particular, the whole unaltered clause may be employed in such a way as to refer to or otherwise to allude to the upshot of a successful use of Language. Thus, should I say, 'If he comes, he will find the door barred', the utterance of the words 'If he comes' do not themselves issue in a statement, question, order, or anything of the kind; rather, they indicate a condition for my asserting that the door will be barred, *viz.*, the condition that would be stated to be satisfied by the words 'He comes (is coming)'. The clause is used to allude to what would be asserted by the transformed clause. I think this is commonly true.[8] The upshot is that a subordinate clause is a sequence of expressions among which is at least one which has in a convention pertaining to the language a use indicating that the uses of the other occurring expressions are to be converted in the illustrated way, *e.g.*, to refer to an indicated conventional upshot.

I repeat that these suggestions for the definitions of *phrase* and *clause* are rough and are intended to be only provisional and experimental.

4. PRODUCTIVE, EFFECTIVE, AND ENDOTYCHISTIC USES OF
LANGUAGE, AND THEIR MEASURES OF SUCCESS

[Included within the three general types of action are uses of Lan-guage that we have called productive, effective, and endotychistic, *e.g.*, conjecturing, giving gifts, and calculating. Special attention is

---

[8] I subscribe to the spirit of Frege's analysis of subordinate clauses in terms of 'oblique reference' (see 'Sense and Reference' esp. pp. 65–78 in *The Philosophical Writings of Gotlob Frege*, ed. Geach and Black), though I think we still need better explanations and classifications of 'oblique reference'.

drawn to the products, effects, and achievements that are the measures of success of such types of action. The dominating fact regarding products of Language is that they, like all conventional products, are produced in their productions. Products of Language have various properties, *e.g.*, form, truth-value, relative vagueness. A well-formed theory of Language would provide means for resolving a product of Language into simple elements. We may call these *elements of Language*. Elements of Language are *contributed* to the product that is the upshot of a successful productive Language act by the *realization* of a use of words. Different uses may contribute the same elements. In the limit, an element of Language is to be defined by mention of a particular condition of success which may be indicated by the realization of a use of words. It is argued that all conventional products are products of Language. Such products provide standards for proving the identity of non-conventional upshots; *e.g.*, the written music may be used to prove the identity of the music played. It is argued that the effects of effective uses of Language are irreducibly conventional. Though effective uses of Language may sometimes be replaced by hybrids of productive conventional ways into other effect-producing acts, as when we replace acts of *appointing* with acts of *nominating*, it would be a mistake to equate all effective uses of Language with such hybrids. The productive uses of Language which may thus replace effective uses of Language are called *residual* uses of Language. They are to be defined in terms of the effective uses of Language from which they are extracted by noting that certain conditions of success for the latter are not conditions of success for the former; *e.g.*, the nominee need not, as an appointee must, be willing to accept the position. Language achievements are also irreducible. Normally, however, they are introduced by detachment or abstraction from other uses of Language, whereupon they may be reabsorbed into many different types of action, both conventional and non-conventional. Thus acts of making formal calculations are normally abstracted from acts of reckoning, whereupon they may be reabsorbed into many different types of action, such as measuring area. These latter types of action may sometimes be analysed as hybrids of conventional endotychistic action into other types of (conventional or non-conventional) action. It may be thought that, since we normally acquire the use of Language with some one language, for most of us most uses of Language originally contained an endotychistic part. That notion is mistaken, for the agent normally does not acquire the supposed endotychistic use of Language except by abstraction from other effective and productive uses of Language. The arguments of this section suggest that behaviourally the most primitive uses of Language are effective.]

Uses of Language classify into the three conjecturedly exhaustive types of action that we have called productive, effective, and endotychistic. This classification is according to the 'measure of success', *viz.*, whether the act if successful produces or contributes to producing a product, an effect, or is an achievement. To substantiate my claim, I shall now consider examples of each, arguing by the way that the kinds of action in question are of the type in question and are uses of Language. Let us begin with endotychistic uses of Language, or, as I now call them, calculative uses of Language.

Examples are caculating in the formal sense and writing a name, one's own or another's, both types of action thought to be done either on an inscribable surface or merely in the air with the finger. Let us especially consider writing a name. This clearly is a kind of *action* which an animal can do only if he knows how to write names, requiring that he conform to an orthographic-cum-morphological rule; furthermore, in conforming to the rule the agent indicates that he is writing a name, and the act is therefore apparently conventional; it is, finally, a use of Language, for the movements in question are inscriptional. Such acts need not aim for such conventional effects as the validation of documents: one might simply doodle names. Since, as we stipulated, the agent might do the act, without wishing to leave visible traces, by merely moving his finger, writing a name qualifies as endotychistic. Here, then, is a proven example of an endotychistic or calculative use of Language.

Effective uses of Language are of many kinds, and examples are almost too easy to find. We may mention the following: *validating* a document, *appointing* a trustee, *giving* a gift; there are other interesting types which involve reciprocal action on the part of others, *e.g.*, *endorsing a contract, choosing sides* in sand-lot football. Let us concentrate on giving a gift, which we may call *gifting*. This is clearly a type of proficient behaviour that an agent is enabled to do only by conforming to rules by which he shows that he means another to have an item which is his to give. Gifting appears to be a type of conventional action. This is borne out by observing that the conditions of success, *e.g.*, that there be an object which is property of the agent, that there be another who is willing to receive the object, are shown by the formula employed by the agent. Since we may do this kind of thing in writing, gifting qualifies as a use of Language. Is it effective? If an act of gifting succeeds, an effect necessarily ensues, *viz.*, the ownership of an object is altered. The effect, of course, is nothing visible or palpable, but it is an effect nonetheless, one, to be sure, that depends upon conventional action. Be clear that the effect in question is not one which goes beyond the immediate purpose of the act done. The conventional act of gifting would fail were the ownership not altered. Moreover, the effect is entirely conventional; it will ensue if only the agent conforms to the rule and all the conditions of success are satisfied, including the essential one that the intended recipient be willing to receive the object. If the agent knew that this condition or any other was not satisfied he would in advance also know that no gift could be successfully given. I have been maintaining, and shall argue more fully below, that gifting in itself is a quite conventional thing; that is part of what sets it off from that other kind of taking into possession by one party of property formerly belonging to another that we call stealing. Gifting must carry the conventional brand, something an observer can 'understand'. The ensuing effect is nothing other than or additional to a conventional effect.

Examples of productive uses of Language are promising and conjecturing. These, we have already argued, are types of productive conventional behaviour (see no. 7 of Part IV). Since they may clearly be done in writing, they qualify as examples of productive uses of Language.

I wish now to turn to the respective measure of success of each of the types of use of Language, which we may call Language products, effects, and achievements, taking them up in that order.

The dominating fact about Language products is that they, like all conventional products, are produced in their productions. One makes the most fundamental kind of practical identification of a promise or a conjecture in acts which if successful would produce the promise or conjecture. The contrast is with such non-conventional upshots as editions of magazines or symphonies which we most fundamentally identify in copies or in performances—objects distinct from the editorial or compositional labours by which the works in question are produced. This fact, that Language products are produced in their productions, reveals a peculiarly intimate relation between Language upshots and the acts which produce them, which at once accounts for the main features of Language products, engenders difficulty, and invites confusion.

The chief difficulty is to effect a separation between the act and the product. One identifies the upshot *pari passu* with identifying what the agent is doing in producing it. We must all the more, then, take care to see that the upshot, the promise, is no more the making of the promise than the chair is the making of the chair. The same conventional upshot could be produced in different acts. Descriptions appropriate to the acts are not always appropriate to the upshot, nor conversely. The act might be deliberate, hesitant, careless, or illtimed; but not the upshot. An upshot, *e.g.*, a conjecture, might be

355

plausible, borne out, or have logical consequences; but not an act of conjecturing.[1]

The ease with which the distinction between an upshot and the act which produces it is passed over is what most of all invites confusion. To take a case, failure to mind the distinction abets a recently fashionable but enormously wrong-headed kind of analysis of Language which would hold that whenever we use Language we are acting to attain a multiplicity of purposes and to produce a multiplicity of upshots.[2] I allow that an agent may sometimes succeed in producing two Language upshots in the same act; e.g., in addressing two different people, I may with my words succeed in conveying to one a statement and to the other a question, and therewith produce two distinct upshots. Still this kind of case is rare, and in no way confirms the sort of theory I have in mind, though it may be wrongly taken to support it. This kind of theory would hold that all Language uses may be 'reduced' to the multiple performance of a few 'basic functions'. Adhering to such a theory, one might then analyse promising as a mixture of asserting, directing, and the expression and/or prompting of feeling on the part of the two parties. The asserted statement might be that the agent may be trusted, or that he is bound to do as he promised, or simply that he will in fact do as promised, or perhaps all these together; the promiser might further be held to *express* feelings of sincerity and to essay to create feelings of trust in the promisee; and, still more, the promiser may be held to be directing the promisee to trust him and be directing himself to do as promised. Only one madly in search of false simplicity which is not simplicity at all could pursue such a contorted and obviously distorting analysis. Nonetheless, the path is prepared by two root confusions into which one might easily fall, both of which are encouraged by the fact that Language upshots are identified in the acts which produce them. First, there is a confounding of the upshot(s) with certain of the conditions of success, commitments, and other conditions whose fulfilment is certainly shown by a successful Language act. If one produces a promise, it is certainly shown, hence implied but not asserted, that someone was promised something, and that the agent has put himself under a certain obligation. Second, there is a confounding of the upshot with the *way* in which the agent does the act in which the upshot is produced. Thus one might heatedly make a

---

[1] I hold that, while what I call statements are in the first instance *true* or *false*, it is acts of asserting statements which are in the first instance *necessary*. To understand this we need a firm grasp on the distinction between the statement and the act of asserting a statement.

[2] See, *e.g.*, Ogden and Richard, *The Meaning of Meaning*, Chap. X; C. L. Stevenson, *Ethics and Language*, Chap. II; I. Copi, *Introduction to Logic*, Chap. Two.

statement in the course of or as the conclusion of an argument. The purpose of the act is not the expression of feeling nor the deducing; it is only the making of the statement. But, unless we are careful to distinguish the act from the upshot, we might naturally be led to say that the agent is not only stating but also (on the same level, in one and the same way) expressing and deducing, *etc.*

A special phase of this, particularly though not exclusively relevant to our consideration of Language upshots, is that we should not confuse the upshot with the (conventional or non-conventional) further effects that an agent may happen or wish to have by producing the upshot. Suppose it be the agent's purpose to convey information to another: in doing this he would most likely make a statement (as I shall call it); but he might succeed in the latter and fail to convey the information, in which case he would fail in his act. A condition of success for the act of conveying information may be that the respondent should 'understand' the agent. The agent must secure 'uptake', as Austin has styled it (*op. cit.*, p. 116). The respondent understands the agent by correctly identifying the upshot produced; and if he misidentifies the upshot, he misunderstands the agent. It thus seems to me that in the standard case it is the agent, not his upshots, who is understood or misunderstood. A productive Language act may succeed, an upshot be produced, and no one else actually be capable of understanding the agent.[3]

Confident of our capacity to distinguish a Language upshot from a producing act, we may observe that these products have their own properties, some of them highly characteristic. Thus every such upshot will be of some type—conjecture, promise, question, or what have you. Again, instances of many but not all types of upshots have *forms*, in the sense of being subject-predicate or relational, singular or universal, *etc.* Included here are conjectures, assumptions, generalizations, and what I call statements; excluded are such things as cheers (if cheers are upshots) and also probably promises and orders. The characteristics of type and form are, with other properties, determined by the producing act. Reviving an old term, we may call them

[3] Still, persistent failure of anyone to understand would be strong evidence but not yet proof that the agent had failed to produce an upshot. He does the act only by conforming to conventions, by which conformity he indicates conditions of success; it must be that others could become familiar with those conventions by observing the fulfilment of the indicated conditions; if all persistently fail to identify an upshot, that is evidence that one of the indicated conditions of success is not met. Still, uptake is not necessary. Historical illustrations are found in the notorious difficulty that orthodox modes of thought have had in comprehending the ideas of action at a distance and of the wave-particle. The theories which are built around these ideas seem to clash too directly with earlier ways of thinking about interaction between bodies or the spatial descriptions of material things, and yet they are apparently coherent.

'primary characteristics' of upshots. There are still other character-istics pertaining to upshots which are not thus determined, *e.g.*, *truth-value*, whether or not a promise is *kept*, and so on. The examina-tion of such characteristics belongs to the detailed study of Language, and we shall not go into it here. Indeed, in the sequels to this volume, I shall make a detailed investigation of only some of the features of what I call statements. It would be interesting to inquire whether Language products are susceptible of characterizations as better or worse, and I would like to pause briefly over that issue.

The question at bottom is whether there are any sorts of considera-tions which quite generally bear on the assessment of conventional upshots. In seeking to answer the question, we must take care not to hold that an upshot is worse just because it is obscurely, ineptly, or peculiarly produced. We must distinguish the quality of how one says something from the quality of what one says, if what is said admits of quality at all. So the question is this: Is there any possible characteristic of upshots that would frequently leave them open to criticism, other things being equal? Well, special kinds of upshots might be regarded as unfortunate for any number of reasons. A promise which cannot be kept; a false statement, *etc.*; but these characteristics are peculiar to certain kinds of upshots, and we should like something rather more general, some fairly common type of 'descriptive characteristic' possession of which by an upshot would frequently lead us to depre-ciate it as not fully acceptable. I believe that an instance of what we are looking for is *vagueness*. 'Vague', as I have already pointed out (p. 317), is a term that initially applies not to Language acts but to Language upshots, and it seems to be applicable to almost all kinds of upshot. One might, with elegance, crispness, and precision, make a quite vague statement, promise, question, *etc.*; *e.g.*, though one enunciates clearly it is not clear what the true conditions are, or whether I am promising only you or you and him both, or what state-ments might qualify as answers to the question. It is notable that we have ways of indicating this in the producing acts, *e.g.*, by employ-ment of the word 'rather' of the suffix 'ish' in 'reddish'.

A vague upshot, I take it, is one of uncertain identity, at least as that would be measured by appeal to some familiar standard of determinateness. The conditions of success are not sharply indicated. But, it must be stressed, there can be such want of determination only if we are looking at the matter through a system which allows us, and perhaps calls upon us, to make distinctions among conditions of success. We must have some way of crystallizing sharp lines out of bands of conditions of success. We are, for instance, apt to suppose that 'several' leads to vague upshots because we also have expressions like '11', '47', and '22'. Now, be clear; vagueness as described is not badness, nor is the assertion of a vague statement always to be regarded as unfortunate. Vagueness, in the first place, is only one consideration among possibly many others bearing on the assessment of upshots; it may sometimes be better to make a vague promise than one which it would be almost impossible to keep. At all events, vagueness is not an 'intrinsic' fault, which latter idea seems as alien to conventional upshots as it does to numbers, though it does apply to other kinds of upshots like pieces of music. Indeed, in delicate circumstances we often *wish* to make vague statements. And, as noted, we have linguistic means available for doing so. That we should scorn an upshot as vague, take 'vague' as an 'evaluative term', depends upon what we want it for, and reflects its unsuitability for certain purposes. Thus, the use of 'several' might lead to an upshot which was unsatisfactory because too vague if, when requested by the University administration to say how many students I have in a class, I replied with 'several'; for though this answer might be unexceptionably true, it leaves too many questions unanswered for the purposes of the administration.

The rudimentary theories of Language which we already have available as offshoots of formal logic and grammar all point in the direction of an analysis according to which Language products would be resolved into complexes of elements. I believe that any fully formed theory of Language will arrive at that position. The achievement is intimated by the observed relation between Language products and their producing acts, and would be the most striking mark of that relation. Consider an example, a question that we might ask by saying, 'Is that boy English?'. Presumably there is something in the upshot, shown by the sentence employed in the producing act, that marks it out as a question; additionally it contains a reference indicated by 'that boy' and a characterization indicated by 'English'. Fastening on these latter two items, it is clear that these are not simple constituents or elements of the upshot. *That boy* is presumably different from *The boy*, although both are references having something in common; furthermore, references (as indicated by 'John' in 'John will do it') have elements in common with addresses (as in 'John, you shall do it!'), though not all these elements are shared; finally, the characterizations *English* and *French* are obviously alike in some respects and different in others. The general conclusion is that items like references and characterizations, regarded as constituents of conventional upshots, are not elements but more like *radicals*, in the chemical analogue. They are complex parts requiring complementation. How, then, to find the elements? I cannot tell the whole story here, but let me anticipate how it would go.

Our theory of Language products must depend upon our theory of producing Language acts. Now the acts consist of elements included among which are elements of movement. But these elements are not elements of sense, for the same kinds of movement may have different senses. The sense of the act, rather, is determined by the uses those movements have. The elements of the Language act, I submit, are the units of sense or the uses which, as I put it, are *realized* in the Language act by making movements having those uses. Clearly, the same elements of sense (uses) may be realized in different Language acts. Let us now confine ourselves to productive Language acts. For at least two reasons, it is evident that the uses realized in the act are distinct from the elements of a produced upshot. First, the Language act consisting of its elements—the uses— might fail, but then there is no upshot produced consisting of its elements. Second, we might produce the same upshot by way of realizing different uses; *e.g.*, I might make a statement with the words 'John came' which I could also make with the word 'yes', where 'yes' has a very different use from 'John' or 'came' or the two together. It is likely that some peoples have uses available in the conventions of their languages not available in some other languages, yet we might still effect translations from one to another, and say that the same statements, questions, *etc.*, were made, asked, *etc.*

How, then, do we determine that the same thing was said in these Language acts which have different sense? The realization of any use in a Language act indicates a package of conditions of success. Now we may in two different Language acts indicate the same total assemblage of conditions by realizing different uses. In that case, the two Language acts, though distinct in sense, say the same thing. Suppose now that the acts are successful; they produce the same product consisting of the same elements. The immediate suggestion is that we may define the elements, which may be elements of Language upshots, by specifying single, particular conditions of success, just as we may define the elements of sense—uses—by specifying packages of such conditions. The similar manner of defining uses and Language elements shows the tight dependence of the latter upon the former. I formulate that relation by saying that the agent *contributes* such and such Language elements to the upshot by *realizing* such and such use of words. The similar manner of theoretically identifying the two kinds of element does not, for all that, imply that they are the same. They are governed by different criteria of existence. While we practically identify and establish the existence of an element of sense—a use—in a Language act, we practically identify and establish the existence of a Language element in an upshot. If a productive act is unsuccessful, we may establish the existence of a use in the act, but we cannot establish the existence of contributed elements in an upshot, because there is no upshot produced.

It is pretty obvious that a theory of the elements of Language action is a theory for grammarians, and will always be applied relative to a given language or family of languages. A theory of Language elements, though it be constructed relatively to the theorists' way of individuating conditions of success, is more abstract and general, and will in principle be applicable to conceptualization in general, regardless of the languages employed. It may, in particular, be utilized to define those components which we have been calling references, forms, modalities (uses of Language). However, not all the properties of Language upshots may be resolved into Language elements, but only those which are determined by producing acts, *i.e.*, only those we have called *primary characteristics*. Whether or not a promise is kept or a statement is false, for example, is not determined by the contributed Language elements.

Hitherto I have formally distinguished Language products from conventional upshots in general. But I have already suggested that all conventional upshots are products of Language. I should now like to review the argument for that conclusion. Since we are concerned with products and not achievements, the object is to be defined independently of the movements by which it is produced. The identification of the purpose must therefore make no reference to the movements by which it could be attained. Presumably then there is no limitation on the movements by which the agent would indicate the conditions of success and produce the upshot. Hence he might employ inscriptional movements; *ergo*, the act would qualify as a Language act.

It remains that not all upshots are conventional; hence not all upshots are products of Language. But we argued that non-conventional upshots depend logically upon the existence of conventional upshots, hence products of Language. That is so, we conjectured, for two connected reasons. First, one produces a non-conventional upshot, *e.g.*, a symphony, only by producing one or a number of conventional products, *e.g.*, what would be set down in a musical score. Second, proof of the identity of a non-conventional upshot would consist in making a favourable comparison between the production of the upshot, *e.g.*, the musical performance, and what we called a diagram, *e.g.*, as recorded in a score, which is a conventional product, hence a product of Language. If this line of reasoning is correct, it establishes that all upshots, conventional or no, depend upon the use of Language.

I come now to Language effects. These are, of course, a species of conventional effect. It seems to me probable that all conventional effects are Language effects, for the argument in support of the claim that all conventional products are Language products would seem to apply equally for conventional effects. Be that as it may, I have already argued that conventional effects are indeed effects, and irreducibly conventional. We must earnestly resist assimilating conventional effects to conventional products and appreciate that effects produced by successful effective Language action are inescapably conventional and not just physical consequences of the producing behaviour. The effect is *not* an upshot, and it is conventional. I should like to consider these two points in turn.

Take a successful act of gifting, and suppose the alleged effect, that the property is altered in respect of ownership, is really an upshot. How are we to identify that upshot? The product cannot be the object given, for that must exist independently of the act; the existence of the object is indeed a condition of success for the act, and therefore not the measure of the success of the act. Questing for an upshot, we might be tempted to follow an analogy from economics. The supposed product is to be construed as rather like what is added to a pair of shoes when it is marketed. But that surely is only an economist's *façon de parler*, introduced to keep the theory simple and neat. The shoes themselves do not lose their identity in being marketed —we would complain if they did. Perhaps then it is like framing a picture. To be sure the frame is something added, but the framed picture is not a different picture. The attempt to suppress the effect in favour of products seems unavailing.

In holding that the effect is irreducibly conventional, I mean two related things. First, it could be produced solely by conventional means. It is sufficient that an object be given as a gift for change of ownership. Second, it is not a mere physical consequence of the act; it is not, as Austin put it, in '*pari materia*' with the act, which is only to say that the affected object need not itself physically alter. A man purchases a house as it is, and if it changes before he takes it over, he may have grounds for legal action; now as a result of this effect's having occurred, the buyer may later come to paint the house a different colour—conventional effects have their sequels in the physical world—but that is another matter.

Conventional effects, unlike conventional products, may be brought about otherwise than by actual animal agency. We must distinguish the conventional effect that immediately ensues upon the presentation of a gift or the legitimate transfer of civil power from the non-conventional effects that result from theft or usurpation. But we also know that the mere passage of time may legitimize and give conventional sanction to the holding of property or power originally stolen. But the non-conventional effecting of conventional effects probably depends upon there being institutions by which these changes could be conventionally produced. The reason is this: These effects must have a conventional sanction which involves their being recognized by at least some interested animals; but that the interested parties should accord such conventional recognition, if only tacitly, would seem to depend upon their having acquired a capacity for conventional behaviour. There would be no distinction between property and stolen goods unless there were known ways by which property could be exchanged, created, *etc.*; stolen goods could therefore evolve into the property of their possessor only if there were known ways by which property could be exchanged, created, *etc.*

We must now consider the relation between effective and productive uses of Language. Some might argue that conventional effects are a confusing superfluity. They would propose that effective uses of Language are really conventionalized hybrids. According to the proposed pattern of analysis, the Original Way of such an act would be conventional but non-effective, where the Original Purpose would be effective but non-conventional. We thus achieve a separation, allowing us to dispense with conventional effects. The argument would consist in examples. Gifting would be analysed as a hybrid of an effective, non-conventional Original Purpose of *getting property into the hands of another* and a productive, conventional Original Way of *proffering* the object. *Appointing* would be analysed as a hybrid of *nominating* (a type of productive conventional action) into *getting a man into office* (a type of effective non-conventional action). According to this mode of analysis, only the productive part of the alleged hybrid action would be of special interest to the student of the nature of Language, and that would be a simplifying convenience.

The question is whether the illustrative analyses are sufficiently persuasive to carry the argument. I contend that they are not. The convenience would be bought at the cost of impoverishing our theory, and would result in a truncated conception of Language itself. There are two arguments against the proposal.

First, effective uses of Language cannot be completely replaced by hybrids. Effective uses of Language, such as gifting, are among the first we acquire; surely most of us learn how to give gifts before we learn how to proffer gifts. Such types of action as gifting come into our lives at relatively primitive levels when we begin to turn natural inclinations into conventional channels, and we are never entirely free subsequently of the need to do that. To analyse as hybrids such relatively primitive acts would be distortion. The reductionist force latent in this suggestion must be corrected or we risk either impoverishing our theory or employing it as a Procrustean bed.

The second argument is tied up with our observation that

363

conventional effects are irreducibly conventional. According to the proposed analysis of gifting, the indicated (non-conventional) effect was the *taking into possession* of the proffered article by the intended recipient. But surely the effect of a successful act of gifting is not a mere taking into possession, but, at the very minimum, a *rightful* taking into possession. This is more correctly put by noting that the object itself is affected, but in an entirely conventional way. The conclusion is that even to the extent that conventional effective action may be replaced by hybrids with conventional productive Original Ways, the effective Original Purpose remains irreducibly conventional. Therefore, we cannot dispense with conventional effects in favour of conventional products.

This established, it is unquestionable that, at a certain stage of conceptual development, effective uses of Language may be sometimes replaced by hybrids of conventional Original Ways into conventional Original Purposes. One who has learned that discovery registered by a suitable claim confirms possession quite as well as does gifting, may also learn to forego gifting in favour of proffering gifts. Proffering becomes one way among many of affecting the ownership of property, and, if the effect is actually sought, that may come to be regarded as the measure of success of a hybrid act.

Now this is a process of replacement. It is a possibility created by a growing sophistication in the supposed agent. Doubtless it is never fully realized. At all events, such a process is no warrant for *analysing* effective uses of Language as hybrids, and for the two reasons we have already reviewed.

This process is interesting in itself, and I should like to investigate it in somewhat greater detail.[4] Let us call this a process of *detaching* the (conventional) effect from the act. And let us denominate as a *residual use of Language* what will figure as the Original Way in the replacing type of hybrid action. It remains to consider, first, the conditions under which the process of detachment may occur; second, the character of the residual use of Language; and third, the relation between the residual use of Language and the detached conventional effect which would normally ensue.

The essential conditions for detaching a conventional effect are (1) that the supposed agent be able to conceive of the same kind of effect being produced by other uses of Language and (2) that he have learned to do acts of a kind which might be expected to produce

---

[4] In lectures VI and VII of *Doing Things with Words*, Austin draws our attention to this process among others in his examples of transitions from *primitive performatives* to *explicit performatives*. According to my definitions, the indicated explicit performatives indeed turn out to be performatives, whereas the indicated primitive performatives are of different categories.

the effect though they may actually fail to do so. The first may come to be satisfied in the course of the agent's acquiring capacity in other uses of Language by which (*e.g.*) property may be exchanged, conferred, or created, *e.g.*, by claiming discovery. Again one may learn that office-holders may be elected as well as appointed. The second condition would come to be satisfied in the course of the agent's learning to cope with failure. A condition of success for giving a gift is that the intended recipient should be willing to receive, and the agent must believe that condition is satisfied if he is to do a genuine act of gifting. But the agent cannot *make* the other willing to receive. Stimulated by the refusals of his gifts, the agent might come to learn to effect the desired change of ownership by *offering* objects where at least his act of offering will not be frustrated by the donee's reluctance. Offering is a kind of conventional act which could succeed even if the indicated effect does not ensue. Having learned to make offers, one may learn to make offers (1) as a *means* of effecting a change of property, or (2) as the Original Way in a hybrid act whose Original Purpose is to effect a change of property, or (3) even in the hope that the offers will be refused. Similar relations obtain between *appointing* and *nominating*. Appointing, which is a kind of conventional act, may fail and the appointment not be made; but nominating, another kind of conventional act, can succeed even though the appointment does not take; later, when our supposed agent learns about nominating, he can make appointments by nominating, or make nominating appointments which latter is a hybrid replacement for acts of appointing.

Let us now consider the character of the residual use of Language. It is got, so to speak, by detaching the effect from the effective use of Language. That will show itself formally by the fact that we shall explain the residual action in terms of the effective action. Here we naturally look to the conditions of success. What stimulates the agent to acquire the residual use of Language is his want of knowledge or even positive disbelief that certain conditions for the effective use of Language are satisfied, *e.g.*, that the intended recipient is willing to accept. Then he must think that an effective act must fail, in which case he could not so much as attempt it. Wishing to do something, he does an act of a kind for which the supposed condition is not a condition of success. We identify the purpose of the residual use of Language by deleting specific items from the (necessarily incomplete) list of conditions proposed as a typification of the purpose of the effective use of Language. We may dub this kind of definition *attenuation*. Definition by attenuation may be used to typify many sorts of action, both conventional and non-conventional. A necessary but not sufficient characterization of a residual use of Language is that it be definable by attenuation from an effective use of Language. Having acquired such a use of Language, *e.g.*, proffering or nominating, I may succeed in such an act without thinking that my respondent will accept, even knowing perhaps that he will not.

Such uses of Language are oftentimes productive. I may make the same offer or nomination over and over again, provided the proffered object remains unaccepted and mine to give, or the office unfilled. It seems, moreover, that such uses of Language are not calculative, for if the attenuated effective use of Language did not require specific movements for success neither does the residual use of Language. It is not so far excluded that residual uses of Language might sometimes be effective. But I cannot find an example. At any rate such a use of Language could be progressively further attenuated until we reached a productive use of Language. In view of all this, I *stipulate* that a residual use of Language *must* be productive. The fact that we can progressively attenuate effective uses of Language into what are finally productive uses of Language misleadingly encourages the false view that effective uses of Language may be eschewed in favour of or even analysed as productive uses of Language.

Now, my offer is *my* offer and not yours; your offer of the same object to the same man would be a different offer. Similarly, I make my nominations, you make yours, and corporate bodies make theirs. This, I submit, is entirely typical of residual uses of Language. In the sequel, I shall define a performative use of Language as a productive use of Language, the theoretical identification of whose upshots would require a specific reference to the possible agent or agents as agent. The suggested conclusion is that residual uses or Language are performative uses of Language. That, I conclude, is a necessary, though possibly not yet a sufficient, characterization.

We have yet to consider the relations of a successful residual Language act to the detached conventional effect. Normally, the effect will ensue, but it may not. Normally, the agent will wish the effect to ensue, but he may not. But whatever the agent may wish, he must know in advance that the effect might ensue, and we expect him to be prepared to accept it without protest. I may offer the object and offer it again, and it never be accepted, though I must be aware of the fact that it might be accepted, and I cannot justifiably object if it is. I am *committed* to relinquishing the object. We shall discover that every use of Language has its characteristic commitments, and may be partially defined in terms of commitment. A condition for doing the act is that the agent should believe that he would be characteristically committed if the act succeeded.

My view is, then, that success in a residual Language act *commits* the *agent to accept* the effect, in just the sense of 'commit' that he would be committed to keep a promise or to withdraw a proven false statement. The commitments of a use of Language typically reflect the usual demands and associations of what would be the normal circumstances in which such deeds would be done, and the commitments remain in force even when those associations are severed. Standard commitment becomes definitive of the type of action. This is patently what happens in the case of residual uses of Language. Though such deeds may succeed even when the normal conventional effect does not ensue, it is a condition for doing the act that the agent should be committed to accepting the effect should it ensue.

To summarize, I have argued that we cannot by a kind of fractional analysis filter off the conventional part of effective conventional action as a productive residue. But it is remarkable that we can by the process of attenuation get so much into and out of productive uses of Language. Capacity to make these replacements betokens a growing conceptual sophistication. We progressively restructure our ways of thinking to permit the extraction of a conventional upshot, and thereby contrive to separate the conventional aspects of behaviour from the incalculable responses of others and situational constraints.

It remains only to consider Language achievements. Let us call these *calculations*. Calculations are normally registered as inscriptions; but that is not necessary, it sufficing merely to make the calculation with, say, the index finger in the air. Calculations, too, are an irreducible category, which would be eliminated at cost of impoverishing our theory. But here also there are forces of dissolution similar to but of opposite direction from those which worked against conventional effects. Take the case of successfully writing a name. Some might say that the name is written only in the course of validating documents or such like. This latter is a kind of conventional effect which could be done with a stamp or by a secretary, or *viva voce*. So, it may seem, there is no conventional achievement of name writing, which, it might be urged, is simply *a way* of doing conventional acts, or, better, a hybridized conventional, in which all that need be conventional is the Original Purpose. But that confuses name writing with signing, and leaves out cases where one simply writes his name, as in doodling. He means to write his name, and we may observe mistakes he makes in doing so; but he does not mean to write his name as a way of doing something else. Even in doing this kind of act, one might concentrate on getting his letter-writing movements round and full, as one actually does in the course of trying to acquire a decent hand, and when learning to spell.

The argument fails, but it does point to something interesting and true. Normally, one learns to make calculations by abstracting from other kinds of act. Generally one achieves the idea of a formal

367

calculation subsequently to acquiring the act of reckoning. The transition made, the supposed agent may then be taught other ways of reckoning, say by machine or 'in the head'. The original type of action may then be replaced by hybrid calculation reckonings. At the same time, the abstracted calculation may come to be done collaterally to or hybridized into other types of action, both conventional and non-conventional: the calculation is re-absorbed into wider practices of diverse kinds. Thus calculations may contribute to acts of measurement. The wide use of arithmetic and other formal calculi in theoretical endeavour, not to speak of the even wider use of writing, shows how far this process of absorption can go. In such cases, the calculations themselves tend to become a kind of anchoring test procedure. Calculative uses of Language, though they unquestionably have a (rather uninteresting) life of their own, are most noticeable on account of their affiliations with other uses of Language and theoretical endeavour at large.

Normally, though not invariably, a calculative use of Language results as a detachment or abstraction from another use of Language; it may then be absorbed into other uses of Language. By analogy, this sheds light on another issue. We first acquire Language in learning to speak the tongue of our mentors. For example, I learned Language by learning to ask questions, *etc.*, in American English. On analogy with calculative uses of Language, it might be argued that speaking English is a type of conventional behaviour, and that learning Language is really a matter of acquiring a mastery over hybrid uses of Language. That would be silly. In learning to ask a question, I must have been able to know what I wanted to know, but I need not have known I was asking in English. My act would have been *misidentified* as *questioning in English*; it was simply questioning. The imitative gurglings, sputterings, and sometimes enunciatings of the infant which prefigure speech do not qualify as conventional behaviour. To see what went wrong, allow the (somewhat doubtful) analogy to calculation. Now the calculative use of Language did not live as a partner with the use of Language from which it may have been abstracted. It was acquired (as we suppose) only subsequently and upon abstraction. So, too, *if* making English sounds were regarded as conventional behaviour, it would be acquired as such only upon abstraction from the uses of Language which we may learn in English.

Returning from this digression, I venture one highly speculative suggestion. We noticed that some productive uses of Language result from a process of detachment of the effect from effective uses of Language. I think that this is very often the case. We also observed that calculative uses of Languages are often a result of abstracting from other uses of Language. This seems not to be the case only when the supposed agent has already attained a quite high degree of sophistication. The suggestion is that behaviourally the most primitive uses of Language are effective. This suggestion will be borne out by later investigations.

5. PERLOCUTIONARY ACTION [1]

[Acts of any kind that are done by way of a collateral Language act are styled *perlocutionary acts*. The characterization of an act as perlocutionary in no way contributes to the identification of the act but rather describes how the act is done, *viz.*, by use of Language.

The idea of perlocutionary action, though obvious in the abstract, is often missed in practice, chiefly because Language action is itself rare and separated only with difficulty from its normal perlocutionary connections. The possibility of re-establishing these connections is assured by the commitments which contribute to the definition of a use of Language. Some types of verbal jests, deceptions, *etc.*, are usefully analysed as perlocutionary acts. Acts which are done by way of collateral lexical acts, whether or not they also be done collaterally to a Language act, *e.g.*, acts of calligraphical decoration, are styled *perlexical acts*.]

Just as we must distinguish the use of Language from what is collateral thereto, so we must also separate Language from that to which it may in its turn be collateral. One may want to bring another to believe or to do a certain thing, and he may do so by transporting the other into certain circumstances or he may *tell* him. In the latter case, Language is employed, but only collaterally to the act of bringing the other to believe or act. The Act done is not a Language act. However, Language contributes, and a full, true *description* of the act could not neglect that feature. Acts which are done in this way, *viz.*, by way of a collateral Language act, I shall describe as *perlocutionary acts*.

It is necessary to be able to draw a distinction between the use of Language and perlocutionary action if we are to have any hope of achieving an understanding of Language as a form of behaviour. Since Language may contribute to almost all the affairs of the tolerably sophisticated conceptualizing agent, the attempt to theorize about Language in the total context of its possible collateral connections would force us to consider practically all kinds of action

---

[1] 'Perlocutionary' is Austin's term, which I first adopted from notes taken down by Chas. Caton from Austin's Oxford lectures entitled 'Words and Deeds', since published as *How to do Things with Words*. I use the term to cover only what Austin classifies as C-a cases (*op. cit.*, pp. 102, 110). Austin's C-b perlocutionaries will be subsumed under the heading of locutionary hybrids.

together and would militate against the isolation of the contribution that is specifically ascribable to Language. At the same time we must be prepared to account for the collateral utility of Language in larger spheres of life.

The term 'perlocutionary', when applied to an act, *describes how* the act was done, *viz.*, by use of Language. The term does not, therefore, in any way contribute to the (typal) identification of the act. We identify the act by saying *what* was done by use of Language. Now Language purposes may be hybridized as Original Ways into possibly non-conventional Original Purposes. Examples of such types of action are *persuading, informing, arguing*. Such types of action (which Austin calls C-b perlocutionary acts) are *not* perlocutionary under the adopted definition, for in these cases the use of Language is essential and figures in the identification of the action. We shall consider these types of action in the next section under the name of locutionary hybrids.

Though the idea of perlocutionary action seems perfectly obvious in theory, it is all too readily overlooked in practice and sometimes discerned only with difficulty. The chief reason for this has already been touched on. While the use of Language is enormously important and evidently visible in the affairs of the human animal, Language acts *simpliciter* are relatively rare. We are moved by sheer weight of statistics to the view that Language is never found except in some perlocutionary setting. It might even be argued that every Language act must have *some* further effect. That, if true, would not prove that Language cannot be separated from its effects, for otherwise it would prove too much; it would lead us to the conclusion that acts of any and every kind are really of some further kind. Effects are relevant only so far as they are sought or intended, but then it is part of the agent's purpose that those effects should ensue. But even the first observation does not threaten the distinction between the use of Language and perlocutionary action. First, as I have been insisting all along, Language acts are possible, as seen in our examples of the ambling naturalist and numerically curious spectator. Second, it is necessary to effect the distinction in order to explain how Language does contribute to the affairs of life.

But can it be done? A formidable challenge to the distinction between Language and perlocutionary action would consist in asking us to reflect upon the normal and natural setting of Language. One might argue that Language is instituted primarily for the sake of its typical further connections, which we would neglect at our peril. It is part of the idea of promising that a promise should be kept; it is part of our idea of stating that a statement should be made as true, and the speaker is accordingly liable before the world. The point is well taken. Surely it is a condition for making a promise that one should know that he is committing himself to do the promised deed. One who would make a statement must recognize that he is liable for the truth of what he says, in the sense that he ought to withdraw the statement should he discover it to be false. We have such types of action as promising and stating partly because it is convenient in life that commitments might be thus conventionally engendered. Language cannot be its own rationale.

We have already encountered this matter of commitments. For the sake of defending our distinction between the use of Language and perlocutionary action, one thing must be clearly understood. The performance of a Language act does not automatically assure fulfilment of commitment. One may fail to speak the truth or to recant falsehood, or one may renege on a promise. But the supposed agent has still (successfully) made the promise or otherwise there would have been no reason for him to have kept the promise.

Thus we might and must sever the connections between a use of Language and meeting the commitments it engenders.

On the other side, a specification of commitment will always contribute to the definition of a use of Language. A condition of doing a Language act of type L is that the agent should not disavow commitments of a kind which are definitive of L. These commitments are, as it were, like hooks by which a use of Language may be attached to various activities, and are fitted to secure a dominating kind of perlocutionary connection.

The upshot of this is that, while the bearing a use of Language may characteristically have on the affairs of life may account for its being as it is, this does not obliterate the distinction between Language and perlocutionary action. The distinction, far from being suspect, is an indispensable tool for discussing the relation between Language and life at large.

'Perlocutionary' is one term for describing action. This type of description comes into effect when we wish to explain such things as jests, deceptions, and the like. We shall look into these more thoroughly in the next section but one, but I wish to say something about them here. Any form of action may occasion a joke or invite deceit, not only the use of Language. One way in which this happens is that one does an act of type K with the purpose of or collaterally to amusing or deceiving others. Where K is a use of Language, the act is perlocutionary. Contrastingly, one may do something of type K (*e.g.*) (1) *jokingly* or (2) *with the hope that it will amuse* or (3) make a joke on K. In case (3) it would be wrong to say that K is done collaterally to something else. Rather, the agent does an act of a kind related to but different from K. I shall call such types of action parasites, and I shall examine parasitical uses of Language in no. 7. In cases (1) or (2), the agent is indeed imagined to be doing an act of kind *K*. However, the indicated description, *e.g.*, 'jokingly', is not a collateral act description. It follows that where *K* is a use of Language, *jokingly* or *with the hope of amusing* are not to be regarded as instances of forms of being perlocutionary. Similarly it would probably be wrong to analyse the concept of *understanding*—what Austin calls 'uptake'—in terms of perlocutionary action. Normally, we do not speak *in order* to be understood. Sometimes we may speak *in the hope* that we shall be understood or even in the hope that we shall not be. That we normally *should* be understood whether or not we seek it or hope it results simply from the fact that this is conventional behaviour, and that we must make what we mean to say identifiable in our movements. Also, success in perlocutionary action is *usually* contingent upon the agent's interlocutors understanding his collateral Language act.

Any Language act is done by way of a collateral lexical act. Invoking the nesting principle of collateral action (Part II, no. 14), it follows that any perlocutionary act contains as a part a collateral lexical act. Let us call any act that is done by way of a collateral lexical act a *perlexical act*. Our conclusion was that every perlocutionary act is a *perlexical act*. The converse does not hold. One may, in stark disregard of sense, mouth meaningful words, with the further purpose, say, of recovering breath or quieting the pulse. Words perhaps are available for the task, but the sense of the words is adventitious. Calligraphical decoration is another instance.

6. LOCUTIONARY HYBRIDS [1]

[Conventionalized hybrids, whose Original Ways are uses of Language, are called *locutionary hybrids*. *Informing*, *persuading*, and *explaining* are examples. Locutionary hybrids are not to be confused with effective uses of Language. Locutionary hybrids always involve something beyond that use of Language which is the Original Way. Lexical action, whether or not collateral to Language, may also be hybridized into other types of action, yielding lexical hybrids.]

'Perlocutionary' is a term descriptive of and not identifactory of action. It draws attention to the fact that the agent did whatever he did by way of using Language. He might have attained the same purpose in some other way.

---

[1] 'Locutionary' is another term I take from Austin. I would have preferred 'Language hybrids', as being more in line with the terminology of 'Language', 'Language act', *etc.*, but an adjective seems to be demanded, and I can find none better than 'locutionary'.

But we may so identify an act as to imply that the use of Language is necessary but not sufficient, *e.g.*, when we say that the agent *informed* someone of such and such. Here the use of Language, whatever it may be, is amalgamated, as the Original Way, into a hybrid. The result would be one species of what we have called conventionalized hybrids. We may call this species *locutionary hybrids*.

A type of such action is that of *obreption* or verbal deception, *i.e.*, lying. Other comparably broad sub-categories are *communicating* and *persuading*. If I am to succeed in *persuading* someone to do something, normally I must tell him what I would like him to do, but that is not sufficient, for I must also get him to do it. Why does Language figure at all? Because to persuade is to get one to do something in consideration of stated reasons.[2] A short sample listing of types of action might be suggestive:

Uses of Language (*Original Ways*)	*Locutionary Hybrids*	(*Original Purposes*)
Tell	Persuade	Induce
Offer	Cajole	Coax
Offer	Inveigle	Entice
Complain	Entreat	Seek assistance
Report	Convey	Make known
Note	Explain	Make familiar or comprehensible
State	Explain	Make familiar or comprehensible

This listing makes it quite clear that available language for identifying locutionary hybrids does not often imply univocal determination for either the Original Way or Original Purpose, and that the same use of Language and the same Original Purpose may be variously hybridized.

Among my hybrids are some which have provoked considerable philosophical concern, most notably *explaining*. My listing prefigures an 'analysis', possibly controversial. Since I have already said something about explaining (see nos. 9 and 23 of Part II), and shall return to the topic in a sequel, I shall not argue for that 'analysis' here. That locutionary hybrids should excite interest in the philosopher is entirely natural, seeing how they bridge the domain of conceptualization with broader realms of theory and action, and are

[2] This point is implicit in Mr. J. N. Garver's article 'On the Rationality of Persuading' (*Mind*, 1960, pp. 163–74). Apart from an obscure hint in the right direction intimated in this article, Austin's use of the notion of a C-b perlocutionary act is the only notice that has been taken of this idea of a locutionary hybrid in the literature with which I am familiar.

thus much before the mind of philosophers who would want to talk about theory and action in terms of what Language is appropriate thereto.

Success in a locutionary hybrid act requires more than success in the use of Language alone. If the Original Purpose is attained only with the inducement of belief in another or with the initiation of activity, the act will not have succeeded if these effects are not forthcoming. But surely I may not make a doubting Thomas believe simply by telling him. Among the conditions of success for the act are ones additional to those which are indicated by conformity to convention. Nor generally is success assured if all these additional conditions are satisfied. It may take the Holy Spirit to breathe belief into the soul of the sceptic. It follows that locutionary hybrids need not be fully conventional, and most commonly will not be. Locutionary hybrids are therefore not effective uses of Language contrary to what we might have been tempted to suppose. The effect produced by a successful act of persuading is not a conventional effect, such as change in ownership.

In the last section, we introduced a generalized notion of perlexical action, where every perlocutionary act is perlexical, but not conversely. That suggests that we might introduce a similar related idea of lexical hybrid action.

Whenever an agent does a locutionary hybrid act he does so by way of a collateral lexical act. Suppose now we hybridize that lexical purpose into some other non-conventional Original Purpose. I call the result a *lexical hybrid*. Lexical hybrids are clearly not locutionary hybrids. But here we do not have any converse relationship either: locutionary hybrids are generally not lexical hybrids, for generally the Original locutionary Way may be attained by way of alternative lines of lexical action. The exception is when the Original Way is already a hybridized conventional purpose.

Are there any natural examples of lexical hybrids? Writing nonsense poetry might be a case. There are, moreover, kinds of action which seem to call for analysis in terms of multiple purposes, some of which are lexical and others locutionary hybrids. In improvising a fugue on B-A-C-H at the piano, the composer might be held to be doing a doubly hybrid act for which the common Original Purpose is the production of music and the Original Ways are (interrelatedly) lexical and locutionary; an alternative analysis would cast the act as a doubly hybridized lexical purpose into a Language purpose into a music-making purpose, or again as a hybrid of a lexical purpose into a music-making purpose into a Language purpose (the composer writes the music in playing it). I would be inclined to argue that the writing of poetry always involves lexical hybrid purposes. For surely it is always a part of the poet's purpose to arrange his words in such a way as to please the ear or the eye regardless of the sense. Allowedly, this is usually only *one* of the poet's purposes. Depending upon *genre*, he must also more or less attend to the intervening machinery of Language, where what he may be striving for most of all is a certain ephemeral kind of accommodation of sound to sense.

Lexical hybrids are comparative rarities. Locutionary hybrids, on the other hand, are common beyond measure. We must know how to spot them, in order not to mistake them as uses of Language. However, since they usually involve something which goes beyond the bare use of Language, they will be the subject of only occasional and peripheral comment in the balance of this work and its sequels.

7. PARASITICAL USES OF LANGUAGE

[The fact that one may use Language with the intent to deceive does not conflict with our characterization of a Language act as self-identifying. An act of lying, say, is not a Language act but a locutionary hybrid. That raises a question concerning the nature of the conventional Original Way, which is use of Language. Usually this use of Language will not be what it is meant to seem to be to the supposed interlocutor, *e.g.*, straightforward assertion, though it has a certain dependence upon that use of Language. It is argued that expressing a belief that one does not have is a use of Language different from but dependent upon expressing a belief that one does have. The former use of Language is called a *simulation*; such acts simulate expressions of belief. Such a simulation is defined by the conditions of success that define the simulated expression of belief, plus the additional condition of success that what is expressed by a simulated expression of belief should be false. Simulation may enter into deception insofar as the agent may do the simulation by perverting the conventions by conformity to which he would do an act of the simulated kind. The relation of simulation is not peculiar to Language, and may be illustrated from other types of action. There are other similar dependent forms of action including those of practising, pretending, exemplifying. Types of action which are dependent in the illustrated way are called *parasitical*, and the types of action upon which they depend are called *hosts*. A type of action P is parasitical if and only if there exists a type of action H (the host) where (1) a condition of doing P is that the agent know how to do H and (2) the conditions of success for P and H are the same except for a specific finite number of conditions $(C^i, \ldots, C^p)$ which are conditions of success for P but not for H and where each C^i is either a contradictory of some condition of success for H *or* is a condition

375

on the measure of success for acts of type H. Parasitical uses of Language are types of action which are in this way dependent upon other (host) uses of Language. Parasitical uses of Language may be cross-classified, first, according to the host and, second, according to the types of conditions $C^i, \ldots, C^p$. The latter mode of classification gives such categories as simulating, pretending, exemplifying, practising, paradoxing.]

Our stipulation regarding the self-identifying character of conventional behaviour (Part IV, no. 3), and with that the subsequent definitions of conventional behaviour and Language, may have seemed to some to be in direct conflict with the undeniable fact of verbal deception, e.g., lying. How, it might be asked, can it possibly be maintained that the lying agent makes his purpose identifiable in his act, when actually his choice of words is calculated to mask his purpose? Yet surely there is Language here. The agent, admittedly, is acting contrary to known conventions, exploiting them and his interlocutors' good faith, abusing Language, to be sure, but only by using Language. At best, it would seem, our definition of Language is too narrow.

The objection is a threatening one, and the difficulty is not easy to get round. Austin was even inclined to remove such 'abuses', 'etiolations', 'parasites' entirely from the field of his investigation, and what he does have to say about such cases does not stabilize the situation very much (*op. cit.*, pp. 22, 104f., 121).

The objection intimates that if our definition of conventional behaviour is not wrong, then it is too narrow. In response to this thought, I was once inclined to elaborate the original stipulation as follows: A purpose, P, is conventional only if an agent can act to attain P only by acting in such a way as would normally cause others to think that he was acting so as to cause others to think that he was acting in such a way as to attain a purpose, P', that could be attained only by an agent's taking means enabling others to recognize his purpose as P', where P may or may not be P'.

All that is true. But it is unnecessary to build it into the definition of conventional behaviour. We may avoid the complication by exploiting the observation that conventional acts of almost all types may be done in disregard of any effects they may have on interlocutors.

Take the case of lying. An act of lying has an ineliminable nonconventional part, *viz.*, to get another to believe something. That part of the purpose could be attained without use of Language, e.g., by simulating a look of despair. Success in deceptions necessarily involves bringing about such effects. One may of course collaterally use Language for attaining the purpose. Again, Language may be hybridized as the Original Way into the Original Purpose of creating belief, in which case the act would be a locutionary hybrid. Acts of deliberate lying are perhaps best described in this way. In any event we are trafficking with further non-conventional purposes, which we originally stipulated must be disregarded and which were cut off from our definition of conventional behaviour. I submit, then, that attention to the distinction between Language and other types of action to which it may be collateral or into which it may be hybridized obviates cluttering our definition of conventional behaviour as well as dubious and dangerous retreats to the 'normal'. (See I. Hungerland, 'Contextual Implications', *Inquiry*, 1961, esp. pp. 236f.).

We observed that lying is perhaps a locutionary hybrid. How are we to identify the use of Language which enters as the Original Way? This remains a hard question, well able to instil the diffidence Austin apparently felt.

Normally when I tell someone something I tell him what I believe. But when I lie, I do not believe what I tell. In order for the deception to have any chance, the Language act of telling which is part of the deceit must look very like a Language act of telling non-deceitfully done. Are the two imagined Language acts of the same type or not? The issue turns entirely upon how we are to reckon in the agent's beliefs. Let us provisionally call the types of Language act under investigation *expressions of belief*, under which will fall *asserting*, *conjecturing*, *guessing*, *predicting*, but not *assuming*, *considering*. The question is, must one have the belief one expresses? At first glance, it would seem not. Whether or not the agent had the belief, he could presumably employ exactly the same words and therefore presumably indicate exactly the same conditions of success. To the objection that belief must figure somewhere in the picture, the advocate of this position could possibly respond that satisfaction of the normal condition of positive belief is intimated but not actually entailed by other conditions of success, *e.g.*, that the agent should not actually disavow willingness to withdraw in case what he said was shown to be false.

I would welcome this proposal. But, alas, it leaves us without any understanding of the difference between expressing beliefs that one has and expressing beliefs that one does not have. There is certainly such a difference and, I would argue, it is a difference in the use of Language. My method of getting you to see this is familiar. Since any kind of Language act may be done on its own, we must consider cases where an agent is talking to himself without any further purpose in view. Here I think that it is obvious that saying to oneself what one does believe is a very different thing from saying to oneself what one does not believe. There is a close analogy to conventional expressions of feeling, attitude, sensation, *etc.* A condition for one's

377

telling oneself that he feels a pain is that he should feel the pain. Now saying to oneself that one does not believe it—it is not an expression of uncertainty or of contrary belief—it is an expression of a belief that one does not have, *e.g.*, it is not a denial or a negative assertion. What, then, is the difference between the two kinds of expression of belief? The two must differ in at least the respect that the agent in the one case believes and in the other disbelieves what he says. Generalizing this case, I shall call Language acts of expressing mental states one does not have *conventional simulations*. Simulations are always simulations of something. Types of conventional simulation are uses of Language which simulates uses of Language. We may now signalize the distinction between the simulation and what it simulates by calling the one a *simulated expression of belief* (pain, *etc.*) and the other an *expression of belief* (pain, *etc.*) *tout court.*[1]

I hold that the simulation differs from what it simulates in the essential condition of whether the agent does or does not believe what he expresses. Are the alternative conditions conditions of doing or conditions of success? Since a reflective agent cannot but know what he believes, they cannot be conditions of success. The conditions in question are therefore presumably conditions of doing. But according to our theory, the difference between the two types of action must be marked by some difference in the defining conditions of success. What is that? The difference, I submit, is this: A condition of success for a simulating expression of belief (pain, *etc.*) is that what the agent expresses must actually be false, whereas this is not a condition of

---

[1] I am advocating a strong form of the thesis that positive belief of what one says is a necessary condition for successful assertion. Some may find this repugnant. I could reply: 'But "assertion" is a technical word!' That would be a cheat. I hope that my use of 'assertion' tallies with contemporary philosophical usage. Besides, the doctrine carries over to other kinds of 'expression', *e.g.*, of pain or emotion. I rest my case upon the above-indicated 'way of getting you to see', *viz.*, by supposing that Language acts of the type in question are detached from their normal perlocutionary connections. Others have argued for a weaker version of the same thesis, by invoking those connections. I think chiefly of Nowell-Smith (see 'Contextual Implication and Ethical Theory', *Proc. Arist. Soc. Supp.*, 1962, pp. 1–18, esp. pp. 12–15). He takes his start from the assumption that the purpose of assertion is to convey information, where *A*'s saying *p* to *B* gives *B* reason to think that *p* is true. Nowell-Smith convincingly argues that that could be so only if *B* were entitled to infer that *A* believes what he says, *i.e.*, that *A*'s assertion implies that *A* believes *p*. These observations may indeed explain the existence of the assertion use of Language as well as the character of that use of Language by way of an upward reference to the normally perlocutionary purposes of communicating, informing, *etc.* But I deny that these normal perlocutionary connections have a definitional strength. This objection is weakened by Nowell-Smith's acknowledged use of 'imply' and related terms in broad, rather vapid senses. At all events, I am willing to maintain a stronger thesis without calling for support from the perlocutionary superstructure of Language.

success for the simulated expression of belief (pain); otherwise all other conditions of success are the same. Two results follow: First, we would define a conventional simulation by adding one condition to the indefinite number of conditions of success which define the simulated use of Language. Second, we can give sense to 'what the agent expresses' where the simulation fails solely on account of the truth of what he expresses, for, 'what the agent expresses' may be defined as the measure of success of the simulated use of Language. The resultant of these consequences is that we should define simulations in terms of what they simulate.

So far I have been appealing to a difference which I presume any user of Language would feel between the two kinds of Language act, were he simply talking to himself. A further argument for the distinction is found in the consideration that the two kinds of action typically make differing collateral contributions to the attainment of further purposes or may enter into different locutionary hybrids. We are not engaged in sheer logical prestidigitation solely for the sake of elucidating cases of deception. We might, for example, invent a game where the winner is the player who says the most false things in a minute. He fails to score whenever the condition of falsehood is not satisfied. Again, one may spoof or lie, or a teacher may test students by offering them the opportunity to catch him out; and then of course there are 'multiple-choice questions'. In all these cases, acts simulating expressions of belief are performed in the course of doing something else, where simple expression of belief would not have done at all.

I anticipate two objections to this account of simulations. First, a true and familiar philosophical principle enjoins us from making the success of an assertion depend upon its truth-value; by extension, we should not allow the success of an act simulating assertion to depend upon its truth-value. My reply is simply that assertion and a simulating expression of belief are different types of action. The success of the simulation depends upon its truth-value only by depending upon the truth-value of what it simulates. There is no principle which enjoins us from making the success of the simulation depend upon the truth-value of what is simulated. There are reasons for the opposite policy. Simulations depend upon what they simulate; a reference in the definition of a simulation to the truth-value of the supposed simulated action marks the character of that dependence.

A second, more challenging objection is simply an allegation of fact: One can say what he does not believe and succeed even though his belief is false; examples are acts of making assumptions. Now, I allow that there could be a type of action we could call simulation of assertion that would not thus depend upon the falsehood of the simulated assertion. But if we concentrate on the particular use of Language that so often contributes to the hybrid purposes of lying and setting multiple-choice questions, then surely the acts in question would fail if what the agent actually believed were false. A commitment engendered by the successful setting of a multiple-choice question is that at least one of the options be false and at least one be true; otherwise the examinee can neither succeed nor fail in answering the question; so the examiner must order certain of the options in the belief that they are false, and if he is mistaken in this, the question fails. Similarly an act of lying would fail if what the agent says is true, even though his suspicious interlocutor believes the contrary and thus deceives himself.

Conventional simulations may be made expressly identifiable as such by use of an expression, e.g., by the multiple-choice format. But simulations are conspicuous for the contribution they make to the ends of deception. For these ends it is important that the agent's Language purpose should not be evident to his interlocutor and that the conventional simulation should not be readily identifiable as such. But our account of Language requires that the act, being a conventional act, should be made identifiable as such. Yes, but not necessarily *readily* identifiable as such. An onlooker who knew enough about the agent could tell from the agent's words what he was saying and what he was doing. The onlooker sees while the interlocutor does not see what conventions control the agent's act. The agent in short conforms to conventions which he hopes will not be penetrated by his interlocutor; he does that by perverting, hence exploiting, conventions which he presumes are familiar to his interlocutor, hoping to give the impression that he is conforming to the perverted conventions. Thus, the agent contrives to secure that his interlocutor should misidentify what is said.

So far we have confined our attention to conventional simulations. But the idea of a simulation can be generalized to include non-conventional cases. I can simulate a cry of pain. Here again, it is a matter of my behaviour showing something that is not the case. We cannot, however, automatically extend our definition to non-conventional instances, for the important reason that the success of non-conventional behaviour does not in general require that the agent should take measures to show anything, and so there is no easily stated relation between an item of a kind of behaviour and action which simulates what that kind of behaviour would show.

Once we have widened our net to catch non-conventional simulations we are bound to drag up a number of different but similar-looking creatures. Examples are practising, pretending, and illustrating (which latter may always have to be conventional). Whenever someone practises, he practises doing something. We do not know what he is doing until we know both that he is practising and what he is practising. Similarly for pretending. There is almost nothing that one cannot practise or pretend doing. Here, then, are fairly systematic ways of generating new, dependent types of action out of old. I propose to call all these *parasitical* types of action. Practising, pretending, simulating are sub-types of parasitical action. The definition of any particular type of parasitical action is always relative to some other type of action—that which is practised, pretended, or simulated. We call that type of action upon which the parasitical type parasitically depends the *host* type of action.

There appears to be a common kind of relation between parasite and host that one may be inclined to describe as follows: In doing parasitical acts one acts as if he were acting in some other way, and that he should act as he does presumes that he could have acted in the other way. So far this but illustrates the general point that capacity to do one kind of action often presumes the capacity to do acts of some other kind. But the cases considered are all such that the dependence and subsequent relations between the parasite and host types of act are of a peculiar and fairly specific kind. Speaking impressionistically, we might say that the dependent type attempts, as it were, to impersonate the other; the one tries to take the other's place; but in such a way that if this were to happen universally the dependent use itself would succumb. Hence 'parasite' and 'host'. The parasite depends upon the host, whose existence it implies, but the host does not depend upon the parasites that feed upon it. The parasite lives upon the host. Were there no action of host-act kind, there could be no parasite of the kind in question. One cannot act parasitically without first having acquired the host type of action, but not conversely; the host affords the possibility of the parasite. In this case the relation is one of vicarious identification.

This is *very* impressionistic. It would be gratifying if we could secure a more concrete statement of the relation between parasite and host framed in the terminology of our theory. Suppose that I should be practising kicking field goals. Apparently most of the conditions of success for actually kicking field goals carry over, *e.g.*, that there be a ball. But one thing is sure: I could not do such an act in the actual course of a game, unless for some reason I thought the game was not going on.

We have already met this kind of situation in our discussion of residual Language acts. We described these as *attenuations* of some other kind of act. A type of action K' is an attenuation of a type of action K if the conditions of success of K and K' are the same except for a specifiable, finite number of types of conditions $(C^i, \ldots, C^p)$

which are conditions of success for K but not for K'. We may then define K' as K without the conditions $(C^i, \ldots, C^p)$.

The dependence of K' upon K may usually be accounted for by appeal to the defeasible character of success in action. While we can never give a complete list of conditions of success for a type of action, we may assume that there is a totality of conditions which we can progressively and discretely attenuate, where this recaptures the actual process by which new types of action may be generated out of old. Now practising doing K is not simply an attenuation of K. That there be a game in progress is not merely not a condition of success; rather, that there *not* be a game in progress *is* a condition of success. Here the relation of dependence is also clearer. Since the possibility of kicking field goals contributes to the definition of playing a game, the condition that there not be a game in progress marks a dependence of the practising upon the kicking. A way of capturing a good part of that is to say that one could not attempt to practise kicking a goal without knowing how to kick goals; *i.e.*, a condition for doing the one is that the agent know how to do the other.

I propose the following generalization: P is parasitical upon H if (1) a condition of doing P is that the agent know how to do H, and (2) all the conditions of success for P and H are the same except for a specifiable, finite number of conditions of success, $C^i, \ldots, C^p$, for H whose denials are conditions of success for P.

That is at most one kind of parasitical relation. It does not directly apply to simulations. The additional condition of success for the simulation, that what would be shown by the corresponding host act is not the case, is not the contradictory of any condition of success for the host act. It is rather a condition on what would be the measure of success for the host act. So we must add, as an alternative second condition, that one of the $C^i(\epsilon\{C^I, \ldots, C^p\})$ is a condition of success for P but not for H, where a statement of the C^i requires reference to the measure of success for acts of the H-kind.

Fusing both cases, I would define a parasitical type of action, P, as a type of action for which there exists another type of action H, such that (1) a condition of doing P is that the agent know how to do H and (2) where the conditions of success for P and H are the same except for conditions $(C^I, \ldots, C^p)$, which are conditions of success for P but not for H and where each $C^i(\epsilon\{C^I, \ldots, C^p\})$ is either a contradictory of a condition of success for H *or* is a condition on the measure of success for some act of type H. H is called a host. The definition permits a host to have numerous parasites.

If P is a parasite on H, where H is a use of Language, P would appear to have to be a use of Language, though I do not see how to demonstrate this. We call such a use of Language a *parasitical use of*

382

Language. There may be cases where *P* is a use of Language and *H* is not, *e.g.*, *giving examples.* If so, I shall call them *conventional parasites,* and they will be said to be conventionally parasitical upon the host. Parasites are of many kinds, as seen already in our use of the terms 'practising', 'pretending', 'simulating'. The classification would naturally proceed in terms of the conditions separating hosts from parasites. Practising would seem to involve conditions on the immediate environment of the act different from those which define the host. In giving an example, it appears, the agent would seem to be willing to disavow the commitments of the corresponding host act. Pretending is interesting for the fact that the agent may pretend to do something by doing it.[2] That shows that the variant condition cannot be a condition of success, and must therefore be on the measure of success of the host act. But it also has something to do with the agent's state of mind. The condition is, I think, none other than that the agent should in performing the pretence be *indifferent* to the character of the achievement, effect, or product that would result from a successful host act. We have already discussed simulations. So-called paradoxes such as found in utterances like 'This statement is false', or in the posting of a 'No-signs-posted' sign or in the playwright's naming a character 'Miss Named' are types of parasites which are always parasitical uses of Language. They would seem to have the common feature that a condition of their success is that performance of the parasitical (paradoxical) act should either result in the failure of a condition of success for the host action or result in the supposed measure of success of the host action having some incriminating property. This will be gone into more thoroughly in the sequel.

Not every kind of dependence in the realm of Language is parasitical dependence. Residual uses of Language are dependent upon the effective uses of Language from which they are attenuated, but not as parasites; *making assumptions* (in any of the explicit, verbal senses) would seem to be similarly dependent upon *asserting* (whatever asserting turns out to be.) But parasitical dependence is a quite widely applying idea, and I should like to consider only one rather curious and notorious instance from contemporary philosophy.

Philosophers have agitated themselves over the status of utterances containing a referring use for which the agent knows there is no referent; *e.g.*, 'The present king of France is bald'. All seem agreed that we want to avoid spurious referents, 'immanent' or ideational.

---

[2] I consider only cases of pretending to *do* and not, *e.g.*, to be, and then only cases where what one means to do is to pretend to do something (*e.g.*, carry a bloody head), not cases where one means to do something else (*e.g.*, to divert attention) *while* pretending. See the Austin-Anscombe symposium on this topic, *Proc. Arist. Soc. Supp.*, 1958.

Russell holds that the want of a referent falsifies the statement. Strawson holds that the existence of referent is a 'presupposition', *i.e.*, a condition of success, hence a condition for there being any statement at all. I would accept the last except for the difficulty of saying what the example is an example of. To understand it, we must *know* that there is no present king of France. So let's accept that, turning our backs on the ignorance which both Russell and Strawson must suppose for *their* purposes. Now, if we knew that there were no referent answering to 'The present king of France', we would not attempt on either Russell's or Strawson's analysis so much as to make the kind of statement that they both suppose we would—one cannot assert either in the knowledge that what he says is false or in the knowledge that his act must fail. On the other side, if De Gaulle were crowned by the Pope the day before, the example would be useless and even an embarrassment for the purposes of our philosophers. My answer to the question I am asking, which is different from the one both Russell and Strawson are asking (for where they presume ignorance I presume knowledge), is that the philosopher's example is an example of a parasite (hence a parasite on a parasite). The illustrated type of utterance is, in particular, parasitical upon singular subject-predicate assertion, where the distinguishing condition of success is the contradictory of a condition of success for such assertions, that there presently exist a king of France.

Conciliant with the strategy of this section, I would stress the following: Both conventional parasites and parasitical uses of Language are indeed uses of Language. For that reason, the odd conditions of success that set them off from their hosts must in particular acts be indicated by conformity to conventions. But parasitical Language acts are powerful instruments of deception. That is so because isolated conditions of success, such as those which set a parasite off from its host, are seldom assigned to particular expressions by the conventions of our language. Conventions generally secure that packages of conditions of success are indicated by employment of an expression. These may easily be singly attenuated, supplemented, or interchanged. Existing conventions are therefore naturally exploited for purposes of parasitical action and easily perverted for purposes of perlocutionary deceit.

8. WAYS OF USING LANGUAGE

[The distinction between what kind of act is done and how it is done carries over to the use of Language. Anything that contributes to how a Language act is done, *i.e.*, anything the mention of which serves to describe in contrast with identify a Language act, is called a *way of using Language*. This covers ever so much that is different, including the expressions and the language employed, the style adopted, the manner of delivery, the motives of the agent, and, of course, the underlying nests of collateral acts. Acts of all kinds may be done in conventional ways; *e.g.*, in acting *politely* the agent shows how he means to act in the movements he makes. Such movements qualify as expressions, and they may possibly have uses in conventions which pertain to a language. That is especially evident when what is done in a conventional way is itself a Language act. One may then 'regretfully' *apologize* or 'therefore' *assert*, where the words employed show that the agent is apologizing in such a way as to show his regret or is asserting as the conclusion of an argument. Mention of the uses thus realized does not contribute to the fixing of the identity of the act but rather describes the conventional way in which it is done. In such cases, the uses are said to be *act-adverbially realized*.]

In no. 4 of Part II we drew a general distinction between what kind of act is done and how or in what manner an act is done. To say what kind of act is done is (in our terminology) to identify it as a kind. To say in what manner an act is done is (in our terminology) to describe it. According to this way of speaking, the mention of anything that does not contribute to the specification of the purpose of an act describes the act and says something about how it was done. 'How an act is done' obviously covers much that is different, including physical manner of performance, the state of the agent, his motives and attitudes, the success or failure of the act, and of course everything which relates to the underlying nests of collateral acts by which the act is done.

The distinction between the *what* and the *how*, and therewith also the distinction between identification and description of action, carries over to the use of Language. Here we meet with special, characteristic modes of act-description, having to do with the choice of expression and language, the adoption of style, relative articulateness, and grammaticality. Still more interestingly, one may say his piece with certain conditions or qualifications attached, or *as* (*e.g.*) the conclusion of an argument, or *in* (*e.g.*) answer to a question. The test is this: if what is mentioned is not taken to affect the identity of the act or the resulting conventional product or effect, then that part of the act draws attention to the *how* and not the what, and to mention that part of the act would be act-description. For example, if the same statement which I make in English in answer to a question or as the conclusion of an argument could have been made in French in a newspaper report on the habits of Americans, then that shows that 'in English', 'in answer . . .', 'as a conclusion . . .', and 'in a news-paper . . .' serve to describe and not identify their respective acts.

For sake of convenience, I shall call anything which may affect how a Language act is done, the mention of which would describe the act, a *way of using Language*. Actually, I shall apply the term 'way of using Language' only in respect to those features of Language acts that would be determined by the elements of the act. I shall not, for example, speak of a *successful* or *unsuccessful* way of using Language. I shall, for all that, employ the term 'way' to refer to much that is different, including everything that relates to the choice of convention, style, and the underlying nests of collateral acts. In the sequel to this volume, where I take up the topics of Language rules, expressions, and styles, we shall be much occupied with *ways* of using Language.

We sometimes speak of *conventional ways* of behaving, *e.g.*, conventional ways of eating, walking, talking. Such an employment of 'conventional' may mark a different contrast from the one that was defined in Part IV. When we say that the major walks in a conventional, military way, we certainly do not mean to say that he takes his steps by indicating that he means to take his steps in a certain way. But sometimes, surely, the conventional way in which an act is done is conventional in precisely our sense of 'conventional'. If I do something in a polite way, then I must show that I mean to do it in a polite way. A test for this is to consider the possibility of converting the manner into part of the purpose, *i.e.*, to consider an agent whose purpose it is to appear to act in the indicated manner: if the resulting act would be a conventional act, then the conventional manner under examination is conventional in our sense. Suppose, for example, it is the agent's purpose to show himself to be a polite man, as it may be his purpose to show himself to be a member of a certain class—he will move in the right way, and say the right things to the ladies at the right time. In order to succeed in such action his movements must indicate the conditions of success, *e.g.*, that this is a lady whom he believes to be of a certain age, *etc.* He must show that he means to be polite. The indicated kind of action is admittedly mercifully rare, for generally politeness is a matter of the *how* and not the *what*—of the way in which one behaves—whereas we have taken as a case an example of an act where the agent's very purpose is to be polite. But by seeing how the way can be converted into the purpose, we are better able to see that it too is conventional in just the sense we have explained. If acting to be polite is a kind of conventional action, then when one acts politely, one is polite by virtue of conforming to conventions.

When the conventional manner is conventional in the right sense, this will be indicated in the agent's movements. More specifically, the agent's movements must indicate conditions of success. But these cannot be conditions of success for The Act, *i.e.*, conditions definitive of the purpose; they can only be conditions of success for a collateral act, *i.e.*, conditions definitive of one of the collateral purposes. Normally, such movements are made in conformity with some familiar convention. Such movements are expressions as we have defined that idea (see pp. 307f.). Often they take the form of gestures. But they may be words having uses in conventions pertaining to some natural language, such words as 'regretfully', 'May I?' and so on.

The conventional movements in question must indicate conditions of success, and the conventional contribution they make to the act may be defined by listing those conditions. Such lists of conditions we say define *uses of words* (see pp. 307f.). It follows that the movements in question have uses.

We have noticed that a conventional manner may be converted into a conventional purpose. In that event, the same conditions of success would be indicated, only now as conditions of success for the act. I have chosen to describe that process as one of *realizing* the use in the act. (Where, of course, the use may be realized, the conditions indicated, even if the act fails.)

How now are we to describe what happens when the indication of the conditions affects the manner in which the act is done? It is interesting that in Indo-European languages we often do this by use of an adverb which modifies, as it were, the whole act, whether the act be a Language act or of some other kind, *e.g.*, 'regretfully', 'consequently'. Trading on this, I shall say that the use is *act-adverbially realized*. Notice that it is not the use itself which is act-adverbial, for it may also be realized to indicate the purpose; it is rather the *realization* of the use which is act-adverbial.

Almost any kind of act may be done in a conventional manner; for that reason I have so far kept the discussion quite general. We may also use Language in a conventional way, and that is certainly the most conspicuous kind of case. Here, too, it is most natural that the uses be act-adverbially realized by employment of words which smoothly blend into the flow of other words employed to indicate conditions which define the purpose of the act. Thus we may 'would you be so kind to' request, or 'regretfully' protest, or 'consequently' assert. This makes it fatally easy to misconstrue the contribution of these words. We must not, in the imagined cases, suppose that they alter the conventional purpose or affect the 'content', *i.e.*, the conventional product or effect that may be produced by the act. To be sure, the same words in the same uses may contribute to the conventional purpose and affect the content of some conventional act. We shall go into this in the next section. But in the imagined cases, they affect only the way of using Language. Failure to appreciate this difference between a conventional *what* and *how*, and to understand how the *way* may be carried by familiar expressions, has contributed to the popular but faulty way of thinking about Language alluded to on p. 356. Missing the difference, one might come to think, for instance, that when I make a statement as the conclusion of an argument, or with feeling, I am not only stating, but, on the same level, in the same way, *also* deducing and expressing feeling. That would be a confusion of what I do (as identified by specification of the purpose) with how I do it; or, again, a confusion of what I do with those additional facts about myself I show in doing the act. In the case of Language, it may cause us to ascribe to the upshot or effect features which properly belong to the acts by which they are produced.[1]

I conclude this section with the speculative thought that the explanation of our having conventional ways of using Language is that these contribute mightily to the attainment of (usually non-conventional) further (perlocutionary) purposes to which the use of Language is itself collateral. I am more likely to get another to do something if I show him conventional respect; I am more likely to convince another if I show him that the alleged fact 'therefore follows'. Finally, the organization of human knowledge into theories is very much a matter of assembling conventional materials in conventional ways, *e.g.*, as mathematical theories, for this facilitates test, proof, and application.

9. HYBRIDIZATION INTO LANGUAGE

[Collateral act ways of using Language may be hybridized as Original Ways into the use of Language. If the Original Way is not itself conventional, the resulting hybrid is only partly conventional. An example is an act of ordering a beverage in French. If the Original Way is itself conventional, the result is a (totally) conventional act. Such occurs when a use that is normally act-adverbially realized is

---

[1] The part of Austin's *How to do Things with Words* I find least satisfying is that which concerns so-called 'expositives', *e.g.*, as found in such locutions as 'I hold', 'I say', 'I define', 'I assume' (see esp. Lecture XII, pp. 160ff.). He observes how these overlap all of his other categories of performative force. What I feel he may fail to appreciate sufficiently is that many of the locutions are most characteristically employed in what I call act-adverbial realization. This makes me think that many of his intimated examples of expository illocutionary force are spurious. I allow that these same uses may be converted and realized to .indicate conditions of success of The Act, and I am then quite prepared to think that the resulting uses of Language are usually performative, but then they are not 'expositive'. See next section.

converted into the purpose. If the expressions in question have inscriptional variants or equivalents, hybridization results in a use of Language. Such uses of Language are often but not always of a kind we may wish to call 'performative'.]

In the last section we noted that Language acts may be done in various ways, including by way of certain lines of collateral action. Thus one may order a bottle of wine by way of uttering a French sentence: 'Je voudrais une bouteille de bon vin rouge'. Such a type of action may be hybridized as the Original Way into the use of Language. Thus it might be one's purpose to order a bottle of wine in French. To attain the purpose it is now not sufficient that the agent should order the bottle of wine, as he might do, in French or English or by pointing to a bottle; our convivial tourist is supposed to be wanting to show his French, and should his French fail, then so will he, no matter how completely the stigma is washed away by the excellent wine which the English-speaking waiter finally brings.

In the example, the Original Way is not itself conventional, and the resulting hybrid is therefore only partly conventional. But it is possible that a conventional way of using Language may be hybridized into the use of Language. I may invite someone into my house in a polite way, e.g., by making a polite gesture. In other circumstances, when protocol matters much, I might also come to want to issue polite invitations, by hybridizing the conventional Original Way into the conventional Original Purpose of *inviting*.

Hybridization always yields a new type of action. The hybridization of a conventional Original Way into an Original Language Purpose yields a new type of conventional behaviour. It may be that the conventional way may be done inscriptionally; that is, it may be that the expressions by employment of which the word uses composing the way are act-adverbially realized have inscriptional variants or equivalents. If so, hybridization results in a new use of Language.

Examples are readily found in the converted force of such words as 'I assume' and 'therefore'. Often when a speaker says, e.g., 'He is coming, I assume', the 'I assume' shows that the agent is saying his piece in a somewhat qualified way.[1] But if pressed, the speaker might change his tune a little, saying, 'Well, I *assume* he's coming', where his words now make clear that he is doing something of a different kind, *viz.*, making an assumption.

We similarly move from making statements as conclusions of

---

[1] See, esp., J. O. Urmson, 'Parenthetical Verbs', reprinted in *Essays in Conceptual Analysis* (ed. Flew). I am here drawing attention to what Urmson calls 'pure parenthetical uses'; see pp. 193f.

deductive argument to setting forth formal deductive proofs of statements. In both cases the equivalent of the word 'therefore' is apt to occur, but with altered 'force'.

What do I mean by saying that the 'force' of the words 'I assume' or 'therefore' alters? Surely not that the meaning of these words changes. Meaning is determined by the conditions of success that would be indicated by employment of the expressions. That remains the same over the transition from a conventional way to a conventional Original Way. What changes is the use of Language, to the determination of which the meaning of (*e.g.*) 'therefore' or 'I assume' now contributes.[2]

In the sequel I shall define what some philosophers (following Austin) have called performative uses of Language as productive uses of Language among whose conditions of success are that the act be performed by one or another of a small number of specifiable agents. In the last section we observed that Austin was inclined to confuse conventional ways with performative uses of Language. Accepting the suggested definition of performative uses of Language, we can now penetrate to the root of the confusion. Conventional ways, signalized by such words as 'I hope', 'I suppose', 'I think', may be hybridized into Language. If the parenthetical, conventional qualification is to be taken as a mark of the particular speaker's attitude, caution, feeling, the resulting hybrid is special to him and hence, if productive, performative. (The hybrid will be productive if the Original Purpose is.) It does not always happen thus—witness our example of 'therefore'. But it is very common indeed. The consequence is that many words, like 'I believe', 'I suppose', may be employed in precisely the same sense both to effect act-adverbial modification and to signalize performative uses of Language. Normally, the latter occurrence is secondary to the former.

SNEAK PREVIEW

The foregoing analysis of the use of Language as a type of action affords a basis for the articulation of a General Theory of Language, whose developments I have, somewhat tediously, been anticipating by advance references to 'the sequels'. I should now like to sketch in the main lines of that theory. Everything follows from our definition of a Language act as one the movements constituting which indicate all the conditions of success for the act, and from the idea that the uses of particular meaningful movements (expressions) may be

[2] Austin might put it by saying that 'I assume' now affects the illocutionary force of the locutionary act.

explained by listing conditions of success that the making of those movements in a Language act would indicate.

The General Theory has a number of stages each rather more abstract and encompassing than the previous. The first stage is, as it were, taxonomic; it consists of a rough classification of types of Language action, which types I call *uses of Language*. This gives way to a more abstract analysis for resolving Language acts into elements of sense—what I call *uses of words*—that are structurally isolable by reference to a body of convention. This in turn is absorbed into a still more abstract theory of *Language elements* that can be defined independently of the conventions of any language. All these items—uses of Language, uses of words, and Language elements—are introduced so as to be definable by listings of indicatable conditions of success.

In the second sequel the General Theory is applied for developing a theory of the products and effects of successful Language action. Attention is concentrated on a somewhat factitious but centrally situated productive use of Language, to be called 'assertion', whose products are to be called 'statements'. It turns out to be relatively easy to formulate explicitly a theory of statements. This theory quickly shows itself to be a powerful instrument for conducting the abstract theory of the use of Language. That comes about as follows: Most uses of words which may contribute to assertion also contribute to Language acts of other kinds, and most uses of words which contribute to Language acts of other kinds can be made to contribute to assertions. Now an assertion if successful produces a statement consisting of Language elements in terms of which the contributing word uses would be explained. The abstract theory of statements can be codified mathematically, where the formulas representing a statement also represent the Language elements constituting the statement. We thus also achieve an abstract, codifiable theory of the use of Language having wide, though not unlimited, applicability. (The limitations are due to the fact that not all uses of words may figure in assertions, and not all Language elements can be elements of statements.)

Let me now fill in a bit. A use of Language is a type of action, to be further differentiated as a species from the genus of Language in much the same way that (*e.g.*) conventional behaviour is differentiated from conformative behaviour. Uses of Language are identified vernacularly by familiar verbs and verb phrases such as 'promise', 'request', 'conjecture', and 'give examples'. These types of action are indefinitely various and their classification is necessarily amorphous; indeed, there is no hope for a proper classification according to the strict taxonomic requirement of a finite number of independently definable, mutually exclusive, and collectively exhaustive categories. What can be done is to introduce broader technical categories under which different uses of Language may be subsumed, including categories for relating one use of Language to others. Here, too, nothing approaching a strict classification can be achieved. However, fairly systematic methods may be employed. These methods fasten chiefly but not exclusively on conditions of the agent and characteristic commitments, the presumption being that our vernacular identifications of uses of Language more or less naturally reflect that kind of consideration.

A Language act is typally identified by saying under what uses or kinds of uses of Language it falls. The conditions characteristic of a use of Language either are among the conditions of success which would be indicated in the movements constituting the Language act or are conditions for doing such an act. But there are other conditions of success for the act in addition to those that are characteristic of the use of Language. As a general rule, certain expressions are employed to indicate the other conditions. The conditions of success are then generally brought together into packages and indicated collectively by the use of particular expressions, where some of these packaged conditions are characteristic of the use of Language and others not. At all events, the expressions that carry these packages of conditions may be employed in different Language acts, this being assured by the structure of the body of conventions that make up the language in question. These packages of conditions define what I call *uses of words*, which, as I have already suggested, may approximate what some linguists mean by 'sememes'. Now the determination of a use of words is relative to a convention in conformity with which an expression may be employed to indicate a package of conditions. These conventions always pertain to bodies of convention, or languages; and in so-called natural languages this packaging normally proceeds in characteristic if complicated ways. The net result of this is that particular uses of words are defined and the notion applied only in relation to a language or a small number of languages. Briefly explained, the theory of word uses is a theory for resolving a Language act into natural elements determined relative to the conventions of a language.

Since a Language act is made identifiable as a kind by employment of certain expressions, it follows that the theory of Language uses available to the speakers of a given language may be absorbed into the more general and abstract theory of the uses of words available to those speakers. Word uses may be classified into various kinds, where one such kind is to indicate the type of Language act or use of Language. Some of these classifications of word uses may, of course, be more pertinent to the speakers of one language than to the speakers of another.

A constraint upon the theory of word uses would be that a Language act could be analysed into a finite number of elements that concurrently indicate a *complete* set of conditions of success. This remark makes sense only if the conditions indicated by the realization of certain uses of words require complementation by conditions that might be indicated by various other uses of words. The theory of complementation—what I have called a theory of 'conceptual valence'—results in a partial criterion of sense and nonsense and has application to a number of other classical issues in theory of Language. It enables us, for one thing, to make precise and explain the ancient dictum of the 'unity of the proposition', a dictum inspired by the existence of meaningful, composite expressions. What binds the Language act and its product together into something more than a mere listing of terms is not the existence of Fregian 'Functions' (see *op. cit.*, pp. 54f.) or Russellian verbs (see *Principles of Mathematics*, no. 54), but the fact that some terms indicate conditions which require complementation with conditions indicated by other terms. Thus, the conditions of success that would be concurrently indicated by the occurrence of a predicate 'is blue', *e.g.*, that we could perform certain tests upon otherwise indicated objects, require the complementary indication that there be one or several objects which at least are capable of having colour and to which the tests may be applied. That could be variously (and differently) indicated by use of a so-called referring expression or by a so-called quantifier.

This theory of word uses, being relative in application to the expressions employed and a body of convention, raises questions about rules of Language and the classification of expressions, and also questions of a grammatical complexion such as those over the definitions of the 'parts of speech'. Many of these questions will be scouted, often in a pretty abstract way, though never actually answered.

The determination of a use of words, we saw, is relative to convention. It is interesting that we can 'translate' 'what is said' in conformity with one body of conventions so that we can imagine that 'the same thing' would be said in conformity with another body of conventions. This is usually facilitated by the overlapping applicability of a given classification of word uses. But it is doubtful whether the overlap is ever complete. How then can we translate?

Another problem is this. It is possible to draw a distinction between the saying of what is said and what is said by saying it if one is successful. A speaker may, for instance, make the same promise by uttering different words having different senses (uses), *e.g.*, by saying

'I promise to . . .' or by simply saying 'yes' in response to a question. How then can we make out the distinction between what is said and the saying of what is said?

The two questions are answered together with our theory of Language elements. One may say something and fail, in which case nothing is said. But success is assured if all the indicated conditions of success are satisfied. It seems, furthermore, that what is said is always determined by the saying, even though there might be different ways of saying the same thing. The solution is that we may identify what is said by simply listing the indicated conditions of success subject to the stipulation that they all be satisfied. Now, since the same thing may be said in different ways, in different languages, by way of realizing different uses of words, it is essential that we identify what is said not in terms of packages of conditions of success but in terms of isolated, particular conditions of success. By listing these we, as it were, resolve the supposed upshot or effect into its elements. These we call Language elements. Each Language element is defined by mention of a particular condition of success.

It is now clear that we have (1) absorbed the theory of word uses into the more abstract theory of Language elements (2) in such a way as to avoid relativization to any particular bodies of convention,[1] (3) while at the same time moving away from the analysis of the relatively concrete Language act into the analysis of the abstracted products and effects of Language.

Because the partitioning of Language into uses of Language would seem an endless affair, it would be fruitless to embark upon an examination of all uses of Language under the pretence that it could be exhaustive. But in our taxonomic investigations it turns out that some uses of Language are more central than others, in that the less central may be characterized relative to the more central. These investigations intimate that there may be a most central use of Language of

---

[1] Of course, how I individuate conditions of success is relative to my ways of thinking and therefore also possibly indirectly relative to the conventions of my language. But that does not matter, so long as I have some way of saying under what conditions speakers would regard their acts as failures. It may be that the theorists of another tribe would have a list of Language elements different from mine. Some of their single conditions would be complex conditions for me, and *vice versa*. We would then, indeed, have different *theories*, but both of the theories would be generally applicable to the analysis of Language however used and wherever found. I might, for example, think of the existence of a movement as resolvable into a number of conditions regarding what was moving, where and when it started and stopped. Someone from another tribe might, differently, think of what I call a moving object as a cross-section of the movement. But presumably I can analyse his Language and his language in my terms, and he can analyse mine in his.

all, this being no other than the somewhat artificial but easily illustratable use of Language that philosophers have sometimes called *assertion*. By fixing the boundaries and the features of this use of Language, assertion, we might come into position to explain many other uses of Language in a fairly systematic way, by charting their locations relative to the central region of assertion. This possibility plus the fact that assertion is of first-water interest in itself gives strong motive for undertaking a systematic examination of assertion, which is what I shall attempt in the second sequel to this volume. I proceed in the usual way, imposing narrow limits on the idea of assertion in terms of commitments, conditions of the agent, *etc*. Assertion comes out as a productive use of Language, the satisfaction of the criterion of success for which implies that there be tests available by application of which the product—called a 'statement'—may be (conclusively) verified and falsified. Assuming the satisfaction of other conditions implicit in the delimitation of assertion as a use of Language, we may define a statement as an ordered pair of such tests—the verification and the falsification tests—subject to the one general condition that if either test could be successfully applied the other could not be. The notion of test is itself explained in terms of (1) the occasions for applying the test, (2) the procedures involved in application, and (3) the conditions of successful application. This explanation can be easily cast into a mathematical form, and therewith also the definition of a statement. In immediate utilization of this 'criterion of identity' for statements, we may give test-theoretical definitions of the notions of *truth, equivalence, consequence, necessity*, as these characteristics attach to statements. It is argued that we can isolate a small number of basic types of test in terms of which countless other types may be defined, chiefly by imposing conditions on the occasions for applying tests, these conditions to be stated in terms of the successful applicability of other tests ultimately of the basic kinds. Algebraic formalism is introduced for referring to tests in terms of the basic types of tests. This affords means for (1) defining forms of statement in terms of forms of verification and falsification tests, and (2) defining subject-matters or theories in terms of selections of basic tests,[2] yielding a classification of kinds of theory, and (3) defining a variety of concepts affiliated with traditional metaphysics. We achieve, in short, a full theory of intensional logic-cum-formal metaphysics.

The theory takes on immediate application to the analysis of Language in the following way. The conditions for applying verification and falsification tests which we can refer to with the formalism

[2] A good part of the contemplated volume consists in applying the theory to itself.

are conditions for the existence of tests. But the existence of tests is a condition for the existence of statements. The existence of a statement is the measure of the success of an assertion. But now the assertion succeeds just in case all the indicated conditions of success are satisfied. It follows that the conditions for applying a test that are referred to by the formalism are *also* among the conditions of success that are indicated by the expressions employed in the assertion. The same part of the test formulas which may thus be taken to fix conditions of success for assertion may also be thought of as fixing the Language elements constituting the statement. Because the expressions employed in the assertion may occur with the same uses in other types of Language act and because the Language elements constituting the statement may occur in other types of conventional upshot or effect, the net result is that our relatively well-articulated theory of tests is immediately converted into an abstract theory of the use of Language. While this theory surely does not *cover* the whole field of Language and must be supplemented with apparatus of a less highly codified kind, it may be employed over the whole field of Language and at various levels of abstraction.

INDEX OF AUTHORS

INDEX OF SUBJECTS

Action—(*cont.*)
  individuation of, 26 f., 37, 40–44,
    50, 134, 174, 177, 221, 312
  inhibiting, 28, 32, 56, 130
  parastical, 158, 381–84
  particular identification of, 37,
    49, 50, 119, 179, 216, 220 ff.
  parts of, 25–27, 68, 140 f., 179,
    328, 330
  primary features of, 178 f. (*see*
    Showing)
  principles and theory of, xi, 101 f.,
    134, 150, 153, 193, 251
  typal identification of (*see also*
    Purpose, specification of),
    34, 47, 49, 51, 80 f., 122, 125,
    131 f., 172, 174, 177, 179,
    216, 222, 370
  verbal index to, 32–34, 48, 60, 68,
    324
Activity, 138, 140, 161, 187 n.,
    236 f., 239, 371
  action and, 39 ff., 131
  completion of, 168
  failure in, 131
  rational, 112
Adjective, rank of, 283 n.
Agent, 12, 35, 38, 49–52, 54, 58,
    60–63, 65, 67, 72 and n.,
    73 n., 77, 79–84, 87–90, 106,
    132, 136, 176, 179, 192 f.,
    205 f., 229–31, 236–40, 261 f.,
    311
  and behaviour, 92, 98, 101, 108,
    128, 142, 145, 147, 160 f.,
    238, 241 f., 248–50, 254–59,
    261–65, 332–37, 340–42, 386
  conceptualizing, 77–84, 106, 128,
    132, 165, 251, 266, 301–5,
    307, 309, 315, 319, 335, 369,
    378
  conditions of the, 123, 158, 179 f.,
    205, 293, 302, 392, 395
  elements of, in action, 140, 157 f.,
    174 f., 298
  reflective, 95, 100 f., 113, 128 f.
  self-conscious, 101 n., 113, 128,
    266

Ambivalence, 110, 339 f., 348
Analogy, argument from, 13
Analysis, 172 f.
Animal, 21, 24, 203, 329
  movements, 11–15, 18, 21–27, 29,
    35, 37, 47, 70, 174–77, 181,
    201, 204, 339
  sequence of, 25–27, 35, 37, 174,
    177, 201, 336 f., 392
  subject, 14
  what happens to, 23, 30, 60, 62
Arbitrariness, 290
Arguments, 92–101, 103 f., 385
Arguing, 370, 385
Arithmetic, 368
Art, critical judgement in, 186
Assertion and statement, 9, 98 ff.,
    123, 162, 216–20, 288, 317 f.,
    356–58, 378 and n., 379 f.,
    383–85, 389, 391, 395 f.
  true and false, 219, 356 n., 358,
    367, 383
Assumption, 2, 322, 357, 379, 383,
    389
Attenuation, definition by, 365 ff.,
    381 f.
Aversion, objects of, 74
Avoidability (*see* Responsibility)
'Aware of', 12, 71
Awareness (*see* Consciousness;
    Knowledge, Knowledge prac-
    tical; Knowledge, of what
    one is about), 63, 67–71, 75 f.,
    78, 81, 83, 85 f., 116, 125 f.,
    165, 169, 181, 206, 211 f., 220,
    224, 254, 296
  appreciative, 169 ff.
  and belief, 69, 75 f., 136
  and purpose, 127
  of facts and of objects, 69 f., 72
    ff., 80, 82, 128 f., 167
  of facts as reasons, 65 f., 69, 86–
    91, 97, 110, 149, 181, 184,
    188, 190, 192, 261 f., 265

Behaviour, 1, 4, 9–12, 18, 21 ff., 29,
    32, 66, 93, 181, 201 f., 237,
    249, 285, 307 n., 321 ff.

Principles—(*cont.*)
109–13, 148, 151 ff., 188, 251 f.
rules and, 236 f.
Productive purposes and action (*see also* Language, uses of), 163 f., 232, 308 f., 312, 315, 317, 319
Products, 154 ff., 159–65, 179, 308 ff., 312, 353 ff., 357 ff., 383
conventional, 309, 313, 334, 353, 355, 362, 364, 385, 387
individuation of, 162
Language, 342–45, 352 ff., 358 f., 361 f., 391, 393 ff.
material, 162 f., 312
non-material (*see* Upshots)
tests for existence and identity of, 342, 395
Promises, 38, 163, 274, 305, 309, 312–15, 317, 322, 324 f., 331–334, 355–58, 370 f.
Property, 38, 160, 267, 309 f., 334, 362–65
Proposition (*see* assertion and statement)
unity of, the, 393
Psychoanalysis, 196 f.
Psychology, 15 ff., 203 f., 230
'purposes', 5, 12, 49, 51–54, 56, 58
'with the purpose of', 52 f.
Purpose (*see* Action, elements of; Conditions of success for; Conventional; Effective; Endotychistic; Hybrid; Intention; Productive), 115 f., 131, 173
attaining, 35, 37 f., 52 f., 56, 75, 77, 105, 118, 121 f., 135, 141, 154, 159, 165, 171, 195, 288, 291, 336, 388 f.
of collateral act, 140 f., 143
conventional (*see* Behaviour)
converting way into, 386
criteria for presence of, 35 f., 56 ff., 63 f., 67, 69 f., 76, 79, 83, 91 f., 115–18, 122 f., 129,

132, 175, 194, 196, 201, 387
double, 38, 135, 144, 177, 356
explaining, 51 ff., 55–57, 65, 117, 194
having a, 62, 65, 74, 121 f.
identification of, 49 ff., 55, 57, 115 ff., 117, 119–26, 128, 132, 137, 175, 204, 294, 296, 298 f., 301 f., 306, 335
immediate (*see* Action, collateral), 141 f., 144, 149, 337, 354
location of, 56 ff., 116
and motive, 188, 195
Original (*see* Hybrid), 144, 182 n., 297, 300, 332, 363 ff., 367, 370, 373 f., 377, 389 f.
parts of, 140 ff., 144, 386
productive, 163
and reasons, 92, 126
specification of, 35–38, 48, 51–55, 58, 64, 67, 91 f., 116, 118, 122, 125, 130 f., 137 f., 140, 143, 149, 153 f., 178, 194, 204 f., 298, 385, 387 f.
ultimate (*see* Action, collateral), 120 f., 141 ff., 149, 176, 337
unconscious, 195 f.
verbal index of, 34, 37, 55

Quantifiers, 393

Radicals, 359
Reading and Spelling, 226 n.
'Reason', 52, 65, 67, 85 and n., 86
Reason (*see also* Acting for; Acting with; Explanation)
having a, 84–87, 89 f., 95, 97 ff., 190, 265
justification of, 84, 107 ff., 112 f., 151 ff.
and motive, 166, 188 f., 194 f.
one's, 18 n., 85, 89 ff., 96, 190, 256
operation of, 113
practical (*see also* Awareness; Syllogism, practical), ix, 18, 65 f., 84 ff., 93, 99, 103
principles of (*see also* Principle of

Rules—(*cont.*)
for succeeding, 156, 240, 242 f.,
271 ff., 279 f., 291 n., 303–6,
312, 319, 341
'That's the rule', 238, 240, 245,
249–52, 254, 258
of tongues, 279 f.
of translation, 124, 279 f., 393

Sanctions, 251, 363
Saying:
the same thing, 360, 394
something, 19, 272
and what is said, 393
Scepticism, 7 f., 11, 16
Scholasticism, 7
Searching (scanning, exploration),
230 f.
Self-consciousness, 63 f., 73 n., 74–
79, 77 n., 116, 126, 128, 265
f., 293 f., 296 f., 304, 306, 319
one's view of himself, 101 n., 113 f.
Self-interest, 106, 110, 113 f.
Semantics (semasiology), 348 n.,
349 n.
Sensation (*see* Perception and)
Sense (*see* Use, meaning), 346,
349 n., 360
and nonsense, 338, 393
Sentences, 320, 342–45
complete and incomplete, 350
individuation of, 347
'sentence', 344
Showing, what an act shows: 179 f.,
288, 323 ff., 386
Simulation (*see* parasites), 378–83
conventional, 378 ff.
Socratic assumption, The, 277
Speculation, 7, 17
Speech, 112, 323 ff., 327, 329,
345 n., 348 f.
act, 323 f., 330
parts of, 393
Statement (*see* Assertion;
Gerundive statements)
'Statement', 5
Statutes, 273 ff., 276
appealing to, 275, 277

Stimulus-Response Theory, 18 f.,
77 n., 198, 203 f.
Style, 144, 386
of linguistic modality, 322
Substances (second), 44 n., 45
Success (*see also* Behaviour, proficient; Conditions of; Rules
for succeeding)
conception of means and ends,
146
criteria of, 164, 395
and failure, 4, 36, 57, 61 f., 65, 67,
83, 118, 119 n., 123, 125,
128 f., 131, 153, 164 f., 178 f.,
224 ff., 228, 303, 324, 383,
385 f.
knowledge of, 164 ff.
measure of, 18 n., 105 and n.,
122, 146, 154, 156, 159 ff.,
182 f., 225, 228, 231, 308 f.,
342, 354 f., 362, 364, 379,
382 f., 396
as object of desire, 105 and n.
presumption or implication of,
38 f., 55, 61, 121, 130 ff., 154,
158
what makes an act succeed, 136,
153 ff., 226 ff., 271 f.
Syllogism, 94
deliberative and explanatory, 94
ff., 98, 100, 102
doxastic, 94 f., 98 ff., 102
practical (*see also* Reason,
practical), 18, 65, 92–103,
188
major and minor premises of,
92 f., 95, 97–103, 188
Symbols, 344, 349 f.
Syntax (*see* Grammar)

Technicality (*see* Usage, technical)
Testimony, privileged, 76 ff., 82 f.,
125, 128 f.
Tests (criteria), 395 f.
for action, 13, 75, 80, 172, 177,
339
for existence, 49, 125, 360
and identity of objects, 42, 56,

DATE DUE

MAY 1 4 1971			
AUG 4 1972			
FEB 9 1973			
Feb 7			
GAYLORD			PRINTED IN U.S.A.